Eighteenth-century poet James Thomson has long held an important place in English literary history, yet almost no critical attention has been directed toward the distinctive influences that his Scottish background had upon his work. Most English and American critics have simply ignored the issue, emphasizing Thomson's links to classical and English sources; many Scottish critics have applied a definition of "Scottishness" so narrow that they never considered Thomson a true Scot, and accused him of abandoning his heritage to embrace the ascendant English literary culture.

In *James Thomson, Anglo-Scot*, Mary Jane W. Scott reevaluates the works of this significant eighteenth-century poet, revealing the true extent of Scottish influences on his work. She presents perhaps the first close critical study of Thomson's juvenile poems, uncovering an early awareness of his Scottish roots and revealing how this greatly alters reading of Thomson's subsequent work. Offering a new perspective on his "exile" in London, Scott recovers for Thomson a place in the Scottish literary canon by outlining the extensive influences his work exerted over the course of Scottish poetry.

James Thomson was born in the Scottish Border Country and spent over half his life there. His work reflected his quiet, religious upbringing as the son of a Calvinist minister. The influences from this rural Scottish childhood and his Edinburgh student years did not fade when the poet emigrated to London; they were fundamental to his poetry, to the subject matter he chose, and to the language and style of his verse. In London, James Thomson fulfilled his potential and became, in Samuel Johnson's estimation, a gifted poet "without imitation"—an original poetic voice with a keen sensitivity to beauty and nature.

By the time of his death at the age of forty-eight, Thomson had become a very popular writer who would profoundly influence later poets including Robert Burns. *James Thomson, Anglo-Scot* restores this poet to his rightful cultural place, expanding the definition of literary "Scottishness" to include one of Scotland's most accomplished writers.

Mary Jane W. Scott studied at Emory University and in Scotland at the University of Edinburgh, where she received a Ph.D. from the School of Scottish Studies.

JAMES THOMSON,
ANGLO-SCOT

JAMES THOMSON,
ANGLO - SCOT

by Mary Jane W. Scott

The University of Georgia Press

ATHENS AND LONDON

© 1988 by the University of Georgia Press
Athens, Georgia 30602
All rights reserved
Designed by Mary Mendell
Set in Linotron 202 Baskerville
The paper in this book meets the
guidelines for permanence and durability
of the Committee on Production
Guidelines for Book Longevity of the
Council on Library Resources.
Printed in the United States of America
92 91 90 89 88   5 4 3 2 1
Library of Congress Cataloging in Publication Data

Scott, Mary Jane W.
  James Thomson, Anglo-Scot.

  Bibliography: p.
  Includes index.
  1. Thomson, James, 1700–1748.   2. Poets, Scottish—
18th century—Biography.   3. Scotland in literature.
I. Title.
PR3733.S37   1988   821'.5 [B]   87-13757
ISBN 0-8203-0973-7 (alk. paper)

British Library Cataloging in Publication Data
available.

FOR PATRICK

While virgin Spring, by Eden's flood,
　　Unfolds her tender mantle green,
Or pranks the sod in frolic mood,
　　Or tunes Eolian strains between.

While Summer with a matron grace
　　Retreats to Dryburgh's cooling shade,
Yet oft, delighted, stops to trace
　　The progress of the spiky blade.

While Autumn, benefactor kind,
　　By Tweed erects his aged head,
And sees, with self-approving mind,
　　Each creature on his bounty fed.

While maniac Winter rages o'er
　　The hills whence classic Yarrow flows,
Rousing the turbid torrent's roar,
　　Or sweeping, wild, a waste of snows.

So long, sweet Poet of the Year,
　　Shall bloom that wreath thou well hast won;
While Scotia, with exulting tear,
　　Proclaims that *Thomson* was her son.

ROBERT BURNS
"Address, To the Shade of Thomson,
on crowning his Bust, at Ednam,
Roxburgh-shire, with Bays"

CONTENTS

Preface   xi

Acknowledgments   xiii

Introduction   1

1   Scottish Nature and Nurture: Thomson's Border Youth   16

2   Edinburgh Years: Education, Apprenticeship, and
     Enlightenment   35

3   The Juvenile Poems   64

4   The Scottish Background of *The Seasons*   96

5   *The Seasons* as a Scottish Poem of Natural Description   113

6   *The Seasons* as an Anglo-Scottish Miscellany   146

7   The Language of *The Seasons*   182

8   Life, *Liberty,* and the Plays: The Scottish Poet in London   204

9   *The Castle of Indolence:* An Anglo-Scottish Allegory   254

     Epilogue   291

     Appendix 1   "A Winter's Day," by [Robert Riccaltoun]   297

     Appendix 2   "Imitation of Shakespeare" ("Winter"),
                    by John Armstrong   301

     Notes   307

     Bibliography   343

     Index   359

PREFACE

James Thomson has long held an important place in English literary history; he and his poetry have been the subjects of abundant critical and biographical comment from his own day to the present. Yet almost no critical attention has been directed toward the distinctive influences which the poet's Scottish background had upon his work. Most English and American critics have simply ignored the issue, emphasizing Thomson's links to classical and English sources; many Scottish critics, especially since the twentieth-century renaissance of Scottish literary nationalism, have applied a definition of "Scottishness" so narrow that they never considered Thomson a true Scot and accused him of "selling out" to the ascendant English literary culture. But James Thomson spent the first half of his life in Scotland, and it was there that he became a poet. This book is both a biographical and a literary-critical study; in it, I attempt to discover the Scottish influences—literary and linguistic, environmental, religious and philosophical, cultural and educational, social and political—on Thomson, to examine his works with these in mind, and to show how his "Scottishness" helped to shape his poetic art.

The structure of the book is chronological, moving at each stage of the poet's career between biographical focus and critical focus to demonstrate the vital relationship between the poet's life and art. I begin with a brief survey of attitudes to Thomson's Scottish background over the last 250 years, to illustrate the problem of critical failure to deal with Scottish influences on the poet, and to suggest a broader working definition of "literary Scottishness" than has usually been applied. Chapters 1 and 2 are a revaluation of Thomson's Scottish years—his youth in the Scottish Borders, the religion and literature he encountered there, his student years in the Scottish capital of Edinburgh, and the literary milieu in which he served his poetic apprenticeship. Chapter 3 gives, I believe, the first close critical examination of the poems Thomson wrote during these significant years. Chapters 4 through 7 show how an awareness of such Scottish influences can alter our reading of Thomson's pivotal work, *The Seasons*. I trace specifically Scottish elements in Thomson's landscape description, religious ideas, neoclassicism, and social and moral philosophy; even the language of the poem bears the signs of Scottish humanistic and dialect influence. Chapters 8 and 9 offer a new perspective on Thomson's London life as a Scot-in-exile among a lively "Scottish circle" and find surprising continuities between his Scottish background and his later dramas and poetry. Chapter 9 also focuses on the second of his more Scottish major works, *The Castle of Indolence*, in some detail. The brief epilogue is an attempt to recover for Thomson his place in the Scottish literary canon by outlining the extensive influence his works have exerted over subsequent Scottish poetry.

Properly understood, James Thomson's Scottishness can restore unity to the career of a poet whose life had appeared oddly discontinuous; it can help us also to read his poems (which have too often been taken as impersonal products of eighteenth-century England) with new eyes.

ACKNOWLEDGMENTS

I am deeply indebted to many people, both in Scotland and the United States, for their help in this transatlantic endeavor; I would not have been able to complete my book without their generous assistance.

I would like to express special thanks to Professor John MacQueen of the School of Scottish Studies, University of Edinburgh, who supervised this work in its first form as a doctoral dissertation. I appreciate the confidence Professor MacQueen has shown in me, and I am grateful for the learned guidance and reasonable advice he has given toward the completion of this work. I would also like to thank Drs. R. D. S. Jack, Ian Campbell, and Geoffrey Carnall and Ms. Faith Pullin of the Department of English Literature, University of Edinburgh, for the liberal material assistance as well as encouragement they have provided. Dr. Alexander Law of Edinburgh took the time to hear my developing thoughts on Thomson and to give me guidance especially on Thomson's associations with Allan Ramsay. I am grateful in this regard also to Dr. Nicholas Phillipson and to the late Professor William Beattie of the University of Edinburgh, who listened to my proposals and helped me the better to place the poet in his social and historical context.

Professor Ralph Cohen of the University of Virginia wrote to share his thoughts on Thomson and Scotland. Professors G. Ross Roy and George Brauer of the University of South Carolina deserve special thanks: Dr. Roy, for generously lending his books and his wisdom; Dr.

Brauer, for taking the trouble to read and comment on the *Seasons* chapters of the book.

Many librarians have shown kind interest, especially Mr. C. P. Finlayson, late Keeper of MSS and Rare Books, University of Edinburgh Library, and all the University library staff; Mrs. Norma Armstrong, Edinburgh Room, Edinburgh Central (Public) Library; Dr. William Makey, Edinburgh City Archivist; Mr. James Riley and the staff of the Library of Congress, Washington, D.C.; Ms. Judith Kalata and Mrs. Susan Dean, Special Collections, Newberry Library, Chicago; and the staffs of the National Library of Scotland and Scottish Record Office, Edinburgh, the Thomas Cooper Library, University of South Carolina, and the University of Virginia Library.

Warmest thanks are also due to my friends and family, who have encouraged me throughout this project, particularly my parents, Mr. and Mrs. Thomas M. Wittstock; my children, Nancy and Thomas; and my husband, Patrick G. Scott, whose constant love and support as well as considerable scholarly expertise have enabled me to complete this work.

JAMES THOMSON,
ANGLO-SCOT

INTRODUCTION

In so far as a writer is "Scottish," his "Scottishness," even if he is himself not conscious of it, will show itself in what he writes. This is certainly true of the writer who possesses the honesty of genius, and . . . there can be no literature without this kind of honesty.

JOHN SPEIRS, *The Scots Literary Tradition*

James Thomson (1700–1748) was born in Scotland and spent over half his life there—the first, formative twenty-five years of literary apprenticeship. He was a Scot and a Scottish poet; that he later chose to go to England and write in English should matter very little.[1] Yet Thomson has ever since suffered a sort of literary-critical prejudice which has neglected the importance of his Scottish experience. The standard, albeit facile, approach of the majority of Thomson critics has thus been to treat Thomson as an "English" rather than a "Scottish" poet. One Scots critic and poet has observed that a great many Scottish writers are in fact "disguised" as English, and that fully to understand their work it is essential to rediscover their national identity.[2] Thomson surely represents one of the most important of these Scots who deserve to be free of that ill-fitting literary disguise.

How can we begin to redress such long-standing neglect of the Scottish aspects of James Thomson's art? "Englishness" and "Scottishness" are of course too vague to serve as autonomous literary-critical terms. They have been too often misapplied to literature, especially in the

cause of political nationalism. Accidental, isolated, or superficial factors such as birthplace, setting, or subject matter have too frequently
justified a Scottish label.[3] Still, the concept of Scottishness, its ability to
define the "honesty of genius" of a Scottish-bred writer such as James
Thomson, does have considerable critical value. It carries the broader
significance of all the influences a poet's distinctive national culture
has had on his art—literary, linguistic, geographical and topographical, educational, religious, social, political, racial; in short, of all the
unique traditions and institutions which distinguish the Scottish national identity.[4] Such influences on Thomson are prodigious.

More specifically, the many and varied Scottish influences acting
upon the young James Thomson included his Scottish Calvinist upbringing; his education in the Scottish tradition and early acquaintance with a wide range of literature; the environment of his youth,
not only the Border landscape but also its people; and the complex
social and political circumstances of that crucial post-Union period of
Scottish history. These influences did not fade when the poet emigrated to London; they were fundamental to the formation of his
ideas of poetry and the poet's role, to the subject matter he chose, and
to the language and style of his writings. They would continue to inform the broader philosophies—religious, social, political—governing his works. So far, critical bias has obscured the tremendous impact
of these forces; a revaluation of Thomson, keeping these basic Scottish influences in mind, would therefore be worthwhile.

The critic must first concede that there is no purely "Scottish," other
than Scottish Gaelic, or purely "English" literature independent of
the other. The critical problem lies in discovering, and striking a balance between, the distinctive national traits characterizing English or
Scottish poetry while also keeping in mind the prolific cross-fertiliza-
tion between the two nations, for ultimately, the literary issue cannot
be one of an oversimplified "English *vs.* Scottish" polarity, but must be
more tolerant. Scottish culture of the eighteenth century was Anglicized to a great extent, but it had by no means disavowed its Scottish national identity; rather, elements of English influence were usually amalgamated with Scottish ones to create a uniquely Scottish
product, particularly in literature. James Thomson shared with most
educated Scots of his day many ambivalent feelings about national

identity and its expression in arts and manners. Thomson was never a Scottish chauvinist, nor should his works be distorted by the critic to fit a nationalistic mold, yet he did succeed in bringing Scottish strengths to his poetry, to its great gain. Awareness of his Scottish background is one very valuable clue to the interpretation of his works. Clearly the assumption that Thomson is exclusively an English or a Scottish poet is misleading and not quite fair, so perhaps the broader term "Anglo-Scot" (denoting a Scot by birth and upbringing who has chosen to settle in England and to write in literary English rather than Scots vernacular) is most appropriate and least charged with deceptive connotations. Anglo-Scot helps to convey the critical balance so long overdue in Thomson studies for which this work aims. As shall be seen, Anglo-Scot means far more than either language or locale.

Critical views of Thomson have shifted considerably over nearly 250 years. One useful scheme for outlining the changing emphasis in Thomson criticism might begin with a predominantly British phase in the eighteenth–early nineteenth centuries, characterized by impartial acceptance of Thomson as a post-Union British poet within the dominant English literary culture, with little reference to his Scottish background. The next stage, the "nationalistic" phase of the late nineteenth–early twentieth centuries, saw many critics eagerly seeking the more superficial Scottish elements of the works and often finding themselves in the Kailyard. The current, mid-to-late twentieth-century phase has again brought widespread neglect of Thomson's Scottish heritage, or, at best, an implicit awareness of it, inadequately articulated. Most major Thomson scholars, as well as experts in eighteenth-century literature, this century simply regard Thomson as a poet within the broader tradition of English literature. A brief survey of Thomson criticism from his day to the present centered on *The Seasons* (the most famous and most Scottish of his works) will attempt to pose the problem of critical failure to reckon with Thomson's Scottishness.

The Seasons was one of the most important and influential poems of the eighteenth century: the literati praised its beauties or censured its faults, but they never failed to notice it. Widely appreciated by the British reading public, it proved the most popular poem of the century.[5] In Scotland, whose people were deeply divided on the question of national identity, professional critics of Thomson tended to gather on the Anglicizing side, representing the cosmopolitan, pro-British spirit; they treated *The Seasons* simply as a significant work in English which happened to be written by a North Briton. The Anglicizers in Enlightenment Scotland had a variety of reasons for ignoring the author of *The Seasons*' Scottishness. Some betrayed embarrassment at being Scottish, as did so many "refined" Scots of the time. They may have considered Thomson's educated Scottish background virtually indistinguishable from that of an educated Englishman, or they may merely have felt that the poet's nationality was not relevant to the quality of the poetry itself. For whatever reasons, they strove primarily to treat Thomson's works as significant within a wider British context: Scottish Enlightenment rhetoricians James Beattie, Hugh Blair, and Lord Kames, for instance (all of whom disapproved of the use of the "vulgar" Scots dialect), drew many passages from Thomson's works to illustrate their treatises, along with examples from the ancients, Shakespeare, and Milton. Kames, whose *Elements of Criticism* professed the new critical standard of sensibility, did not approve of Thomson's old-fashioned rhetoric of "writing mechanically without taste." On the other hand, Beattie's "On Poetry and Music" and Blair's *Rhetoric* highly praised Thomson's superior descriptive ability.[6] These Enlightenment rhetoricians thus acknowledged (if implicitly) Thomson's Scottish heritage: Kames, in recognizing Thomson's traditional, neoclassical rhetorical training, which was central to Scottish education well into the eighteenth century; Beattie and Blair, in praising Thomson's natural-descriptive genius, which has long been recognized as a special feature of Scottish literature, both Scots and Gaelic, long before it appeared in English literature. Beattie's admiration for Thomson's piety and didacticism also paid tribute to the poet's Scottish Calvinist religious upbringing, which early shaped his moral values as well as his moral tone.

The great majority of Thomson biographers and critics of that period, both Scottish and English, scarcely mentioned the poet's national origins as a significant factor. These critics, including Patrick Murdoch (Thomson's close friend and classmate), Robert Shiels, John Aikin, Robert Heron, John Scott, John Pinkerton, and Joseph Warton, all concentrated on *The Seasons* as a product of post-Union Britain and made scant reference to its Scottish aspects.[7] They were right to focus attention on the merits of the poem itself without allowing potentially destructive nationalism—Scottish or English—to distort their critical vision, as would occur in the following century. But where the character of the poem owed much to specifically Scottish as distinct from English or "British" influences, as in *The Seasons,* such a stance was inevitably inadequate.

There were some, however, who did consider it important that the author of *The Seasons* was a Scot. These nonprofessional critics and admirers of the poem tended also to be Scottish patriots who hailed it as a particularly Scottish achievement and Thomson as a Scottish literary giant. Those whose views are recorded include Robert Fergusson, Robert Burns, and the eleventh earl of Buchan. Scots vernacular poets Fergusson and Burns both regarded Anglo-Scot Thomson highly and praised him as a Scottish hero. Fergusson's Cape Club customarily marked Thomson's birthday with readings, songs, and speeches; in certain such circles in Scotland in the late eighteenth century, Thomson's birthday occasioned the same patriotic celebrations as Burns's does today.[8] Fergusson, who of the eighteenth-century Scots poets best blended Scots with Augustan poetic idioms, must have appreciated Thomson's neoclassicism as well as the energy and realistic impact of his descriptions. Burns and Thomson had much in common, particularly: deep love for nature, for the Scottish scenery and its sentimental associations, as expressed in their descriptive poetry; awareness of man in nature; and strong humanitarian concern. Many echoes of Thomson—not only themes and scenes, but also phrases and constructions—are found in Burns, who wrote two poems very revealing of his attitude to Thomson. One, in formal English, praises him as a Scottish bard:

> So long, sweet Poet of the Year,
>   Shall bloom that wreath thou well hast won;
> While Scotia, with exulting tear,
>   Proclaims that *Thomson* was her son.

The other, in satirical Scoto-English, attacks those Scots who neglected Thomson in his lifetime and the dearth of patronage which

drove him to England and mocks the belated recognition of the poet
in Scotland:

> Dost thou not rise, indignant Shade,
>   And smile wi' spurning scorn,
> When they wha wad hae starv'd thy life,
>   Thy senseless turf adorn.[9]

In their respect for Thomson, Burns and Fergusson were not acting
as professional men of letters attempting to influence public taste;
they could simply appreciate good poetry, especially that which grew
from the same Scottish roots as their own. Although they themselves
chose to write in Scots, Fergusson and Burns demonstrated that vital
acceptance of the ascendant Anglo-Scottish culture in proudly embracing Thomson as a Scottish poet.

   Another Scottish patriot and amateur critic, James Steuart Erskine,
eleventh earl of Buchan, fanatically promoted Thomson with Burns
as the two chief bards of Scotland and organized Thomsonian Border
fetes for the Ednam Club. His enthusiasm led to occasional inconsistencies; he showed a typically Scottish split consciousness about the
poet's status as a British or a Scottish hero. While his Romantic
vagueness and bursts of Scottish chauvinism did not allow for a thorough, detailed study of Thomson's Scottishness, he did raise two
important issues: personal (the significance of Thomson's childhood
in rural "Tiviotdale," placing Rousseau-like emphasis on early environment in fostering genius) and, particularly, sociopolitical
(Border Scotland's relationship with England, her traditional love of
freedom, as Thomson had expressed in *Liberty*). The earl also contributed to Thomson studies through his strong influence over the periodical *The Bee*, which published Thomson letters as well as articles of
biographical interest.[10]

   In addition to these eminent Scotsmen, there must have been
countless anonymous readers in Scotland who revered Thomson as a
national poet. Of such John Wilson wrote, refuting Wordsworth's
"elitist" theory of Thomson's readership: "Mr. Wordsworth ought to
know that all over Scotland, 'The Seasons' is an household-book. Let
the taste and feeling shewn by the Collectors of Elegant Extracts be

poor as possible, yet Thomson's countrymen, high and low, rich and poor, have all along not only gloried in his illustrious fame, but have made a very manual of his great work. It lies in many thousand cottages . . ."[11]

Surprisingly, the professional literary critics of the period who were most sensible of fundamental Scottish influences on Thomson were two Englishmen. John More[12] elaborated on environmental factors of harsh Scottish climate and topography and their impact on *The Seasons,* noting the realism of the winter description and incidents such as the shepherd dying in the snow, taken directly from the poet's Scottish experience. He expressed amazement that a Scotsman could have become the "father of descriptive poetry," that "it was reserved for him, who had his birth and education among the bleak and desart wilds and hills of North Britain, to present the world with a graphical map of the year, to which there is no parallel, in this, or perhaps any other language." More's references to Scotland's "bleak and desart wilds" and harsh winters clearly carried negative cultural implications, but at least he acknowledged that Thomson's Scottish experience, however "bleak," had great bearing on his work.

Perhaps the fairest, most enduring, and intelligent Thomson critic of the eighteenth century was Dr. Samuel Johnson. His biography of the poet was drawn from Shiels's and Murdoch's, but his assessment of the poetry itself was his own candid view. Johnson, when asked to write his *Lives of the Poets,* noticed at once that the publishers had omitted Thomson's name from the list of subjects; as Thomson was a Scot, this seems to have been a deliberate snub to a rival publisher in Edinburgh who had recently completed a *Lives* series of its own. Johnson insisted that his *Lives* include Thomson, Scot or no.[13] Like Burns, Johnson decried the narrow Edinburgh literary coterie which had rejected young Thomson and forced him to go south: "[Thomson] easily discovered that the only stage on which a poet could appear, with any hope of advantage, was London; a place too wide for operation of petty competition and private malignity. . . ." He saw the importance of the Scottish landscape in *The Seasons,* particularly in "Autumn," where the poet "delights to recollect" the Jedburgh area. He fully appreciated Thomson's genius as a descriptive poet and praised his blank verse: "His

numbers, his pauses, his diction, are of his own growth, without tran-
scription, without imitation. . . . His is one of the works in which blank
verse seems properly used. . . ." The qualities of Thomson's poetry
Johnson most admired—his gift for descriptive poetry and his original
language—in great part represented the poet's Scottish heritage.

Most notably, Johnson was the first critic to call attention to Thomson's revisions, the empirical, creative process, as a characteristic of *The
Seasons.* He analyzed the effects of the many revisions, which tended to
remove the poem farther away from its Scottish origins and often
resulted in loss of what he called "race."[14] In Johnson's *Dictionary,* one
definition of race was "A particular strength or taste of wine, applied by
[William] *Temple* to any extraordinary natural force of intellect."
Among the *Oxford English Dictionary*'s definitions are "A particular class
of wine, or the characteristic flavour of this, supposed to be due to the
soil . . ." and "Of speech, writing, etc.: A peculiar and characteristic
style or manner, especially liveliness, sprightliness, piquancy" (and also
quoting Temple). Johnson, exploiting Temple's pun on the vintner's
term in applying it to Thomson, meant not only the poet's original
genius, his "racy" and immediate description, but also the distinctive
"racial" or native quality of his expression; thus, as J. Logie Robertson
has interpreted it, the race or unique flavor of Thomson's language,
particularly in earlier versions of *The Seasons,* seems to have grown
from its native elements: Scotticisms or northern derivatives, and more
colorful, "vigorous," even balladlike diction.[15] The race which Johnson
perceived had almost certainly to do with the fact that Thomson was a
Scots speaker. Even the poet's early clumsiness with formal English
diction, resulting in some awkward but expressive usages, added race.
Johnson's was the first attempt to explain, in terms of Scottish influence, the originality of Thomson's poetic language; like others who
have appreciated Thomson's Scottishness, he regretted the loss of race
he observed in the otherwise useful revisions. His less positive remarks
on *The Seasons* and *Liberty* unfortunately invited misinterpretation—
notably by the earl of Buchan[16]—but in truth the praise as well as the
honest criticism offered by Scotophobe Dr. Johnson was a compliment
to Thomson and to Scotland.

In the early nineteenth century, broader British attitudes continued to dominate Thomson criticism; by now, some information about the poet's youth and Scottish connections had begun to emerge through publication of new editions, memoirs, letters, interviews, and articles in such periodicals as *Blackwood's, The Gentleman's Magazine, Edinburgh Review,* and *The Bee,* but as yet no more comprehensive consideration of Thomson as a Scot had appeared. While most writers on Thomson in this period (such as William Hazlitt, Harris Nicolas, and Anglo-Scot Thomas Campbell)[17] did not emphasize Thomson's nationality, a trend was becoming apparent whereby critics increasingly endeavored to place *The Seasons* in a historical, "developmental" context, measuring its social and moral relevance rather than its literary quality.[18] This trend eventually encouraged both English and Scottish nationalism as critical motives; such national awareness was necessary, yet the resulting criticism was often narrow-minded and distorted and threatened literary standards. Misdirected, even absurd nationalistic claims (like Bulwer-Lytton's proclamation on the distinctively Scottish "fog" passage in "Autumn," "This is *description!*—and this is national—this is English!")[19] became commonplace in Thomson criticism by the late nineteenth century.

John Wilson ("Christopher North"), a Scot, represented this spirit of Scottish literary nationalism when in *Blackwood's* he asserted that those best equipped to appreciate *The Seasons* were the Scottish peasants, who "saw" the way Thomson did, knew the landscape and life he depicted, and had similar, almost "religious" intuitions about nature.[20] Wilson's idea about peculiarly Scottish attitudes to nature was intriguing, but he failed to go beyond this generalization, actually to define that Scottish way of seeing and describing. One wishes he had more usefully applied his Scottish literary patriotism to his otherwise fine treatment of the language and structure of *The Seasons,* but at least national awareness was there, that the poem was somehow unique and perhaps better for being Scottish.

Through mid nineteenth to early twentieth century, the developmental approach grew to become the norm in Thomson criticism, whereby literary patriotism was a prime motive. Though *The Seasons* declined in popularity, it was ever in the critical eye as part of a larger tradition; there was a flood of critical comment, much of it superficial or idiosyncratic, but its nationalistic bias did serve to raise essential points about Thomson's Scottish background in relation to his work. Most Scottish critics, and a number of English ones, now acknowledged that certain aspects of Thomson's poetry were directly influenced by his having been a Scot. Detailed discussion of the abundant Thomson criticism of this period is not possible here, but a brief overview will touch on key issues worth following up.

The matter of Thomson's childhood environment in rural Scotland, raised in the eighteenth century, continued to be a major topic with nineteenth-century critics, especially Scottish ones. Most mentioned the influence of Border life and landscape on the poetry: some commented on Thomson's fidelity to real Border scenes and incidents, others on Scottish landscape as a more generalized "inspiration" for the poet's descriptive mood and manner. All praised the importance of Thomson's fresh contribution to natural-descriptive poetry in English.

More significant was the growing tendency, within the historical-critical view, to place Thomson as a nature poet in an older tradition of specifically Scottish nature poetry. Stopford Brooke and William Bayne held the vague racial premise that the "Celtic spirit" was responsible for the traditional feeling for nature in Lowland poets like Thomson (modern scholars Kurt Wittig and Derick Thomson have since made a stronger case for Celtic influence on Lowland literature).[21] Some, such as Brooke and Bayne, rightly associated the Middle Scots art poetry of Henryson, Dunbar, and Douglas and the descriptive element of the Scottish ballads with Thomson's natural description "for its own sake," though as Brooke concluded, the matter of Thomson's relationship to older Scottish literature had "not been enough investigated,"[22] and so it has remained. J. C. Shairp and G. Gregory Smith believed that Thomson inherited certain stylistic characteristics from earlier Scottish descriptive poetry, such as "intimacy" and realism, and introduced these into English poetry. Other stylistic devices of older Scottish poetry were also ascribed to Thomson, such as the "cataloging" method of describing complex scenes, which Scots geologist-critic Hugh Miller appreciated for its Scottish application of meticulous empirical scientific method to descriptive poetry. John Veitch placed Thomson in a tradition of Anglo-Scottish nature poetry which he traced back to William Drummond of Hawthornden.[23]

Critics in the last century also began to pay more attention to the Scottish aspects governing the poet's diction. Léon Morel, in his general study of Thomson's language and style, analyzed the Latinate diction, though without reference to its roots in Scottish vernacular humanism, and remarked only briefly on the Scotticisms in the juvenilia and their rarity in the later works. Veitch ventured an over-simplified but suggestive explanation for Thomson's occasionally awkward diction; noting Thomson's reliance on "book-gotten epithets," he observed that "English was not [Thomson's] native language—that to a Scotsman one hundred and fifty years ago English was a foreign language to be learned. . . ." His view was echoed by Henry Grey Graham and taken up in the twentieth century by such scholars as David Nichol Smith, John Butt, and Geoffrey Carnall. This awareness of the complexity of the Scottish linguistic situation, presupposing a split between spoken and written language, would prove vital to a deeper understanding of Thomson's poetic diction.[24]

While Thomson did at times "let the roughness of the bothie invade his work" (G. Gregory Smith), such roughness was part of that race some critics found attractive. J. Logie Robertson, who applied a specifically Scottish definition of race to Thomson's poetry, corroborating Dr. Johnson's observations on loss of race in *Seasons* revisions, completed two key editions of Thomson. He edited *The Seasons and The Castle of Indolence* (1891) from the stance of Scottish literary nationalism and not only noted racy Scotticisms but also documented passages with Scottish thematic or literary associations. This edition remains a valuable guide to Thomson's Scottish language and subject matter. Robertson's Oxford Standard Authors *James Thomson: Poetical Works* (1908; reprinted five times) was long the standard *Seasons* text until James Sambrook's Oxford edition of 1981 appeared. Robertson's annotation of the OSA edition was focused considerably less on Scottish interests than his earlier edition. Oddly, Robertson, who was himself a Scots poet under the pseudonym Hugh Haliburton, remarked scornfully on Thomson's sole Scots poem, a juvenile verse elegy which he nevertheless published, that the "doggerel stanzas in the Scottish dialect are surely not Thomson's." Did this comment represent some deep-seated uneasiness about the propriety of Thomson's use of Scots, or simply the honest critical opinion that the "Elegy upon James Therburn" is bad Scots verse?[25]

Such inconsistencies abound in Thomson criticism of this period, mostly born of complex nationalistic or patriotic motives; while confounding, they often served to emphasize the matter of broader Scottish cultural influence on the poet. The central critical paradox is embodied in two of the major biographies: lives of James Thomson are included in both the "English Men of Letters" series (G. C. Macaulay) and the "Famous Scots" series (William Bayne).[26] Each raises tantalizing questions about Thomson's Scottishness, but these have not yet been pursued, even by twentieth-century scholars. So where does Thomson belong? Indeed, by its very Anglo-Scottish nature, Thomson's North British cultural heritage was paradoxical. Robertson, quoting Thomson himself, best summed up the poet's dual allegiance: "He was by no means an aggressive Scot. His patriotism was for Britain. . . . Yet one likes to remember that, as he wrote to a fellow-countryman, 'Britannia includes our native kingdom of Scotland, too.'"[27] Despite all the contradictions, superficiality, and bombast of much of the nationalistic criticism of the later nineteenth–early twentieth centuries, recognition of Thomson as a Scot was at least explicit; the significance of the poet's Scottish nationality had now been established.

In the twentieth century, the developmental trend in Thomson criticism has shifted away from a heavily nationalistic bias toward a more literary and philosophical view. Thomson's Scottishness, so often taken for granted or deliberately ignored, seems once again disguised as English literature, as it had been in the eighteenth century, but this critical masquerade is no longer justifiable on grounds of contemporary social or political expediency, as it had been in that post-Union era. Indeed, the opposite is true today; with a renewed upsurge of Scottish nationalism, one might expect greater critical interest in the crucial matter of Scottish influence on so-called English literature. Yet in this century, astonishingly, the major Thomson scholars have failed to address this issue with any conviction. Douglas Grant's biography *James Thomson* is a very useful life of the poet but spends remarkably little space on his Scottish years. Hilbert Campbell in his recent general study of Thomson is sympathetically aware of the importance of those formative years and their Scottish influences but adds little new on the subject. Ralph Cohen's substantial works on *The Seasons* and its critical reception, *The Unfolding of "The Seasons"* and *The Art of Discrimination*, leave the impression that he does not place special importance on either Scottish influences and references in the poetry itself or on Scottish critical attitudes toward it. Percy G. Adams's edition of *The Plays of James Thomson* simply reprints an eighteenth-century edition without critical comment. Alan D. McKillop's admirable scholarship on Thomson, particularly his *Background of "The Seasons," Background of "Liberty,"* and annotated editions of *The Castle of Indolence and Other Poems* and *James Thomson: Letters and Documents*, interprets the facts in light of broader European and British thought, with awareness of the Scottish background largely implicit. James Sambrook's definitive critical editions of *The Seasons* (Oxford, 1981) and *Liberty, The Castle of Indolence and Other Poems* (1986) likewise take little note of Scottish sources and influences. The latter does, however, represent a significant Scottish contribution in its sensitive edition of Thomson's juvenile poems. These works[28] and many others which have appeared in recent years are certainly extremely valuable to Thomson studies, yet none has directly confronted the vital issue of the relationship between Thomson's Scottishness and his art.

Some of the more interesting twentieth-century insights into that aspect of Thomson's work have appeared in more general literary studies. Patricia M. Spacks appropriately treats *The Seasons* as a nature poem which is also a hymn to the Creator; nature and religion were, of course, the two chief thematic influences of Thomson's Scottish youth. Hoxie Neale Fairchild deals thoughtfully with Thomson's Scottish Calvinist upbringing and its impact on the poetry and outlines Thomson's religious thought from the juvenilia through the *Castle*. Marjorie Hope Nicolson examines religious and scientific aspects of *The Seasons*, acknowledging the importance of Thomson's early education in shaping his mature philosophy; Herbert Drennon's study of Thomson and Newtonian science supplies more information on the poet's first contacts with Newtonianism in Edinburgh. Literary historians Maurice Lindsay, Agnes Mure Mackenzie, C. E. de Haas, Kurt Wittig, and John Speirs all place Thomson's work within the tradition of Scottish natural-descriptive poetry and praise Thomson as the poet who carried the theme of nature, vividly and realistically described, south of the Border and into Augustan English poetry. Wittig in particular finds evidence of the influence of both Scottish landscape and literature. John Butt remarks on the many references to the supernatural in *The Seasons*—unusual in Augustan poetry and Thomson's Scottish contribution. A. M. Oliver concurs and convincingly approaches Thomson as a "Scottish Augustan." Morris Golden treats Thomson from a psychological perspective, suggesting that the crucial event of Thomson's life, his migration from Scotland to England, set the pattern for the themes and images of adventure, potential, life process, and progress which recur in the poetry. Terence Tobin includes Thomson in his important survey of eighteenth-century Scottish dramatists, where he notes Scottish influences on the poet's dramatic forms and themes and his "ponderous" diction. John MacQueen establishes Thomson's place among the poets of the early Scottish Enlightenment.[29]

Perhaps the most provocative general study of Thomson this century is that of Scot David Nichol Smith, who sees Thomson's nostalgia for his homeland as the catalyst for *The Seasons*, which he deems a true poem of the Scottish Borders. He holds that Thomson, no less than Burns, could only have written the highly original poetry he did because he was a Scot. He also articulates a crucial point about the poet's diction (taken up by John Butt) which critics had long evaded when he evaluates Thomson's Latinate poetic language in light of the poet's Scottish humanistic education. Unlike Maurice Lindsay, who thoughtlessly censures Thomson's Latinisms, Nichol Smith and Butt could appreciate Thomson's Latinate diction as the expressive and natural literary language of a Lowland Scot writing in English.[30]

Each of these diverse, fresh critical insights is a worthwhile contribution to Thomson studies; together they begin to create a composite portrait of Thomson the Anglo-Scot. Still, the subject of Thomson's Scottishness itself remains at best an undercurrent in the mainstream of Thomson scholarship. It seems time to attempt a more comprehensive study, with the goal of cultivating a greater understanding of Thomson's works themselves from the Scottish perspective. Partly through biography, partly through literary criticism, the aim here will be further to identify the nature and extent of Scottish influence on the particular genius of James Thomson.

1 SCOTTISH NATURE AND NURTURE: THOMSON'S BORDER YOUTH

$\mho\mho\mho$

Most people know that James Thomson was a Scot, born and raised in Scotland. The facts of his early years in the Borders and Edinburgh have been dutifully documented in biographical and source studies of the poet, and few details need be added. But what do these bare biographical facts signify? Recent studies, useful though they are, leave a serious gap; none has attempted to look beyond the facts, to explore the complex cultural implications of the poet's Scottish experience. The task here will thus be to look at the details of Thomson's life from a different—Scottish—viewpoint to try to discover the significance of those statistics for those who appreciate Thomson's poetry. Such an approach will lead, not to a narrow or nationalistic view, but rather to a broader and more enlightened interpretation of the poet and his work. Placing Thomson in his relevant cultural context will show how he drew sustenance from his Scottish roots and how he ultimately grew beyond them to carry Scottish strengths to Anglo-Scottish, British poetry.

James Thomson's grandfather was Andrew Thomson, gardener to Andrew Edmonstoune of Ednam, Roxburghshire, a small village on the River Eden about three miles from the English Border. In fact, there were several gardeners in Thomson's family, and in youth he gained an appreciation of their art, that affinity with and improvement of nature so closely akin to his descriptive poetry. He was always carefully observant of the varied landscape, in detail and in prospect view, and his descriptions would manifest a trained eye.[1] Further, his

early awareness of the psychological and emotional effects of landscape gardening would have parallels in Scottish Enlightenment aesthetic philosophy; he put this philosophy into practice through his
poetry of natural description.

The poet's father, the Rev. Mr. Thomas Thomson (1666–1716), was
born in Ednam; very little is known of him. His family was of humble
means, and he chose the respectable career of the church. He studied
at the College of Edinburgh (later, the University), and was licensed to
preach in 1691; his first charge was his home parish of Ednam. Here
he married and started a family. In November 1700 he moved to the
parish of Southdean, remaining there until his death. Nothing more
is recorded of his character than the conventional reference in Patrick
Murdoch's (1762) biography of Thomson: Thomas Thomson was
"highly respected . . . for his piety, and his diligence in the pastoral
duty. . . ."[2] In his student days, a university education did not necessarily liberalize one's religious and philosophical attitudes, and
Thomas Thomson was among the generation just before a Moderate
trend swept Presbyterianism—and carried with it the young James.
Biographers have reasonably speculated that the elder Thomson was
of the old-school, high-flying "Antedeluvian" persuasion, severe, superstitious, and mistrustful of polite letters. He had been chosen to
serve at Ednam by a group of Covenanting Presbyters; he had close
associations also with the Marrow Men.[3] Murdoch's words "diligence"
and "piety" may be revealing of the poet's relationship with his father
(the biographer was James's intimate friend); they convey filial respect
but little affection. James himself never mentioned his father in extant
writings, affectionately or otherwise, in contrast to the love he openly
displayed for his mother in letters and in the poem he wrote upon her
death. It seems likely that father and son clashed over issues of both
manners and morals. Mr. Thomson may not have approved of his
son's attempts at poetry, as the Kirk deplored idleness, particularly in
the pursuit of poetic fancy; nor can he have been happy with James's
poor academic record at Jedburgh Grammar School, or his friendships with the liberal local gentry. While easy-going James does not
seem to have been of a particularly rebellious nature, the pressures
imposed by a strict minister-father might well have compelled him to

seek more congenial secular companions and interests. James Thomson eventually did reject many old-style Scottish Calvinist beliefs, but it is important to keep in mind that the more rigorous themes and tones of the religion of his youth, under the influence of father and Kirk, continue to reappear alongside the more Moderate philosophy he came to espouse throughout all his works.

The mysterious death of Thomas Thomson provides an important clue to the religious tenor of the poet's youth and helps explain his deep-rooted superstitions. The minister was summoned by the inhabitants of Wolflee ("Woolie") House on the lands of the Elliots of Stobs near Southdean to exorcize an evil spirit. While performing the exorcism he was struck by a ball of fire, left speechless, and soon died. Thomas Thomson died on February 9, 1716, possibly from apoplexy or a heart attack or possibly from a fever contracted in the winter expedition during a fierce Border epidemic; his death was locally attributed to Satan, and it is said that Mr. Thomson himself was convinced of Satanic intervention as were the terror-stricken onlookers. Apparently the alleged supernatural cause of his father's death greatly reinforced young James's already superstitious nature; he was even afraid of being left alone in the dark, and thus became the butt of many a practical joke at college. He must have been strongly imbued with those fears and superstitions attending orthodox Scottish Calvinism, particularly in rural areas like the Borders, right through the eighteenth century. In *The Seasons,* although the poet carefully distances himself from such "peasant" beliefs, superstition about spirits and unexplained natural phenomena, sometimes even linked with the wrath of God, is a recurrent theme.[4]

What more did James Thomson learn from his father? James Thomson would prove both a preacher and a teacher in his religious-didactic *Seasons* as well as in *Liberty* and *The Castle of Indolence.* The impulse to exhort his readers to practice virtue and to avoid sin surely derives even more from his early experience at the foot of his father's Scottish Calvinist pulpit than from abstract Augustan social concern. In many passages his very style echoes the rhetoric of the pulpit: its intensity of emotion, its power of literal and vivid descriptive imagery, particularly when portraying hell-like scenes so popular with Scottish preachers.[5] The central religious message of *The Seasons* ultimately affirms much that is orthodox in Scottish Calvinist doctrine, even if considerably more Moderate overall than Thomas Thomson's own beliefs. *Liberty* and *The Castle,* too, advance ideas of progress and the work ethic held to be congenial to the Scottish Calvinist spirit. Along with the poet's earliest religious indoctrination, his first introduction to literature, including the Bible and other religious texts, and also his initial acquaintance with the humanities would have been at the hands of his father. James Thomson was first exposed to all these influences as a son of the manse of Southdean.

The poet's relationship with his mother is somewhat better known, as she lived on into his early manhood. Beatrix Trotter was the daughter of Alexander Trotter of Fogo in Berwickshire and Margaret Home and was co-heiress of the lands of Wideopen or Widehope on Kale Water east of Jedburgh. She was also distant cousin to Lady Grisell (Home) Baillie, poetess daughter of the earl of Marchmont; this kinship would prove useful to James when he sought his fortune in England. Mrs. Thomson is said to have been a loving mother, lively and imaginative, and an enthusiast in her spiritual fervor. She seems to have inspired her son with the beauty and power of religious emotion. Thomson's warm portrayal of cozy cottage life in *The Seasons* suggests a happy childhood at home, the father's concerned discipline tempered by the mother's benevolence. While Thomson's father instructed the children in religious literature, Mrs. Thomson is said to have taught them another sort of literature, the Border ballads and songs. Her influence on her son's poetry can perhaps best be seen in such qualities as his religious and aesthetic sensitivity, benevolent moral intuition, and vivid imagination—in a word, his sensibility. Soon after her husband's death Mrs. Thomson and her family settled permanently in Edinburgh, where James was a university student. Mother and son seem to have been close, and she died to his great grief just weeks after he went to London.[6]

James Thomson was born, probably in Ednam, on or around September 11, 1700 (O.S.), two months before his parents moved to Southdean. He spent his childhood in Southdean, where economic, political, and geographical factors combined to have particular impact on this, his formative period. Scotland, a poor country largely dependent on agriculture, suffered a series of famines, and from 1697 until 1705, and again in 1709, the harvests were inadequate to maintain the population. Many Scots starved or emigrated. Border famines and consequent poverty owed partly to the primitive Scottish farming methods of the time, before "improving" English ways gained favor. Resistance to change was deep-rooted, reinforced as it was by Scottish Calvinist religious beliefs which tended to leave too much to Providence—the adult poet Thomson would grow impatient with Scottish "indolence" and counter such debilitating reliance on Providence with Virgilian "improving" philosophy laced with hearty Whig materialism. While not directly dependent on agriculture, Thomas Thomson's large family still counted to a great extent on the prosperity and generosity of the parishioners and possibly, too, on income derived from Wideopen lands. Growing up in such difficult times, James would come to know at close hand the hardships and privations of Lowland peasant life.

The greatest obstacle to Scottish improvement in Thomson's day was the country's inexorable climate. Roxburghshire, full of rivers and streams, was liable to destructive flooding, especially in spring thaws. Winters often brought sharp winds and severe snows; summers were mild but wet and misty, with bad thunderstorms. Southdean was exposed, lacking shelter from the elements, and so especially vulnerable to the vagaries of a harsh climate. Not only were crops frequently endangered, but people's lives were also in peril from flood and storm as well as starvation.[7] This environment made a lasting impression on young James; his superstitions, his belief in a controlling Providence working through nature, his constant awareness of nature's inscrutable power are all elements of his religious philosophy which, while present in Job and orthodox Scottish Calvinism, also owed much to his childhood experience of the natural world. Such interplay of religion and landscape would lend the force of truth to his most compelling descriptive poetry.

The geographical situation of Southdean is isolated, desolate; the surrounding moors, variegated with woods and rich farmlands, contrast dramatically with the bald, bold Cheviot Hills to the south.

Border light creates peculiar atmospheric effects; Kurt Wittig has described it as eerie, "unearthly," and felt it enhanced his own appreciation of the mood of the Border ballads. The impact of this wild, romantic scene on the poet Thomson, the emotional associations it held for him, cannot be overemphasized, since the Southdean landscape itself surely taught him to see and to describe nature in his particular way; his poetry distinctly reflects this early Scottish lesson.[8]

Southdean's very isolation also helped to shape young Thomson's personality, reinforcing his natural shyness and in turn affecting the poetry, where social life is seldom to the fore.[9] The setting would certainly have fostered a contemplative temperament, congenial to Scottish Calvinist spiritual introspection, along with an intimacy with the natural world. Again, the vital communion of religion and landscape was an inspiration. Paradoxically, too, Thomson's childhood isolation might have provoked a reaction, encouraging young Thomson's growing attraction to new, more exciting, and sophisticated people and places which culminated in his move to a convivial life in London.

Southdean is about seven miles from the English Border at Carter Bar. For centuries it was on the route of the Border raiders; it was as vulnerable to political as to climatic upheavals. After the Union of Crowns such raids abated, but religious strife prevented peace; only in the eighteenth century did the area grow tranquil. With the Union of 1707 the population dwindled, as Borderers at last felt free to move to the intimidating, attractive south. James Thomson would have grown up amid conflicting attitudes toward England: his Border home was the very site of long-standing antagonism with England, and its people had developed a strongly nationalistic, independent spirit; yet it was in such close proximity to England that when peace came, Scots Borderers were readily lured there in the hope of a better life. In time, Thomson himself would follow this course.

The Southdean landscape was also rich in classical associations, which made their impression on the poet. Great similarity has been seen between this Border scene, particularly in summer, and Mantua, the land of Virgil, young Thomson's model and mentor.[10] Virgil was a northern Roman poet, of Gallic, Celtic ancestry; Thomson's identification with Virgil may have been partly to do with the perception that both were provincial, northern poets with certain "Celtic" links.[11] Roxburghshire itself, and especially the Jedburgh area, had once been overrun with Romans, who left artifacts, roads, and ruins which fired the imagination of the boy Thomson; these reinforced in a concrete way his "Scoto-Roman" ethos—the ideal whereby many Scots identified themselves, in his day, with ancient Roman civilization. Thomson adopted this Roman spirit with enthusiasm. So his affinity with Virgil was more than simply literary; it was based on historical and topographical and also cultural factors as well.

Scottish environmental influences acting upon the young James Thomson, then, were strong. What of more specific early literary and linguistic influences? Clearly James grew up in a literate household where he encountered a variety of literature even before he began his formal education. His father tutored him at home, with the Bible and Shorter Catechism as primary "texts." The Bible was the poet's first acquaintance with formal literature and proved a major thematic and stylistic influence on his poetry. While Thomson, his family, and his friends probably spoke Scots in everyday conversation, the poet would have become familiar with formal literary English through his biblical studies—the authorized version was the lyrical King James. The language he heard from the pulpit, too, was heavily Anglicized.[12] The Rev. Mr. Thomson's library would have included, in addition to theological works, sermons and tracts, perhaps some college texts of philosophy and the humanities, and religious-allegorical works such as *Pilgrim's Progress*. Thomas Thomson almost certainly did not encourage his son's endeavors in the belles lettres, however; even apart from the Kirk's deep distrust of imaginative literature, there was actually very little art literature generally available in Scotland at the time. In James's youth, English books were only just beginning to arrive in quantity in Scotland; the boy began to seek literary stimulation not at the Southdean manse, but where these books could be found, in the homes of his learned friends Sir William Bennet, the Elliots of Minto, and his tutor, Robert Riccaltoun.

Less formal sorts of literature were also available to young Thomson in the Borders in the form of chapbooks and ballads. Chapbooks, in English or crude Scoto-English, treated many subjects: Scottish history and heroes (such as Barbour's *Bruce* and *Sir William Wallace*); religion (including sermons and Covenanting tracts); superstition and prophecy (closely tied in with religion); songs and ballads; pastoral romance; Middle Scots poetry (such as David Lindsay's works); and other literature. Some of the more severe religious chapbooks may have provoked a reaction in the boy James against strict, old-style Scottish Calvinism while subconsciously reinforcing his superstitions. Others aroused his interest in the wider world, past and present; geography and history became lifelong avocations and figured centrally in his works. He would also have learned to enjoy such literary modes as allegory, pastoral, and didactic verse from the chapbooks. The Border ballads taught him by his mother were another native literary resource, and this folk literature helped develop his facility for describing action and process in the natural world, as well as his awareness of important ballad themes, the supernatural and the providential acting arbitrarily through nature, which became significant themes in his own poetry.

The poet's formal education began at a local village school in Southdean or possibly neighboring Chesters. The basics of Scottish primary education were usually taught in so-called English schools, and the work, with a little writing and mathematics, was mostly reading; the Bible and Shorter Catechism were commonly used as textbooks from which the children learned to read English.[13] Thus religion and the formal English language were taught simultaneously from the start, and as a son of the manse Thomson would have had an earlier start than most pupils. At the age of twelve, he entered Jedburgh Grammar School, one of the best schools in the Borders at that time. The boy may have boarded in Jedburgh, travelling the eight miles home at weekends. Jedburgh's setting in a richly wooded, fertile area is in striking contrast to the isolated, bleak foothills of his home in Southdean. Here in Jedburgh, Thomson began to write poetry; the change to a softer, prettier landscape seems to have inspired him. His juvenile poems are mostly set in idealized, "beautiful" pastoral scenes rather than stark or "sublime" ones; he would return nostalgically to the native sublime in his first major poem, "Winter."

Jedburgh Grammar School was held, in Thomson's day, in a part of the old Jedburgh Abbey. The master was a Mr. James Brown, of whom little is known. A strong superstition concerning his death in about 1720 or 1721, not unlike that of Thomas Thomson, survived well into the nineteenth century. Brown was a good and pious man, but his wife was a "mischievous witch" of evil character. He reproved her, so she and other witches drowned him in the River Jed; "witnesses" reported that he sang the Twenty-third Psalm while being led by a rope to the water and that, at his death, fairies danced atop the abbey steeple.[14] So while young James Thomson had moved to a larger town and a more enlightened academic environment, he had not escaped the atmosphere of quasi-religious superstition which still permeated rural Scotland and made such a lasting impression on him.

The Grammar School was a Latin school probably founded in the fifteenth century. There was also an English school in the town, but the older, more prestigious Latin school almost certainly maintained the traditional curriculum, based on the humanities. Its pupils were required to use the Latin tongue at all times, or at least during school hours. Despauter's Latin grammar was probably Thomson's text, or, given his early attraction to literary English, he may have studied from one of the updated versions of Despauter which taught English along with Latin, texts which were forerunners of Thomas Ruddiman's *Rudiments* (1714ff.).[15] In addition to grammar, he learned the comprehensive rules governing classical rhetoric from Despauter and Vassius; his sound education in rhetoric would prove itself in the care with which he worked the intricate, expressive language of his poetry, following the rules when decorum required, departing from them when genius inspired. Among the Latin authors Thomson probably studied at school were Virgil, Horace, Ovid, Terence, Sallust, Lucan, Quintus Curtius, and, most notably, Scottish Latinist George Buchanan. Buchanan's *De Prosodia Libellus*, setting forth the rudiments of Latin prosody, was appended to Despauter; his *Psalms, Tragoidiae*, and *Historia Scotorum* were a major part of the curriculum in most Scottish schools (Thomson would also later own Buchanan's *Opera Omnia*). Respect for Latin language and Latin culture in general was so deeply rooted in Scotland by Thomson's day that it had become part of the native tradition.[16] "Vernacular humanists" sought to preserve and perpetuate Roman culture in Scotland, and Thomson was from youth impressed by their ideals. An understanding of Thomson's classical education is essential for full appreciation of his poetical diction, subject matter, and artistic method. Thomson was a Scottish Augustan and humanist and as such a representative, not of a new classical revival as in Augustan England, but of an ancient and continuously evolving line of Scottish Latinist literary culture.

In addition to Latin, Thomson also studied elementary Greek and some arithmetic. Although very little science was taught at the start of the century, Thomson would have learned some natural philosophy as well as moral philosophy and history through his diverse readings in Latin prose. The Kirk exercised strong control over the curriculum of Jedburgh Grammar School, a joint burgh-parochial school; religious studies complemented the humanistic program, with Latin devotional readings from, for instance, Buchanan's Psalms and Greek lessons from the New Testament. The Bible and Shorter Catechism were used for prayers and readings and, along with Scripture and theology, also taught lessons in English.[17]

Growing out of this Latin curriculum in Scottish schools was a pertinent extracurricular activity, the production of school plays. Jedburgh Grammar School probably staged such plays; many accounts of these come from Border schools. The plays were in Latin, served a pedagogic purpose, and were usually excruciatingly dull. One of the most popular with zealous masters was Alexander Hume's *Bellum Grammaticale,* where the various parts of speech assume roles; pupils also acted in Terence's *Eunuchus* as well as dramatized extracts from Ovid, Juvenal, and other authors.[18] Such efforts were likely Thomson's first acquaintance with the drama. If a wooden linguistic allegory like *Bellum Grammaticale* was his earliest idea of a play, one can scarcely wonder that his own neoclassical tragedies sometimes lacked life.

Young James had the reputation of being a backward pupil, and his literary talent was certainly not apparent to his school fellows—nor would it be obvious at first to his university classmates. But the evidence suggests a quiet, shy nature and perhaps a pedantic approach to study rather than real dullness. As a schoolboy he must have been inquisitive, reading a great deal and absorbing knowledge and experience which would form the basis of his life's work. He would have had access to the grammar school's books and perhaps also to the new library opened at Jedburgh's English school in 1714. He also owned a number of works of English literature of an early date which possibly belonged to him while a schoolboy, including Donne's poems (1669), John Hughes's edition of Spenser (1715), and Milton's *Paradise Lost* and *Paradise Regained* (1711, 1713). Although his parents probably did not encourage him to read such imaginative poetry, Thomson acquired a passion for English literature during his school days in spite of their disapproval. During this time, his own earliest poems were conceived.

Thomson's boyhood attraction to English polite letters was nurtured most especially by his friendships with neighbors of refined and liberal taste whose libraries were open to him and who inspired him to love and imitate Augustan English poetry. Chief among them were Sir William Bennet of Grubbet and the Gilbert Elliots (first and second baronets) of Minto, and the humble but brilliant farmer-clergyman Robert Riccaltoun. After 1707, communication between England and Scotland began to improve. Scots members of the United Parliament such as William Bennet and, later, Gilbert Elliot of Minto (second baronet) were leaders of the Anglicizing movement in Scottish culture; they brought back to Scotland English books and literary tastes as well as English styles in gardening and dress and new English ideas in religion and philosophy. Such tastes and views were eagerly adopted by a rising generation of educated Scots at home such as Riccaltoun. Young Thomson was fortunate to know such broad-minded men; they gave him encouragement and tuition as his father would not in literature and in more liberal attitudes generally, and with their help he transcended the isolation of the Scottish Borders to become part of the wider Anglo-Scottish culture.

Thomson probably met Sir William Bennet the Younger of Grubbet (second baronet) through the poet's mother, whose Wideopen property was just north of the lands of Grubbet on Kale Water. Bennet, master of the elegant seventeenth-century Marlefield House, was renowned for his gardening skill and devoted much effort to the improvement of the estate. When Thomson visited there, the Marlefield gardens were probably rather formal, in the fashion of the period, but Bennet may well have experimented early with the more natural landscaping style the poet would so admire in England. Thomson would write nostalgically to Bennet from London in 1725, "I see you att the verge of your creation forming in your mind some beautifull scheme of new improvements to bless the country 'round you," adding his own translation of lines written by Scottish Latinist poet Sir William Scott of Thirlestane for Bennet: "Happy the house with such a master crown'd! / Happy the woods! the fields! and happy all around!"[19]

Bennet was a colorful character. Like his father and grandfather, he was active in local civil and religious affairs. He served in the Scottish Parliament (1707–1708) and succeeded to the baronetcy about 1710. Bennet, who led the militia in the defense of Kelso from the Jacobites in 1715, was an ardent Whig, probably of the Squadrone faction; that is, he would have preferred some sort of devolution for Scotland rather than rule from London by an all-powerful Scottish secretary. He seems also to have sympathized with the Opposition Whig, anti-Walpole faction, as Thomson would later do. He may have had reservations about the Union as a "nostalgic patriot" member of the nationalistic Royal Company of Archers, but he generally accepted it; Scotland's Anglicized Whig gentry, along with the Moderate Presbyterian clergy, generally were allies in their pro-Union stance, while many old-style, "high-flying" ministers like Thomas Thomson opposed the Union.[20] In coming to adopt a complex set of religious and political views so similar to Bennet's, Thomson was thus in a sense rejecting the deeply held values of his minister father. Of course, most of Thomson's acquaintances in the Borders were Whigs, and the Whigs were the party allied with the Presbyterian church; he himself naturally assimilated Whig views. William Bennet was undoubtedly the individual most responsible for fostering political interest in young Thomson. Though he did not become politically active until later when he lived in London, Thomson's lifelong allegiance was to the party which in Scotland came increasingly to stand for support of Great Britain along with Anglicization, rather than militant Scottish nationalism.

In literary matters as in political ones (and indeed the two were closely linked in the issues surrounding the Union), William Bennet was a curious mixture of the old and the new. He tended to admit of more liberal and "British" ideas with toleration and broadminded-ness, yet he was also part of a circle of nostalgic-patriotic Latinist poets, a group which included a fair number of Jacobites and Episco-palians and many fellow members of the Archers. He had a good reputation as a Latin poet, though little of his work survives, as he was sometimes indolent and neglected to write down his extempore verse—and too often in truth preferred his bottle to his pen.[21] The old soldier Bennet espoused the Roman ideal in both literature and life and represented that significant element of Scottish culture which identified Scotland with Rome and promoted the continuation of the living Latin literary tradition.

Bennet was well known for his refined critical sense and for his generous support of Scottish poetical efforts. He was an intimate friend and patron of Allan Ramsay who, like Bennet, recognized po-tential Scottish benefits from the Union but at the same time dis-played deep Scottish patriotic sentiment. Ramsay often visited Mar-lefield and he wrote several poems in praise of Bennet and his estate, which he lavishly described as Edenlike.[22] The myth that Bennet was the author of *The Gentle Shepherd* probably grew from his having of-fered advice to Ramsay about the work; other traditions claim that Sir William Bennet the Elder (first baronet) was the model for "Sir William Worthy" while his son was "Patie," and that Marlefield itself was the setting for the Scots pastoral.[23]

Bennet invited young James Thomson to Marlefield in his summer holidays and extended the same generous hospitality to the boy as he had to the man of letters, Ramsay. Bennet was Thomson's first patron and encouraged him to write poetry in English. Thomson almost cer-tainly met Ramsay at Marlefield, and many of his juvenile poems show a clear debt to Ramsay. Thomson was enthralled with lovely, Edenlike Marlefield and its good laird; his early works "A Poetical Epistle to Sir William Bennet of Grubbat Baronet" and "Upon Marle-feild" convey his sincere appreciation. He was grateful to Bennet for opening a whole new world to him, a world of Scottish Latinist culture, Moderate religious belief, new aesthetics of landscaping, Opposition Whig political intrigue, and, especially, Augustan English literature.

Thomson's relationship with the Elliots of Minto was of a similar character. The first Sir Gilbert (1651–1718) was at Minto during Thomson's boyhood; the younger Gilbert Elliot (1693–1766) went to Leyden in 1712 and then to Edinburgh in the 1720s, where he was a member of the Worthy Club. Thomson's uncle and his cousin Robert were gardeners at the Minto estate on the Teviot; also, his closest boyhood friends, the Cranstouns of Ancrum, about six miles away, had connections there.[24] Many benefits would accrue from Thomson's close association with the learned and talented Elliot family. At Minto, famous for its extensive library, Thomson would have become acquainted with a cosmopolitan culture in literature, art, and music and with people of refinement and taste. Here he would have found encouragement in his poetical efforts; the elder Sir Gilbert was a literary scholar and connoisseur, the younger an amateur poet. He may also have learned from his relatives employed there some of the technical and aesthetic aspects of landscape gardening reflected in his poetry. Here, as at Marlefield, he would have encountered the complexities of Scottish-English politics; the elder Sir Gilbert voted against the Union, while his son was strongly pro-British and an ally of the Campbells of Argyll.

Thomson had many more friends in the Borders, of humbler means than the Bennets and Elliots but nonetheless important in his life. Among them were the Rev. Mr. John Cranstoun of Ancrum and his sons John and William. Thomson's lively letters to William (who became a physician) in the 1720s and 1730s are the best source of information about the poet's early manhood and the period of his emigration south. With these friends of youth, he shared the pleasures of rural life which he celebrates in *The Seasons*.

Perhaps the Border friend who had the most abiding influence on young James Thomson was Robert Riccaltoun (1691–1769), whom Thomas Thomson himself chose to be his son's tutor and companion. Riccaltoun, who had studied at Jedburgh Grammar School and Edinburgh University, returned to farm his family's lands in Hobkirk Par-

ish, adjoining Southdean. He later became a minister of the Church
of Scotland (licensed 1717) and in 1725 took the living of Hobkirk,
where he remained all his life. Even as a young farmer Riccaltoun had
a reputation for uncommon intelligence and imagination as well as
good-natured kindness. His shy pupil Thomson was quick to learn
under his tuition and particularly followed his tutor's guidance in the
matter of writing English poetry. Riccaltoun was himself a poet and
later "modestly acknowledged . . . that he had considerable influence
in discovering and prompting the poetical talents of Thomson." His
method of fostering literary creativity in his pupils was to discourage
self-indulgence or extravagant fancy and to reward simplicity and
common sense; he taught that one should write, with discipline, about
subjects one knew. This was sound advice, for what did the boy James
Thomson know more about first-hand than religion and nature, the
subjects of many juvenile poems and of course the central themes of
The Seasons?[25]

Riccaltoun's direct literary influence on Thomson has often been
acknowledged. Thomson himself praised a poem by Riccaltoun,
probably "A Winter's Day" or a similar poem of winter description
now lost, as a primary model for his own "Winter." Yet Riccaltoun's
chief influence on Thomson was a more subtle one, as the tutor
helped to shape the boy's religious and philosophical understanding.
Riccaltoun became known in later years as a distinguished Moderate
divine; his prose works included essays on philosophy and Christian
theology and a lengthy exegesis of the Book of Galatians. James
Thomson very probably met with these ideas, similar in so many ways
to his own mature thought, in a germinal state while he was under
Riccaltoun's tutelage.[26]

Riccaltoun's philosophical "Essays on Human Nature" treat mainly
of theories of knowledge. He advised men to avoid abstract metaphysics and to approach knowledge through observation; man should
thus proceed empirically toward truth via the scientific method of
Locke, Newton, and later Hume (whom Riccaltoun greatly admired).[27] As an empiricist and Moderate Presbyterian Riccaltoun allowed himself, unlike many old-style Scottish Calvinists, to delight in
the aesthetic pleasures the senses afford: "beautiful colours, figures,

or arrangement and position of material objects, and the wonderful variety of sounds" pleased him (and strike a note congenial to readers of *The Seasons*). But, he insisted, reason must control and interpret these sense perceptions. Maintaining a humanistic view, he respected the power of the mind to arrive at valuable knowledge about man himself and about the objects and processes of life. He held reason to be very powerful, its power extending to "imaging" (imagination) or the deduction of, for example, "all the invisible causes of the several alterations we observe on the face of the earth, throughout the different seasons of the year. . . ." He held that the mind is obliged to "improve" itself by degrees and to reach its ultimate goal of truth in God in the afterlife. This concept of intellectual perfectability is the very "rising mind" which plays such an important role in Thomson's works and especially in *The Seasons*.[28]

Riccaltoun, being close to the earth as well as to the heavens, drew his concrete images liberally from nature and often from the tamed, "improved" nature he knew as a farmer. He believed that "making images" could lead to much of our "real and most useful knowledge." So James Thomson's earliest poetical exercises could be considered an integral part of his educational process, stimulating the boy to observe nature closely and to make images from it in the poetic mode of natural description. The greatest truths to be so expressed were of course religious ones, which provided his descriptive poetry with its religious-didactic motive. Riccaltoun often invoked the conventional title of God as "Author," as Thomson would do in *The Seasons*, comparing divine with literary creation. He affirmed the power of "inspiration," that special God-given genius for "imaging," and so must have strengthened Thomson's confidence that his own writing of poetry was God's will. Assurance of God's will was a necessary condition to be met in a Scottish Calvinist's choice of occupation or "calling," and surely Riccaltoun's was an early instance of such a Moderate attitude applied specifically to imaginative literature in Scotland. Riccaltoun detected this creative sensibility in his protégé Thomson and indeed taught him that poetry and religious faith could happily coexist.[29]

Riccaltoun's treatment of scriptural revelation in the "Essays on Several of the Doctrines of Revelation," typical of his literary bias, emphasized the concept of "images." He took these on two levels: natural images (the natural world as imperfect image of the spiritual); and literary images (individual biblical images carrying the added resonance of symbolism). The pagan authors, he said, often knew and described the same natural images as did biblical authors but simply lacked the divine inspiration to interpret their full spiritual truth. One example is Virgil's Golden Age, which is the same literal image as the Paradise of Genesis; this parallel narrative tradition would inform Milton's *Paradise Lost* and, later, Thomson's *Seasons*. Significantly, Riccaltoun readily reconciled classical literature with Christian revelation and saw them as complementary traditions. His was a characteristic Moderate attitude, conceived in Scottish humanism; he genuinely respected those "greatest and most learned" classical authors who recorded the truth as they knew it.[30] It is hardly surprising, then, that his pupil Thomson chose the Old Testament, Virgil, and Milton as primary models for his own imaging of man's relationship to God and nature.

Riccaltoun's study of biblical "images" had been influenced by empirical science and particularly by the work of amateur scientist and theologian John Hutchinson (1674–1737). Hutchinson sought to reinterpret biblical symbols by seeking their parallels in nature. He focused especially on Moses' account of the Deluge (an important image in *The Seasons*) and cited geological evidence to support the Scriptures; his vivid description of elementary chaos recalls Thomson's fog sequence in "Autumn," where the poet invokes the "Hebrew Bard," as well as the thaw scene in "Winter." Duncan Forbes of Culloden was another disciple of Hutchinson, and if Thomson read his works it was probably at Forbes's recommendation. Riccaltoun and Forbes, both Hebrew scholars, affirmed Hutchinson's insistence that the Bible should be read in the original Hebrew to discover its deepest truth; Thomson echoed this view in his preface to the second edition of "Winter" (1726).[31]

While the empiricist Riccaltoun believed that man could learn much about God through His creation, he very firmly rejected as inadequate the contemporary systems of natural theology or physicotheology.[32] Reason was not all-powerful: in the way of Job, *Paradise Lost*, and *The Seasons*, Riccaltoun defined the limits of reason and made the

leap to faith via a fundamentalist and basically orthodox Scottish Calvinist reliance on scriptural revelation. While his God was a God of
love and had much in common with Shaftesbury's benevolent deity,
Riccaltoun asserted orthodoxy in his unequivocal rejection of deism
or any notion of a mechanistic universe. He upheld belief in a God
actively at work in the world through Providence, a tenet of Calvinism
also central to *The Seasons'* world-view. Further, he professed orthodox
belief in an active devil. His superstition, like Thomson's, was considerably relieved by common sense, but it was nonetheless a real part of
his religious belief and not at all surprising in one raised in rural
Scotland at that time.[33] Riccaltoun's moral philosophy, too, had more
in common with Scots Thomson and Francis Hutcheson than with
Shaftesbury; ultimately, God's laws as revealed in revelation prevailed
over man's reason and intuition about good and evil. Nonetheless,
Riccaltoun was an optimist and believed that however mysterious or
malevolent God's predetermined plan might appear to man's limited
reason, it was all wise in its fullness, which the rising mind could know
in eternity. Just such tempered religious optimism has been seen as
the overall (no less) vision unifying Thomson's *Seasons*.[34]

Robert Riccaltoun's views on philosophy and theology bear striking
resemblance in many points to Thomson's own mature thought. His
eclectic ideas reflect the intellectual climate of his age and Thomson's:
traditions and new developments in Scottish Calvinism, Moderate adaptations of Scottish Christian humanism, and the first stirrings of the
Scottish Enlightenment. While Riccaltoun showed strongly Moderate
leanings, he consistently maintained tenets basic to Presbyterian
Christian orthodoxy; he was no heretic. Likewise, his pupil Thomson
took account of current ideas of physicotheology, its extreme of pantheism, and also deism, but finally reasserted faith in the traditional
God. Thomson indeed retained throughout his life a discernible Scottish Calvinist structure of thought. His complex Scottish Calvinist outlook would reach far beyond specifically religious ideas to inform his
general attitudes to man in nature and in society. It is illuminating to
discover a parallel Scottish expression in prose of the eclectic religious
and moral philosophy of *The Seasons* in the poet's own teacher and
mentor, Robert Riccaltoun.

James Thomson's friendships with Riccaltoun and other men of

God and letters, his religious and educational experience, his family life, his place in the Border community and as a solitary figure in the Border landscape were clearly to have lasting impact on both the subject matter and the style of his works. Here, in the Scottish Borders, he would first become acquainted with his enduring literary models— the Bible, the classics, Scottish folklore and literature, and formal English poetry and prose. Here he would come to know intimately his primary source of inspiration, the natural world. Here was his essential "Scottish context," which would soon expand to include Edinburgh.

2 EDINBURGH YEARS: EDUCATION, APPRENTICESHIP, AND ENLIGHTENMENT

James Thomson's student years, the decade 1715 to 1725, were crucial years not only for him personally but also for post-Union Scotland. It was a time of change, exciting if unsettling, for a young man coming up to Edinburgh University. This was the time of Thomson's higher education, when he continued his study of the classics and also met with modern ideas in philosophy and science as well as more Moderate theology, the foundations of his mature thought. It was a time when he met many new people and made influential contacts in literary, artistic, and political circles. It was the decade of his serious apprenticeship in poetry and of his first published work. It was, too, a period of inner conflict and growth as he struggled to choose between the callings of divinity and poetry. Thomson's Edinburgh years are rather thinly documented, yet the pattern of his life there can be drawn from an examination of the broader contemporary Edinburgh context—its university, its social and political life, its literary milieu.

In the early years of the eighteenth century, Scotland itself, like the adolescent Thomson, was seeking its own identity in an age of transition. The Scottish church was experiencing gradual but momentous changes in outlook; Moderatism came to predominate, but not without bitter opposition from conservative, old-style Presbyterians. Edinburgh University had undergone sweeping reforms as recently as 1708, and its curriculum was changing to accommodate the revolutionary philosophies of Locke and Newton. The Union of 1707 was sealed just eight years before James Thomson arrived in the Scottish capital, and though the poor country had not yet felt its economic benefits, Scots were hopeful; town life began to revive, and the "improving" impulse grew stronger. Many Scots simply equated improvement with Anglicization, but while British culture was ascendant, a nationalistic countermovement gained strength as well. The Scottish identity crisis was most clearly reflected in the burgeoning literary culture: English (Anglo-Scottish), Scots vernacular, and Scottish Latinist literature each promoted its own brand of patriotism. The Jacobite risings of 1715 and 1719, causing turmoil and endangering Edinburgh itself, drew attention to that other deep division in the Scottish political consciousness.

Young James Thomson, it is said, first came to Edinburgh with great reluctance; the shy boy from the provinces, insecure about his academic abilities and social skills, left home just as Jacobite unrest threatened both Edinburgh and the Borders. It was in 1715 that he first matriculated at Edinburgh University. At university, as at school, he was thought a bit dull by his classmates; he stayed a university student for ten years, and was in some ways immature,[1] as his juvenile verses, with their artless religious enthusiasm alternating with Calvinist rigor, their naive love-themes, and their over-eager eclecticism show. Yet he gained a store of learning and valuable experience at Edinburgh which gave him the confidence, by about 1720, to offer his first poetical efforts to peers and public and soon afterward to brave the wider world of London.

Thomson lived in the crowded, noisy Old Town of Edinburgh—vastly different from the orderly, spacious New Town envisioned by his nephew, architect James Craig. Young James probably took university lodgings at first, but soon after his father died in 1716, his mother and family moved to Edinburgh and he may have lived with them for a time. On the advice of a friend, the Rev. Mr. William Gusthart of Crailing and Nisbet, Mrs. Thomson mortgaged her Wideopen property and came to the town to live "in a decent and frugal manner." Her family was large and she was not wealthy, but she kept a comfortable if humble home; her testament lists ample furniture, linens, and pewter and one book, "an old incompleat Bible in quarto." The family was helped with expenses by James's award as Lowland bursar for the

Jedburgh Presbytery.[2] Later, the boy may have shared a room in town with his friend from Ancrum, John Cranstoun, Jr. Cranstoun, who later became a minister, is said to be the source of an anecdote dramatizing Thomson's debilitating superstition: Thomson's bed-mate, at the urging of fellow-collegians who knew his fears, played a joke on him and left him alone in the dark; on awaking, James was so terrified that he ran to his landlady, crying for help.[3]

Despite his insecurities, however, Thomson seems to have led a fairly normal student life at Edinburgh. He studied, participated wholeheartedly in various clubs and especially literary societies, and generally seems to have had a good time. A letter to Dr. William Cranstoun (1724) shows him amused with Edinburgh society: "yet I am but little conversant in the Beau Monde viz Conserts balls assemblies and wher beauty shines and Coxcombs admire themselves." He could not afford to indulge in such entertainments, nor would the Kirk have approved; more important, he felt that such worldly pleasures would interfere with his poetical aspirations:

> If nature had thrown me in a more soft and indolent mold had made me a Shapely or a S[r] Fopling Flutter if fortune had fill'd my pockets (I suppose my head is empty enough as it is) had I been taught to cut a caper to hum a tune to take a pinch and lisp Nonsence with all the grace of fashionable stupidity then I could— what could I have done?—hardly write. but however I might have made a shift to fill up an half sheet with ratt me demme etc. interspers'd with broken Charrecters of ladies gliding o'er my fancy like a passing Image o'er a Mirror.

Young Thomson also showed his enthusiastic appreciation for female beauty and wit here; he was an ardent admirer of the "lasses" all his life. His juvenile love verses in fact approach "Nonsence with all the grace of fashionable stupidity," yet a strain of rich sensuality sometimes breaks through their conventionality. There is no evidence, however, that any youthful infatuations were requited. Though he enjoyed the lively society of the town, Thomson was certainly no libertine; when not engaged in academic or literary pursuits, he found innocuous pleasure in meeting friends in the "Typenny cells," or ale-cellars. Living in Edinburgh, he was very much in the shadow of the Kirk as well as of his mother, so his student days were surely innocent.[4]

Edinburgh University itself in the early eighteenth century was small and poor, but, unlike Oxford, had adopted in 1708 the Continental model of professorial teaching which fostered a more progressive spirit of intellectual curiosity. Good command of Latin was essential, as all lectures were given in Latin; when Thomson matriculated for the M.A. course in autumn 1715, he was admitted as a *Superveniente,* one of those students so well grounded in Latin that they were allowed to exempt Professor Dundas's first-year class and enter a second-year course, Professor William Scott's humanities class. Thomson repeated Scott's class the following year; disturbances in the university caused by the recent Jacobite rising as well as the personal trauma of his father's death in February 1716 must have set him behind in his work. In 1717 he entered Professor Colin Drummond's logic and metaphysics class. Drummond taught according to a rather dull traditional Aristotelian curriculum; his course included rhetoric in the old style based on strict adherence to the rules of Aristotle and the humanists.[5] The study of classical rhetoric, long a central element of Scottish education, proved a pervasive influence on Thomson's Scottish Augustan poetry. The strictures of decorum or appropriateness, correctness or accuracy, and imitation, of which description is one type, governed that traditional canon. In practice, young Thomson's early enthusiasm (under the influence of Horace and Longinus, filtered through Addison's *Spectator*) often led him to bend the ancient rules of decorum and correctness in an age of changing rhetorical values, but he was always aware of those rules.

Thomson's fourth-year course was that of Professor Robert Stewart, who taught natural philosophy, or science, and ethics. Thomson especially enjoyed this class, and it influenced his developing thought, as Stewart embodied the new philosophical spirit of the reformed university. The pedagogic link between science and ethics was a significant one; Thomson would frequently represent moral ideas with scientific imagery in his poetry. It is even highly probable that by 1719 Stewart was teaching Newtonian philosophy. Edinburgh had been the first college in Europe publicly to profess Newtonianism, under David Gregory, and here the new science flourished.[6] The empirical scientific method particularly appealed to young Thomson, who would delight in directly observing and describing nature in poetry. His fellow-student and friend George Turnbull would later articulate such faith in empirical and ethical "education through things" and its manifestation in the arts, including descriptive poetry, in his "common sense" philosophy of the Scottish Enlightenment.[7]

Robert Stewart's Newtonian curriculum was at first centered on the *Principia,* and only after Thomson's student days did he treat the *Optics* in depth, so it is no surprise that Thomson's juvenile poetry has little noticeably Newtonian light or color imagery while it does make symbolic reference to gravity and attractive force. More important, Stewart spent much of his course discussing the religious implications of Newtonian science. This was typical of contemporary science teaching at Edinburgh, where mathematics and astronomy lessons also introduced theological and metaphysical, along with technical, concepts.[8] Thomson made a conscious effort to reconcile this new science with Scottish Calvinist orthodoxy, and this is evident in his poetry; even as a young poet and prospective divine he, like other physicotheological poets of the age, was trying to arrive at a satisfying and sound union of science with orthodox faith. Newton's laws, as well as his light and color imagery, could be found to reinforce theological concepts and symbols, so admiration for Newton's discoveries was logically also admiration for God's universal scheme and a worthy theme for poetry.

While at Edinburgh University, then, Thomson learned the valuable lesson that theology, philosophy and science, and poetry were congenial disciplines, and he set out at once to prove it. He has been called "the first Scottish Newtonian poet."[9] Shortly after leaving Edinburgh, he wrote the famous "A Poem Sacred to the Memory of Sir Isaac Newton" (1727), where influence of both *Principia* and *Optics* is clear. Years later, George Turnbull urged the poet to write a lengthy descriptive and philosophical poem on the beauties of the Newtonian system, though this never materialized. Thomson's empirical impulse, his use of Newtonian light and color imagery and symbolism, his identification of Newtonian gravity with the ethical and religious concept of universal harmony, his concern with the deeper moral significance of nature's laws generally inform *The Seasons, Liberty,* and *The Castle of Indolence.*[10]

Beyond Thomson's formal scientific curriculum, it is enlightening to record an event which took place on March 6, 1716, the only specific incident from this decade portrayed in the mature poetry. On that date, the aurora borealis made a dramatic appearance over Scotland, and Thomson probably witnessed it. He may have been in Edinburgh or in Southdean following his father's death. Such a phenomenon, traditionally held to be an ominous portent and coming so soon after his father's strange death, must have made a strong impression on the superstitious boy. His description of the aurora in "Autumn" is strikingly similar to an eye-witness account of the sighting over Edinburgh:

> The Sky grew very bright on a sudden; and from the several Parts of the Heaven, the Light collected it self into so many several Points, which (with great haste) flew unanimously toward a Center, which seem'd directly over the Town . . . The Light at this Meeting was prodigiously great, though not lasting; when the several Points seem'd just upon each other in the Center, they appeared to clash with great Fury, then retired, seemingly half a Dozen or Ten Yards, then flew in again; particularly the Points from the *East* and *West,* which perfectly, as it were, fought and run into each other, which always gave the greater Brightness. At this Mixture, there appeared all the Colours of the Rainbow.[11]

Young Thomson's very will to overcome his own debilitating superstition likely motivated him to study the new science with such enthusiasm and, more broadly, to try to reconcile the scientific laws of nature with religious belief. He ultimately hoped to identify himself with the "Man of philosophic Eye," the "sage" ("Autumn," ll. 1133–1134), who rose above fear and superstition through informed reason.

In 1719, Thomson completed the four-year M.A. course at Edinburgh University, but, as was the custom of the time, he did not take the degree. The college emphasis was more on learning than on graduation itself, an attitude which prompted students to explore subjects outside the prescribed syllabus. The university offered a number of optional public lectures which Thomson may have attended, such as James Gregory's mathematics class, which was Newtonian in the Gregory family tradition, and perhaps Charles Mackie's class in the Faculty of Laws on universal history and Greek and Roman antiquities, subjects which fascinated Thomson and which would become the themes of *Liberty* and several of the plays.[12] Thomson was always highly ambitious to learn about things which interested him, and even outside of these university courses he eagerly sought to improve himself. He did not lack for improving facilities in Edinburgh. He joined university debating and literary societies whose chief object seemed to be to divest their members of Scotticisms. He also found time to indulge his own poetical pursuits and to read voraciously. The Edinburgh University Library was a valuable resource, and its holdings included much English and Middle Scots literature. The Divinity College library, too, held a wide-ranging collection. Edinburgh was at this time the Scottish center for publication and distribution of a variety of literature in Scots, English, and Latin, providing a rich fund of learning for Thomson and his keen contemporaries. Scottish publishers and editors such as Thomas Ruddiman, James Watson, and Allan Ramsay, acting as literary patriots, made important Scottish neo-Latin and Scots vernacular works more readily accessible. English periodicals such as *The Tatler* and *The Spectator* were also available and offered popular versions of current ideas in philosophy, science, theology, and aesthetics; they served as improving guides for ambitious Anglo-Scots. It would not be too much to assume, for example, that Addison's series of *Spectator* essays on "The Pleasures of the Imagination" served as a sort of handbook for James Thomson and his colleagues in their serious study of English letters.

While Addison himself did not invent the new rhetoric, with its growing emphasis on more subjective criteria of taste and sensibility, his advice certainly helped to shape its character. English Augustan poets had already been treating the strict classical rules with some freedom, though the intellectual formulation of the new rhetoric was a phenomenon of late eighteenth-century Scotland, as Lord Kames, Hugh Blair, James Beattie, George Campbell, and others of their generation worked a compromise between old-style objective rhetorical strictures and more subjective standards. These standards reflected the fresh scientific spirit of empiricism; the subjective sense experience of pleasure could help to determine aesthetic value. Scottish Enlightenment philosophers such as Francis Hutcheson, Thomson's friend George Turnbull, and Turnbull's pupil Thomas Reid further held that man's moral sense could be disposed to cultivation through the aesthetic sense, though these two "senses" were separate and distinct. Thomson, educated in Scotland during the formative years of the Scottish Enlightenment, was perhaps the earliest poet actually to practice wholeheartedly what these Scottish rhetoricians and philosophers would preach. The empirical ethos and the new rhetoric of the Enlightenment were both basic to his poetry of description. His philosophical and aesthetic ideals were both "common sense" and "sensible" ones.

However "enlightened" in his literary views, though, Thomson still intended to study divinity with the ultimate goal of becoming a minister of the Scottish church. Momentous changes were taking place within the church at this time, as Reformation attitudes were rapidly giving way to the more tolerant, rational Enlightenment outlook of the Moderate element.[13] Old-style beliefs were far from dead in Thomson's years at divinity college, however; the student-poet would continue to encounter both sides of Scottish religion, the rigorous, dogmatic older Scottish Calvinism and the more liberal Moderate philosophy, and to experience and try to come to terms with the tensions between them in that time of transition.

Thomson matriculated at Divinity Hall in 1719. His undergraduate years, a time of intense literary activity, had culminated in a substantial body of juvenile poetry and the publication of three poems in the *Edinburgh Miscellany* (1720). Yet there are no extant poems from the period of 1721 to 1725; he may have found that he had to restrict his poetical efforts while at Divinity Hall due to lack of time and perhaps also the Kirk's lingering disapproval of imaginative literature. Art-literature, and especially drama, had long been abhorrent to Scottish Calvinists, who even in the early eighteenth century provided scant encouragement for the arts. There was already, though, growing acceptance of poetry by some, particularly verse of religious purpose such as physicotheological poetry. This growing acceptance came in part through increased contacts with England and in part through liberal trends within the Scottish church and society itself. Even as Moderatism tempered Calvinist severity and many old tenets fell away, Scottish Calvinists still inherited an introspective, soul-searching propensity and an emotional, mystical sensibility which had characterized their religious faith. Such subjective dispositions, newly freed from strict doctrinal constraints, were naturally enough drawn to poetry; such had been the case in Puritan England in the previous century, and a similar liberating process now gave rise to religious poetry in eighteenth-century Scotland. Poetry could express deep religious feelings in a fresh and imaginative way; it could function as an emotional outlet, a means of sharing in God's creative power, and a legitimate act of praise as well as be a means of teaching others about God.[14] Elements of both religious sentimentality and heavy didacticism, products of this Calvinist habit of mind, are evident in Thomson's juvenile poetry and reappear even in *The Seasons* and later works. More positively, this spirit inherited from Scottish Calvinism— the emotional sensitivity, the impulse to praise the Creator and to share in His Creation through description—inspires the best of Thomson's religious poetry in *The Seasons*.

What precedents were there for a Scottish minister aiming to be a poet? A rare early role model was Alexander Hume (ca. 1560–1609). His *Hymnes, or Sacred Songs* were all religious-didactic pieces except for the famous "Of the Day Estivall," a poem of exquisite and sensuous natural description. The religious-didactic purpose of poetry as Hume saw it was essentially the same as Thomson and many of his contemporaries conceived it to be; however, more than a century of religious strife, marked by increasing distrust and censure of literature by the Scottish Kirk, had intervened. Paradoxically, poetry— even explicitly religious poetry—was not so generally well tolerated in Scotland in 1700 as it had been in 1600. A major theme underlying Thomson's years as a prospective divine, as evidenced in the juvenilia, is his personal struggle to reconcile his ministerial calling to his poetic vocation. In his student days in Scotland, this resolution was not so easily reached as it might have been by mid-century, when Robert Blair would publish his *The Grave*.

Blair makes the obvious contemporary comparison to Thomson as religious poet. He was Thomson's fellow student at Divinity Hall; he became a minister and remained in Scotland. He began *The Grave* in youth but did not publish it until 1743, when the milder religious climate was more favorable to art-literature. While Blair's mentor Isaac Watts had long been comfortably established in the dual role of minister and poet in England, Blair was very cautious about submitting his *Grave* to the eye of the public, and especially of the Kirk. Even by 1743 he harbored doubts as to the propriety of a minister publishing poetry. Blair's *Grave* is a poetical sermon, preaching the message that man must ever be prepared for death. *The Grave* was representative of the mid-eighteenth-century Evangelical Revival in Britain; Blair recognized that Scotland was fertile ground for such revival.[15] His evangelical fervor in the poem frequently leads to gloomy or sentimental emotional excess; its often horrendous literal-mindedness, its vivid and concrete use of unsavory graveyard imagery bear the influence of Scottish Calvinist sermon rhetoric. In general, *The Grave* manifests a negative, sensational side of old-style Scottish Calvinism handled with considerable poetic license. Thomson's *Seasons,* on the other hand, generally represents the more Moderate outlook, where reason and benevolence predominate.

There is kinship, nonetheless, between the evangelical *Grave* and the enlightened *Seasons. The Seasons* never completely forsakes the old-style Scottish Calvinism of the poet's youth; rather, certain passages could almost have inspired *The Grave* itself, as Thomson preaches a stern morality, attacking vanity and warning "fond Man" to prepare to die. The sermon tone, the forceful didacticism are the same. The vein of emotional indulgence and sentimentality, important in Thomson's juvenile poetry as well as in *The Grave* and an indirect spiritual product of the Scottish Calvinist temper, also runs right through *The Seasons,* though moderated with Augustan reason. Both poets share a peculiar credulity, a genuine belief in the supernatural largely absent from contemporary English poetry; such superstition permeated both the folklore and the unenlightened religious beliefs of Scotland. Both *The Grave* and *The Seasons* are in blank verse; in fact, when Blair and Thomson were students at the university, there seems to have been among Edinburgh students a particular vogue for descriptive poetry in blank verse.[16] Further, both poems use sound patterns liberally and effectively to reinforce sense.[17] Both poems are not only religious but also natural-descriptive poems in the Scottish tradition. Both Blair and Thomson, who shared a common background and education at Edinburgh University's Divinity College, found a creative outlet in poetry for their philosophies and their feelings: Blair, writing from an old-style viewpoint within the orthodox Presbyterian ministry, and Thomson, writing from a more Moderate stance, without.

Much of the divinity course which Thomson and Blair undertook was almost certainly old-fashioned, perhaps dull; many early eighteenth-century professors of divinity were said to have been so tedious in their learned orthodoxy that this in itself provoked their students to think for themselves and adopt more liberal views. Little formal course work was actually prescribed. Ecclesiastical history was not required, and Hebrew was neglected during the century. Only Professor William Hamilton's course in divinity was mandatory,[18] and while this was a fairly rigorous, traditional course, it sparked a spirit of religious inquiry, and Thomson and his fellow students appreciated and profited from it. Hamilton's wisdom, kindness, and candor earned him the love and esteem of his students, and Thomson always spoke of him with affectionate respect.[19] The learned Professor William Hamilton was a religious conservative, but he had an open mind and kept well informed of current theological trends. He came from a Covenanting background and hoped that his students would show "charitable respect" for the stern Kirk fathers, but his own enlightened toleration led a suspicious Robert Wodrow to remark, " 'it's thought he is departed from the Calvinistic doctrine taught in the Church, though he hath the wisdom to keep himself in the clouds.' " Wodrow also borrowed the term "New Light" to apply to Hamilton's students. Hamilton so inspired a new, broad-minded, and liberal attitude in his students, including Thomson, that he has been called the first true teacher of the Moderate generation.[20]

Hamilton's training went beyond theology into rhetoric and homi-
letics to prepare his students for the pulpit. He would assign his students a variety of exercises, including lectures and homilies and also
scriptural exegeses designated "exercises" and "additions." These pre-
sentations he criticized freely, "lopping off luxuriances, and repre-
hending with kind severity everything that savoured of bombast or
vulgarity."[21] It is said that about 1720 James Thomson delivered a
Psalm exercise so extravagantly poetical that Hamilton "told him,
smiling, that if he thought of being useful in the ministry, he must
keep a stricter rein upon his imagination, and express himself in language more intelligible to an ordinary congregation."[22] Thomson's
fellows, amazed at his display of genius, tried but failed to prove that
the poetical exercise was a plagiarism; thereafter they greatly admired
him.[23]

Hamilton kept meticulous records of how each of his students performed the tasks he had set them, and this record is happily extant in
the professor's notebook.[24] He divided his students into a number of
groups, or "Societies," to do their various so-called exercises, additions, and lectures or homilies. James Thomson was a part of Group 4
from 1719 until 1723, joined in that group by Patrick Murdoch in
1721 to 1723; Murdoch later became an Anglican clergyman and was
Thomson's lifelong friend, biographer, and editor. Also in Group 4 in
1721 was one "Will. Riddall," probably the William Riddell who was
the lamented subject of Thomson's juvenile elegy "A Pastoral betwixt
Thirsis and Corydon upon the death of Damon." Thomson delivered
a number of exercises, additions, and lectures in his years at Divinity
Hall. On January 13, 1723, for example, he gave a homily on Matthew
10:29–31 (God's loving care of both sparrows and men), and on
March 28, 1724, another homily on Matthew 26:29.[25] Professor
Hamilton's notebook also contained a book list, evidently a catalog of
the theological library. Notably, the list included many books which
treated of theology and natural history together, such as Derham's
writings, Ray's *Wisdom of God in the Creation* and *On the Chaos and Deluge,* and Woodward's *Essay on Natural History.* Clearly, physicotheology
or natural religion had increasingly come to be taught in reinforce-
ment of Christian revelation and was considered a legitimate and sig-

nificant subject of study in Thomson's time as a divinity student, even though Scottish Calvinist orthodoxy did not sanction it wholeheartedly and even Moderates like Riccaltoun had reservations about its use. As a student in Scotland, Thomson thus learned to see religion and nature—and the scientific study of nature—in harmony and to view the natural world from a religious standpoint.[26]

Thomson stayed on at Divinity Hall until late 1724 or early 1725, nearly completing the required six years of study but not taking the trials for licensing as a minister. By that time he had certain plans in mind; he knew he wanted to write poetry and possibly envisioned a solution similar to that of one of his early models in English verse, Isaac Watts, of adopting the dual vocation of minister-poet, an aspiration more readily attainable in England than in Scotland. He had not, at that point, abandoned the ministry, but at the same time England and a literary life beckoned.

In 1725 Thomson's formal education, after ten years as a student in Edinburgh, was complete. His education as a poet, however, had only just begun with his university course-work. Beyond the curriculum, simply living in Edinburgh in the early eighteenth century was an education in itself for young Thomson. Developments in Scottish society and culture had lasting impact on the impressionable boy from the Borders and would profoundly influence his way of looking at life, literature, and his native land. The recent Union of 1707 had greatly intensified Scotland's crisis of national identity. To many Scots the Union represented final political loss to England.[27] Other Scots hopefully expected economic benefits from the Union, but these were not immediately forthcoming, and for the first two decades of Union Scotland suffered burdensome taxes and regulations and loss of trade. Unemployment was high and industry and agriculture languished. Many people escaped from a life of poverty in Scotland by emigrating to England or abroad. Ultimately such conditions motivated a constructive improvement campaign within Scotland, leading directly to the Scottish Enlightenment later in the century, but the greatest fear of many Scots—loss of Scottish cultural identity in the rising tide of post-Union Anglicization—was swiftly becoming a reality.

Thomson himself was brought up a staunch Whig and Hanoverian, as were most Presbyterians of the time; it did not necessarily follow, though, that he was strongly pro-Union at first. The issue was complex. Thomson would have heard both sides of the Union debate from his father, William Bennet, the Elliots of Minto, Riccaltoun, and others. Bennet, a Squadrone Whig, was probably ambivalent about the Union himself, though like most he ultimately supported it. Bennet and many Scots like him saw a parallel between the Union of Scotland with Augustan England and the relationship of Rome to her provinces in the Roman Empire;[28] such Scots perhaps did not wish to be thought a "province" of London but determined to make the best of the Union by working for the good of Great Britain, the new Augustan Empire. Though James Thomson would later show increasing admiration for Roman Republican virtues of native independence, patriotism, and national autonomy as well, at this early stage he largely shared Bennet's pragmatic views in identifying united Britain with "Empire." During the Jacobite rising of 1715, Thomson certainly sympathized with the ruling Hanoverians. He was probably caught up in the university's upheaval when the rebels bore down on Edinburgh; he surely shared in the general Whig mood of mockery mixed with nervousness, which letters and publications of the time betrayed.[29] This earlier Jacobite threat laid the basis for his later experiences; in 1745 to 1746, when the Jacobites mounted their major offensive and Thomson was living in London, he would relive certain anxieties he had felt in 1715.

Even as a student in Edinburgh, James Thomson had many friends in high places. He had become acquainted with leaders in Whig political circles from both major factions of the party, the Squadrones (who wanted some form of Scottish home rule) and the Argathelians (supporters of the duke of Argyll, who preferred centralized rule of Scotland from London). Through David Mallet or perhaps William Bennet, Thomson may have met John Ker, duke of Roxburghe; he was the Squadrone leader and served as Third Secretary (secretary of state for Scotland) from 1716 to 1725. Roxburghe was an Opposition Whig from the poet's home county and subscribed to *The Seasons* (1730). Thomson's close friend and mentor Duncan Forbes of Culloden, an Argathelian Whig, became Lord Advocate for Scotland in 1725. Associating with such powerful Scotsmen as these, young Thomson no doubt followed with great interest the intricacies of Scottish politics and Scottish-English relations.

Politics and literature were especially closely linked in post-Union Scotland, when literature became the arena for the debate over national identity after the political issue had been officially settled with the treaty of Union, and literary language both reflected and reinforced cultural divisions. In Edinburgh, Thomson's own political awareness and his poetical ambitions grew strong together and informed one another. The national consciousness was not merely a dichotomy, as it is usually characterized, but was split three ways. Advocates of Scots vernacular, Scottish neo-Latin, and Anglo-Scottish poetry each held their own views on literary patriotism and Scottish identity which they voiced in the many literary societies which sprang up in the capital city during the period and in their newly revivified Scottish literature itself.

Poetry in Scots was generally linked with ardent Scottish patriotism, nationalism, and opposition to Union. Scots as a literary language was beginning to experience a far-reaching revival in the early eighteenth century, thanks to publishers such as Ruddiman and Watson and the dynamic author, editor, and antiquarian Allan Ramsay; literary-patriotic societies such as Ramsay's Easy Club promoted the vernacular revival and its goals. The Easy Club actually grew so aggressively nationalistic that it was seen as a threat to the Union and was dissolved in 1715. Thomson was apparently never drawn to such an overtly nationalistic group and showed little interest in writing Scots verse himself, though as a boy he did at least once try his hand at it (see Chapter 3).

A second element of Scottish literary-political society, also strongly patriotic but from a slightly different standpoint, was the Scottish neo-Latinist circle of poets and scholars. Directly descended from the Renaissance Scottish Latinist culture and still dedicated to perpetuating the Roman ethos in Scotland, it identified Scotland with ancient Rome and fostered so-called vernacular humanism. In Thomson's day Scottish classicism was kept alive by a small number of Latinists, mainly of

Tory-Jacobite and Episcopalian allegiance, but also including some Whigs and Presbyterians such as Sir William Bennet. Thomas Ruddiman brought together the Latinist element of Edinburgh society in his Society for Improving Classical Studies (founded 1718), a group which discussed philosophy and law and celebrated the Scottish Latinist literary tradition. Many divinity students attended its meetings to debate religious questions and study Latin culture,[30] and Thomson may have been among them. Thomson himself left no extant attempts at Latin verse; he spoke disparagingly of contemporary neo-Latin poetry in commenting on a poem by Professor John Ker of Aberdeen, translated by Mallet, who was once Ker's pupil. He wrote to Mallet: "How dare you immerse Yourself in his [Ker's] Utter Darkness. Death! to sing after a Cuckow; and abett the Murderer of the Classicks. . . . The Muses blush that these, and several Others, should be called in Imitation of the Latin Jargon; which, rather than imitated should be eschewed. . . ." This light-hearted remark cannot help but suggest that Thomson actually saw Scottish neo-Latin literature as a futile and obsolete exercise. He may have felt about Latin as about Scots, that it was now inappropriate and outdated as a formal literary language and would limit the scope as well as the audience of the literature. His attitude was fairly justified given the poor quality of much contemporary Latin verse; he probably believed, along with the English Augustans he emulated, that true neoclassicism would be better represented by good English imitation than by inferior modern invention. Nevertheless, his comment seems curious, since he was profoundly influenced by the Scoto-Roman ethos and especially since his own poetical language is pervasively Latinate, aureate.[31]

The third segment of early eighteenth-century Scottish society was that of the Anglicizers, the ascendant culture comprising a Whig-Presbyterian majority and the one most congenial to Thomson himself. These Anglo-Scots had a variety of motives for adopting English ways. Many sought higher social standing by rejecting "provincial" Scottish language and accent; they were actually ashamed of their nationality. Other more practical Scots knew that writing in English would attract a wider literary market. Still others had more noble motives for embracing English language and literature; optimistic about Scotland's improvement through Union with England, they were truly patriotic North Britons who felt pride in Scottish potential and hoped not only to gain from but also to contribute to wider British culture. These Anglo-Scots, Thomson among them, prepared the way for the Scottish Enlightenment, which was both nationalistic and cosmopolitan. Thomson, of course, chose English as the medium for his poetry, but he did not simply mimic Augustan English poetic language and forms; rather, he adapted them, combining them with many distinctively Scottish strengths, to make his own contribution to British poetry in an act of positive patriotism.[32]

In the Edinburgh context of Thomson's student years, one central figure exemplifies the cultural complexity of the period. One can learn much by becoming acquainted with that archetypal Scot and literary man of the age, Allan Ramsay. Ramsay is often portrayed as a cultural schizophrenic driven by mixed motives, torn among sentimental Jacobitism, Scottish jingoism, and Anglophilia; this rather negative stereotype, however, cannot account for the wide-ranging accomplishments and influence of that eclectic genius. Ramsay's role in reviving older Scottish literature and encouraging new, as editor of *The Ever Green* and *The Tea-Table Miscellany* and as a Scots poet, was invaluable. He also had close ties with the Scottish Latinists, particularly as member and bard of that same Royal Company of Archers to which William Bennet belonged. Ramsay was certainly not immune to Anglicizing fever, either; many of his poems (though not his best) are in English, and even his Scots poems were very much influenced in both language and form by Augustan English poetry. Ramsay's poetry, so prolific and varied, *was* his politics, reflecting to some extent all three facets of Scottish culture. Officially he was a Whig and was realistic in accepting the Union and optimistic that Scotland could improve itself. James Thomson surely shared many of Ramsay's complex feelings about Scotland; his juvenilia attest to his admiration for Ramsay and his poetry, though Thomson would ultimately choose for himself a different resolution. Thomson probably met Ramsay first at Sir William Bennet's Marlefield House; he almost certainly knew him in Edinburgh. The main feature of Edinburgh literary society in the early eighteenth century was its many "improving" clubs, and Ramsay's influence on Thomson may have come through a group with which they both seem to have been associated, the Worthy Club, a literary and convivial society of eminent Scots. Ramsay belonged, of course, and among its other members were several of Thomson's friends, including Duncan Forbes, Sir Gilbert Elliot of Minto, and artist William Aikman. David Mallet also knew Ramsay and helped him collect material for the *Tea-Table*.

Out of Thomson's and Ramsay's acquaintance arose a curious and long-lived legend. As Ramsay frequently read drafts of his *The Gentle Shepherd* (1725) to friends to solicit their critical comments, authorship of the pastoral drama came to be attributed to various people who no doubt did offer some advice about it to Ramsay. One suspected "author" was William Bennet, and it has likewise been suggested that the setting of *The Gentle Shepherd* closely resembles the Marlefield estate, which Ramsay so loved. Another candidate was William Hamilton of Gilbertfield.[33] The most intriguing of these tales claims that James Thomson himself wrote *The Gentle Shepherd*. If young Thomson was associated with the Worthy Club in some way, as seems likely, and if he attended their meetings, he might well have been a party to the literary-critical sessions on the evolving *Gentle Shepherd*. Descendants of Thomson's family even speculated that he may have contributed to Ramsay's work; a "near relation" reported in the early nineteenth century that Thomson's nephew, the Rev. James Bell of Coldstream, who once projected an edition and life of the poet, had "strong grounds for believing Thomson to have assisted Ramsay in writing The Gentle Shepherd." Published attributions to Thomson began to appear in the late eighteenth century, and the authorship question continued to be debated on textual, stylistic, generic, and thematic grounds until into the twentieth century.[34] The fact that both Ramsay and Thomson had set out, in the Scottish tradition, to revitalize Scottish nature poetry surely reinforced the myth. The similarity of their goals for Scottish poetry can be seen by comparing Ramsay's important preface to *The Ever Green* (1724) with Thomson's preface to "Winter" (1726). The legend that Thomson actually wrote *The Gentle Shepherd* takes several variations but generally holds that young Thomson, having written the pastoral himself, felt it would be better received under the name of the eminent man of letters Ramsay. He thus proposed to Ramsay that he "father" the work and lend it his name. While these stories are utterly false, that they arose at all suggests Thomson's intimate links with the Ramsay circle.

Apart from Ramsay, a number of other Worthy Club members would figure significantly in Thomson's future. The Worthy Club may even have been the group described by Patrick Murdoch of "certain learned gentlemen, into whose hands a few of Mr. Thomson's first essays had fallen," who reportedly criticized stylistic improprieties while overlooking the novice poet's enthusiasm and originality. But Worthy Club members were not all negative in responding to Thomson's juvenile verse; some of those "learned gentlemen" must be counted as major influences on his career. Thomson already knew Sir Gilbert Elliot of Minto from Border days. He almost certainly knew Duncan Forbes of Culloden in Edinburgh. Forbes is said to have seen some of Thomson's poetry in Scotland, and he would prove a friend and mentor to the poet after he arrived, poor and bewildered, in London.[35] Thomson would also become a good friend of Forbes's son John, or "Jock."

Portrait artist William Aikman was also a "Worthy"; he had studied in Italy and returned to Edinburgh in 1712. His departure for London in 1723, where he would enjoy the patronage of the duke of Argyll, was commemorated in verse by Allan Ramsay. Later in London, Aikman and Thomson would be close friends. In addition to two later oil portraits of Thomson done in London (ca. 1725–1726) and showing the poet already growing corpulent and unattractive, Aikman had done a sketch of Thomson as a younger, handsome man; this early sketch is tentatively dated ca. 1720, that is, while Thomson was a divinity student in Edinburgh.[36] Thomson's relationship with Aikman may have sparked his lifelong interest in fine art. When Aikman died in 1731, both Thomson and Mallet responded with elegies for him. Through Aikman and the Worthies, Thomson also knew the artist's cousin, Sir John Clerk of Penicuik, second baronet. Years later, Thomson would be called upon to exercise great tact in commenting on Sir John's uninspired verse *The Country Seat*, which he had sent in draft to Aikman to solicit the opinion of the poet of *The Seasons*.[37]

Other Worthies Thomson probably knew were poets Dr. Alexander Pennecuik of Newhall and Romanno, author of *Description of Tweeddale* (1715) and several verses of natural description, and his nephew Alexander Pennecuik. The Worthies often met at Newhall House, where Thomson may even have met an occasional visitor there, John Gay.

The deep-rooted ambivalence of Edinburgh literary society can best be seen in another of its clubs, to which James Thomson certainly belonged. This was the Grotesque Club, which met to foster "improvement" in (English) arts and letters. Young Thomson certainly needed improvement in formal English; his early letters and manuscript poems are liberally sprinkled with Scotticisms, solecisms, and irregular spellings.[38] He would "improve" rapidly, however; with practice his writing grew increasingly polished and his early letters home from London, from the time when he was writing "Winter," had attained a certain elegance. Such improvement cannot have been an easy task for the apprentice Scottish poet. In such clubs as the Grotesque, members democratically submitted their work to their fellows for criticism, and such outspoken censure must have been painful for the shy and self-conscious Thomson. When he eventually did present his poetry to the club, it was not much appreciated. Mallet, also a Grotesque Club member, later recalled of Thomson:

> ["Winter"] was written by that dull fellow, whom [Alexander] Malcolm calls the jest of our club. The injustice I did him then, in joining with my companions to ridicule the first, imperfect, essays of an excellent genius, was a strong motive to make me active in endeavouring to assist and encourage him since. . . .[39]

Clubs such as this, where zealous Anglo-Scots tried to surpass the Augustans in propriety, strongly discouraged any deviation from strict neoclassical poetic norms, any trace of peculiarity or originality. Thomson's juvenilia certainly did not always fit the proper or decorous Augustan mold, though some of them do display an element of creativity perhaps less deliberate than naive, a spark of enlivening enthusiasm which the literati overlooked. Thomson's juvenile poems are mostly mediocre, but his rejection by early Edinburgh audiences

was surely also due to his very originality, or, as the Scottish Enlightenment rhetoricians would call it, his untutored "genius." Thomson
bore candid criticism with good nature and persisted with his poetry
while making plans to go south to England to seek a more receptive
audience.[40]

Little is known of the Grotesque Club itself except for a notice
Aaron Hill printed in his *Plain Dealer* (August 28, 1724), sent to him
by one who styled himself "Fergus Bruce." This was clearly someone
concerned with Scottish social improvement through English language—possibly Allan Ramsay,[41] Joseph Mitchell, or even Mallet:

> A Society of Young Gentlemen, most, if not all of them, Students
> in the University of *Edinburgh,* who from a Sympathy of Affec-
> tions, founded on a Similitude of *Parts,* and *Genius,* have united
> themselves into a Body, under Title of THE GROTESQUE CLUB; the
> Reason of which Name, I shall explain in a future Paper [unfor-
> tunately, he did not]. Their Business, to express it in the Words of
> one of their own Members, is, *A Friendship that knows no Strife, but
> that of a generous Emulation, to excell, in Virtue, Learning, and
> Politeness.*[42]

Along with this, Hill printed the anonymous poem ["The Works and
Wonders of Almighty Power"], which has since been attributed to
Thomson. "Fergus Bruce" afterward thanked Hill for his recognition
of the club (*Plain Dealer,* September 28, 1724).

As fellow-members of the Grotesque Club, students Thomson and
David Mallet (1705?–1765) began their lifelong friendship. Mallet,
son of a gardener from Abercairny, Perthshire, was a pupil of John Ker,
later professor of classics at Aberdeen. Mallet's real name was "Mal-
loch"; he changed it to the more English "Mallet" after settling in
London. He also succeeded, unlike Thomson, in removing all trace of
Scots accent and dialect from his speech. How he and Thomson remained such good friends is a mystery; Mallet, who often showed
himself to be an egotistical, unscrupulous opportunist, was very different from Thomson and even "more inferior to his amiable friend
in heart than in genius. . . ."[43] Yet he and Thomson shared a great
love of poetry of natural description, they had many friends in com-

mon from student days, and they held similar political views. Mallet, who went south in 1723, proved helpful to Thomson when he arrived two years later.

A third Edinburgh literary club, with which both Thomson and Mallet were associated even though they were not official members, was the Athenian Society, and it offers the fullest record of Thomson's early poetical activity. This club was better known than the Grotesque by virtue of its several publications. The society, labeled "Mitchell's Club," was led by Joseph Mitchell (1684–1738), a contemporary of Ramsay. Later, Mitchell's adverse criticism would cause both Ramsay and Thomson to fall out with him. Mitchell was a poet and arbiter of taste among rising young Anglo-Scottish poets. One of these, Thomson's colleague John Callender of Craigforth, wrote for *The Edinburgh Miscellany* (1720) a fulsome "Epistle to Mr. M[itchel]l" ("To thee, dear Friend, who prun'd my flutt'ring Wing, / Inspir'd my Muse, and taught me how to sing"), invoking Mitchell to

> Clap but my Cheek, it will afford Delight,
> And when I err, but set me in the right;
> Approve my first my criminal Essays,
> And, with good Words, correct my Infant Lays.

Mitchell had planned to become a clergyman but chose instead a literary career. His early poetry like Thomson's was much influenced by Isaac Watts, whom he knew, and generally by the emotional element in Calvinism. Like so many of his Scottish contemporaries, Mitchell eventually went to London to practice his art, where he joined Aaron Hill's circle. Mitchell would become the only critic who, for his disparaging remarks on "Winter," genuinely angered the genial Thomson. While still in Edinburgh, however, Mitchell seems to have offered encouragement to the younger poet.[44]

The Athenian Society sponsored several volumes of verse, and it is revealing of the Scottish literary scene at the time to look at these more closely. Among them were a collection of five translations of Horace's "Epistle to Nero" and the no longer extant *Scots Miscellany*, with a verse by Mallet. Both collections, ca. 1719, have been described as mediocre.[45] Another volume, published in London for the Athenians, was more noteworthy; it was entitled *Lugubres Cantus: Poems on Several Grave and Important Subjects, Chiefly Occasion'd by the Death of the late Ingenious Youth John Mitchell,* by Joseph Mitchell, John Calendar [Callender], et al.[46] This volume was a collection of elegiac and religious-meditative poetry in memory of the younger brother of Joseph Mitchell, who died in 1719, and also a "Mr. Foord." It served to publicize both the poetic accomplishments and the patriotism of the ascendant Anglo-Scottish literati, as the preface declares:

> It may be sufficient to tell, that besides the Charms of Nature and Friendship, which are conspicuous in these loose and careless Performances, the Zeal we have for our Country's Honour and Interest, and the Encouragement we are dispos'd to afford our Youth, who begin of late to shew a noble Genius, and discover a generous Emulation in the Study of all polite Accomplishments, particularly Poetry, put us upon this Method; and we hope, since we are as good Friends to the Publick, and as seldom uneasy to it, as any Set of Mortals, no Body will deny us the Privilege of Acting as well as Thinking freely, when we have a Mind.

> 'Ere long (if the Prospect we now have of our rising Generation in *Scotland* deceive us not) the World may have the Satisfaction to know, and be better entertained by them, in whose Name this Preface is compos'd. . . . J. Hume (p. iv)

The society's serious "Method" was thus to bring the "rising Generation" of Anglo-Scottish poets to public notice. Though none of Thomson's early poems appear in *Lugubres,* those of several of his colleagues do. Among John Callender's verses, for instance, is an "Epistle to Robert Blair," who was Callender's good friend. Other contributors were the Scots R. Boyd, C. Cunningham, and Robert Duncan, Thomson's former classmate in Professor Scott's class of 1715.

Among the prefatory verses in *Lugubres* are those by "A. [Ambrose] Philips" and "E. [Edward] Young," indicating some close connection between the Edinburgh Athenian Society and the "rising Generation" of descriptive-meditative poets in England. Philips was also the author of the descriptive verse letter "A Winter Piece" (1709), an influence on

Thomson's own "Winter." Thomson would come to know Young personally in England in later years. Philips's poem "To the Author of the First Part of the Lugubres Cantus" (Mitchell) shows sympathy with the tribulations of aspiring Scottish poets:

> But most they are expos'd to publick Spite,
> Who in a rude and sullen Country write.
> Ungenerous Minds, with Prejudice possest,
> Despise the Brave, and make their Works a Jest:
> While others meanly reckon Nothing fine,
> Can in a poor abandon'd Nation shine;
> That foggy Air th' aspiring Genius checks,
> And adverse Fate a noble Spirit breaks.
> As if the Oak on Mountains could not rise,
> And Palms oppress'd shoot faster to the Skies.

He calls on these poets to, "In spite of Censure and Misfortune rise, / Dear Youth, your rugged Land to civilize," and finally concedes, "That we must own the *English* Muse is yours, / With as much Right and Liberty as ours." Young, in his "To Mr. Mitchell," hails the new Anglo-Scottish effort: "Our hopes and fond Endeavours now succeed, / *Edina's* Bards begin to raise their Head." Indeed, *Lugubres* was published in London with an eye toward bringing this fresh Anglo-Scottish talent to the attention of English audiences, patrons, and publishers, and Philips and Young clearly intended to offer the young Scots a boost in this.[47]

The most important production of the Athenian Society was *The Edinburgh Miscellany* (Edinburgh, 1720),[48] where James Thomson's first published verses appeared. It, too, boasted of its primary aim of promoting new Anglo-Scottish poetry. Its preface, by one "W. C.," is rather condescending and apologetic for the poor quality of some of the verses in the volume:

> . . . we have ventur'd to publish several juvenile Poems, where the Dawings [*sic*—Scotticism] of a good Genius appear'd, merely to encourage the Authors, and raise a generous Emulation amongst their Companions. Perhaps our Fondness to cherish the sprightly

Youth, has occasion'd some Blunders here and there in this Volume, which we wou'd not have indulg'd in the Performances of more grown People. . . . (Preface, pp. ii–iii)

Certain members of the elitist Athenian Society may have been among those "learned gentlemen" who, according to Murdoch, so severely ridiculed Thomson's early verse. Still, the society's motives were "generous" and Scottish-patriotic. Their mission was to disclose

those various Seeds of Wit, which lay suppress'd in many a Bosom; and has rear'd numberless Conceits and curious Fancies, which the natural Rudeness and Asperity of their native Soil wou'd have with-held, or at least not have permitted to rise above the Ground. . . . As we are conscious of the Integrity and Generosity of our Endeavours for the Honour of our Country and the Improvement of the Youth, so we dread not the Fury of those who think 'tis modish and witty to censure. . . . (Preface, pp. i, iii)

Many of the *Edinburgh Miscellany* poems themselves articulate the Athenian Society's goals in fostering Anglo-Scottish poetry; they show awareness of Scottish potential despite cultural setbacks, desire to build on Scottish strengths not merely to imitate but to equal and exceed English accomplishments, and patriotic optimism that Scotland could "improve" itself. As John Callender summed it up,

In spite of our hereditary Snows,
Our Winds and Ice a noble Fervour glows
In *Scottish* Breasts, which, if improven, vyes
With *English* Warmth produc'd in clement Skies.

It is fascinating to find that, while all the *Miscellany* poems are in English and their very presentation had a patriotic purpose, they were not confined strictly to the pro-British or pro-Hanoverian viewpoint, nor did they support wholesale Anglicization. "Holy Ode" by "A.," for example, links Scottish national identity with Jacobitism. A militaristic "Poem Upon the Young Company of Archers" by Thomas Boyd urges Caledonian youth to defend Scotland's ancient glory against old English foes and employs the obvious "thistle" versus "thorn" imagery.

The patriotism the *Edinburgh Miscellany* represented was, then, of a special nature, thoroughly Scottish and clearly unwilling for Scotland to sacrifice her national integrity to Great Britain. The patriot-poets of the Athenian Society hoped to prove that Scotland was separate but equal to England in the field of literature in English. James Thomson himself was always such a Scottish literary patriot.[49]

Contributors to the *Edinburgh Miscellany* (some signed, some anonymous) came from diverse backgrounds: many were students, such as Thomson and Mallet; some were members of the progressive women's club, the Fair Intellectual Society; others were older Scottish poets whose works were reprinted from earlier publications such as Watson's *Choice Collection* (including Robert Ayton, George Mackenzie, and James Graham, marquis of Montrose). James Thomson's contributions to the *Miscellany* were subtitled "By a Student in the University" and initialed "T." They are "Of a Country Life," a significant proto-*Seasons* descriptive poem (pp. 193–197), "Upon Happiness," a long religious-philosophical piece (pp. 197–203), and "Verses on receiving a Flower from his Mistress," a trivial courtly love verse (pp. 203–204). They are certainly not prepossessing as poetry, but they offer valuable insights into the growth of Thomson's genius. Mallet's poems, subtitled "By a Youth in his Fifteenth Year" and initialed "D.M.," are "A Pastoral, Inscrib'd to Mr. [Joseph] M[itchel]l," a pastoral dialogue (pp. 223–228), "Chapter II of Solomon's Song," a scriptural paraphrase (pp. 229–231), "The Grove or Interview," modeled on Ramsay's *The Morning Interview* (pp. 232–233), and "Epithalamium on the Marriage of a Friend" (pp. 259–263). Poems in the volume signed "B" are said to be by Robert Blair. Other contributors included John Callender of Craigforth, a Mr. Hepburn, James Arbuckle, Robert Symmer (variously Simmer, or Seymour), fellow student of Thomson and Mallet and later a member of Thomson's Scottish circle in London, and a Mr. Hume. This may have been Henry Home, Lord Kames himself,[50] though this is not certain; while there were many Humes in the university community at the time, including the "J. Hume" who wrote the preface to *Lugubres Cantus*, it is intriguing to speculate that Thomson might have known Lord Kames in youth. Thomson would create a new poetry that was in many ways the early embodiment of the Enlightenment literary theory of Kames's *Elements of Criticism* (1762).

Thomson's club life in Edinburgh, his membership in the Grotesque Club, and his associations with the Athenian Society and the Worthy Club were perhaps the most significant and far-reaching educational experiences of the young student-poet in Scotland. Men he met through these societies would remain his lifelong friends and confidants. What he learned in these literary and social groups, in ideas and attitudes, in patriotism and politics, in language and literature, would continue to influence his life and his art. Thomson, riding the first wave of the Scottish improvement tide, would become by far the most successful poet of his generation of Anglo-Scots.

By 1725, then, James Thomson was well prepared to embark on a career as a poet, or a divine, or both. His letters to William Cranstoun from the spring of that year reveal much about his plans. He certainly at first hoped for a literary career within the ministry, going to England to write poetry of a religious nature and purpose. In April 1725 he wrote:

> 'twill be prodigiously difficult to succeed in the business you know I design. however come what will come I shall make an effort and leave the rest to providence. ther is I'm perswaded a necessary fix'd chain of things, and I hope my fortune whatever it be shall be link'd to diligence and honesty . . . succeed or not I firmly resolve to pursue divinity as the only thing now I am fitt for. now if I can't accomplish the design on which I came up [to London] I think, I had best make interest and pass my tryalls here so that if I be oblidg'd soon to return to Scotland again I may not return no better than I came away. and to be deeply serious with you the more I see of the vanity and wickedness of the world I'm more inclin'd to that sacred office.

Thomson was determined to make a popular success of his literary efforts: "I shall do all that's in my powr; act, hope, and so either make something out or be bury'd in obscurity. . . ." Perhaps he even contemplated becoming a minister of the Church of England, as his classmates Patrick Murdoch, Hugh Warrender, and George Turnbull would do; this course might have been better suited to his own increasingly Moderate beliefs. However, Thomson's plan to "pass my tryalls here" in England more probably referred to his taking the Presbyterian trials there at some later date, which of course he never did attempt.[51]

What persuaded Thomson to go to England? Many motives lay behind his move south. The Scottish Kirk still tended to distrust and discourage imaginative literature. Literary patrons and publishers in Scotland were relatively few until the next decade and after. As he later wrote to William Bennet, "If what the Gospel says of Prophets may likewise be aplyed to Poets, (as the word vates implies them both) . . . they have no honour in their own Country." Also, many of Thomson's friends and colleagues, including Mallet, Mitchell, and Aikman, had already departed for England to brave the wider literary and artistic culture, and Aaron Hill's encouragement in publishing ["Works and Wonders"] must have given him some confidence about his own literary prospects. A particularly compelling motive must have been poverty and his desire for material improvement and security. Material success at one's calling, according to Scottish and English interpretations of Calvinism, was sanctioned as a sign of God's approval; Thomson probably sought such concrete assurance that his poetic calling was indeed God's will. His early contacts with the gentry, too, had no doubt cultivated his taste for a more genteel, comfortable lifestyle than that of a poor minister of the Kirk. The poet's mother and family had very little money, and he also hoped to assist them; before long, he was indeed able to help his sisters with profits from *The Seasons*.[52]

As he made plans for a career, Thomson "received some encouragement from a lady of quality, a friend of his mother's, then in London. . . ." This "friend" (the word in Scotland also denoted "relative") was probably Lady Grisell Home Baillie, cousin of the poet's mother. While Lady Grisell apparently offered no monetary aid, she may have helped to obtain a tutorship in England for young Thomson with the sons of Lord Binning. Hoping to pursue his calling as a religious poet, Thomson also sought letters of introduction from several persons, including a "Mr. Elliot" (possibly the "John Elliot" who subscribed to

The Seasons, 1730, probably a relative of the Elliots of Minto), from family friend the Rev. Mr. Alexander Colden of Oxnam, and from an unnamed cousin of the Cranstouns. Mr. Elliot obliged by sending a letter along with some realistic advice, but Mr. Colden, to Thomson's chagrin, offered only his prayers.

But in spite of enormous difficulties and his own doubts and fears, Thomson still resolved to go south to make his way. In his ten years in Edinburgh, between 1715 and 1725, he had learned long-lasting lessons about Scottish culture, old and new. In Edinburgh he completed his formal education in the humanities, philosophy and science, and divinity. He studied the classics and encountered the living Scottish Latinist culture. He learned the old laws of natural philosophy and eagerly embraced the new, Newtonian creed. He was indoctrinated in the stern tenets of old-style Scottish Calvinism and he was also open to the new Moderate spirit within the church. He partook of the rich club life of the city and there found the inspiration for "improvement" in English letters. He discovered, too, an older tradition of Scottish literature, newly revived and frequently Scottish-patriotic in purpose. As his own contribution to this Scottish literary revival, he found the courage to write poetry of his own and to offer it to peers and public. James Thomson grew up in Edinburgh; he felt the growing pains of Scotland itself as his country reached toward Enlightenment. In his Edinburgh experience was the poet's own "enlightenment."

In late February 1725, on a dark, stormy night, James Thomson sailed from the port of Leith.[53] Although he would never see Scotland again, he subconsciously carried south with him a priceless literary and cultural heritage—a complex Anglo-Scottish heritage which would ultimately alter the course of English poetry.

3   THE JUVENILE POEMS

───────────────ᘐᘐᘐ───────────────

The reader of poetry for pleasure, picking up James Thomson's juvenile verses, would find little there to tempt him to read on. For indeed, at first glance, the juvenile poems hold little inherent literary interest. Most are highly conventional, the awkward apprentice-exercises of a schoolboy. Their quality is uneven and they are often gauche and naive, so it is hardly surprising that critics have paid them scant attention for over 250 years. But for those readers who genuinely appreciate Thomson's mature poetry, are curious about its Scottish background, and want to understand it better, the juvenilia merit more than a passing glance. They offer an early and intriguing glimpse of the poet of *The Seasons:* his conception of the poet's role, his poetic aims, his evolving subject matter and style. They also add to a fuller picture of the diverse sources of Thomson's poetry in the Borders and in Edinburgh—specific literary sources as well as more general, cultural ones.

Only in the juvenilia is there to be found proof of direct Scottish literary influence on Thomson's poetry, that of Allan Ramsay himself. Other more subtle and enduring Scottish sources of Thomson's mature thought—religious, cultural, educational, scientific—can also be traced from this stage. Further, these early poems are convincing evidence of certain major conflicts of values within the young poet, tensions which he would spend his whole literary life working to resolve: religious versus secular world-views; country versus city life-styles, and primitivism versus progress; Scottish versus English or British allegiance; and classical versus contemporary values and aesthetic standards. Finally, the juvenilia prove both the problems and the potential of Thomson's poetic language: they illustrate his use of abundant Latinisms in an "aureate" English; his adaptations of biblical language and tone and sermon rhetoric; his Scotticisms; and his occasional awkwardness with English expressions and pronunciations, for even though English was his standard for "proper" usage, Scots, his first spoken language, was still always at the back of his mind.[1]

Thomson's uneasy dual linguistic consciousness led to many a metrical fault, weak rhyme, and unfortunate choice of diction in the juvenile poems. Yet his uncertainty with both formal and colloquial English did leave room for an element of creativity. Young Thomson was groping for a literary language for his eclectic verse, and often his unconventional vocabulary in the juvenilia is surprisingly expressive and accurately descriptive, foreshadowing the language of his mature poetry and well suited to its new, more realistic subject matter and freer blank-verse form. His youthful enthusiasm seems to have allowed a healthy if ingenuous disregard for the rules of Augustan poetry; in any case, unlike so much second-hand, second-rate Anglo-Scottish poetry of the eighteenth century, Thomson's poetry was redeemed to a great degree by his unconventional, original language.

The early poems, except for two blank-verse pieces, are all in either lyric or heroic-couplet form. Young Thomson was seeking an appropriate form, as he was a language, for his poetry. He would develop the blank-verse mode for *The Seasons* and *Liberty* perhaps as a release from the rigors of strict rhyme in a literary language which was at first alien to him, and would return to rhyme only when he was more sure of formal English and had adapted it to his own style and purpose in the mature lyrics and *The Castle of Indolence*.

Since there are so many, and so many mediocre or derivative, verses among the juvenilia, this critical survey will focus only on exceptional or representative pieces. Certainly classical and English literary influences are pervasive in these early poems, but here the emphasis will be on those poems which show significant Scottish influence of sources and analogues or which especially anticipate Thomson's later works. While acknowledging the weaknesses of the juvenilia, one should not forget that they are essentially the exercises of a student-poet trying out various ideas in various modes. They grew from a combination of religious, literary, and philosophical ideals: Scottish Calvinism, Christian Neoplatonism, Newtonianism, classical, neoclassical, and vernacular poetry, and most of all a deep love of the natural world.[2] The significant point to keep in mind is that Thomson acquired this complex of motives as a youth in Scotland; the breadth and diversity of influence is striking, yet it is absolutely typical of post-Union Anglo-Scottish culture. James Thomson's juvenile poems reflect the tensions and the rich texture of contemporary Scotland itself.

Most of the juvenilia are found in the so-called Newberry Manuscript,[3] a holograph of uncertain provenance. The Newberry Manuscript has not been dated with certainty. While most of the poems were probably conceived and written between 1714 and 1720, including some with Border subject matter and rougher versions of two of the *Edinburgh Miscellany* poems, at least one seems to date from as late as 1721. This is the "Pastoral betwixt Thirsis and Corydon upon the death of Damon." Thomson noted in the manuscript that "Damon" was "William Riddell," and one "William Riddal" was a student in the Arts Faculty of Edinburgh University, 1717 to 1720. In 1721 he entered Divinity Hall and was in Thomson's own Group 4 of Professor Hamilton's class societies, but then abruptly dropped from the rolls. If he indeed died in 1721, this could date the "Pastoral" at about that time; the relatively polished style of the elegy, too, suggests a late date among the juvenilia. So while the manuscript poems were written and collected over a long period, the fair-copy manuscript was probably compiled around 1721 as a portfolio for presentation to the Grotesque Club and for private circulation among friends. In fact, Thomson may have given the manuscript to Mallet while they were students; Mallet seems to have had possession of it until his death in 1765. Three early poems which are not in the Newberry Manuscript but which have usually been included among Thomson's juvenilia will be considered here as well: "Of a Country Life" (*Edinburgh Miscellany*, 1720); ["The Works and Wonders of Almighty Power"] (*Plain Dealer*, 1724); and "Lisy's parting with her cat."[4]

The juvenile poems show incredible diversity. They fall into two broad groups, secular and religious. The secular poems include those with specific reference to the Borders or Edinburgh as well as the love lyrics and pastorals; religious poems include the classical-Christian blends, biblical adaptations, and religious-philosophical verses. Some of the poems were written specifically for a local Border audience and clearly grew from the Border youth's homesickness and nostalgia; these same motives prompted him to write *The Seasons* after he had gone to London. The manuscript apparently circulated among Thomson's Border friends; several Border names, among them "John Cranstone," are signed to the last page. Other manuscript poems seem aimed at a more sophisticated readership in the town—literati, fellow students, and club members—and were obviously influenced by town life itself as well as by the work of Allan Ramsay. Still others are religious exercises, written perhaps with an eye toward pleasing family, friends, and divinity professors; in these Thomson was exploring the notion that writing religious poetry could be a form of worship, a means of doing one's spiritual duty and praising God as well as serving a didactic purpose. Particularly interesting are the juvenile pieces which attempt to combine classical-pastoral with Christian themes, anticipating the descriptive-religious genre of *The Seasons*. While Thomson was drawn early on to passionate and pastoral secular verse, as a divinity student he was still perhaps doubtful about its propriety. So he adopted the sermonizing rhetorical device of concluding such poems with a "moral" or prayerlike invocation. These rather self-conscious attempts at preaching and praying, added on like afterthoughts to some of the juvenile verses, led to some undoubtedly awkward pagan-Christian hybrids and even a few passages of the mature poetry suffer from this persistent homiletic urge.

Some of the most appealing of the secular poems are explicitly Scottish in their subject matter. Several highlight the poet's life and acquaintances in the Borders, such as the mock-elegy "An Elegy upon James Therburn in Chatto," the only extant poem of Thomson's in Scots. Although editor J. Logie Robertson expressed shocked disbelief that Thomson could have written the verse, it occurs in the Newberry Manuscript in Thomson's hand and is almost certainly his own. The elegy is rather crudely written: Robertson may have questioned its attribution on these grounds alone, apart from the Scots language and bawdy subject matter. The poem was obviously written for a Border audience;[5] Jamie Therburn (or Thorburn) was evidently someone known to Thomson, and Chatto was a hill and homestead near the poet's mother's Wideopen property. The Elegy is an imitation of the mock-elegies of Ramsay ("Maggie Johnstoun," 1713; "John Cowper" and "Lucky Wood," 1717) and a number of others of the genre in Watson's *Choice Collection,* all of which Thomson would have known. Of these, his "James Therburn" is perhaps most like Alexander Pennecuik's "William Lithgow, his Epitaph" (Watson's *Choice Collection,* 1709) in its rather cruel, heavy-handed satire and coarse treatment of drunkenness and sex; by contrast, Ramsay's and the other Scots mock-elegies are lighter, more jovial, and affectionate in tone. Thomson followed the established convention in employing Scots for low comedy; his poem also recalls the grim humor and personal invective of earlier Scottish flyting literature. Most revealing is the language of "James Therburn." The poet's own emendations work toward more dense use of Scots words, directly contrary to the practice of subsequent editors, who erroneously tried to Anglicize the poem's diction. The young Thomson, doggedly imitating Ramsay's language from the mock-elegies, was thus demonstrating that while spoken Scots may have been the language of his "heart," written Scots was for him a language of the "head"; he evidently had to make a conscious effort to translate the more natural written English of his poem into Scots. This example shows just how complicated the language issue was in Scotland in Thomson's day. While "James Therburn" does not excel as Scots verse, it is fascinating in its links with the Scots mock-elegy tradition and illustrates one sort of exercise aspiring Scottish poets were trying at the time. It proves that while Thomson was probably wise to decide against Scots as his chosen literary language,[6] he did at least once try his hand at it.

Ramsay's influence is also apparent in four more secular poems. The two odes "Upon the Hoop" and "Upon Beauty" praise "our dear Caledonian ladies," who "grace fair Edina's street" wearing hoop and tartan to enhance their "native beauties." Ramsay's patriotic ode in English couplets, *Tartana, or the Plaid* (1718) was Thomson's immediate model here. Thomson himself was particularly fond of Scottish ladies, always preferring them to Englishwomen:[7]

> Should you go search the spacious globe throughout
> You will find none so pious and devout
> So modest chaste so handsome and so fair
> As our dear Caledonian ladies are
> ("Upon the Hoop," ll. 9–12)

A tartan-clad Scots lass is the goddess of beauty in "Upon Beauty"; in her train follow the "British ladies." The poem makes an admiring acknowledgment to Ramsay and *Tartana:*

> Around her shoulders dangling on her throne
> A Bright Tartana carelessly was thrown
> Which has already won Immortal praise
> Most sweetly sung in Allan Ramsay's lays
> ("Upon Beauty," ll. 90–93)

The verse also recalls Ramsay's "On our Ladies being dressed in SCOTS Manufactory at a publick Assembly" ["Let Meaner Beauties use their art"] and "In Praise of Scottish Ladies." Thomson's poetic patriotism echoes Ramsay's, where Scottish allegiance supersedes British.

"Upon Beauty" is not simply an imitation of Ramsay; it also belongs to an older tradition of Scottish courtly love allegory, predating Spenser and best represented by Dunbar's *Golden Targe.* Dunbar's allegory was written in aureate (formal, Latinate) Scots; Thomson's poem is in neo-aureate (formal, Latinate) English. Thomson's dream-vision shares with Dunbar's a Scottish immediacy of natural description going beyond courtly love convention, with Thomson's setting owing certain realistic details to the landscape of the Borders. Thomson's descriptions of women even here display a sensuousness approaching sensuality which recurs in such mature passages as "Summer"'s "Damon and Musidora"; his "Goddess" of beauty is clearly descended from Dunbar's "Dame Beautee." Thomson concludes this predominantly secular ode with a "prayer," typical even of the secular verses in the juvenilia:

> May all the blessings mortalls need below
> May all the blessings heaven can bestow
> May ev'ry thing thats pleasant good or rare
> Be the Eternal portion of the Fair.
> ("Upon Beauty," ll. 120–123)

More manuscript poems influenced by Ramsay are the two Aesopic fables "The fable of a sick Kite and it's Dame" and "The Fable of a Hawk and Nightingale." Another such fable listed in the manuscript index, "[The Do]g and a Piece of Flesh," has been lost. Ramsay wrote a number of Aesopic fables in Scots rhymed couplets which were published in 1722 to 1730 but probably in local circulation and available to Thomson earlier. These followed in a long tradition of animal tales and Aesopic fables in Scottish literature, notably the Middle Scots *Morall Fabillis of Esope the Phrygian* (1621) by Henryson, which Ramsay much admired. Traditionally, Scottish animal literature in both folk and art modes has treated beasts with great sympathy and affection as companions to man as well as emblems of the human condition. Dunbar, Henryson, Ramsay, Thomson, the Gaelic poets, and later Burns all wrote in this tradition, which gave rise to what has become a critical commonplace in Scottish literature—the popular perception that Scottish writers were somehow especially disposed to love animals as their fellow creatures in a sometimes hostile world.[8] Such sentiment on Thomson's part is amply illustrated in *The Seasons* and is but one aspect of that warm humanitarianism which permeates the poem. While Thomson's juvenile Aesopic fables are not among those versified by Henryson or Ramsay, they have much in common with those Scots fables.

Aesop's fables themselves enjoyed a popular revival in Thomson's day and he chose to rework two of the better-known classical tales. The conventional moral of "The Hawk and Nightingale" is one of self-interest—hawk catches nightingale and, though it is small, pragmatically declares it better than nothing; Thomson's version takes a more cynical turn, emphasizing the hawk's false expectations, vanity, and disappointment: "thou'rt nothing but a throat." This theme, echoed elsewhere in the juvenilia, arises from a Scottish Calvinist, flesh-denying moral rigor, with its Joblike warning not to put too much stock in delusive earthly expectations. Further, Thomson's startled hawk is drawn with a hint of sly wit also seen in Henryson and Ramsay. Thomson's contemporary John Callender had contributed a version of this same fable to *The Edinburgh Miscellany.* Popular adaptations of such fables were apparently a favorite exercise in English poetical composition practiced by Thomson and his young colleagues in their Edinburgh literary societies.

"The sick Kite," about a dying predatory bird who belatedly asks for divine assistance, emphasizes more strongly than the original version of the fable the idea of "fate" or determinism acting through nature by God's hand. Such harsh Providence would become a frequent *Seasons* theme. The atmosphere of the fable is gloomy and superstitious. Even in this early fable, Thomson envisions a deity ("gods") transcendent over man and nature and preaches that it is wrong to try to share in his omniscience. This is the "angry" God of orthodox, old-style Scottish Calvinism, just and vengeful. Thomson's fable bears comparison with another bird allegory, Henryson's "The Preiching of the Swallow." Both fables cast strong biblical overtones, Thomson's echoing Proverbs 1:20–31. Thomson, like Henryson, recognizes man's ability to know something of God's predetermined ways through nature but firmly sets the limits of human knowledge.[9] So while they are clothed in the conventional neoclassical trappings of Aesopic wisdom, Thomson's animal fables reveal a significant religious dimension as well: they reflect the poet's background within the Calvinist bibliocracy and anticipate certain aspects of his mature religious and moral thought.

Three other secular Scottish poems are of explicitly Border subject matter. These were probably conceived—if not written—at an early date in the Borders: "Upon Marle-feild," "A Poetical Epistle to Sir William Bennet of Grubbat Baronet," and "Upon Mrs. Elizabeth Bennet." "Upon Marle-feild" is a conventional piece in the country-house poem tradition and may owe something to George Mackenzie of Rosehaugh's set of verses CÆLIA's *Country-house and Closet,* particularly "The Palace" and "The Garden" (Watson's *Choice Collection,* 1709). It borrows certain lines directly from Pope's *Windsor Forest* (1713) and the influence of Virgil and Milton is also discernible. Resemblance to the Scots lyric "Leader Haughs and Yarrow," attributed to Robert Crawford (1690–1733), has also been noted in the details of its description: both poems depict a great house which is beautiful beyond the poets' powers to describe, in an idyllic landscape where "Flora" dwells, flowers "rise" and "rear their head," and birds with "narrow throats" sing.[10] The poem is perhaps of more biographical than literary interest; here, Thomson shows something of his lifelong fascination with gardens—their poetical description and their psychological impact. At Marlefield he first cultivated his interest in the "improved" landscape and pondered man's place in it. Thomson pays tribute, too, to Marlefield's greenhouse: "Immortal Authors grace this cool retreat / Of antient times and of a modern date" (ll. 33–34). This was perhaps the place where he himself retreated to read and discuss literature from Sir William's library and also where "modern" authors such as Bennet's friends Allan Ramsay, William Hamilton of Bangour, and the Scottish Latinists gathered.[11] The estate's "real nymphs" (l. 30) were probably Bennet's daughters. "Marle-feild" concludes with the couplet "O may this sweet this beautifull abode / Remain the charge of the Eternal God" (ll. 37–38); again a secular poem in Augustan heroic couplets turns suddenly to prayer, the typical gesture of the religious-minded young poet himself.

Along with "Marle-feild," Thomson's tribute to his patron and friend "A Poetical Epistle to Sir William Bennet of Grubbat Baronet" was probably among the earliest of the juvenile verses. Thomson compares himself to Virgil and Bennet to Virgil's mentor Maecenas. It is interesting to see with what apparent confidence young Thomson could presume to compare himself, a poor minister's son, with the rural poet Virgil; the simile illustrates just how pervasive was the Roman identity of the Scotland of Thomson's youth. Thomson invokes Bennet, the Latinist poet who epitomized that Roman ideal:

> If you'll encourage her [his Muse's] young fagging flight
> She'll upwards soar and mount Parnassus height
>
> . . . .

But if upon my flight your honour frowns
The muse folds up her wings and dying—justice owns
("Epistle," ll. 3–4, 9–10)

In this poem a very different influence is also discernible—that of the lyrics of Isaac Watts. The slightly sentimental lines above, for example, echo Watts's poetic prayer "Asking Leave to Sing": "If thou my daring flight forbid, / The muse folds up her wings . . ."[12] Once again, Thomson has created a composite of classical and Christian themes.

Marlefield is again the setting of a third poem, "Upon Mrs. Elizabeth Bennet." The lengthy verse is surprisingly sensual for a boy of Thomson's age who was also a prospective clergyman. Elizabeth was probably an unmarried daughter of Sir William's, one year Thomson's senior; she was apparently the poet's first infatuation. The poem pours forth highly extravagant flattery in the Sidney-Spenser tradition and also recalls the Scottish Petrarchan love poetry of William Fowler, William Alexander, and William Drummond of Hawthornden. While much of its imagery is conventional, the poem, like "Upon Beauty," shows a strong strain of descriptive realism. "Mrs. Elizabeth Bennet," too, concludes characteristically with a neoclassical "prayer."

The juvenilia count among them several more such conventional courtly love verses on a more modest scale: "Verses on receiving a Flower from his Mistress"[13] (in both manuscript and *Edinburgh Miscellany*); "Upon the Sparkler!"; and the "[Fragment: Upon a Flower given me by ———]." Two more secular love poems belong more properly to the classical pastoral tradition: "An Elegy upon Parting" and "A Pastoral betwixt Damon and Celia parting." These are likewise highly derivative exercises, yet judging both from the passionate realism which occasionally breaks through their conventionality and from Thomson's penchant for semiautobiographical poetry at this stage, the "loves" he poetically addresses were probably actual ladies. It is the lovesick student-poet himself, for example, who is so dejected that "Yea, books themselves I do not now admire" ("Elegy upon Parting," l. 24). This prefigures a similar lover's complaint in "Spring" (l. 1016).

Thomson's early experiments in the comic, mock-heroic mode also have specifically Scottish settings. "A Description of ten a-clock of night in the town" is an amusing picture of Edinburgh's nocturnal perils of drunkenness and "gardy-loo." In English mock-heroic couplets, it suggests the influence of Gay and Swift[14] in addition to the influence of the native tradition of low Scots humor and looks forward to the boisterous Edinburgh scenes of Robert Fergusson. Another, lighter comic verse is the delightful mock-epic "Lisy's parting with her cat," about the poet's favorite sister Elizabeth and her pet. Although not in the Newberry Manuscript, its subject matter is an incident from the poet's youth, possibly from the time when he lived with his family in Edinburgh, around 1716 and after. The mock-epic vehicle was no doubt suggested by Ramsay's *The Morning Interview* (1716), itself an imitation of Pope's *Rape of the Lock.* Thomson's unexpected talent in this vein is later glimpsed in such passages as the hunting burlesque in "Autumn" and the caricatures in *The Castle of Indolence.* "Lisy" demonstrates genial wit, detailed description, and great familial affection. The poem is in blank verse, rare in the juvenilia; the only other blank verse is ["Works and Wonders"], which likewise does not occur in the manuscript. "Lisy"'s style is polished and suggests that in its present form it may not be a strictly juvenile poem but one which the poet later reworked.[15]

The pastoral, foreshadowing *The Seasons'* realism of natural description and love of rural life and frequently also coupled with a religious theme, is perhaps the most significant genre represented in Thomson's juvenilia. The predominance of pastoral verse in *The Edinburgh Miscellany* bears witness to its popularity as a poetic mode among Thomson's Scottish contemporaries. Thomson's juvenile pastorals were generally much influenced by Theocritus and Virgil and by English adaptations by Milton, Pope, Gay, and others. There was, of course, a long line of Scottish pastoral poetry as well which Thomson would have known, descending from Henryson's *Robene and Makyne,* to the Scottish Petrarchans and Drummond, to the pastoral lyric verse which flourished particularly in Thomson's native Borders, to the Scots and English pastorals of Ramsay. While there are too many pastorals among the juvenilia to treat each individually, some deserve closer attention, such as the dialogue "A Pastoral betwixt Thirsis and Corydon upon the death of Damon by whom is [meant] mr: william riddell," the poem which helped to date the Newberry Manuscript. The lamented "Riddell" was "a faithfull true and constant freind [*sic*]" (l. 39) and fellow-student of Thomson's who praised him so warmly. Damon/Riddell is portrayed as a poet-swain amidst a group of such "circling swains" who met to "sing" and socialize—perhaps the Grotesque Club? The character Corydon, chief speaker of the dialogue, seems to be Thomson, whose usually "chearfull presence" (l. 3) and poetical efforts amused the group. The elegy praises Damon as a learned young man and a poet who "In charming verse his witty thoughts array'd" (l. 34). Riddell was also, briefly, a fellow divinity student of Thomson's, hence: "He was a pious and a virtuous soul / And still press'd forward to the heav'nly goal" (ll. 37–38). In composing this elegy, Thomson may have been influenced by the "Poems on several grave and important subjects" of his colleagues Joseph Mitchell, John Callender, and others in *Lugubres Cantus*. His verse is much like the kind of conventional elegy his contemporaries in Edinburgh were practicing at the time.

Thomson chose the pastoral dialogue form, based on Theocritus and Virgil, for his elegy. The poet also owed something to Milton's *Lycidas* and perhaps more to William Drummond of Hawthornden's pastoral elegy "To the Exequies of the Honourable, Sr. Antonye Alexander." Thomson's and Drummond's elegies both employ heroic couplets, and there are verbal echoes of Drummond's verse in Thomson. Pathetic fallacy, though conventional, is stronger in both Scottish elegies than in *Lycidas*. Generally, Thomson would have found a great deal to admire and emulate in the poetry of his fellow Anglo-Scot Drummond, who himself had influenced Milton, one of Thomson's chief models. Other echoes in Thomson's elegy are Pope's pastoral "Winter," which also influenced Thomson's "Winter," and the elegies of Isaac Watts. Allan Ramsay's serious pastoral-dialogue elegies in Scots such as "Richy and Sandy" (1719?) and "Keitha, A Pastoral" (1721) also show kinship with Thomson's elegy. By Thomson's day, in fact, there was a substantial body of formal Scottish elegiac verse in English, Scots, and Latin which would have been available to the apprentice-poet.[16]

Thomson's rhetorical style in the "Pastoral" elegy is fairly confident. The diction is heavily Latinate, reflecting his Virgilian model and, more broadly, the Scottish classical tradition to which the poet was educated; for example, phrases such as "desponding looks" and "impending woe" help to create the heavy elegiac mood. This formal poem is typical of many of the juvenile poems, where Thomson seems to have worked with a rather limited stock of words and particularly rhyme-words, which he used in competent if uninspired combinations. Surely this restraint was due to his uncertainty about standard English.

But Thomson did not always try to adhere strictly to pastoral convention in the language or description of the juvenilia. Two of the pastoral-descriptive poems, set in rural Scotland, are especially interesting and even original, as they anticipate *The Seasons*. "The morning in the country" shows the influence of "L'Allegro" in its diction and many of its descriptive details. But while Thomson's exercise is largely derivative, the portrait of the shepherd wrapped in his plaid with "dear crook" and dog is drawn directly from Scottish Border life. Allan Ramsay's work, too, certainly inspired Thomson to create a rural descriptive verse of his own and specifically to treat of Scottish scenes in "native" pastoral poetry.[17] Judging from the extent of borrowing and the somewhat awkward style (grammatical lapses, stilted or imprecise diction, tortuous inversion to fit the heroic-couplet scheme), this poem is probably an early one, possibly even begun in the Borders. The most significant point about this novice exercise is that here, albeit in borrowed language, Thomson deliberately set out to portray a real and familiar Scottish scene.

A similar "native" pastoral, far better and probably later in date, is the significant "Of a Country Life."[18] One of the three *Edinburgh Miscellany* poems, it does not occur in the Newberry Manuscript and was possibly composed for presentation to the Grotesque Club or Athenian Society. In this poem one sees the first hint of Thomson's talent for descriptive poetry, his "primitivistic" equation of rural life with innocence, and the germ of specific scenes, descriptions, and diction of *The Seasons*. Again, it is a derivative exercise, where the poet attempted to cast real Border experience into familiar literary models. In doing so, he was experimenting with the new, more realistic native pastoral mode being promoted by Gay in England and Ramsay in

Scotland while at the same time keeping in mind his primary model for the pastoral, Virgil.

"Of a Country Life" is immediately modeled on Gay's *Rural Sports* (1712–1713; revised 1720), an English georgic patterned on Virgil's *Georgic* II extolling rural life and praising man's ability to order and control nature. Thomson's poem also adopts the Horatian thematic convention, taken up by Virgil, of the "happy swain"; this motif was a favorite with Scottish poets, who lived in a predominantly rural society. Variations on this theme included William Drummond's "The Praise of a Solitarie Life," George Mackenzie's "The Praise of a Country Life," Ramsay's "The Happy Man" and Sir William Worthy's Song in *The Gentle Shepherd* (III.i), and Dr. Alexander Pennecuik's "to my friend inviting him to the Country." Pennecuik's lines "Sir, fly the smoke and clamour of the town, / Breathe country air . . ." are echoed in Thomson's opening. The same classical "happy man" theme recurs in a number of Thomson's later verses in addition to *The Seasons*. "Of a Country Life" is revealing of the kind of poetical exercise Thomson and his contemporaries were practicing, the problems he encountered with the English poetic language at this stage, and the homesickness for the rural Borders he felt as a student in "noisy," "smoaky" Edinburgh.

"Of a Country Life" is set "on the banks of soft, meandering Tweed." The first section of the poem (ll. 1–20) describes the sounds of the country, opening with a conventional contrast of "Clamours of the smoaky Towns," their "rude Noise" with pleasant rural sounds. The next passage (ll. 21ff.) moves to more visual description as the poet pictures each season in miniature. He uses conventional, strongly Virgilian language in these brief cameos describing spring, summer, and autumn ("painted Flow'rs," l. 26; "bearded Groves" which "portend" the sickle, ll. 31–32; reaping of the "Honours of the Plains," l. 34). In dramatic contrast, his description of winter is more fully detailed and original:

> Anon black Winter from the frozen North
> Its Treasuries of Snow and Hail pours forth;
> Then stormy Winds blow thro' the hazy Sky,
> In Desolation Nature seems to ly.
> The unstain'd Snow from the full Clouds descends,

> Whose sparkling Lustre open Eyes offends.
> In Maiden-white the glit'ring Fields do shine,
> Then bleating Flocks for want of Food repine,
> With wither'd Eyes they see all Snow around,
> And with their Fore-feet paw and scrap the Ground,
> They chearfully do crop th' insipid Grass;
> The Shepherds, sighing, cry, Alas! alas!
> Then pinching Want the wildest Beast does tame.
> Then Huntsmen on the Snow do trace their Game.
> Keen Frost then turns the liquid Lakes to Glass,
> Arrests the dancing Riv'lets as they pass.
> ("Of a Country Life," ll. 35–50)

This foreshadows *The Seasons*' "Winter" in many details and scenes: storms, shining fields of snow, suffering sheep pawing the ground, wild animals "tamed" by the harsh season, the hunt, frozen waters. Thomson's knowledge of the hardships of rural winter based on his experiences in the Scottish Borders and revealing his own benevolent, sympathetic feelings is manifest in the realism of this description. This juvenile winter passage well illustrates two characteristic themes of *The Seasons* and of Scottish nature poetry generally: the especially realistic and detailed descriptive treatment of winter, Scotland's longest and most severe and immediate season; and genuine sympathy with animals as comrades and fellow sufferers in a difficult environment. After these seasonal views, Thomson follows Gay's lead in treating the country sports of angling, hare coursing, and fowl hunting. Again, these scenes are prototypes of *The Seasons:* the angling scene would recur in "Spring," the hunting scene in "Autumn." Typically here Thomson is most accurate and original in describing action and movement in nature. The pastoral scene which follows is probably an idealized Border setting. The poem concludes with a "prayer" characteristic of the juvenilia: "But grant, ye Pow'rs, that it may be my Lot / To live in Peace from noisy Towns remote" (ll. 107–108).

"Of a Country Life" is a surprisingly carefully worked poem, given the poet's youth and inexperience and the difficult poetic tasks he set himself. The verse, despite its occasional awkwardness of expression, shows more originality of descriptive diction than Gay's more polished georgic. The young poet was obviously struggling to find a fresh means of recreating the sounds and sights of Border life. "Of a Country Life" was indeed written with real Scottish Border life in mind, and Thomson's "foreign" English literary language, charged with the new demands of native pastoral, produced some very striking effects. Much of Thomson's diction here is Latinate, of course, echoing his Virgilian model; he even uses the occasional Latin word in its original sense, such as "insipid" (l. 45, describing the grass as tasteless) to gain precision. But the most notable quality of Thomson's unusual diction is its attention to sound.

Sometimes he chose words simply to fit rhyme or meter; occasionally his word choices betrayed Scottish pronunciations (for example, "Plough" [pleugh] rhymed with "renew," ll. 19–20; "haste" with "last," ll. 63–64). Sound sometimes even precludes sense, and sound effects play an integral part in the descriptive function of the words themselves. Dense patterns of onomatopoeia, alliteration, assonance, and consonance are pervasive and emotionally persuasive. His description of country noises illustrates this close attention to sound effects:

> Nought but soft *Zephyrs* whisp'ring thro' the Trees,
> Or the still Humming of the painful Bees;
> The gentle Murmurs of a purling Rill,
> Or the unweary'd chirping of the Drill;
> The charming Harmony of warbling Birds,
> Or hollow Lowings of the grazing Herds;
> The murm'ring Stock-Doves melancholly Coo
> When they their loved Mates lament or woo;
> The pleasing Bleatings of the tender Lambs,
> Or the indistinct mum'ling of their Dams;
> The musical Discord of chiding Hounds,
> Whereto the echoing Hill or Rock resounds;
> The rural mournful Songs of love-sick Swains,
> Whereby they sooth their raging am'rous Pains;
> The whisling Musick of the lagging Plough,
> Which does the Strength of drooping Beasts renew.
> (ll. 5–20)

Abundant, well-chosen participles in "extended onomatopoeia" imitate sounds and actions ("whisp'ring," "Humming," "murm'ring," "purling," "chirping," "warbling," "mum'ling," "chiding," "lagging"). Careful alliteration reinforces sense ("murm'ring . . . melancholly . . . Mates"; "Rock resounds"; "Songs of love-sick Swains . . . sooth"). Most notable is the deliberate use of assonance and consonance, in addition to alliteration, in exploiting sound-metaphors, or the associations between certain sounds and the emotional responses they evoke ("Murmurs . . . purling"; "charming Harmony . . . warbling," itself a harmony of sounds; "hollow Lowings," echoed in "Spring," l. 207; "pleasing Bleatings"). Even the "indistinct mum'ling" of the "Dams," a rather odd image, is aurally effective, as the multisyllabled Latinism joined with the more colloquial verb imitates a "mumbling" sound.[19] Such imitative sound effects function, of course, in Augustan English verse as well, but, more to the point, they are inherent in the very nature of the Scots language, and Thomson very frequently chose English words with sounds suggestive of familiar Scots words to enhance their connotative impact. Examples are the unusual "flounces," l. 65, related to the Scots "flounge," and "wither'd," l. 43, in the Scots sense of "trembling." By choosing such emotive and imitative words to use along with his more formal Latinate English vocabulary, Thomson was consciously striving to lend immediacy and very often achieved innovative and accurate description. The ways in which Thomson worked with language in "Of a Country Life" point directly toward his method in the mature poetry and especially in *The Seasons.*

"Of a Country Life" affords a tantalizing glimpse of Thomson's mature art: his adaptation of Latin and English literary models to his own Scottish experience; his creation of a combined Latinate and colloquial language, with its striking and unexpected descriptive power; and his close observation of man and animals in the complex natural world. Here, in this prototype of *The Seasons,* is the earliest true picture of James Thomson's poetic genius.

In addition to these secular juvenile poems, the other major group of Thomson's early poems are those of an explicitly religious nature: religious pastorals, religious-philosophical or meditative poems, and purely religious exercises such as scriptural paraphrases. Each type is revealing of young Thomson's religious background and beliefs. While such notes as the stern, old-style Scottish Calvinism of the poet's father's generation are relatively rare here,[20] they are by no means absent; witness the uncompromising religious and moral implications of his animal fables, which condemn vanity and greed and allude to concepts of determinism, Providence, and divine retribution. Such tenets, preached in the poet's didactic mode and echoing powerful pulpit rhetoric, also recur in the later works. Thomson's vein of moral rigor, his acute awareness of man's fallen state, is clearly a product of his strict religious upbringing; so also is the strong emotional, mystical strain, where the influence of Watts in particular and the Calvinist temper in general is obvious. Thomson's early religious verse also shows Moderate influence in keeping with current liberal trends in the church; identifiable Moderate traits here and in Thomson's later poetry include a Christian humanistic spirit of trust in man's reason to reinforce revelation, interest in physicotheology and empirical science, influence of secular literatures, attraction to Christian Neoplatonic philosophy and figurative language, and a prevailing religious optimism emphasizing God's love rather than His wrath. Still, these various new ideas were firmly tempered in Thomson, as in most of the Moderates, by orthodox awareness of the limits of reason in the face of God's omniscience and His omnipotence. Even here in the juvenilia the nature of Thomson's mature religious thought becomes clear: it is eclectic and bears the influence of both old-style and more liberal religious beliefs as well as of many secular disciplines, yet it is ultimately based in the deep-laid foundation of conventional religious faith of his youth.

Some of the juvenile poems introduce explicitly religious themes cast in the traditional pastoral mode. In these religious pastorals Thomson attempted to fuse classical conventions with the language and themes of the Bible and of hymns or meditative literature. Such classical-Christian pastoral poetry was a popular genre with Thomson and his colleagues, as seen in the *Edinburgh Miscellany*. Thomson's juvenile religious pastorals do not entirely succeed in creating a convincing poetic blend, yet they are evidence of the debt Thomson owed his early models in the Renaissance tradition such as Drummond and

Milton and exemplify the Scottish poet's thorough grounding in the ideals of Christian humanism. They look forward to a more powerful and successful synthesis of classical and Christian poetry in *The Seasons*.

Among these poems combining Virgilian with biblical and Miltonic elements are "A Pastoral Entertainment described," "A Dialogue In praise of the pastoral Life," and "A Pastoral betwixt David Thirsis and the Angell Gabriel upon the birth of Our Saviour." The first two are heavy-handed and probably of an early date. The third, a pastoral dialogue celebrating the birth of Christ, is more effective at blending religious with descriptive poetry. Miltonic "Paradise" inspires Thomson's vision of the redeemed Christian world; there are other close Miltonic verbal echoes as well. Two pre-Miltonic, Scottish analogues for Thomson's "upon the birth of Our Saviour" are poems by William Drummond of Hawthornden. His "The Angels for the Natiuitie of Our Lord" is in the plain style, very like the angelic chorus in Thomson's poems. In contrast, Drummond's "For the Natiuitie of Our Lord" is more aureate, like the shepherds' song in Thomson's same verse; Thomson's and Drummond's poems share similar strongly Neoplatonic light imagery as well, which calls to mind an even earlier Scottish nativity poem, Dunbar's aureate "Of the Nativitie of Christ." Compare, for instance, Drummond's,

> O than the fairest Day, thrice fairer Night!
> Night to best Dayes in which a Sunne doth rise,
> Of which that golden Eye, which cleares the Skies,
> Is but a sparkling Ray, a Shadow light.
> ("For the Natiuitie of Our Lord," ll. 1–4)

with Thomson's,

> Thou fairest morn that ever sprang from night
> Or deck'd the opening skies with rosie light
> Well may'st thou shine with a distinguish'd ray.
> ("upon the birth of our Saviour," ll. 33–35)

Another parallel to Thomson's nativity pastoral is Watts's "The Nativity of Christ" ("Shepherds, rejoice"). Thomson's chorus of angels (ll. 17–20) follows the same lyric form as Watts's verse; Thomson's concluding line "Sheepherd let's go and humbly kiss the Son" (l. 40) echoes Watts's "Go, shepherds, kiss the Son."[21]

Isaac Watts, the English Calvinist clergyman and poet, is one early role-model for young James Thomson who has thus far received very little critical attention, yet his influence, particularly on the juvenilia, is significant. The poetry of Watts, like that of Thomson, was shaped by his strong classical education and reflects admiration for Virgil as well as Milton. Watts, like Thomson, also owed much to the Cambridge Platonists and Shaftesbury. Watts's verse is primarily lyric and some might call it banal; similar sing-song rhythms and trivial rhymes recur in many of Thomson's early verses. Watts, however (unlike Thomson), intended many of his lyrics to be set to music. The avowed purpose of Watts's poetry is to praise his Creator; he does so with humility and wonder, treating the natural world with respect and love as a vital stepping stone for the ascendant spirit toward this Christian Neoplatonic deity. Watts's relationship with God is deeply personal; therefore, the poetry, like young Thomson's, is mostly subjective. Watts's beliefs were imbued with sentimentalism, or that "sublime" religious emotionalism heightened with awe and fear which paradoxically ran parallel to austerity in the puritan disposition. Just these sorts of feelings occur in Thomson's juvenile religious poetry and on a personal level might be traced back to the poet's own mother, who was a religious enthusiast. Although not a Scottish influence himself, Watts was clearly much admired by Thomson's generation of divinity students and novice Anglo-Scottish poets. Joseph Mitchell dedicated his *Jonah* (1720) to Watts, and an "Ode to the Rev. Mr. Isaac Watts" by "D.V.M." (Mallet?) is found in *Lugubres*. The English divine's nonconformist beliefs showed the same tendency toward moderatism and religious optimism, even alongside of the mystery and awe which would increasingly characterize eighteenth-century Scottish Calvinism and indeed Thomson's own views. As he celebrates in his poem "Two Happy Rivals: Devotion and the Muse," Watts succeeded in reconciling his religious faith with his poetic vocation—this was young James Thomson's very goal.[22]

Scriptural paraphrases, another sort of religious poetry, were the basis for the exercises required of divinity students in Thomson's day, as Professor Hamilton carefully recorded in his notebook of class assignments. Such scriptural paraphrases proved to be useful practice pieces for poetically minded students, and Thomson and his colleagues often used the Bible as a convenient text for embellishment. Thomson's early verse paraphrase of the "Song of Solomon Chap:I ver:7" is such a reworking of Scripture into competent Augustan pastoral verse. Another is "A Hymn to God's power," a rendering of Psalm 148. Thomson's version owes much to Richard Blackmore's *Creation*, book VII, and especially to Watts's version of Psalm 148 in the same lyric form. A third juvenile scriptural piece, a verse paraphrase of Psalm 104, shows the most talent and originality.

Thomson's "Psalm 104 Paraphrazed" treats of what became known in his day as physicotheology: the knowledge of an all-powerful God through His Creation and the sacred role of all Creation, and particularly the poet, to praise Him. In the poem's opening, young Thomson chooses to address God as "Author"; with this metaphor the poet seems again to be striving to reconcile his callings of poetry and divinity through physicotheology, which was to become a central unifying theme of his poem of religion and nature, *The Seasons*.

In Scotland, as in England, Psalm translations and paraphrases had long been a favorite literary pastime. Among Scots and Latinist as well as Anglo-Scottish poets, Psalm 104 ("Bless the Lord, O my soul") was an especially popular subject. George Buchanan's Latin Psalms, including "civ," had been studied in Scottish schools for many years, and they were emulated by a host of other Scottish Latinists. David Murray of Gorthy wrote an English version of Psalm 104 (1615), and George Mackenzie wrote a Metaphysical-style interpretation in rhymed couplets of the popular psalm. One version of the metrical psalms themselves was a Scottish production of King James VI & I [and Sir William Alexander]. Thomson's own "Psalm 104" in heroic couplets follows the exposition of Tate and Brady's metrical psalms (1696) most closely and demonstrates his eye for accurate and original natural description.[23] His rhymes are mostly well chosen; a few apparently uncertain rhymes (such as "Thee"/"die," ll. 99–100) probably represent Scottish pronunciation. While the iambic pentameter occasionally lapses, the psalm is vigorous and vividly descriptive.

The diction and imagery Thomson chose to recast the psalmist's descriptions of nature is typically eclectic. Along with biblical formal conventions ("Thou" address, archaic *st* verb endings), strongly Latinate vocabulary predominates, borrowing Virgilian descriptive epithets (e.g., "*rocky caverns fruitfull moisture weep,*" l. 24; "He doth the clouds with *genial moisture* fill," l. 42, italics mine) and periphrasis ("bleating kind," l. 30; "feather'd nation," l. 36). Much of the Latinate language also strikes a Miltonic note ("primogeneal light," l. 5; "Ethereal road," l. 11, and other descriptive details, particularly light and cosmic images). Thomson's characterization of the flood, "Shrinked within the limits of their shoar," l. 22, may echo George Mackenzie's "Psalm civ" ("The trembling Floods soon shrunk within their Shore," l. 20). Much of the language of "Psalm 104" is of similar character to that found in "Of a Country Life"; that is, full of deliberate and unusual sound effects and using an original and accurate descriptive vocabulary of onomatopoeic and imitative words. Clearly, then, the young poet made the popular Psalm 104 his own song of praise, forging a fresh poetical language to bring the metrical psalm to life in descriptive poetry while also professing his life work: "I'll to Gods honour consecrate my lays / And when I cease to be I'll cease to praise" (ll. 111–112). The creativity of language and thought of Thomson's "Psalm 104" won the praise of English critic, patron, and politician William Benson, who encouraged the novice poet to go to London to pursue his poetic vocation.[24]

Finally, the early religious poems include a group which might be called religious-philosophical verse. They borrow much from the ideas and the imagery of near-contemporary metaphysics to profess a predominantly orthodox religious viewpoint. One important religious-philosophical poem, ["The Works and Wonders of Almighty Power"], was not in the juvenile manuscript and was first published anonymously in *The Plain Dealer* (1724) as

conceiv'd, and express'd, with all the Clearness, Depth, and Strength, of an *experienc'd Philosopher,* by a Member of this Grotesque Club, who was in his *Fourteenth Year only,* when he compos'd, in Blank Verse, a Poem, now in my Hands; and founded on a Supposition of the Author's sitting, a whole Summer Night, in a

Garden, looking upward, and quite losing himself in Contemplation, on *the Works, and Wonders, of Almighty Power.*—If this was a
Subject, naturally above the Capacity of so very a Boy, to what a
Degree does it increase our Wonder, when we find it treated, in
this Masterly Manner![25]

It is no wonder that the poem seemed to Aaron Hill to have been
written by an "experienc'd Philosopher": it has since been discovered
to be a close paraphrase in verse of several passages of Shaftesbury's
Moralists, a philosophical rhapsody (1709).[26] The poem is in blank verse;
blank verse was certainly the appropriate form for a paraphrase of
Shaftesbury, who deplored rhyme. There are no blank-verse pieces in
the Newberry Manuscript, and the only other traditionally included
among the juvenilia is "Lisy's parting with her cat." ["Works and Wonders"] is probably of a late date among Thomson's juvenile poems,
despite Hill's claim that the poet was only fourteen years old. Hill's
dating may be an error resulting from the fact that Thomson's numeral 9s often closely resembled 4s; at age nineteen, Thomson was a
student at the university and writing poetry prolifically. It is possible
that ["Works and Wonders"] was the same "discourse on the Power of
the Supreme Being" in "sublimely elevated" blank verse which Thomson composed as an exercise for his divinity class—the very one which
Professor Hamilton censured for its overly poetical, "improper" style.
Even at the time, Thomson's fellow students suspected that exercise as
a plagiarism but could not prove it.[27]

The theme of ["Works and Wonders"] is physicotheology. Beyond
the influence of Shaftesbury and the Cambridge Platonists, Thomson's interpretation, its religious enthusiasm and emotional tone,
probably owes much to Watts. Thomson again proclaims his role as
physicotheological poet:

> Yet may I, from thy most *apparent Works,*
> Form some Idea of their wond'rous Author;
> And celebrate *thy Praise,* with rapt'rous Mind.
> (ll. 18–20)

While young Thomson's paraphrase made few changes in the ideas of
the deist Shaftesbury, ultimately he did depart from his model to

make his own characteristically humble moralistic statement, reflecting conventional Scottish Calvinist awareness of the limits of reason:

> But, 'tis too much, for my weak Mind to know:
> Teach me, with humble Rev'rence, to *adore*
> The Mysteries, I *must not comprehend!*
> (ll. 37–39)

Another religious-philosophical poem, "A complaint on the miseries of this life," is much closer in tone and in theme to the stern, old-style Scottish Calvinism of the poet's father;[28] here, young Thomson shows deep consciousness of the depravity of the Fallen World. Biblical influence is obvious; the poem carries the message, as well as specific echoes, of Job and also alludes to Ecclesiastes ("Yea what is all beneath the sky / But emptiness and vanity," ll. 23–24). The poem's theme—"fading fleeting joys" of earthly life, the body as a dark prison of the soul versus bright heavenly happiness—also reflects conventional Christian Neoplatonism. Thomson's verse indeed has a strong seventeenth-century flavor; its imagery recalls, for example, such poems as William Drummond's "What Haplesse Hap had I now to bee borne" ["The Court of True Honour"] and "Why (Worldlings) doe ye trust fraile Honours Dreames." The lyric form of Thomson's verse as well as its flesh-denying theme, emotional tone, and details of diction and Neoplatonic imagery also suggest the influence of Watts. Thomson's poem, lamenting "In the lone grave I long to rest" (l. 27), especially bears comparison with the work of Robert Blair. Like Thomson's "complaint," Blair's *Grave* preaches the message of Job; Blair, too, wrote under the strong influence of Watts, who was his mentor. Blair, anticipating the release of death, concludes *The Grave* with the conventional symbol, also in Watts, of the soul as a bird, homing to heaven; Thomson also hopes that death will free him to "sweetly singing soar away" (l. 18). Many contemporary verses in this same vein, such as John Callender's "The Elevation" (*Edinburgh Miscellany*), show the popularity of such "enthusiastic" religious lyric poetry in Scotland. Thomson's world-weary complaint concludes with a typically Calvinist prayer, placing ultimate faith in God's word of revelation as man's best guide through "corrupt life" to heaven.

By far the most complex and richly textured of the early religious-philosophical poems is the lengthy "Upon Happiness."[29] This poem bears examination in some detail, as it directly anticipates much of Thomson's mature philosophical and moral thought as well as poetical methods. "Upon Happiness" is one of the three *Edinburgh Miscellany* poems. The poem relies not on a single source but is eclectic; as a synthesis of a variety of religious, philosophical, and scientific influences it illustrates one popular contemporary mode of thought in Scotland in the young poet's day. Briefly, the speaker of "Upon Happiness" contemplates earthly life and the means to happiness, sleeps, and enters a dream-vision wherein he climbs steep Mount Contemplation. He observes vain men and their delusive pleasures as the poem moves from first-person narrative to direct, didactic address. He expounds the joys of virtue and horrors of eternal damnation while holding the orthodox Scottish Calvinist line that this virtue will not of itself guarantee election to heaven (i.e., predestination). The tone shifts again to enthusiasm as the speaker pledges to devote himself to God's service to find the greatest earthly happiness. He describes in near-mystical terms the ultimate happiness of the beatific vision: God is Light, the goal of the "rising mind," Neoplatonic form of perfection, center of all bliss. The speaker ultimately finds such overwhelming brightness beyond his humble powers to "drink in"; he has reached the temporal limits of human reason and knowledge. He descends Mount Contemplation and the vision ends.

A variety of prose sources and analogues can be found for "Upon Happiness." John Norris of Bemerton's essay "An Idea of Happiness" (6th edition, 1717) seems to have set the philosophical pattern of the poem. Norris was an Anglican divine, a disciple of the Cambridge Platonists who was associated with the Athenian Society in London, the group said to have been the model for the Edinburgh Athenians.[30] Thomson distilled the abstract philosophy and framework of ideas from Norris, along with many close verbal borrowings, and placed them in a dream-vision vehicle adopted from other sources. Another fruitful source was *The Spectator* essays, which frequently presented Neoplatonic thought in a more easily digestible, popular manner. Some of these essays are in a dream-vision format, among them numbers by Addison, Steele, John Hughes, and Henry Grove; details of

Thomson's poem particularly resemble points of Grove's writings. Grove (1684–1738), an English Presbyterian divine, was also a poet; he was a friend of Watts and a disciple of Isaac Newton. Significantly, he has been called a philosophical "connecting link" between Shaftesbury and the Scottish philosopher Francis Hutcheson[31] and, as shall be seen, Thomson forges this philosophical connection in his poetry.

A more immediate source for Thomson's interpretation of Christian Neoplatonism could be found in the writings of Scottish Calvinism itself. The Scottish church, and particularly the Moderate faction, was powerfully influenced by Neoplatonic philosophy; Hutcheson, for instance, was a follower of Shaftesbury, and Robert Riccaltoun's views on happiness also drew to a great extent upon Christian Neoplatonism. In his "Of Happiness and Perfection in general, absolute and limited," Riccaltoun distinguished between the "limited, dependent" happiness man can know on earth as he "improves" himself by degrees via the scale of ascending knowledge, and the "absolute, independent, and every way perfect happiness" the intellect achieves in the knowledge of God in eternity. Even writers in the old-style Scottish Calvinist tradition were affected by the mystical element of Christian Neoplatonism. The works of the Rev. Mr. Thomas Boston of Ettrick, for example, make an instructive and revealing parallel with Thomson's own in their Scottish Calvinist interpretations of the themes and images of Christian Neoplatonic thought. Boston was a representative figure of older Scottish religion in Thomson's day; a friend of Duncan Forbes and likely of the churchmen in Thomson's father's circle, he was a prolific writer on Presbyterian theology, so his writings can serve as a useful reference point throughout this study. Boston's *Fourfold State* (1720) is one instance where he employs a great deal of conventional Neoplatonic imagery to describe the fourth spiritual state of eternal life; like Thomson in "Upon Happiness," however, Boston was ultimately at a loss for words to describe the beatific vision (although he could graphically depict the horrors of hell). Significantly, Boston's conception of the Neoplatonic rising mind is the same as Thomson's; it takes the extreme form of "empirical immortality"; that is, the infinite advance of knowledge even in the afterlife. This unusual interpretation, also found in the philosophy of George Turnbull, is the one which Thomson himself prefers in his treatment of the Neoplatonic improving intellect in "Upon Happiness" as well as in the later poems. Thus the Christian Neoplatonic ideal of happiness and its expression in traditional figurative language, while primarily associated with Shaftesburyian optimism and Newtonian science, was also compatible with old-style Scottish Calvinism and its vision of the fourth state of eternal life and of the progress of the individual soul.[32]

Christian Neoplatonism was a popular theme not only with prosewriters but also with poets. An early Scottish exponent was Florence Wilson (1500–1547).[33] His Latin "Ode" was published, with his *De Animi Tranquillitate* (3rd edition, 1707), by Ruddiman, and Robert Blair translated the "Ode" into English, possibly while a student with Thomson in Edinburgh. William Drummond's religious poems, too, which Thomson's "Upon Happiness" echoes in many details, are pervasively Neoplatonic. Among English poets who drew extensively from Neoplatonic ideas and imagery were Blackmore and Watts. Blackmore's "Happiness Discover'd" is thought to be a major source for Thomson's poem.[34] The religious lyrics of Watts were also a likely source of inspiration, particularly for the second, more sentimental and mystical portion of "Upon Happiness" where there are abundant verbal echoes of Watts's Neoplatonic rapture.

As the eclectic philosophy of "Upon Happiness" evolved from a variety of sources, so too did the poem's form. "Upon Happiness" follows on a long line of religious and "knightly quest" allegories. There are innumerable literary analogues for Thomson's semiallegorical dream-vision vehicle. Shakespeare's *Midsummer Night's Dream* and *Twelfth Night,* as well as Milton's *Comus,* all Neoplatonic in theme, may have suggested to Thomson the magic-spell, sleep, and dream sequence (ll. 88–93); such supernatural scenes would naturally have appealed to a Border Scot brought up on similar folklore.[35] The poet also, of course, drew upon a strong tradition of Scottish allegory. Scottish poems such as David Lindsay's *The Dreme* and Alexander Montgomerie's *The Cherry and the Slae* were well-known examples of the dream vision, and one such allegory in particular, Gavin Douglas's Middle Scots dream vision *The Palice of Honour,* seems likely to have influenced Thomson in both "Upon Happiness" and later in *The Castle of Indolence.* The *Palice*'s dream framework and surprise awakening, its journey up a steep mountain, its affirmation that only virtue leads to true honor, and its religious message all find parallels in "Upon Happiness."

The motif of a difficult ascent to reach some transcendent good, with the attendant danger of slipping down, is highly conventional. Thomson uses this theme to symbolize the individual, Scottish Calvinist, lonely spiritual ascent to perfect happiness in eternity. Among allegories depicting such a quest are Spenser's "An Hymne of Heavenly Beauty," and plainer versions include John Bunyan's *Pilgrim's Progress,* surely known to Thomson from childhood, and its Scottish counterpart, John Burel's *Passage of Pilgrimer* (Watson's *Choice Collection,* 1709). The most striking contemporary analogue is Allan Ramsay's *Content: A Poem* (1721),[36] an allegorical dream vision possibly itself influenced by Douglas's *Palice of Honour.* Thomson's "Upon Happiness" bears marked resemblance to Ramsay's poem; both are in English heroic couplets, and there are many verbal echoes of Ramsay in Thomson's poem. The speaker of *Content* falls into a "gentle slumber" and "mimic fancy op'd the following scene," just as Thomson's speaker, "While mimick Fancy did her Vigils keep; / . . . Unto my Sight a boundless Scene did ope" (ll. 22, 36). Like Thomson's speaker, Ramsay's undertakes an uphill journey, spurning the world's "Fantastic Joys," which Thomson calls "our Joys, / . . . fantastick Toys" (ll. 70–71). Ramsay's speaker sees vain men fail to gain audience with the goddess Content; finally, by practicing virtue, he achieves true earthly happiness, or content. Thomson almost certainly knew Ramsay's poem and set out to write his own, more religiously oriented equivalent.

Looking ahead, "Upon Happiness" as an expression of Christian Neoplatonic religious and moral philosophy within the traditional allegorical dream vision can be seen as a significant prototype of Thomson's *The Castle of Indolence.* Thomson's "vision" in "Upon Happiness" is twofold: the opening, first-person narrative (ll. 1–93), followed by the direct-address, didactic portion (ll. 94ff), which builds to a high emotional pitch. This pattern approximates the two-part structure of *The Castle,* narrative quest and "sermon." The metaphorical pattern of the first, pilgrimage sequence of "Upon Happiness" borrows much from Thomson's literary models in dream vision and allegory. Abun-

dant visual, concrete images for vanity also recall Scottish pulpit rhetoric, with its graphic descriptions of sin to serve a didactic purpose.
But it is in the more insistently didactic second part of the poem (as in
Canto II of *The Castle*) that Thomson's heritage of Scottish Calvinism
is most apparent: its sternly moralistic, sermonlike tendency as well as
its emotional, mystical aspects. Biblical influence is most obvious here,
and the intensifying rhetoric of the pulpit resounds as the tone builds
from heavy didacticism ("Behold the GOD-HEAD just, as well as good, /
And Vengeance pour'd on Tramplers on his Blood," ll. 118–119) to
enthusiasm ("Then sure you will with holy Ardours burn, / And to
seraphick Heats your Passion turn," ll. 122–123). Thomson is orthodox in his characterization of the deity as "awful" (l. 106), "just, as well
as good" (l. 118), omnipotent through "Providence" (l. 127), and the
ultimate source of all "Happiness." The young poet is clearly aware
here of the limits of reason on earth and of the mystery of God's
divine plan. In this second part of "Upon Happiness" are the strongest verbal echoes of Thomson's models Job, Milton, Watts, and the
Scottish Calvinist divines. But even along with these, the influences of
contemporary empirical philosophy and science on Thomson's conception of God and His plan here also demonstrate the poet's disposition toward a more Moderate, rational, and optimistic outlook than
that of his father's generation. Thomson's God is, even at this early
stage, the "GOD of Nature" (l. 113) to whom the young poet could
relate most intimately and to whom he would dedicate *The Seasons*.

Appropriately, the diction and imagery of "Upon Happiness" are
eclectic. Along with diction from the poet's diverse literary, philosophical, and religious sources is the abundant language of philosophy and
science: "Appetite as fixed as the Pole," "extended Will" (Descartes);
"*Æther*," "*Preludium*" (Norris); "attracting Centre" (Newton); "*Atmosphere*"; "Compass"; and so on. Such terminology frames the dream
vision and conveys the metaphysical nature of the poet's quest. Significantly, Thomson begins his poem with a Ptolemaic—earth- and man-
centered—image, comparing the sun circling the earth to his own
thoughts in search of "Th' attracting Centre of the humane Mind" (ll.
15–18). Such a world-view was the basis of George Buchanan's *De
Sphæra*, a text which Thomson would have known as a schoolboy. The

poet concludes "Upon Happiness," however, with a modern, scientifically accurate Copernican image—sun-centered and corresponding to the Neoplatonic symbol for God-centered perfection and harmony. Thus has the young poet's intellect "improved" and "risen" from earthly to spiritual goals. In *The Seasons* and *Liberty* Thomson would equate religious-philosophical universal harmony and benevolence with related concepts of Newtonian gravity or "attraction." In "Upon Happiness," his rising mind, his ascent up Mount Contemplation, has led the speaker, as the divinity student Thomson himself, to complementary philosophical and scientific truths—truths which would reinforce, rather than diminish, his religious faith in a transcendent God.

"Upon Happiness" is yet another of young James Thomson's exercises in personal reconciliation; here, he was trying to reconcile not only the art of poetry but also the rapidly changing disciplines of philosophy and science with his still-strong Scottish Calvinism and religious vocation. While clearly over-ambitious for such a youth, the poem shows Thomson bravely attempting to synthesize widely various material and, within a primarily religious poem, to make it his own. He would succeed at such a task in *The Seasons*. "Upon Happiness" makes elaborate testimony to Thomson's growing self-confidence as a poet and, above all, to the impressive breadth of literature and learning which it was his good fortune to experience in Scotland.

James Thomson's juvenile poems, while not strikingly original or precocious apprentice-pieces, do reveal the wide range of ideas and influences, both old and new, acting upon the boy poet in post-Union Scotland. To a great extent he found himself caught between the old and the new in a difficult time of cultural transition; he was an adolescent struggling to find his poetic voice, living in a land which was itself struggling to reestablish its own identity. Yet the personal and cultural tensions reflected in his first poetical efforts tell us much about James Thomson himself and also about his national background, and these poems show how such tensions ultimately proved positive motivating forces for his growth as a poet.

Thomson's juvenile poems affirm his traditional Scottish Calvinist faith and many hint at a new, more secular and Moderate outlook as well. They show scientific interest, both Cartesian and Newtonian. They demonstrate his debt to classical ideals, yet also reflect changing contemporary aesthetic standards. Especially, the juvenile poems show how Thomson drew strength from Scottish literature: the traditions of Scottish nature poetry, allegory, elegy and religious verse, Scottish Latinist literature, folk literature, Ramsay and the Scots vernacular, and Anglo-Scottish poetry. He brought these native strengths together with English influences such as Milton, Pope, Gay, Watts, and the Authorized Version and also the philosophy of Shaftesbury and the Cambridge Platonists to create an original Anglo-Scottish amalgam, a rich cultural mix indeed.

In these early poems, young Thomson would not ultimately commit himself to either old or new, Scottish or English. Should he write religious poetry, as a proper prospective divine, or should he incorporate more secular, liberal, and rational ideas into his poetry? Should he rely on his tried and true classical mentors and models, or imitate the latest English literary modes? Should he extol the primitive, rural life he knew as a boy in the Borders, or celebrate the city? Was he, in fact, Scottish or British? Growing from the same cultural roots as the germinal Scottish Enlightenment itself, James Thomson adopted what proved to be the Enlightenment solution to the dilemma of his identity as an individual and artist: he borrowed the best of both worlds, old and new, Scottish and English, and brought these influences to bear on a poetry which was all the stronger for its dauntless eclecticism. This eclecticism would characterize even his mature poetry.

In short, James Thomson's poetry grew from a solid foundation of Scottish experience and education, which taught him to be conscious of the past yet open to and informed by new ideas, full of respect and love for the Scottish heritage yet also receptive to English influence. Thomson's juvenile poems prefigure in countless ways the poet's later works. They are important proof that his attitudes to life and art were born in Scotland. They demonstrate the limits and the potential of Thomson's chosen literary medium, his determination to forge a new poetic language for his new poetry of religion and nature. They show just how substantial and significant were the Scottish influences on the poet, and in illustrating those influences they help the reader to appreciate more fully the mature vision of James Thomson, Anglo-Scot.

4 THE SCOTTISH BACKGROUND OF *THE SEASONS*

⚒⚒⚒

Even though James Thomson did not go down to London with the poem "Winter" in his pocket, as legend has it, he did go with a headful of ideas on religion, science, philosophy, and literature and a heart full of nostalgia and love for his native Scotland. Thomson carried the germ of *The Seasons* with him when he left Scotland; it is no wonder that his first major poem, begun just after he arrived in England, is the most thoroughly Scottish of all his major works.

What elements of the native Scottish literary tradition did Thomson bring to England and to *The Seasons*? They are many and complex. First, much of the Scots "art" literature of the Middle Ages and Renaissance is dominated by religious-didactic purpose, often expressed from a surprisingly personal, subjective stance as the narrator places himself within the poem. *The Seasons,* too, is governed by religious-didactic motives, and the peripatetic speaker, the subjective "I" who occasionally appears, is Thomson himself. Second, these older Scots poets worked in that distinguished tradition of Scottish classicism, or vernacular humanism, to which Thomson was heir. Third, the literary language which the Makars and their seventeenth-century successors created for themselves was an eclectic blend of vigorous Scots, aureate Latinate diction, and Southern English; the trend was toward expansion and enrichment of poetic language, and such was also Thomson's method. Most important, these Scots poets very frequently chose the theme of natural description as the vehicle for many of their works; Thomson would make this theme a major art form in Anglo-Scottish poetry.

Abundant detailed, accurate natural description, not purely "for its own sake" yet carrying far greater than conventional weight in the overall scheme and significance of the poetry, was a prominent subject of formal poetry in Scots as well as in Scottish Gaelic and folk literatures long before it was a major feature of English poetry. The presentation of particulars and details within the landscape, the strong strain of realism even in works of a basically allegorical or symbolic nature far surpassed any such descriptive interpretation in the English tradition even by Thomson's day. That there is in fact a long-established tradition of Scottish natural-descriptive poetry has become a generally accepted critical assumption in Scottish literary studies. What are some of the more specific traits of this tradition? Scottish poetry of natural description has shown such characteristics as a penchant for portraying dramatic contrasts or paradoxes in the natural world; a deep sense of man's camaraderie with animals, provoking frequent literary parallels of animals' with man's situation and related to a more general attitude of humanitarian sympathy; keen color sense; and a tendency to describe the harsher, more violent aspects of nature, especially the Scottish winter season. All of these qualities are significant in *The Seasons*. It was this descriptive theme in Scottish literature, primarily, which Thomson adopted and brought to the poetry of Augustan England. A brief survey of the descriptive tradition in Scottish poetry will offer some insight into Thomson's choice of this theme for his *Seasons*.

Seasonal description in poetry was never exclusive to Scotland, of course. Complex symbolic seasonal schemes in the visual arts as well as poetry have featured in Western European culture from classical times. But in addition to such conventional, stylized seasonal portrayals, there developed a more realistic strain of winter description within Old and Middle English alliterative verse. *Sir Gawain and the Green Knight*, for example, which is probably a Northern Midlands work, is set chiefly in winter and draws sharp contrasts between indoor warmth and outdoor cold, spring and winter; these physical conditions correspond to the poet's moral themes. Description of vivid winter scenes in poetry seems to have been a characteristic of alliterative and not simply Scottish verse. Still, long after alliterative verse on the Old English pattern had died out in England, it continued to survive and thrive in Scotland. The heavy alliteration which was part of the formal intricacy of Scottish and Irish Gaelic poetry perhaps disposed medieval Scots poets also to employ so much alliteration and their partly bilingual audiences to appreciate it.[1] So this continuing interest in alliterative verse and the particularly realistic manner of describing winter seem to have survived together in Scots poetry. Even after the true alliterative verse line went out of use in the north, a tendency to use abundant decorative alliteration, especially in passages of natural description, along with a preference for winter or other such scenes of violent nature stayed strong in Scots poetry.

What were the native roots of this poetry of natural description in Scotland? Even if the genius for such nature poetry is not a "racial" quality, as some Victorian critics rather rashly claimed, it is true that societies tend to see things in certain ways as their artistic culture evolves in response to many factors such as geography and climate (important influences on the Scottish winter theme), politics, education, history, and religion. Aesthetic response is thus conditioned by a variety of external circumstances. But if a Scottish literary predilection for description could in fact be traced, it might have had its source in the Celtic strain and was thence communicated from the Strathclyde Welsh to the Scots poets of the Lowlands.[2] Recent scholars claim that certain resemblances, such as the prominent nature theme, do in fact occur between Scottish Gaelic and Lowland literatures. They further assert that "bilingual" influence in the Lowlands extends not only to poetic themes but also to prosody and language,[3] carrying with it the alliteration and words for natural features such as "brae," "cairn," and "glen." Oral transmission in bilingual Border areas could thus account for certain cross-cultural similarities which Gaelic and Lowland Scots poetry share; for example, their close visual description of small scenes; their vivid concretizing imagination; their extensive personification, dynamically with description; their precise detailing, often through "cataloging"; their respect for the natural world, heightening descriptive impact; and their concern for strict form, including intricate sound effects. These characteristic methods of Scottish Gaelic poetry are all part of *The Seasons,* a "Lowland" poem of nature influenced through the Scots tradition.

Much has been made of the importance of winter in Scottish nature poetry and rightly so, for this subject does seem to figure most prominently and with the most originality and realism. The reason for its appeal to Scottish poets is surely the very real and immediate presence of the inclement northern climate itself. Winter was a ready subject; poets naturally tended to incorporate such immediate environmental experience into their natural-descriptive poetry, especially since pastoral conventions of more temperate southern climes were simply not appropriate for them. The contrast between realistic Scottish winter scenes and conventional, stylized Mediterranean spring or summer scenes was marked in the work of such poets as David Lindsay, William Dunbar, Robert Henryson, and Gavin Douglas.

Henryson exploited this northern winter tradition; his *Testament of Cresseid* and fable "The Preiching of the Swallow" are often cited as illustrations. The poet-narrator opens the *Testament*'s prologue by placing himself within the icy Scottish winter season, then retiring to his fireside. Such portrayal of the striking contrast between outdoor cold and indoor comfort is an important motif in Scottish winter poetry and characterizes several of the *The Season*'s cottage scenes. The "Preiching," set in Scotland, aims to teach the moral significance of the nature it depicts. The poem represents the belief which would be the basis of physicotheology: that God is manifest in His Creation and can be known through nature. Both Henryson and Thomson, along with the other Scottish descriptive poets, placed very strong emphasis on the "book of nature" as chief teacher of moral and spiritual truth, with realistic and pleasing natural description as the best vehicle for expressing this truth. Thomson also follows Henryson's lead in qualifying this lesson from nature; both poets make it clear that earthly knowledge of God is limited and will be fulfilled only in eternity.

In the "preiching" proper, birds function as both real animals and allegorical personifications; Henryson's method of enhancing description with extensive dramatic personification of nature is also Thomson's. Henryson shows that sympathy with animals which runs

right through Scottish literature; a variation of the dual real-alle-
gorical role of animals works in *The Seasons* as well, where Thomson
describes birds and other animals for their own sakes and as members
of the various Creation and also as parallels to the human situation.
Four brief seasonal cameos are prefixed to Henryson's fable. Although there are details of realistic description in "Somer," "Harvest,"
and "Ver" and some conventions in "Wynter," the first three seasons
are mostly stylized, conventional, and Mediterranean while "Wynter"
is more realistic and immediate.[4] "Wynter" is the most recognizably
Scottish of the scenes, most clearly based on the poet's own experience
of the wet, windy, and cold season. Significantly, Henryson's denser
use of northern alliteration and of vernacular, less-aureate Scots diction complements his Scottish "Wynter" description, much as Thomson's use of stronger alliteration and more colloquial language height-
ens many of the more vigorous and particularly Scottish scenes in *The
Seasons*, thus demonstrating the link between the alliterative and
native winter descriptive traditions in Scottish poetry.

Perhaps the Middle Scots Makar of closest affinity to Thomson himself was Gavin Douglas. His *Eneados* (1513; Ruddiman edition, 1710)
becomes a thoroughly Scottish rendering of Virgil's *Aeneid,* a faithful
translation into Scots by a Scottish classicist, filtered through perceptive and keen Scottish experience to give it greater descriptive force,
and at times greater poetic force, than the original. Both Douglas and
Thomson borrowed freely from conventions of dynamic personification and abstraction, combining these with fresh description drawn
from personal observation of nature. In Douglas's *Eneados* prologues,
wholly of his own composition, occur his most extensive seasonal passages, showing distinct influence of Scottish experience. Prologue
VII, which has been compared with Thomson's "Winter,"[5] typically
and subjectively depicts the harsher aspects of winter in realistic,
strongly alliterative Scots vernacular terms. Prologues XII ("May")
and XIII ("June"), in contrast, are more conventional, Mediterranean
settings described with more aureate diction. Douglas delighted in his
descriptions for their own sake to a far greater extent than even
Henryson. Within the *Eneados* proper, natural description plays a
more important role than it had even in Virgil. Douglas enhanced

Virgil's descriptions of storms, floods, and mountains with details from his own Scottish experience, much as Thomson would enhance *Georgics* themes with Scottish experience in *The Seasons*. Both Douglas and Thomson appreciated Virgil's descriptive skill, and both Scottish poets owe something of their profound awareness of the physical world to the *Georgics*.[6] Further, the elements of superstition and the supernatural, while present in Virgil, assume an even greater importance in both Douglas and Thomson than in their Virgilian models; this theme of superstition in poetry, while by no means exclusively Scottish, did tend to linger in Scottish poetry long after it had lost importance in English literature. Such references to superstition and the supernatural by Thomson's day and even after were distinctive in that behind them lay an element of genuine belief, reinforced by the long survival of such attitudes in Scottish folklore and religion. English poet William Collins, in "An Ode on the Popular Superstitions of the Highlands of Scotland" (1749), for instance, acknowledged this theme as a particularly Scottish one.[7]

Douglas's poetry represents the most significant and successful attempt to develop the Middle Scots literary language to its fullest potential as a medium for natural description. Virgil's dignified, controlled epic gains vitality with Douglas's particularly northern descriptive connotations; the strength of Scots for concretizing individual scenes and for recreating action powerfully reinforces Virgilian imagery. Douglas was far more liberal in using aureate diction than were his fellow Makars, borrowing abundant Latin words, especially from his primary source, and also introducing many Southern English words and constructions into his elevated literary language. His enrichment of Middle Scots for fullest expressive, particularly descriptive force is thus highly comparable to Thomson's approach in the eighteenth century, as he introduced Latinate and Virgilian vocabulary as well as his own coinages, compound epithets, and expressions deriving from spoken Scots to expand formal literary English for his new poetry of nature.

Throughout the sixteenth and seventeenth centuries many more Scottish antecedents to Thomson in seasonal and descriptive poetry appeared; these gained in purely descriptive, as distinct from symbolic, emphasis. Alexander Montgomerie was a master of sensuous description, and his *The Cherry and the Slae* demonstrates close observation and representation of nature. Alexander Hume's "Of the Day Estivall" depicts an ideal June day; Thomson in "Summer" would also adopt the "ideal day" framework. Hume's delightful verse is an early instance of poetic natural description for its own sake, of pure concentration on the natural scene as a subject; while not explicitly religious, it conveys a love of nature as God's work without being didactic or dogmatic. William Drummond, too, made sympathetic natural description the vehicle for much of his meditative verse. Certainly many of Thomson's better *Seasons* descriptions join nature with implicit religious feeling in this way without belaboring underlying didactic aims. King James VI & I composed four "Seasons" sonnets[8] which nicely illustrate the particularly Scottish pattern of seasonal poetry. He explicitly stated his purpose of recreating the sense experiences of each season, making them tangible to the reader. His sonnets are miniature prototypes of Thomson's *Seasons;* his blend of seasonal convention with details from his own experience clearly anticipates Thomson. "Springtyme" refers to that Virgilian eternal spring which is an important ideal in Thomson; "Somer" is replete with conventional heat and light imagery, like that which governs Thomson's "Summer"; "Harvest" portrays reapers, the human "industry" of Thomson's "Autumn"; and "Winter," with its sustained and transformed water imagery, denser alliteration, and especially Scottish realism prefigures Thomson's own picture of "Winter."

Art and folk literatures in Scotland have long enjoyed a fruitful interaction; they have influenced one another in, among other things, modes of natural description. Along with the established tradition of formal Scottish nature poetry, another strain of Scottish literature should be considered an indirect influence on Thomson's descriptive art—the Border ballads. The ballads convey descriptive immediacy and lively action; they are close to nature and exhibit a strong pictorial and color sense. Thomson captures the ballads' sense of drama and energy in his portrayal of the natural world, dynamically and dramatically, in process. Even certain images are common to Lowland Scottish art and folk literatures and also to Thomson; one example is the unconventional image of hell as a Scottish winter landscape—damp, murky, and foggy rather than fiery—which occurs in the ballad "The Daemon-Lover" and in Douglas's *Eneados* and likewise in Thomson's *Castle of Indolence* (II.lxxviii).[9] In the ballads, in the poetry of the Makars, and in Thomson's *Seasons,* descriptions of winter and wild nature are thus particularly vivid. Other qualities of the Border ballads also compare with the conception of *The Seasons:* their strong fatalism in the face of nature's mysterious forces—Thomson's Providence acting through nature is at times precariously close, in a poem of predominant Augustan optimism, to the ballads' fatalism, as in the tale of "Celadon and Amelia"; ribald or grotesque humor, as in the "Autumn" hunt burlesque; and preoccupation with the supernatural, which appears surprisingly often in Thomson. Formal devices of strong alliteration and emphatic, dramatic pauses, also characteristic of the ballads, likewise work effectively in *The Seasons.*

By Thomson's day, then, there had evolved a complex tradition of Scottish poetry of natural description, a tradition which would gain new vigor through two strains of development: the Scots vernacular revival, led by Allan Ramsay, and the upsurge of Anglo-Scottish interest in descriptive verse. Ramsay, in his preface to *The Ever Green* (1724), thus praised Scottish nature poetry of the "good old Bards" in his volume:

> Their Poetry is the Product of their own Country, not pilfered and spoiled in the Transportation from abroad: Their Images are native, and their Landskips domestick; copied from those Fields and Meadows we every Day behold.
>
> The Morning rises (in the Poets Description) as she does in the Scottish Horizon. We are not carried to Greece or Italy for a Shade, a Stream or a Breeze. The Groves rise in our own Valleys; the Rivers flow from our own Fountains, and the Winds blow upon our own Hills. I find not Fault with those Things, as they are in Greece or Italy: But with a Northern Poet for fetching his Materials from these Places, in a Poem, of which his own Country

is the Scene; as our Hymners to the Spring and Makers of Pastorals frequently do.[10]

Indeed it had been the practice of many Scottish poets merely to borrow conventional Mediterranean pastoral imagery for their nature
scenes, especially of spring and summer. However, a number of
young Anglo-Scots writing in Ramsay's day were equally unhappy
with this facile borrowing of foreign descriptive imagery, so they tried
consciously to incorporate more realistic native Scottish imagery into
their poetry. Ramsay's own example and advice were undoubtedly
taken to heart by Thomson and his contemporaries as they committed
themselves to reviving Scottish poetry of natural description.

An added incentive for these young Scots was surely the new enthusiasm for Newtonian empirical science at Edinburgh University which
taught them to see nature with a clearer, more closely observant eye.
The value of first-hand observation and experience had earned increasing scientific and philosophical respectability, and in this intellectual atmosphere it is no wonder that poetry based on real, empirical
experience of the natural world—descriptive poetry—began to gain
such favor. One could know, learn, and feel through the senses; one
could recapture this experience as well in poetry. The choice of James
Thomson and his generation to write poetry of natural description
was thus also a natural outgrowth of their broader scientific education
in pre-Enlightenment Scotland.

Two contemporary Anglo-Scottish verses, both about the Scottish
winter, are said to have been direct influences on Thomson's *Seasons*.
As both are of uncertain provenance, the extent of their influence on
Thomson, or of his work on them, cannot be proven. Nonetheless,
they are fascinating examples of the new type of Anglo-Scottish descriptive poetry being written in Thomson's day by two men who were
his friends.

Robert Riccaltoun wrote a verse describing a winter scene which is
known to have inspired James Thomson to begin his own "Winter":
"Mr. Rickleton's poem on winter, which I still have, first put the design
into my head. in it are some masterly strokes that awaken'd me." "A

Winter's Day," first published in Savage's *Miscellany* (1726), was long thought to be this verse; there, it was attributed to the "author of the celebrated ballad of William and Margaret" (David Mallet) "in a state of melancholy," but it was later published in the *Gentleman's Magazine* (1740) as "Written by a Scotch Clergyman. Corrected by an Eminent Hand." The "Scotch Clergyman" has never been identified with certainty, yet the poem is counted among Riccaltoun's publications. The "Eminent Hand" was almost certainly the unprincipled Mallet who, in a letter to John Ker, claimed the poem as his own;[11] attribution to the "Scotch Clergyman" may have been added at Thomson's insistence. Thomas Somerville, minister of Jedburgh, reported that Riccaltoun himself once mentioned a poem he had composed describing a heavy snowfall on Ruberslaw Hill which had suggested the winter theme to Thomson. This poem, however, may not have been "A Winter's Day," which depicts neither snow nor a hill; there may have been two winter poems by Riccaltoun, "A Winter's Day" and another on a Border snowstorm now lost. "A Winter's Day," if indeed it is Riccaltoun's, does seem to bear the mark of considerable revision by the "Eminent Hand" of Mallet, who courted the sublime and sensational.[12]

"A Winter's Day," in English heroic couplets and with effective alliteration and assonance, describes what is apparently a Scottish Border scene:

Rough, rugged rocks, wet marshes, ruin'd tow'rs,
Bare trees, brown brakes, bleak heaths, and rushy moors,
Dead [*sic*—for "dread"] floods, huge cataracts, to my pleased eyes
(Now I can smile!) in wild disorder rise.
(ll. 39–42)

The storm is wet and windy; in his letter to Cranstoun, just prior to mentioning Riccaltoun's verse, Thomson too recalled "terrible floods, and high winds, that usually happen about this time of year" in Scotland. The poem's images of dull, fading color and disorder closely resemble Thomson's imagery in "Winter" as he describes the first and second storms and flood; use of extensive personification combined with realistic details in "A Winter's Day" is also similar to

Thomson's. The speaker of "A Winter's Day" embraces the season's "welcome horror" (l. 50), as Thomson does its "kindred Glooms! / Wish'd, win'try, Horrors" ("Winter," 1st edition, 1726, ll. 5–6); the speaker's paradoxical pleasure in the familiar season, his "Black melancholy" mood, is matched in Thomson's "Philosophic Melancholly" ("Winter, 1726, l. 66; transferred to "Autumn," 1730). Thomson's letter also recorded such sentiments attendant on the "beloved gloom" of the "fading" year. References to the Scottish theme of the supernatural also recur in both "A Winter's Day" and "Winter."[13]

Despite their many similarities, there are significant differences between the two poems. "A Winter's Day" is so thoroughly steeped in pathetic fallacy, overpowering some fine descriptive points, that it becomes morbidly self-indulgent; Thomson never allowed his sentimentality to go so far. Thomson ultimately awaits renewing spring, whereas the speaker of "A Winter's Day" seems to wish that winter, "all nature in agony with me" (l. 38), would remain. This exaggerated emotional element, coupled with the heightened "sublimity" of the Scottish winter scene, is surely due to Mallet's influence; it is hard to imagine that the reasonable Riccaltoun, who had warned young Thomson to avoid "luxuriance of diction" and to discipline his imagination, would have composed such gloomy and emotional verse. So whether or not this was the same poem Thomson so admired and emulated cannot be proven; indeed, Mallet's "correction" of the winter piece, like his more sensational *Excursion,* might even have been influenced by Thomson's own "Winter" (1726) itself. All that can be said with certainty is that Riccaltoun once wrote a descriptive winter poem which directly inspired the author of *The Seasons.*

Another Anglo-Scottish winter description believed to be a direct influence on Thomson's "Winter" is likewise of uncertain provenance. Like "A Winter's Day" it may at some stage have been influenced by Thomson rather than vice-versa. The Scottish Augustan "Imitation of Shakespeare" (or "Winter") by John Armstrong, a medical student at Edinburgh University, was "... made when he was very young. It help'd to amuse the solitude of a winter past in a wild romantic country; and, what is rather particular, was just finished when Mr. Thomson's celebrated poem upon the same subject appeared. Mr. Thomson, soon hearing of it, had the curiosity to procure a copy by means of a common acquaintance." Allegedly, Thomson showed the verse to Mallet, Aaron Hill, and Edward Young. Mallet was so impressed that he offered to help Armstrong publish it, but he changed his mind. The poem was not actually published until 1770, and this late statement from Armstrong's publisher is the only "evidence" that the poem was written independently of Thomson, but the tradition has survived that Thomson saw the manuscript of Armstrong's poem only after his own "Winter" had first appeared in March 1726. Armstrong's "Winter" is thus tentatively dated ca. 1725.[14]

Dr. John Armstrong, who later joined Thomson's Scottish circle of friends in London, was a son of the manse from Castleton, Roxburghshire. If his poem were written in 1725, then he would have been only sixteen years old. Armstrong's and Thomson's "Winter" poems have many points in common; their primary source, the Scottish Border winter, was the same. Armstrong's acknowledged model was Shakespeare, and indeed Thomson's "Winter" has been called the most "Shakespearean" of *The Seasons*.[15] The poems could have been written independently of one another, but the similarities in the two blank-verse pieces are so great that they almost certainly resulted from some direct influence of one upon the other. While there is closer correspondence in diction and detail between Armstrong's "Winter" and later editions of Thomson's revised "Winter," suggesting that Thomson was influenced by Armstrong's poem in manuscript and perhaps continued to draw from it in subsequent "Winter" revisions, it remains true that there are many important parallels which have been underestimated[16] between Armstrong and even the first edition of Thomson's "Winter": either Thomson was affected by Armstrong's manuscript poem before his own "Winter" was published (he might even have seen the manuscript in Scotland, in Edinburgh or the Borders), or Armstrong was inspired by the manuscript or more probably the first edition of Thomson's "Winter" and his own verse written in 1726 or later, thereafter to influence Thomson's revisions after the two poets had become friends. Parallels between Armstrong and Thomson's "Winter" (1726) include similar overall thematic development (wetness and Border waters, freeze, snowstorm, thaw, and stormy peril at sea) and similar controlling, "transforming" imagery (water and ice, shape-lessness and disorder), as well as many more detailed points of descrip-tion. In both Armstrong and Thomson (1st edition, 1726) occur such typical Border scenes as schoolboy sports on ice; shepherd and starving flocks; sheep buried in snowdrifts; birds made tame by winter's hard-ship; and cottagers by the fireside telling tales (in Armstrong, specifi-cally ghost stories; made so by Thomson, 1730ff.). The realism of Armstrong's Border observations is striking. Like Thomson, he em-ploys a great deal of personification, effectively to add vigor to the descriptions. An imaginative detail Armstrong uses to contrast with winter's snowstorm is the desert sandstorm (ll. 88–94); in 1744, Thom-son added a similar sandstorm to "Summer" (ll. 759–779). Given so many similarities, who influenced whom? Mallet again plays some sus-picious role. If Armstrong's poem had come first, did Mallet perhaps suppress its publication to safeguard Thomson's accomplishment in "Winter" (1726)? Or, more likely, did Mallet act out of self-interest so that he might borrow from Armstrong's poem for his own *Excursion* (1728)? There are some close resemblances. Despite the claim of Armstrong's publisher to the contrary, it seems most probable that Thomson's "Winter" (1st edition) first influenced young Armstrong, whose poem in turn suggested revisions and additions to his friend Thomson for later versions of his "Winter."

In any case, one contemporary Anglo-Scot who certainly did influ-ence—and was influenced by—James Thomson was his lifelong friend David Mallet. Thomson and Mallet exchanged manuscripts and ideas and influenced one another's blank-verse poems *The Seasons* and *The Excursion*. Their mutual influence probably began as early as their student days in Edinburgh. Mallet, like Thomson, was drawn to descriptive verse, and both liked to experiment with visual effects in poetry; it was Mallet, for example, who suggested to Thomson the "Newtonian" description of gems in "Summer," deriving from both poets' scientific education at Edinburgh University. *The Excursion* speaks high praise for Newton. Thomson's influence on Mallet was the stronger at first; *The Excursion* was written in imitation of early versions of Thomson's "Winter" and "Summer" and in turn affected Thomson's revisions of "Summer." Both poets went beyond strictly physicotheological purpose in their nature poetry to put more emphasis, in the Scottish tradition, on description for its own sake. Thomson encouraged Mallet to include dramatic scenes from nature in *The Excursion,* such as plague, thunderstorm and the guilty man's fears, polar ice and arctic winter—incidents which also occur in *The Seasons,* though Thomson himself generally used such sensational descriptive effects with more restraint than did his friend. Thomson also prescribed the Scottish element of the supernatural, so important in *The Seasons,* to Mallet, who likewise took it to extremes Thomson did not want to attempt.[17]

Whatever immediate impact the poems of Riccaltoun, Armstrong, and Mallet had on *The Seasons,* such works strikingly illustrate the new kind of poetry being written in Thomson's day by young Anglo-Scottish poets. They show that the Scottish tradition of dynamic natural description was very much alive and injecting new vitality into Augustan English poetry of the early eighteenth century. These Anglo-Scots were simply more enthusiastic about the potential value of closely observed and accurately portrayed nature in poetry than were their contemporaries in England, who still tended to rely more heavily upon pastoral and descriptive conventions. Thomson, with his *Seasons,* would prove the best, most famous and influential of this generation of Scottish Augustan nature poets.

What sort of Anglo-Scottish "nature" poem did Thomson intend *The Seasons* to be? He prefixed to his second edition of "Winter" (June 1726) a brief but important preface[18] (dropped in 1730) which, as Thomson's own apology for poetry, is very valuable for the study of his works. In the preface he reaches back, beyond the more immediate Scottish tradition of which he is a part, to acknowledge the sacred and classical sources of his theme and, specifically, to set forth his religious goals in portraying nature poetically. The preface is couched in fairly smooth, witty and urbane Augustan prose, modeled on the *Spectator* style, which the poet had emulated as a student in Scotland. A year as tutor and working poet in London had, by 1726, helped him to work out much of the awkwardness in written English expression which as a Scot he no doubt experienced at first (a refreshing exception is "friskish," a coinage possibly derived from Scots, which remains in the preface). Thomson's Scottish training in classical rhetoric had served him well; in the preface he uses persuasive logic against the enemies of poetry while eloquently arguing its value.

Significantly, Thomson begins by linking the poet's "DIVINE ART" with revelation itself; the Bible is poetry, "the peculiar Language of Heaven." He exclaims, "let POETRY, once more, be restored to her antient Truth and Purity; let Her be inspired from Heaven, and, in Return her Incense ascend thither." Poetry as revelation, as well as a sacred offering of praise from the poet, is already, of course, a familiar theme in Thomson. He goes on to criticize current "notorious abuses of POETRY." He laments that something has been lost in recent English poetry—genuine concern for man's spiritual edification—and he calls for a poetic "Genius" with "the true Interest of Virtue, Learning, and Mankind, intirely, at Heart," to uplift the "DIVINE ART" once more. Thus does he establish the moral and didactic motives so vital to *The Seasons*.

Thomson's image for the barren contemporary literary scene as a "wintry World of Letters" is apt and prophetic: he himself, a Scotsman from a truly wintry clime and a culture considered equally wintry by most Englishmen of his day, would become that very genius who would impart spiritual meaning to "Winter" and to *The Seasons*. He himself would introduce the favorite Scottish theme of natural description as the true "Native POETRY" needed to enliven English verse. Thomson's call for "Native POETRY" strongly recalls Ramsay's preface to *The Ever Green*, two years previous, where Ramsay likewise made a plea for the Scottish descriptive tradition; indeed, *The Seasons*, no less than *The Gentle Shepherd*, is a Scottish product of the need for native pastoral poetry. Echoing Addison and also Francis Hutcheson on the theme of natural beauty-in-variety, Thomson writes:

> I know no Subject more elevating, more amusing; more ready to awake the poetical Enthusiasm, the philosophical Reflection, and the moral Sentiment, than the *Works of Nature*. Where can we meet with such Variety, such Beauty, such Magnificence? All that enlarges, and transports, the Soul? What more inspiring than a calm, wide, Survey of Them? In every Dress *Nature* is greatly

charming. . . . there is no thinking of these Things without breaking out into POETRY. . . .

This recalls the poet's letter to William Cranstoun, nostalgically referring to the variety, beauty, and magnificence of the Scottish nature he
misses in England: "this country, I am in, is not very entertaining. no
variety but that of woods, and them we have in abundance. but where
is the living stream? the airy mountain? and the hanging rock? with
twenty other things that elegantly please the lover of nature?—
Nature delights me in every form. . . ."[19]

Thomson's preface next acknowledges the wider nature tradition in
literature which helped to shape his own concepts of the art: for these
"best . . . POETS," ancient and modern, "The wild romantic Country
was their Delight," as it was his own in Scotland. He praises Job,
"which, even, strikes so forcibly thro' a mangling Translation, is
crowned with a Description of the grand *Works of Nature;* and that,
too, from the Mouth of their ALMIGHTY AUTHOR."[20] He then praises
Virgil's natural description; Thomson's early intimacy with the works
of Virgil profoundly influenced both language and themes of *The Seasons.* He illustrates with his own translation into English blank verse of
a passage from *Georgics* II (475–486), where he compares himself with
Virgil as a "Priest" of the Muses, professing his priestly "Devotion to
the Works of Nature" and adopting the theme of nature for his own
poetry. Job and Virgil are thus Thomson's two acknowledged models
for the sort of poetry he hoped to write; they exemplify the classical-
religious parallel traditions, the Christian humanism, to which Thomson was educated in Scotland and which informs all his works. Thomson's aims in writing *The Seasons,* as expressed in his preface, were "to
give the Reader some of that true Pleasure, which [the seasons], in
their agreeable Succession, are, always, sure to inspire into my Heart,"
and through giving pleasure by lovingly describing nature for its own
sake also to reveal deeper religious truths and to make a sacred offering to the Creator.

The Seasons, then, is many kinds of poem. It is a wide-ranging, detailed, and deeply felt poem of nature in the Scottish descriptive tradition. Not less, it is a religious poem, an enthusiastic prayer of praise as

well as an interpretation of physicotheology from the heart and pen of a Scots divinity student. It is a neoclassical poem, a native georgic. It is a didactic poem, pronouncing not only theological but also philosophical, moral, and scientific ideas. It would become more and more an Augustan public poem, proclaiming sociopolitical views on behalf of united Great Britain. It is at the same time a very personal poem, revealing the poet's own feelings about the natural world he describes, the God he worships. *The Seasons* is all of these and more. In bringing the fruits of his rich Scottish culture to English poetry, Thomson succeeded in creating a new generic blend, an Anglo-Scottish miscellany. The poem's complex interaction of themes, modes, and styles, each influenced by the poet's Scottish experience, makes *The Seasons* James Thomson's unique, and uniquely Scottish, achievement.

5 *THE SEASONS* AS A SCOTTISH POEM OF NATURAL DESCRIPTION

The Seasons is so full of Scottish-inspired scenery that proof of the poem's Scottishness has mostly rested on this evidence alone. While this immediate descriptive, literal level of meaning can now be recognized as just one of many Scottish aspects of the poem, it is certainly a vital element, one which helped to carry on the Scottish tradition of nature poetry itself and one which James Thomson chose to carry into Augustan English poetry. For a great many of the descriptions in *The Seasons* are directly based on Thomson's memories of the pleasing "variety" of the Scottish landscape itself, the sublimity and beauty he missed in England. Further, his experiences in the Border country and his deep feelings associated with it, reinforced by his acquired knowledge of other parts of his native land, inform all the poem's descriptions,[1] the domestic and even the foreign scenes and incidents. The following critical overview will look at *The Seasons* primarily as a Scottish poem of natural description, keeping in mind Thomson's significant contribution to that distinguished tradition and focusing on the more identifiably Scottish features of the various descriptions themselves.

Thomson began "Winter," his first *Season*, with determined emphasis on accurate description based on personal observation of nature. Over several revisions of *The Seasons*, many descriptive passages grew to include scientific, and especially Newtonian, material; the poet also added other kinds of description, such as his own adaptations of conventional and borrowed literature (drawn from Virgil, Milton, the

Scriptures, pastoral poetry, and so on) and much foreign seasonal descriptive material gleaned from geographical and travel literature. To accompany and explain these expanded descriptions, he also added abstract, didactic comment. Such revisions can best be seen in the evolution of "Winter," where changes are most widespread, and best illustrate the types of revisions Thomson made up to and including 1746. Thomson's goal was comprehensiveness of the seasonal vision; his revisions aimed not only to broaden the physical range of *Seasons'* descriptions but also to engender deeper understanding of the subject of those descriptions: the vital relationship between man and nature and both of these to God. Some of the revisions are successful, some not, but the descriptive backbone of "Winter," and of each *Season*, based on the poet's own observation and experience, remains strong.

"Winter" appeared in March 1726. It was published by John Millan and printed by Archibald Campbell, two Scotsmen in London; Thomson tended to prefer dealing with Scots publishers. This first "Winter," a brief 405 lines, was composed soon after Thomson's arrival in England, and in many ways it affords the clearest picture of the poet's adaptation of the Scottish literary tradition of natural, and particularly winter, description to Augustan English poetry. By 1746, after Thomson's final revisions, it had grown to a length of 1,069 lines. The first "Winter" included several passages which were transferred in 1730 in altered form to "Autumn": clouds and light (to "Autumn," ll. 956–963); solitary wanderer in the "withering Copse" (ll. 963–975); "Philosophic Melancholly" (ll. 1004ff.); poet's retreat of "high, embowering Shades" (ll. 1030–1036); moonlit "humid *Evening*" of fogs and vapors (ll. 1082–1102); and "Dew" (ll. 1065–1171). Some of these transfers may reflect Thomson's personal feeling that autumn is the most congenial season for philosophical meditation, as he indicated in a letter of October 1725 to Cranstoun in Scotland: "Now, I imagine you seized w^t a fine romantic kind of melancholy, on the fading of the Year. Now I figure you wandering, philosophical, and pensive . . . while deep, divine Contemplation, the genius of the place, prompts each swelling awfull thought."[2] In an opening passage little altered from the original (1726), personified "WINTER comes, to rule the vary'd Year"; Thomson greets the familiar season:

... Welcome, kindred Glooms!
Cogenial Horrors, hail! With frequent Foot,
Pleas'd have I, in my chearful Morn of Life,
When nurs'd by careless Solitude I liv'd,
And sung of Nature with unceasing Joy,
Pleas'd have I wander'd thro' your rough Domain;
Trod the pure Virgin-Snows, myself as pure;
Heard the Winds roar, and the big Torrent burst;
Or seen the deep-fermenting Tempest brew'd,
In the grim Evening-Sky. Thus pass'd the Time,
Till thro' the lucid Chambers of the South
Look'd out the joyous SPRING, look'd out and smil'd.[3]

This passage recounts the poet's apprenticeship in wintry, rural Scotland and his juvenile attempts at nature poetry based on the familiar Scottish scene. "Lucid Chambers of the South," from which "joyous SPRING . . . smil'd," refers to the attractive warmth of spring sun and might also allude to the "spring" of young Thomson's new life and literary opportunities in the south, in England, which had opened up to him in the spring of 1725. The passage also establishes winter's central paradox of beauty ("welcome," "pure") and horror (gloomy, "rough," "grim"). Each of Thomson's *Seasons* is built around such a central paradox: "Spring," love and pain; "Summer," power and violence; "Autumn," fulfillment and barrenness. Thomson's ambiguous attitude to winter's forces has, in fact, been identified as one Scottish characteristic of the poem.[4] His greeting to winter echoes *Paradise Lost* (I.250), Satan's greeting to hell, thus linking Scottish winter description with the idea of hell, an association also found in older Scottish poetry. "Winter" not only describes the season itself but also reflects the poet's mood at the time he began the poem; it is a two-sided season of both familiarity and sadness. Thomson's mother had recently died in Scotland, and the young poet was grieving and painfully homesick in the strange city of London. Thomson constructed in "Winter" (1726) a well-balanced descriptive and religious poem, and although its shape would grow distorted with the numerous geographical, sociopolitical, and scientific additions he made over the years, the descriptive heart of the original poem remains sound.

"Winter" and all the *Seasons* are full of lively personification of nature enhanced with realistic detail; Thomson's characteristic method was to adopt a literary convention, such as a conventional stylized personification, to his own purposes by making it more realistic and true to nature. Thus he can cleverly exploit the tension between literal (descriptive, detailed) and metaphorical or allusive; his creative use of personification is also in the Scottish tradition both of the Makars and of the Gaelic poets. Like each of the *Seasons,* "Winter" is portrayed through a set of relevant "transforming" images. "Winter" 's imagery is that of pale or drab color or lack of color, deceptiveness, shapelessness and deformity, and especially water in its various forms of rain, snow, ice, fog, and flood. The colorless or subdued-color imagery of "Winter" (and also of "Autumn," as the two more inclement Scottish seasons) contrasts with the strong color imagery of "Spring" and "Summer" and is consistent with the dull hues of the landscape in certain bleak Scottish Border areas such as Southdean.[5] Winter's arrival is typically lacking in color ("wan" rays, l. 49; "long dark Night," l. 50; "sable Cincture" and "Shadows," l. 54; "dun discolour'd Flocks," l. 64; "brown Deluge," l. 77) as well as lacking order ("Untended" flocks, l. 65; "loose disjointed Cliffs," l. 68; "fractur'd Mountains," l. 69; "brawling Brook," l. 69). Here follows the first major descriptive event of "Winter," the personified rainstorm which is the first of three "Winter" tempests. Storms occur in each *Season,* linking them to one another and demonstrating Thomson's skill at describing dynamic nature-in-process:

> Along the Woods, along the moorish Fens,
> Sighs the sad *Genius* of the coming Storm;
> And up among the loose disjointed Cliffs,
> And fractur'd Mountains wild, the brawling Brook
> And Cave, presageful, send a hollow Moan,
> Resounding long in listening Fancy's Ear.
>   Then comes the Father of the Tempest forth,
> Wrapt in black Glooms. First joyless Rains obscure
> Drive thro' the mingling Skies with Vapour foul;

> Dash on the Mountain's Brow, and shake the Woods,
> That grumbling wave below. Th' unsightly Plain
> Lies a brown Deluge; as the low-bent Clouds
> Pour Flood on Flood, yet unexhausted still
> Combine, and deepening into Night shut up
> The Day's fair Face . . .
> (ll. 66–80)

This appears to be a Cheviot scene;[6] Thomson grew up in such an area of rugged mountains, hillside caves, and streams. The element of superstition, too ("Moan" in "listening Fancy's Ear") is Scottish. The domestic scene which comes next is one of several in *The Seasons* portraying cottagers telling tales by the fireside while the storm rages outside (ll. 89–93). It is likewise Scottish, the typical contrast of indoor comfort with outdoor cold and natural violence, and recalls not only older Scottish poetry but also "social" scenes in the late eighteenth-century vernacular poetry of Fergusson and Burns. Compared with such convivial scenes in Scots poetry, those in *The Seasons* are rather restrained and decorous, yet they suggest just how much the rich folk culture of his Border community mattered to Thomson.[7]

A vigorous description of the flooding river follows: this river in spate, roaring down the mountainside, is surely a Scottish one, perhaps the Tweed.[8] This passage was in the original "Winter" and was revised beneficially in 1730 with the addition of adjectives giving more "race" (see Chapter 7). From this scene Thomson abruptly invokes "NATURE! great Parent!" (ll. 106–117), then shifts back to description as the winter's second storm, the windstorm, brews (ll. 118ff.). Here imagery of chaos and weak color is even more pronounced: the sun "Uncertain wanders" (l. 20); "reeling Clouds / Stagger . . . dizzy . . . doubting" (ll. 121–122); air is "fluctuating" (l. 126); stars are "obtuse," "shivering" (l. 127); sky is "palid" (l. 118); moon is "Blank, in the leaden-colour'd East" (l. 124) and "wan" (l. 125). In lines added in 1744, the animals sense the storm's coming (ll. 132–145), echoing *Georgics* I. Thomson's personal observations and innovative language enhance Virgilian descriptions here, particularly his vivid portrayal of the distress of the birds: rooks are "clamorous"; a cormorant "Wheels from the Deep, and screams along the Land"; "circling Sea-Fowl cleave the flaky Clouds." The poet's involvement with and realistic representations of animal life here and throughout the poem owe much to his youthful experiences, growing up close to nature in rural Scotland. In such passages as this, Thomson's skill at choosing apt descriptive adjectives, and especially verbs and verb forms, is also evident. He is best at recreating not merely visual, static nature but action and movement, showing kinship with the dramatic Border ballads; he is able to apprehend the dramatic element in the natural world and to convey it in accurate and animated detail.

The storm at sea (ll. 155–174), greatly expanded from the original, becomes verbose and repetitious, particularly in its patriotic references to British sea-power, but still it retains much lively detail. The storm on land (ll. 175–201) is more within the poet's own Scottish experience; it rages over a landscape of forest and mountains. Thomson, living in London when he wrote *The Seasons*, was far from any real mountains; his homesick letter to Cranstoun wonders, "where is . . . the airy mountain?" in Southern England. Yet there are many mountain scenes in *The Seasons* drawing upon his nostalgic recollection of the wilder landscape of his native Borders. The windstorm surrounds both "Cottage thatch'd" and "lordly Roof," and "Sleep frighted flies." The important element of superstition recurs:

> Then, too, they say, thro' all the burthen'd Air,
> Long Groans are heard, shrill Sounds, and distant Sighs,
> That, utter'd by the Demon of the Night,
> Warn the devoted Wretch of Woe and Death.
> (ll. 191–194)

This recalls Martin Martin's account in *Description of the Western Islands of Scotland Circa 1695* (1703; revised 1716) of the Hebridean superstition of "loud noises" like human voices which the islanders heard in haunted regions.[9] The qualifying "they say," typical of Thomson's references to the supernatural, occurs in all versions of "Winter." The storm intensifies until God ("Nature's KING") commands a calm; the original version, which made more use of personification ("chidden" storm "begins to pant," "dies") had been even more effective than the more abstract revised passage (2nd edition, 1726 ff.). After the storm, personified Nature is exhausted ("weary Clouds," "drowsy World") and sleeps, allowing transition to meditation and thence to a personal prayer ("FATHER . . . teach me THYSELF!" ll. 217–222).

"Winter"'s third storm is a snowstorm (ll. 223ff.) and marks a return to realistic natural description in controlling imagery of disorder, shapelessness, water transformed into snow, and pale color (first "dun," then white, "wild dazzling Waste, that buries wide / The Works of Man," ll. 223 and 239–240). Thomson's snowstorm is drawn mainly from his Border experience; Roxburghshire is an area subject to severe and paralyzing blizzards. The description of the hungry animals—wild birds including a robin redbreast (added 2nd edition, 1726) "Tam'd by the cruel Season," sheep seeking the "wither'd Herb"—is a refinement of the winter scene in Thomson's juvenile "Of a Country Life." Thomson's sympathy with animals, that strain of feeling which features so prominently in Scottish poetry, was seen in the juvenilia and recurs throughout *The Seasons;* here, he urges, "Now, Shepherds, to your helpless Charge be kind . . ." (ll. 265ff.). The poet follows this scene with the horrors of a flock of sheep buried in a snowdrift, then a man lost and dying in the transformed and deceptive snow-covered landscape. Tragic accidents of this kind were no doubt common in rugged, rural Scotland in the eighteenth century. Defoe, for instance, wrote of sheep and cattle starving in the Scottish winter snows; Smollett reported that sheep in the Borders "'run wild . . . and thousands are lost under huge wreaths of snow.'" The swain's awful death (added 2nd edition, 1726) is visualized in such a straightforward, immediate manner, reinforced with strong alliteration, that it recalls the directness and violence of the ballads; it is a horrible scene, especially contrasted with the warmth of home and hearth awaiting the doomed man. The poet seems fatalistically to accept the inevitability of death, as

> . . . On every Nerve
> The deadly Winter seizes; shuts up Sense;
> And, o'er his inmost Vitals creeping cold,
> Lays him along the Snows, a stiffen'd Corse,
> Stretch'd out, and bleaching in the northern blast.
> (ll. 317–321)

Such incidents in "Winter," describing the negative side of the paradoxical season and inspiring the poet's awe and fear, come directly
from Scottish rural life as he knew it.[10] These descriptions lead him
into a long religious-didactic passage (ll. 322–388), but he follows this
with still more wintry horrors.

The next "Winter" scene (ll. 389–413) is an example of Thomson's
drawing from factual travel literature and heightening its impact with
details from Scottish experience and folklore. While the scene itself is
not Scottish, the poet's Scottish background, his "recollected emotion,"[11] predisposed him to dramatize the incident in the way he did.
This blending of foreign with Scottish information and impression
occurs several times in *The Seasons*. Here, his setting is the "*Alps*, / And
wavy *Apennines* and *Pyrenees*," but the conception of the scene also
owes much to Scottish influences:

> Cruel as Death, and hungry as the Grave!
> Burning for Blood! bony, and ghaunt, and grim!
> Assembling Wolves in raging Troops descend
> (ll. 393–395)

These lines seem to speak from an older Scottish poetry. The first two
lines are divided by a strong caesura, and the second line in particular
could almost have come straight from northern alliterative verse; it
follows the characteristic pattern, as the two stresses of the first half-
line alliterate with the first stressed word of the second half-line. The
short-syllabled language, too, is Teutonic rather than Latinate (contrasting with the Latinate "Assembling"). Thomson goes on to describe grisly scenes of wolves preying on horse and bull, human in-
fant, lion, and even "On Church-Yards drear," "to dig / the shrouded
Body from the Grave; o'er which, / Mixed with foul Shades, and
frighted Ghosts, they howl" (ll. 410–413). Again, Thomson clearly
echoes Scottish folk history, with its tone of superstition and fear;
wolves had long been a real danger in Scotland, and the poet himself
surely knew of such atrocities. Bishop John Leslie's *History of Scotland*
(1578), for example, recorded that

> (evin as our nychbour Inglande has nocht ane wolfe, with
> quhilkes afore thay war mekle molested and invadet) bot we now

nocht few, 3e contrare, verie monie and maist cruel, cheiflie in our North cuntrey, quhair nocht only invade they scheip, oxne, 3e and horse, bot evin men, specialie women with barne, outragiouslie and fercelie thay ouirthrows.

The *Orkneyinga Saga* told that "There I saw the grey wolf gaping / O'er wounded corse of many a man." The last wolf in Scotland, which murdered two children, was said to have been killed as late as 1743, long after wolves had disappeared from England. So in creating this gruesome scene, Thomson likely drew from Scottish life and legend, consciously to reinforce an alpine picture and to add to the sublime or sensational character of violent "Winter." The passage, while striking in itself, seems oddly raw and undigested, perhaps too grotesque even for the varied *Seasons*.[12]

The speaker shifts from winter's violence to another, typically Scottish domestic retreat, "A rural, shelter'd, solitary, Scene; / Where ruddy Fire and beaming Tapers join, / To chear the Gloom" (ll. 429–431). After pausing to muse on Greek, Roman, and British heroes or "Worthies" (ll. 433–616), he resumes description (ll. 617ff.) with yet another convivial Scottish scene.[13] Around the fire, merry villagers tell "the Goblin-Story" "Till superstitious Horror creeps o'er all" (another reminder of the supernatural), joke, and dance "to Notes / Of native Music," passing the winter night. Thomson contrasts such innocent pleasures with the corrupt "false inchanted Joy" of city and court entertainment, which he describes in light-filled aureate terms (ll. 640–655); the court's brightness is paradoxical (superficial and artificial yet attractive), as indeed it would have appeared to the rural-bred Scot newly arrived in London.

After a conventional compliment to Lord Chesterfield (added 1744), Thomson returns to pure natural description with the frost passage. Such a scene was on the poet's mind as early as "Of a Country Life," where he pictured "Keen frost that turns the liquid Lakes to Glass, / Arrests the dancing Riv'lets as they Pass." *The Seasons'* passage was considerably expanded as the poet gradually added scientific information as well as foreign geographical material to the basic British scene. Still, the descriptive core of the "freeze" retains its immediacy and even gains force with the accumulation of added details and fanciful "scientific" speculation. These descriptions of the "court" and the "frost," contrasting with the previous harsh scenes, represent paradoxical winter's beauty, and aureate language abounds ("shining Atmosphere," l. 697; "luculent" rivers, l. 710; "crystal Pavement," l. 729; "starry Glitter, glows," l. 741; "Myriads of Gems, that in the waving Gleam / Gay-twinkle," ll. 787–788). Such diction describing the frost reflects back on corresponding aureate language in the court scene. In the frost passage, the controlling "Winter" image of water is again transformed, literally frozen into light.

Following a passage on rural winter sports expanded from the original "Winter," Thomson shifts his focus to the frigid zone and its inhabitants; these arctic descriptions (mostly added after 1738) move in a broad and chaotic sweep. Lengthy additions represent the extremes of winter's violent impact and come from a variety of sources; besides extending the physical range of "Winter" description, they also help to develop the poet's sociological debate between the values of simple, primitive life and modern, progressive civilization; that is, primitivism versus progress. Thomson's descriptions here show some imaginative touches, especially where his own Scottish experience could reinforce his visualization of a scene in the remote frigid zone: for example, he describes the Northern Lights as he may have seen them over Scotland, "By dancing Meteors then, that ceaseless shake / A waving Blaze refracted o'er the Heavens" (ll. 859–864); and the "Snows . . . on Snows," "Mountains on Mountains piled" (ll. 904–910). On the whole, though, the arctic scenes are weighted with the general, abstract, and didactic and lack the immediacy of the poet's first-hand descriptions drawn directly from Scottish personal experience.

Realistic description resumes with the "thaw" (ll. 988ff.), certainly based on a Border scene:

> Muttering, the Winds at Eve, with blunted Point,
> Blow hollow-blustering from the South. Subdu'd,
> The Frost resolves into a trickling Thaw.
> Spotted the Mountains shine; loose Sleet descends,
> And floods the Country round. The Rivers swell,
> Of Bonds impatient. Sudden from the Hills,

O'er Rocks and Woods, in broad brown Cataracts,
A thousand snow-fed Torrents shoot at once;
And, where they rush, the wide-resounding Plain
Is left one slimy Waste . . .
(ll. 988–997)

This passage has been compared with another Scottish poetical scene from Burns's "Brigs of Ayr" ("Aroused by blustering winds and spotting thowes . . .").[14] From the original (1726) version, Thomson kept all the vigor of his description of rivers in spate. The final passage of natural description in "Winter" depicts the personified season victorious over dying nature, the conventional warning to "fond Man" of his approaching "winter" of old age and death. The sermonlike commentary (ll. 1028ff.) anticipates the morality as well as the rhetoric of Blair's *Grave*.[15] In 1730 Thomson replaced a bland conclusion to "Winter" with a more fitting seasonal and symbolic end: "The Storms of WINTRY TIME will quickly pass, / And one unbounded SPRING encircle All" (ll. 1068–1069).

Only after "Winter" (1726) had proved a popular success did Thomson commit himself to completing a poetic seasonal cycle. Next in order of composition came "Summer" (1727) which, as the opposite seasonal extreme, demonstrates several important parallels with "Winter." "Summer," however, was in a significant sense farther removed from the poet's own experience; the shorter, cooler Scottish summer had not inspired Thomson to observe and to describe with the same degree of affectionate accuracy as had pervasive winter, and in the tradition of Scottish nature poets he tended more frequently to draw from outside sources, both idealizing literary conventions and factual geographical and scientific sources, for his "Summer" scenes. Here, classical and Miltonic pastoral conventions play nearly as crucial a role as they would do in "Spring." More remote, sensational "tropical" additions, illustrating the season's extremes not found in Britain, compare with those of the frigid zone in "Winter" and likewise contribute to the primitivism-progress argument. In direct contrast to the Scottish core of "Winter" description, "Summer" is generally the most

British, abstract, and public and the least personal and particular of *The Seasons.*

Thomson's original plan for "Summer" was to depict a typical summer's day. Predominant transforming imagery is of light, heat, and color, and, to a lesser extent, water and storms. The sun becomes the central symbol, embodying the paradox of the season's—and symbolically God's—beneficial and enlivening, yet potentially terrible, power.

In "Summer" the morning breaks on a generalized though surely Scottish scene:

> The dripping Rock, the Mountain's misty Top
> Swell on the Sight, and brighten with the Dawn.
> Blue, thro' the Dusk, the smoking Currents shine;
> And from the bladed Field the fearful Hare
> Limps, aukward: while along the Forest glade
> The wild Deer trip, and often turning gaze
> At early Passenger. Musick awakes,
> The native Voice of undissembled Joy;
> And thick around the woodland Hymns arise.
> Rous'd by the Cock, the soon-clad Shepherd leaves
> His mossy Cottage, where with *Peace* he dwells;
> And from the crouded Fold, in Order, drives
> His Flock to taste the verdure of the Morn.
> (ll. 54–66)

These lines strongly recall the juvenile "Morning in the Country" where, too, the influence of *L'Allegro* enhanced Thomson's first-hand Border observations.

A paean to the sun follows, where the descriptive lines, "On Rocks, and Hills, and Towers, and wandering Streams / High-gleaming from afar" (ll. 89–90) also suggest a Cheviot locale,[16] with its varied mountain scenery and unusual effects of light and atmosphere. In the hymn to the sun (ll. 81–198) Thomson cleverly blends conventional biblical, Neoplatonic, Miltonic, and scientific light imagery with imaginative first-hand description. Appropriately, "Summer," with its emphasis on light and color, is the *Season* where allusions to Newtonian science most

frequently occur. Thomson was writing "Summer" when his hero Newton died (March 1727); the poet interrupted his work on "Summer" to
compose "A Poem Sacred to the Memory of Sir Isaac Newton," where
the influence of the *Optics* is likewise strong. An example in "Summer"
is the important "spectrum" passage (ll. 140–159), which fancifully
describes the breaking up of sunlight into colors, forming multihued
gems deep in the earth. Thomson combines understanding of the
Newtonian spectrum, probably first learned at Edinburgh, with genuine aesthetic appreciation of the colors themselves, "compact" in the
gems; further, gems reflect in their colors the various facets of
nature—amethyst, the purple of evening; emerald, the green of
spring; and so on. This passage, where scientific knowledge joins with
wonder at a natural phenomenon, parallels the Newtonian rainbow
passage in "Spring." Here, and in such passages throughout *The Seasons,* Thomson achieved Scottish Enlightenment intellectual and aesthetic ideals by blending accurate scientific facts with accurate perceptions and feelings about them in descriptive poetry.[17] "Summer" also
shows Newtonian influence of the *Principia,* as Thomson describes
gravity: " 'Tis by thy [Sun's] secret, strong, attractive Force, / As with a
Chain indissoluble bound, / Thy System rolls entire . . ." (ll. 97–99).

After this exuberant hymn of science and sensibility comes another
native descriptive passage (ll. 199ff.), combining, as in comparable
"Winter" scenes, some conventional pastoral imagery with realistic,
probably Scottish, details:

> . . . the potent Sun
> Melts into limpid Air the high-rais'd Clouds,
> And morning Fogs, that hover'd round the Hills
> In party-colour'd Bands . . .
> (ll. 199–202)

This idyll leads into the playful, closely observed description of the
"little noisy summer-race," the periphrastically grouped insects. Their
predators are the "quick-eyed Trout" and "darting Salmon" (ll. 253–
254) and suggest a Border-river recollection. The clever mock-heroic
characterization of the spider (ll. 268–280), with its hint of the Scottish grotesque, is a good example of the poet's hyperbolic vein of

humor. A scientific description of microscopic organisms (ll. 281–317) follows; the poet's rather morbid fascination with this view of minute nature provokes religious-didactic comment (ll. 318–351).

Thomson shifts his focus once again to two rural scenes, the hay making (added 1730) and the sheep shearing (added 1744). The hay making is stylized, portrayed in conventional pastoral imagery, in contrast to the sheep shearing, described with energy and close, loving detail and recollecting a familiar activity of the poet's Scottish Border youth. A paean to rural industry follows, then Thomson describes the heat of noon (ll. 432–464); this passage, demonstrating summer's destructive power, makes skillful use of the pathetic fallacy. Unfortunately, the poet sacrificed immediacy and realism with the removal (after 1738) of a brief but perceptive portrayal of the effects of excessive heat on man; this dramatization of dizziness, double vision, ringing ears, sweating, and shivering (comparable to "Autumn"'s drunkenness scene) was an intriguing psychological as well as physiological handling of distorted, surrealistic sense impressions. "Summer"'s speaker seeks relief from the heat in a shady grove, described in conventional pastoral terms with Virgilian (*Eclogues*) atmosphere. Amid this idealized scene, the poet's description of the waterfall (ll. 590–606) stands out; altered from its original, it lost some "race" and accuracy yet retains the vitality of a directly observed phenomenon and strongly recalls Alexander Montgomerie's lively waterfall description, which makes similar use of the sound effects of alliteration and onomatopoeia, in *The Cherry and the Slae*.

Now a wider geographical vista opens (ll. 629ff.) as the speaker leaves Britain and travels to the torrid zone. This lengthy addition parallels "Winter"'s frigid-zone scenes and like them tends to distort the proportions of the *Season* as a whole. Description here is less realistic: a luxuriant tropical paradise is imaginatively described, and exotic names of places, plant and animal life, and rivers are mingled with classical allusions ("Pan," "Pomona," "Flora") to set the remote and idealized scene. Thomson's conception here was influenced by Job (Chapters 40–41) and more immediately by his correspondence with his Scots friend William Paterson, who lived in the tropics at

Bridgetown, Barbados. Paterson liked to send to Thomson, an avid gardener, various rare and exotic seeds and plant specimens to cultivate at Richmond.

The essential paradox of "Summer" is not forgotten amid this lush landscape, however, as Thomson does not neglect to illustrate the horrors of the tropics, including vicious beasts, sea- and sandstorms, plague, slavery, passion, and violence. These passages, like "Winter" 's arctic extremes, are mostly fanciful rather than realistic and derive chiefly from second-hand sources transformed by the poet's vivid imagination; yet they do contain some effective descriptive details. Even these foreign incidents are not entirely removed from Scottish experience; as in the "Winter" passage on wolves, for example, the element of folk memory probably plays a part. Fierce beasts had existed in Scotland; seastorms were a constant danger to Scots sailors; plague had many times struck Scotland in the not-so-distant past; and even sandstorms, such as the Culbin Sands on the Morayshire coast, had wreaked destruction on Scottish farms and villages within living memory. Again, Scottish life and lore could reinforce foreign factual as well as fanciful descriptions.[18]

"A nearer Scene of Horror" calls the speaker "home" to Britain (ll. 1102ff.) to portray a familiar, temperate-zone thunderstorm. Here, characteristic of Thomson's better descriptions, personification is important and enhances natural drama: "Darkness broods" and "growing, gains / . . . Possession of the Sky"; "wrathful Vapour"; "baleful Cloud"; "War / Of fighting Winds"; "muttering Earth"; "scouling Heavens"; "Tempest growls." The description is not merely visual but powerfully aural as well and demonstrates Thomson's forte, portrayal of nature's events in dramatic, well-paced, and intensifying action:

> The Lightnings flash a larger Curve, and more
> The Noise astounds: till over Head a Sheet
> Of livid Flame discloses wide, then shuts
> And opens wider, shuts and opens still
> Expansive, wrapping Ether in a Blaze.

>Follows the loosen'd aggravated Roar,
>Enlarging, deepening, mingling, Peal on Peal
>Crush'd horrible, convulsing Heaven and Earth.
>(ll. 1136–1143)

The storm is set in a mountainous, rural landscape very like the Borders; along with the Welsh "*Carnarvon*," "*Penmannaur*," and "*Snowden*," the poet specifically mentions the storm's impact in Scotland on "the Heights of heathy *Cheviot*" and also in the "utmost Isles" of "*Thulé*." A description of lightning, raging despite rain and hail, "Ragged and fierce, or in red whirling Balls" (l. 1148), followed soon after by the comment, "GUILT hears appall'd . . . / And yet not always on the guilty Head / Descends the fated Flash" (ll. 1169–1171), might betray the poet's deep fears about his father's strange death—Thomas Thomson was allegedly struck down by a "ball of fire." Thomson's preoccupation with death by lightning was probably an attempt to overcome the old-style Scottish Calvinist superstition that a violent end by natural force, such as his father's, was the punishment of an angry God and to assert his belief in a benevolent deity. He had originally included descriptions of both lightning-struck cattle (perhaps suggested by Martin Martin's *A Description of the Western Islands,* which records such an event in Orkney) and a shepherd killed by lightning, but after 1738 he omitted the shepherd's death as redundant, since the interpolated tale which follows portrays a similar tragic end.

The tale of "Celadon and Amelia" (ll. 1171–1256) is the first of three interpolated tales in *The Seasons*. Description in the story is elevated and idealizing, deriving largely from pastoral convention; the plot is simple. Innocent Amelia is struck down by lightning, and her lover Celadon is despondent until the sun appears and, in pathetic fallacy, he is cheered sufficiently to refresh himself with a swim. Despite the pastoral trappings of the tale, however, the death of Amelia is imbued with balladlike fatalism; the fleeting image of the once-lovely "blacken'd Corse" (l. 1216) recalls the random, grotesque violence which is a recurrent theme of Scottish folk literature. The story of Celadon also echoes *The Cherry and the Slae,* where the speaker, also a melancholy lover, repairs for refreshment to the river, "where Hope grew with Despair."

A transitional passage here, a straightforward commentary on the healthful benefits of swimming, with reference to the Roman *mens sana in corpore sano* (a sound mind in a sound body) philosophy, leads swiftly into the second interpolated tale. In "Damon and Musidora" (ll. 1269–1370) the poet again sets an idealized classical-pastoral scene. In the final version of this tale, there is but one "nymph," Musidora herself, but in the original (perhaps suggested by the Judgment of Paris and also the apocryphal story of Susanna and the Elders), Damon spied three bathing nymphs. Notably, this passage also recalls a similar scenario in Ramsay's *The Gentle Shepherd* (I.ii) where Jenny and Peggy wash semiclad in a Scottish stream while hidden Patie watches. An anonymous song in Ramsay's *Tea-Table Miscellany,* "Song CV" ("On a bank of flowers"),[19] also bears close resemblance to Thomson's tale; this song recounts the story of another "Damon" who sees the sleeping Celia and desires her. She wakes and flees, and he regrets the lost opportunity for love. The original version of Thomson's "Damon and Musidora" kept Damon hidden from the nymphs; he learned of adult love only from afar. The revised version (1744ff.), with its idealizing yet graphic description of Musidora, who this time sees Damon and gives him hope that his love will be requited, has been censured as gratuitously sensual.[20] Thomson's hearty, explicit sensuality here, surpassing conventional epithets for female beauty, recalls the juvenile "Upon Mrs. Elizabeth Bennet." Indeed, the purpose of "Damon and Musidora" within *The Seasons* as a whole is not clear, unlike that of "Celadon and Amelia," which illustrates nature's violence and raises theological questions of the nature of God and His Providence, of "predestination"; nonetheless, Thomson's refreshingly candid treatment here helps to bring predominantly pastoral-conventional "Summer" down to earth.

Now the poem returns to the afternoon of the "ideal day," inspiring a lengthy abstract passage of personal reflection and patriotic panegyric (ll. 1371–1437). Sparse description here includes a picturesque prospect-view of an English scene, "Augusta," or London and the Thames Valley; elements of the landscape are cataloged in the manner often found in Scottish poetry rather than depicted in detail, effectively to display the broader vista. This "Britannia" panegyric is dull and verbose, demonstrating Thomson's weakness, confirmed in *Liberty*, at handling abstract ideas on a large scale without the support of natural description. In this passage Thomson lists heroes of British civilization, including the guiding spirit of "Summer," Newton (ll. 1560–1563), yet he does not mention a single Scotsman; "Summer" had originally included here a brief tribute to Scottish worthies, but this was shifted to "Autumn" in 1730. Thomson's alleged negligence in failing to do his patriotic duty aroused the indignation of Scottish nationalistic critic J. Logie Robertson; yet as John MacQueen points out, every one of the English philosophers celebrated here was a "forerunner" of the Scottish Enlightenment,[21] so their significance for Scotland was by no means lost on the poet. The English roll call leads to a praise of the "DAUGHTERS" of "BRITANNIA" (ll. 1580–1594), recalling the juvenile "Upon Beauty" and "Upon the Hoop," which had paid similar tribute to British and especially Scottish womanhood.

After an invocation on behalf of "Empire," Thomson returns to his ideal summer's day (ll. 1620ff.), again blending convention and personification with more immediate description; "Low walks the Sun," and sunset is painted in rich, aureate terms. Thomson subtly describes the deepening darkness and rising breeze, which carries a delicate "whitening Shower" of thistledown. With nightfall comes another Scottish scene, as "His folded Flock secure, the Shepherd home / Hies ..." (ll. 1664ff.). The poet conjures up the "Fairy People" who gather on such summer nights and depicts the haunts of the "yelling Ghost," the sinister graves of suicides and the "lonely Tower" which rustics avoid at day's end. Although Thomson consciously qualifies these superstitions ("as Village-Stories tell," "So night-struck Fancy dreams"), such fearful scenes of the supernatural were clearly a part of the lore of his youth in the Scottish Borders, recollected with trepidation even in adulthood. Blair's *Grave* would describe such haunted scenes with a similar and peculiarly Scottish sense of credulity.

Welcome light, the controlling "Summer" image, returns, transformed into the glowworm's "twinkle," the star's shine, and then the strange and "wondrous" comet. Another "comet," more properly the aurora borealis, was originally portrayed here but was transferred to "Autumn" in 1730. The comet description which remains in "Summer" (ll. 1706–1729), with its scientifically observed "huge vapoury Train" and "long Ellipsis," was revised in 1744, possibly influenced by the sighting of a major comet in late 1743 or 1744, or by a previous one which had appeared over London and Edinburgh in early 1742. The 1742 comet was witnessed and recorded by Colin McLaurin and Sir John Clerk of Penicuik in Scotland, and notice of it was reported in the *Scots Magazine*. Sir John Clerk also saw the 1744 comet and interpreted it as a presage of the Jacobite rebellion. Thomson's comet in "Summer" strikes the ignorant "fearful murmuring Crouds" in amazement and terror of what it might portend, in contrast to those "enlighten'd Few, / Whose Godlike Minds Philosophy exalts, / [And who] The glorious Stranger hail" (ll. 1714–1716). This passage, like others such as the "aurora" on the same pattern in *The Seasons*, demonstrates Thomson's characteristic qualification of superstition, distancing it from himself and his own beliefs; he obviously desired to rid himself of certain deeply ingrained early fears, and with his growing knowledge of rational philosophy and science to be counted among the "enlighten'd Few." Thus follows his concluding paean to "serene PHILOSOPHY" (ll. 1730–1805) which ascends through reason to the ultimate light of truth, God. "Summer" ends on this brightly optimistic note.[22]

"Spring" (1728) has much in common with "Summer"; it, too, has a greater proportion of pastoral-conventional material than do the more inclement Scottish *Seasons* "Autumn" and "Winter"; like "Summer," "Spring" also has more explicitly English scenes (Hagley Park and, again, Augusta) than do the chillier *Seasons*. Neoplatonic and Newtonian light, and particularly color, imagery is again pervasive. Imagery of gravity also figures centrally in "Spring": Thomson identifies this season's goal of natural harmony, the Virgilian ideal of perpetual spring, with Newtonian gravity and finds the Neoplatonic concepts of the rising mind and the "Great Chain of Being" which coheres through harmony/gravity congenial to Newtonian empirical science. Thomson's friend Scottish philosopher George Turnbull drew this same gravitational image and further proposed a similar empirical parallel between Newtonian physical laws and some universal system of discernible moral laws. Thomson's method is accordingly to examine the effects of the spring season on all nature, ascending the scale of being. The season's theme is love, the crucial paradox love's pleasure and pain.[23]

The description in "Spring" opens (ll. 11–47) with the delicately drawn "trembling" time between winter and spring, followed by warming winds which signal the husbandman to plow and sow; Thomson's avid study of agricultural texts reinforced his first-hand knowledge and perceptions of husbandry acquired in the Scottish Lowlands.[24] As vegetable life quickens, a storm again figures in the seasonal scheme (ll. 143ff.); this time it is not violent, but rather a "lovely, gentle, kind" shower nourishing the earth. With realism and accurate description Thomson portrays the calm before the storm, soft rain, and glowing landscape; a rainbow ("NEWTON . . . / thy showery Prism," ll. 208–209) then appears. Again, the poet combines scientific precision with his delight in the purely visual. He displays knowledge of Newtonian optics from the point of view of the "sage-instructed Eye" and at the same time captures the simple swain's wonder at the beautiful "amusive Arch." The rainbow, biblical symbol of harmony between God and His Creation and this season's theme, reappears in *Liberty* (V.549ff.).

In a clever interplay of the literal with the metaphorical, Thomson recreates the Golden Age in terms of the total harmony of nature in times past, which he contrasts with modern disharmony, the Fallen World of "Nature disturb'd" (l. 307). Thomson's "Prime of Days" joins the pastoral ideal of the Virgilian Golden Age with the Paradise of Genesis and Milton, showing the strength of classical and Christian traditions in parallel which he was taught to revere in Scotland. He goes on to describe the Deluge resulting from the Fall, again combining natural description with conventional religious symbolism, reinforced with the added dimension of scientific speculation. In addition to his primary sources here (Scriptures, Virgil, Milton), the poet would have found precedents in Scottish religious-didactic literature. David Lindsay in his Middle Scots *The Monarche* (Book I), for instance, had depicted the Fall and breaking up of the earth and resulting flood. Thomas Boston, in "proving" the corrupt, depraved "Second State" of human nature, had not only attributed the literal flood to man's sins, but had also described it metaphorically: "Whence is the deluge of sin on the earth, but from the breaking up of the fountains of *the great deep,* the heart of man. . . ." Thomson's chief scientific source here was Thomas Burnet's *Theory of the Earth* (1681–1689); pseudo-scientist John Hutchinson's description of the earth's break-up and flood, similar to Burnet's, was also a possible influence. Burnet further held that before the flood the earth was not tilted on its axis, so that some regions did enjoy "eternal springtime"; but with the flood, in Hutchinson's words, "The course of nature was to be con-trouled and inverted by him, whom they had ungratefully forgotten, the supreme Lord of nature." Thomson likewise asserts that the Del-uge was responsible for disturbing the one "Great Spring" of natural harmony, so "The Seasons since have, with severer Sway, / Oppress'd a broken World" (ll. 317–318ff.).[25]

After pausing to reflect on the cruel Fallen World, Thomson added (1744) a passage on angling (ll. 379–466), often praised for its vig-orous and realistic description in a clever mock-heroic mode. Again, Thomson is at his best describing natural drama. The germ of the angling passage is in the juvenile "Of a Country Life." This scene is clearly a reminiscence of the poet's youth in the stream-filled Borders, perhaps of the Jed; a specifically Scottish reference is to the "flower-ing Elders" (l. 446), by which Thomson means the red elder, native to Scotland and northeast England, that flowers in spring.[26] In the an-gling passage Thomson shows some sympathy for the worm and the tiny fish, although at the same time his enjoyment of the sport is un-disguised; herein lies the paradoxical pleasure and pain of the season.

Thomson's enthusiasm on beholding the beautiful spring landscape prompts him to voice the fundamental dilemma of the descriptive poet: "But who can paint / Like Nature? . . . / . . . If fancy then / Un-equal fails beneath the pleasing Task; / Ah what shall Language do?" (ll. 468–475ff.). Yet he accepts the inevitable, paradoxical joy and frustration of his "Task." He states his aim, not to improve upon God's Creation, but to recreate its true beauties as far as he is able in poetry, and "Yet, tho' successless, will the Toil delight" him (l. 480). Continu-ing in a bitter-sweet vein, he describes an English garden walk with his "Amanda," who was Elizabeth Young, a Scotswoman who was the love of his life; reference to her was added in 1744, when their romantic future was uncertain. The speaker carefully guides the reader through the garden, closely observing bees at work, then viewing the wider prospect, and finally focusing on the flowerbed where he delights in naming individual species in English, Latin, and Greek, cataloging as he describes them in their colorful variety. Here, pastoral convention ("rosy-footed May / Steals blushing on," ll. 489–490) combines with much natural description based on close observation and loving attention to detail. The passage is also an instance of Thomson's practical knowledge of horticulture and landscape gardening, grounded in his Scottish experience, which added to his keen perception of nature and his deep sensibility toward it.

Next the poet's "Theme ascends" (ll. 572ff.) to a lengthy description of spring's effects on the animal world, its paradoxical love and pain. Again, literary influence—chiefly *Georgics* III—and Thomson's own, immediate description blend to portray animal "Love." Thomson is especially accurate, detailed, and affectionate in his description of the behavior of birds in this passage, comparable to the sympathetic robin redbreast and realistic seafowl in "Winter" and the migratory birds in "Autumn." Such feeling for animals, and particularly birds, is also part of the Scottish tradition of animal literature. To this first-hand description Thomson also adds some second-hand material. The lines describing the eagle on St. Kilda (ll. 755–765), a part of Scotland the poet never visited, were revised in 1744 with considerable loss of race from a more sharply visual, vigorous passage;[27] the original did not specifically mention the Scottish locale, and in the revised version the poet seems to rely on the connotative force of the place-name of (St.) "*Kilda*" rather than on any imaginative description itself. The birds in "Spring" ultimately unite in a chorus of love, singing the season's harmony. The love theme then moves to description of spring's effects on the higher animals (ll. 789–830), bull, horse, and sea-creatures; however, unlike his model Virgil, Thomson in his gentle "love-song" declines to go into any detail on the more violent side of animal love.

A Scottish pastoral scene follows, where a joyful shepherd sits watching his flock frisk about the "massy Mound / That runs around the Hill; the Rampart once / Of iron War, in ancient barbarous Times, / When disunited BRITAIN ever bled . . ." (ll. 840–843). This is evidently a description of the Early Iron Age fort on Southdean Law near the village where Thomson grew up, the site of frequent Border skirmishes; it is also a positive reference to the Union of 1707. His love theme then ascends still higher to treat of spring's effects on man. Thomson injects here a compliment to his friend George Lyttelton, whom he held to be the epitome of man in ideal harmony with nature. He describes in glowing terms Lyttelton's English estate Hagley Park (ll. 904–922, 950–962) in one of the most famous examples of Thomson's versatile descriptive skill. Again the speaker—Thomson himself—guides the reader through the vast and varied prospect, with his enumerative or cataloging method. Scots geologist Hugh Miller, who visited Hagley in the nineteenth century, well appreciated Thomson's accuracy in describing the "undulating" landscape of the estate and the poet's understanding of the "osteology" of the scene; Miller also praised Thomson's ingenious cataloging of the main features of the prospect while omitting details which would detract from the overall grandeur of the view.[28] The Hagley passage again shows Thomson's continuing interest in the art and science of landscape gardening; Hagley represents his mature taste for more natural gardens, which had become fashionable, in contrast to the formal ones he would have known in his youth. The selective composition of the Hagley description is also an instance of Thomson's "painterly" technique, possibly influenced by his association with such friends as artist William Aikman and art historian George Turnbull, as well as the poet's personal study of art and artistic theory.

Now Thomson shifts to preach upon, and then to describe, the dark side of paradoxical human love in "Spring," the pain of unrequited love. Pastoral convention and extravagant pathetic fallacy color the description of the dejected lover, yet a strong element of personal experience is also present to lend truth and immediacy: the poet's frustrated love for his compatriot Elizabeth Young. Thomson was revising this portion of "Spring" in 1743–44 at the height of his passion for her. He first describes the lover's realistic response of solitary retirement to "sympathetic Glooms," where even "Books are but formal Dulness, tedious Friends" (l. 1016). The sleepless speaker pours out his feelings in love letters, too, as Thomson himself wrote many passionate letters and verses to Miss Young, his "Amanda." When sleep finally comes, his dreams are tortured. Thomson had written to Miss Young of his own "dear exquisite Mixture of Pleasure and Pain";[29] for him, "These are the charming Agonies of Love, / Whose Misery delights" (ll. 1074–1075) and also inspires poetry. The poet goes on to describe the extreme of abnormal love, that destructive despair which borders on insanity (ll. 1075–1112). This dramatization of the disturbed and distorting psyche compares with the omitted "heatstroke" passage in "Summer" and the "drunkenness" scene in "Autumn"; they are uncannily accurate in their representations of both physical and mental distress. Thomson then places this realistic portrayal in contrast with an idealized picture of "virtuous" love in a happy marriage (ll. 1161–1165), which he so longed to share with Miss Young but never enjoyed. "Spring" then concludes on a didactic note; as in "Winter," Thomson again employs the age-old convention of seasons as stages in a man's life. In married love, the joy and harmony of "Spring" rule throughout life and into the "perpetual Spring" of afterlife.

Completing Thomson's poetical year was the final *Season*, "Autumn," which appeared in 1730 with the first collected edition of *The Seasons.* The poet exclaims:

> . . . Whate'er the wintry Frost
> Nitrous prepar'd; the various-blossom'd Spring
> Put in white Promise forth; and Summer-Suns
> Concocted strong, rush boundless now to View,
> Full, perfect all, and swell my glorious Theme.
> (ll. 4–8)

"Wintry" Scotland had indeed "prepar'd" Thomson to write *The Seasons;* "Autumn" made the cycle "perfect." "Autumn" is second only to "Winter" as an especially Scottish and inclement *Season:* it marks a return to more realistic, directly observed description, in contrast to that of the warmer, more conventional "Spring" and "Summer," and contains a great deal of recognizably Scottish description. The original "Winter" (1726) contained several scenes more properly located in "Autumn"; Thomson transferred these to "Autumn," his own favorite season for contemplation and poetical composition,[30] in 1730. "Autumn" is also the *Season* where Thomson chose to convey his explicit comments and implicit feelings about his native Scotland, as he "fondly tries / To mix the Patriot's with the Poet's Flame" (ll. 21–22). Controlling imagery, as in "Winter," is again transforming water and muted color, shapelessness and disorder. "Autumn"'s central paradox is that of fruitfulness and desolation or decay; the paradoxical emotion of pleasing sadness or "Philosophic Melancholy" which the season inspires flavors much of the description and enhances the poet's sociopolitical message.

"Autumn" enters personified as a jovial swain, "Crown'd with the Sickle, and the wheaten Sheaf" (ll. 1–3). The odd image of "Crown'd with the Sickle" apparently confused one of George Lyttelton's young sons when he first heard Thomson read the passage aloud; the poet explained it rather obscurely as "'a custom the reapers have in Scotland of putting their sickles round their heads in the intervals of labour.'"[31] "Autumn"'s first descriptive passage (ll. 23–42) is a brief but acutely perceived, rich, rural landscape, subtly transforming as the breeze rises. This country scene inspires the lengthy didactic "Industry" panegyric (ll. 43–176) which expounds the Scottish Calvinist work ethic and parallels "Summer"'s patriotic "Britannia" sequence. After these lines on "Industry," Thomson tells the tale of "Palemon and Lavinia," the third interpolated tale of *The Seasons* (ll. 177–310). This tale, set in an idealized pastoral landscape, recounts the story of a poor gleaner in the fields, the once-fortunate and high-born Lavinia, and the nobleman Palemon who loves her and removes her to a better life. The pastoral, while loosely based on the biblical story of Ruth and Boaz,[32] more closely follows the plot of Ramsay's Scots *Gentle Shepherd* (1725), which Thomson surely knew. In Ramsay's Scots pastoral, Patie, a nobleman in disguise, loves the poor but lovely shepherdess Peggy; it is discovered that (like Lavinia) she is high-born. Patie vows to take Peggy away to Edinburgh, where art can enhance her nature, just as Thomson's Palemon seeks to "Transplant" Lavinia to the richer soil of his "Garden" to enhance her natural charms and cultivate their joyful and productive love. This tale shows Thomson's willingness to believe that art—that is, the civilizing, social "arts" as opposed to the representative arts of painting and poetry—can in some cases improve upon nature. Thus in this "Autumn" tale Thomson professes ultimately Virgilian faith in man's ability to control nature through art and industry to bring it to its fullest potential. Such a rural-based "progressive" philosophy would come to fruition in the quest of the Knight of Arts and Industry in *The Castle of Indolence*.

Thomson resumes natural description with a vigorous, compact portrayal of "Autumn"'s destructive storm and flood (ll. 311–343) through transforming imagery of water and disorder; "Winter"'s thaw was followed by similar flooding, a common catastrophe in the Scottish Borders. "Autumn"'s storm, like those of "Winter" and "Summer," is destructive and desolating, a sudden unexplained act of natural violence such as fostered deep fatalism in Thomson's fellow Borderers. Characteristically, however, the poet does not dwell on fatalistic response nor does he attempt to explain the mystery of so great an evil, which he accepts as part of God's hidden plan. His attitude is not far removed from the Scottish Calvinist interpretation of determinism or providence. He goes on in a more benevolent mood to show his genuine sympathy with the ruined husbandman and implores the "Masters" to care for their poor laborers (ll. 341–359).

The acclaimed "hunting" passage follows, depicting another sort of autumnal violence, this time perpetrated by man (ll. 360ff.). "Of a Country Life," after its angling scene (compare "Spring"), had described both fowl shooting and hare coursing. Thomson in "Autumn" again harks back to his juvenilia for the hunt theme and adds a stag hunt to these incidents, which are, to a large extent, based on his own Border observations. Here, typically, the poet's sympathy is with the hunted animals. In one of several attacks on hunters in *The Seasons*, he contrasts man, who hunts chiefly for sport, with the beasts of prey, who must hunt to live; man is the "steady Tyrant," the "worst Monster that e'er roam'd the Waste" (ll. 390–393). A sympathetic description of the hunted hare, which was lively even in the germinal "Of a Country Life," is closely observed and dramatic. The portrait of the weeping stag, whose "big round Tears run down his dappled Face" (l. 454), echoing Shakespeare, is rather more sentimental. While the stag hunt is usually considered an archetypal English scene, it might equally well be a recollection of a Scottish pursuit. Border ballads "The Battle of Otterbourne" and "Chevy Chase," for instance, both open with descriptions of "deere" hunts with hounds in the Scottish Borders, and stag and fox hunting with hounds was recorded as a Border activity from earliest times.[33]

From the hunt itself, Thomson begins a lively burlesque, a caricature of the huntsmen themselves at the hunt board. The rich description begins as a clever mock heroic, a light-hearted satire on the debauched huntsmen, with a strong element of realistic detail. The subjects of the satire probably represent the Tory squirearchy; such coarse, hard-drinking country squires had become something of a literary stereotype by Thomson's day,[34] and the Whig Thomson was no doubt aiming an amusing party-political barb here. He goes beyond comedy, however, to reveal the darker side of the "social Slaughter" (l. 561); he betrays stern Scottish Calvinist disapproval and disgust, underlying his obvious amusement at the orgy. His strong didactic and hortatory urge, anticipating the moral rigor of *The Castle,* surfaces here. In this scene, Thomson ultimately violates the limits of Augustan decorum to display a particularly Scottish sense of humor: the hint of wildness, excess, grotesque exaggeration as the hunters grow inebriated is unmistakably Scottish. Lively social drinking scenes themselves are of course a recurring motif in Scottish literature, especially in the vernacular; examples include Ramsay's "Scotch Drink," Fergusson's "The Daft Days," and Burns's "Tam O'Shanter." Thomson's description is not quite so good-natured as these, though; in its extremes it rather recalls the extravagant skirmishes of the flyting tradition as well as the vein of grotesque in, for example, Dunbar's "The Dance of the Sevin Deidly Synnis" and Smollett's bizarre caricatures. The description is typical of Thomson's ribald, rather coarse comedy and looks forward to the more grotesque descriptions in *The Castle.* Thomson deftly manipulates the deteriorating "wet broken Scene" (l. 560) as transforming imagery of wetness saturates every descriptive detail. His characterization of the hunters' increasingly distorted, drunken sense perceptions is especially accurate and will feel familiar to the modern reader of Hugh MacDiarmid's "A Drunk Man Looks at the Thistle." Thomson's hunt burlesque is a complex blend of diverse elements—mock-heroic satire, comic political comment, wild Scottish humor, a strain of Scottish Calvinist sermonizing, and both real and surreal description—and the result is a highly successful scene.

After brief didactic comment and a conventional pastoral interlude comes the "Orchard" scene (ll. 625–651), a multisensuous description owing something to John Philips's *Cyder* and much more to Thomson's own observations. He first describes the "gentle Race" of pears, a crop grown in abundance in the Jedburgh area in the poet's day, and then apples. After a prospect view of the Dorsetshire estate of his friend George Bubb Doddington, then an imaginary excursion to warm, wine-making climes, Thomson moves into another of his exceptionally realistic descriptive sequences. The very Scottish scene opens with imagery of dampness, lack of color, shapelessness; "doubling Fogs around the Hill" obscure the

> . . . Mountain, horrid, vast, sublime,
> Who pours a Sweep of Rivers from his Sides,
> And high between contending Kingdoms rears
> The rocky long Division . . .
> (ll. 710–714)

This is evidently a description of the mists over Carter Fell, or a neighboring hill such as Ruberslaw, overlooking the Jed Valley of Thomson's Border homeland. The jagged ridge of the Cheviots did indeed mark a "rocky long Division,"[35] the border between the pre-Union "contending Kingdoms" of Scotland and England; the division here is blurred by fog—is this perhaps Thomson's allusion to post-Union blurring of national distinctions, with ambiguous connotations? The eerie phenomenon of the fog's magnification of objects and of the human form, "beyond the Life, / Objects appear; and, wilder'd, o'er the Waste / The Shepherd stalks gigantic" (ll. 725–727), does occur in the uplands of Scotland, and Thomson had probably witnessed it himself.[36] He may also have thought about the Newtonian (*Optics*) implications of such an incident. Another Scot, James Hogg, would describe in his *Confessions of a Justified Sinner* (1824) the same phenomenon occurring at Arthur's Seat in Edinburgh. Thomson also acknowledges the scriptural analogue for his fog description, that of pre-Creation Chaos as portrayed by the "HEBREW BARD" (ll. 731–732) of Genesis.

Making clever use of second-hand descriptive material, Thomson next speculates at length on the origins of the world's rivers, then launches into a descriptive survey of migratory birds (ll. 836ff.), focusing in on those

> . . . where the *Northern* Ocean, in vast Whirls,
> Boils round the naked melancholy Isles
> Of farthest *Thulé*, and th' *Atlantic* Surge
> Pours in among the stormy *Hebrides*.
> (ll. 862–865)

Hence begins the most explicit and extensive Scottish passage in *The Seasons*. Its germ was moved from "Summer" (1727) to "Autumn" in 1730. In the opening Scottish scene, alluding also to *Lycidas,* "*Thulé*" refers to the Orkney and Shetland islands, while the "*Hebrides*" are the western isles off Scotland; these are scenes which Thomson never visited but which he nonetheless vividly describes. The poet has taken most of the factual material for these remote Scottish scenes from Martin Martin's *A Late Voyage to St. Kilda* (1698) and *A Description of the Western Islands of Scotland Circa 1695* (1703, 1716) and has transformed the distant islands into a living landscape. He also depicts the self-sufficient "plain harmless Native," as Martin recorded him, tending his flock and "Herd diminutive" and gathering seabirds' eggs and feathers and fish (ll. 871–878). These Scottish islanders come to represent for Thomson the idea of positive, well-adapted primitivism, or simple "unimproved" existence.

Thomson next displays the imaginative prospect of "CALEDONIA, in romantic View" (ll. 880–893). The passage is probably indebted to David Lindsay's vision of Scotland in *The Dreme* (ca. 1528), and the scene also prefigures later eighteenth-century "Romantic" concepts of Scotland, especially her remoter regions, which works such as Macpherson's *Ossian* would exploit. Like Lindsay, Thomson delights in the rich variety, magnitude, and natural beauty of his homeland. He again catalogs the features of the prospect—"airy Mountains," "waving Main," "Forests huge, / Incult, robust, and tall," "azure Lakes . . .

extensive," "watry Wealth / Full," "deep, and green . . . fertile Vales"—
in a view sweeping from gentle Tweed to sublime "*Orca's* or *Betubium's*
highest Peak." Thomson's reference to the "airy Mountains" echoes
his often-cited letter home to William Cranstoun, where the poet lamented the lack in the English landscape of variety such as he knew in
Scotland.[37] He does not miss the opportunity to inject a personal,
parenthetical tribute to the Border area of his youth, to "the *Tweed*
(pure *Parent-Stream*, / Whose pastoral Banks first heard my *Doric*
Reed, / With, silvan *Jed*, thy tributary Brook)" (ll. 889–891). This
proud prospect leads Thomson into profound reflections on
Scotland's people, her history and culture, her potential for progress
(themes also treated in Lindsay's *Dreme*), as well as her heroes (ll. 894–
949).

Description of the autumn season itself resumes with imagery of loss
of color, as leaves gradually fade and shadowing sunlight weakens (ll.
950–963). Nature's dour countenance, the leaden overcast sky with
thin, pale rays of sun occasionally breaking through, is a familiar one in
Lowland Scotland. The solitary speaker wanders through the autumnal landscape, subtly described in terms of dying, discord (the opposite
of "Spring" harmony), and desolation, falling and fading, loss of color
and shape; the process of the season's gradual transformation is portrayed through the poet's own acute and sensitive observation. The
"desolated Prospect thrills the Soul" as "PHILOSOPHIC MELANCHOLY"
enters (ll. 1003–1081, transferred from "Winter"), personifying the
season's paradoxical mood of pleasing sadness and its attendant benevolent sentiments. Again, Thomson's letter to Cranstoun comes to
mind, where he described the "fine romantic kind of melancholy,"
"beloved gloom," "divine Contemplation" which the Scottish autumn
always inspired in him. The description here (ll. 950ff.) uses much the
same wording and closely parallels the Scottish scene near Ancrum
which Thomson remembered in that nostalgic letter:

> Now I figure you *wandering, philosophical,* and *pensive,* amidst the
> *brown, wither'd groves:* while the leaves rustle under your feet. the
> sun gives a farewell parting gleam and the *birds* 'Stir the faint
> note, and but attempt to sing.' then again, when the heavns wear

a more gloomy aspect, the *winds whistle* and the waters spout, I see you in the well known Cleugh, beneath the solemn Arch of tall, thick *embowring trees.* . . . (Italics added)[38]

Clearly Thomson had that very Border scene in mind in 1726 when he composed this *Seasons* passage.

"PHILOSOPHIC MELANCHOLY" leads the speaker to a high pitch of religious rapture (ll. 1030–1036). Thomson then reasserts hearty Augustan optimism in lines (added 1744, ll. 1037–1081) inspired by a third English "estate" prospect, that of Cobham's (Pitt's) seat at Stowe, again illustrating the poet's educated interest in the "regulated Wild" of landscape gardening. Thomson returns to autumnal natural description as the personified "humid Evening," bringing with it "rolling Fogs," arrives. The moon rises, transforming the whitening landscape of "sky'd Mountain," "shadowy Vale," "Rocks and Floods" which might be a Border scene. The passage which follows (ll. 1108ff.) was originally in "Summer" and corresponds to the "comet" passage in that *Season*; it depicts a "Blaze of Meteors," actually the aurora borealis. This dynamic description of the "Meteors"

> . . . ensweeping first
> The lower Skies, they all at once converge
> High to the Crown of Heaven, and all at once
> Relapsing quick as quickly reascend,
> And mix, and thwart, extinguish, and renew,
> All Ether coursing in a Maze of Light
> (ll. 1109–1114)

is strikingly similar to an account of the aurora sighted over Scotland on March 6, 1716, which the poet himself may have seen (see Chapter 2); the author of that account, William Whiston, also termed the phenomenon a "meteor." Thomson also captures the "contagious . . . Pannic" of the crowd and their terrified superstition that the event is a portent of evil. In the popular imagination, the aurora resembles a bloody battle (ll. 1117–1121); such a cosmic display was traditionally associated with ominous portents. Among literary sources known to Thomson were Shakespeare (*Julius Caesar* II.ii), Milton (*Paradise Lost*

II.533–538, IV.1518), and Marlowe (*Tamburlaine* 2.IV.i),[39] as well as Virgil (*Georgics* I) and William Hamilton of Gilbertfield (*Wallace* VI.I). Thomson portrays the majority of witnesses as ignorant and superstitious, but the poet deliberately qualifies his own superstition and identifies himself with the "Man of Philosophic Eye," the "Inspect sage" who views the "waving Brightness" with curiosity, wonder, and empirical scientific interest.

Night falls, the ultimate image of colorlessness and chaos: "Order confounded lies; all Beauty void; / Distinction lost; and gay Variety / One universal Blot . . ." (ll. 1141–1143). A swain on horseback wanders, lost in the dark, "Full of pale Fancies, and Chimeras huge" (l. 1147), evoking the poet's own early extreme fear of the dark. Like the family of the cottager lost in the "Winter" snow, wife and children await the swain in their cozy cottage. This fearful and dramatic scene recalls the wild ride of Burns's "Tam O'Shanter" and is perhaps based on some real incident in Scottish folk memory.

A new "Autumn" days dawns (ll. 1165ff.), described in aureate terms, and the villagers celebrate harvest home in a "lively Dance" (ll. 1208–1234) inspired by native Scottish country life. Thomson concludes "Autumn" with a panegyric to rural life and an invocation to his chief inspiration, "NATURE": "From THEE begin, / Dwell all on THEE, with THEE conclude my Song; / And let me never never stray from THEE!" (ll. 1371–1373).

With "Autumn" *The Seasons* were complete, first published together in 1730. The collected *Seasons* concludes with "The Hymn on the Seasons." The poet's use of such a "hymn" or prayer recalls his characteristic concluding invocations in the juvenilia; the "Hymn" combines affirmation of Thomson's primary religious purpose with his devotion to natural description in an enthusiastic rendering of Psalm 148, replete with nature imagery. Ultimately, he finds even words and images too limiting to describe his love of God, nature's king, hence his final, forceful gesture: "Come then, expressive Silence, muse HIS Praise" ("Hymn," l. 118). This resonant conclusion invites the reader to reflect with wonder on the wealth of images of the natural world which God has created and the poet has recreated in *The Seasons*.

James Thomson's "natural" choice of the seasonal descriptive scheme for his religious-philosophical poem, his accurate and affectionate handling of the nature theme, demonstrates much more than simple admiration and emulation of his acknowledged models Job and Virgil. It also signifies his deep awareness of and kinship with a venerable Scottish tradition of nature poetry and his assumption of a place within that living tradition. In his poem he drew from Scottish folk memory of people, places, and events; he drew from travel literature about Scotland such as Martin's accounts of the remote Highlands and islands; he drew from Scottish descriptive literary conventions, such as Lindsay's allegories and Ramsay's native pastorals. But most of all—and with astonishing frequency—he drew from personal experience of Scottish life and landscape, recalling time and again realistic details from his own memory of Scotland and coloring them with his complex emotions about his homeland. So the "Scottish" influence on the descriptions of *The Seasons* works on many levels, both general and particular, conscious and unconscious, and is indeed profound.

In yet another important sense, too, Thomson brings his Scottish experience and education to bear on his descriptive theme. His choice of the descriptive mode also reflects his enthusiasm for Newtonian, empirical science and his eagerness to apply its methods to a poetry describing the natural world he so loved. He sought to translate first-hand observation and sense experience into poetry, to "test" this sense experience against his religious and philosophical beliefs, and ultimately to reinforce those beliefs with empirical "truth" recreated in poetry of natural description. James Thomson was thus in the curious yet exciting position of belonging to an older tradition of Scottish nature poetry while at the same time experimenting with a new, empirical sensibility—the spirit of the Scottish Enlightenment in descriptive poetry.

6 *THE SEASONS* AS AN ANGLO-SCOTTISH MISCELLANY

As delightful as it may be, James Thomson's Scottish natural description in *The Seasons* does not serve as his favorite poetical theme simply for its own sake. Natural description becomes the means of the poet's expression and exploration of the poem's central religious purpose; it likewise works to complement and develop the major social, political, and humanistic themes of the complex, miscellaneous poem. *The Seasons* is, therefore, far more than a Scottish nature poem. It is Scottish in many more subtle ways. *The Seasons* is a religious poem, both physicotheological and mystical, professing the Scottish Calvinist poet's sincere, if sometimes inconsistent and ever-eclectic, beliefs. Along with its religious message, *The Seasons* reveals Thomson's equally eclectic philosophy— again, not absolutely consistent, but bearing influence of both Scottish and English thinkers in an ethical and aesthetic system which in many ways anticipates the Scottish Enlightenment. Thomson was a poet interested in people; he was a keen observer of man in nature and society, so his *Seasons* is also a sociological and political poem, a public poem. He was a committed Opposition Whig and a staunch British patriot, but he was also a Scot in England, and his sociopolitical views in *The Seasons* reflect this intriguing perspective. Finally, *The Seasons* is a neoclassical poem. Scottish vernacular humanism taught Thomson to admire the strengths of Roman civilization which helped to shape his own ideals for a united Britain proclaimed in his poem. The influence of Virgil on the language, style, and georgic motif is strong. Like the poem's natural description itself, each of these dimensions of *The Seasons*—religious, philosophical, sociopolitical, neoclassical—represents in some basic sense a part of the poet's Scottishness. These aspects of the varied *Seasons'* vision now deserve closer attention in relation to James Thomson's Scottish background.

Religion remains the primary motivation behind *The Seasons* and encompasses prayer and praise, didacticism and contemplation. Thomson's religious beliefs and attitudes were rooted in his Scottish experience as son of the manse and divinity student. As his preface of 1726 announced, the young poet conceived his role to be a religious one, projected through his "darling Theme" ("Hymn," l. 94) of natural description. In England he could live comfortably in the vocation of poet while keeping the option of becoming a minister as well. Also, the Scottish Calvinist view of work and worldly success at one's calling, as proof that one was doing God's will and was elected to salvation, must have greatly encouraged Thomson, particularly with the huge success of "Winter."

Natural description works directly to carry out Thomson's religious goals. In many instances his description is imbued with religious significance, blending natural imagery with religious symbolism to reinforce one another; in other instances, a purely descriptive passage will provoke religious or didactic comment. Where Thomson joins description with religious symbolism he is demonstrating that skill whereby he is able to enhance personal observation and precise description with subtle reworking of literary conventions; his sources for such conventions were most often the Scriptures (especially the Old Testament), Milton, and Christian Neoplatonism. Examples of such religious-descriptive symbolic sequences include Eden-Fall-Deluge ("Spring," ll. 237ff.); tropical Paradise-serpent ("Summer," ll. 854ff.); pre-Creation Chaos and fog ("Autumn," ll. 707ff.); and hymn to the sun/God ("Summer," ll. 81ff.). Thomson's conception of Eden as the Golden Age again illustrates the parallel classical and Christian humanistic traditions to which he was educated in Scotland. Thomson represents the Fall as "Nature disturb'd," manifested in universal chaos. His indignation at man's fall from order, expressed in Augustan terms, gains force under the influence of emotional and strik-

ingly graphic Scottish Calvinist homiletic rhetoric. His portrayal of
the Deluge combines imaginative natural description with conventions from Genesis and *Paradise Lost,* further strengthened with the
element of empirical scientific data. The Deluge scene is but one illustration in Thomson of that concept, taught by John Hutchinson
and Robert Riccaltoun, of natural "symbols," those real events and
natural phenomena which likewise represent scriptural, spiritual
truths. "Summer"'s tropical Paradise, borrowing from both Job and
travel literature, is a similar blend of literal and metaphorical; Thomson thus achieves maximum expressive power by exploiting the tension between the real and the ideal. The "Autumn" fog scene refers
explicitly to the account of elementary Chaos by the "HEBREW BARD"
of Genesis and closely resembles the description of the phenomenon
in Hutchinson; it was also strongly influenced by Thomson's real experience of the damp, misty Scottish climate. Christian Neoplatonic
symbolism of God as "light" or "sun" combines convincingly with accurate natural description as well as Newtonian science, especially to
inform the *Seasons* of light and color, "Spring" and "Summer."

Thomson's religious aims in *The Seasons* were two: to praise and to
pray to God, and to discover and teach His truth. The element of
prayer and praise permeates the entire *Seasons.* Thomson's personal,
individual relationship with his God (a Scottish Calvinist priority) is
made manifest, as personal pronouns "I" and "me," the poet's own
voice, speak in spiritual contexts: "HAIL, SOURCE OF BEINGS! / . . . To
THEE I bend the Knee" ("Spring," ll. 556–558), and so on. Such personal interjections recur despite the poem's elevated, Augustan, "public" format. Further, Thomson envisions all nature offering continual
praise to the Creator and urges man to join in adoration: "Can he
forebear to join the general Smile / Of Nature? . . . come, ye generous
Minds" ("Spring," ll. 871–872, 878). The praising function of *The Seasons* was, appropriately, much influenced by the Psalms; the "Hymn
on the Seasons," perhaps the most notable illustration of this Psalm
influence, is based, like the juvenile "A Hymn to God's power," on
Psalm 148.

Lines in "Winter" (ll. 106–117) also echo Psalm 148; here, however,
the song addresses not God himself, but "NATURE! great Parent!" This

enthusiastic exclamation and similar invocations to nature ("Oh Nature! all-sufficent!" "Autumn," ll. 1352ff.; "These, as they change, ALMIGHTY FATHER, these, / Are but the *varied* GOD. The rolling Year / Is full of Thee," "Hymn," ll. 1–3; and so on), coupled with the poem's relentless personification of the natural world, have led critics to suspect Thomson of pantheism, or worshiping nature itself as a "God" and blurring the distinction between them. But while Thomson clearly rejoiced in learning about God in His Creation and loved the natural world the more deeply as a Creation of his God, the facile charge of pantheism is unfounded. The poet asserts in numerous *Seasons* passages that God is *not* identical with nature. He sings of "Nature . . . and Nature's GOD" ("Summer," l. 555), a transcendent deity ("Hymn," ll. 37ff.) who is "Nature's KING" ("Winter," l. 197, recurring in *Liberty* III.556). God is not nature but is distinct from it, ruler over it. *The Seasons* in general is much concerned with exploring man's quest for harmony with nature; God ("PROVIDENCE") constantly watches over this earthly struggle, intervenes in it, and offers hope and succor to His creatures ("Winter," ll. 1020–1023). Thomson's conception of the deity as transcendent yet omnipresent, continually acting in the natural world through Providence, thus represents not pantheism at all but orthodox Calvinist "panergism."[1]

Critics focusing on Thomson's deep admiration for the natural laws of the universe have likewise charged him with deism, or worshiping a mechanistic universe set in motion by a retiring "clock-maker" deity. Neither is this a fair claim, despite the poet's knowledgeable respect for the Copernican system, Newtonian physics, and other universal laws; again, he makes frequent reference to a providential God ever active in the world, an orthodox Scottish Calvinist tenet. In one example, Thomson praises the planets and seasons "Minutely faithful: Such TH' ALL-PERFECT HAND, / That pois'd, impels, and rules the steady Whole!" ("Summer," ll. 41–42). These lines in the present tense clearly describe an active deity (revised in 1744, they replaced lines which might well have been interpreted as deistic, "*Seasons*, faithful; not excentric once; / So pois'd, and perfect, is the vast Machine!"). Thomson seems to have realized that his earlier exclamation might savor too strongly of deism and he was careful to alter it, reasserting belief in God's ever-active role in the universe. Similarly, his line "Th' eternal Cause, Support, and End of all!" ("Summer," l. 191) was revised in 1744 from the original "Cause, the Glory, and the End of All" to remove any deistical implications. While Thomson was certainly influenced by Shaftesbury's deistic benevolism, he never wholeheartedly embraced deism. Rather, his views were more closely akin to those of Scottish philosopher Francis Hutcheson, who came from similar religious and educational roots; that is, more liberal, rational, and Moderate but within the philosophical framework of Scottish Calvinist orthodoxy. Among other *Seasons* references supporting Thomson's faith in an active, immanent God are "PROVIDENCE, that *ever-waking Eye*" ("Winter," ll. 1020ff.); "by whose almighty *Nod* the Scale / Of Empire rises, or alternate falls" ("Summer," ll. 1602ff.); "the mighty Hand, / That, ever-busy, wheels the silent Spheres" ("Hymn," ll. 29–30); and "should he hide his Face, . . . / . . . [would] Chaos come again" ("Summer," ll. 182–184, echoing Psalm 104). Even in seemingly random acts of nature God carries out His providential plan, approaching a concept of determinism: Amelia's death is the work of "Mysterious Heaven!" ("Summer," ll. 1204ff.); "Winter" 's storm ceases when "Nature's KING . . . / commands a Calm" ("Winter," ll. 197–201).

Thomson's God, then, is neither pantheistic nor deistic, although the poet knew of such contemporary ideas and the terms in which they were expressed, and his own means of expression was certainly much influenced by them. Indeed, the most "consistent" thing that can be said about Thomson's theology in *The Seasons* is that it is inconsistent and eclectic. Yet throughout *The Seasons* he continued to maintain orthodox belief in the Providence of an ever-active God who is both present in and lord over nature, beyond any operation of mechanism or blind fate, a mysterious God who is both just and benevolent, all-powerful and all-wise. Thomson's metaphors for God are likewise mostly conventional: "LIGHT HIMSELF," "ALMIGHTY FATHER" ("Summer," ll. 176, 186), "GREAT SHEPHERD" (usually a title given to Christ, here applied to God the Father, "Hymn," l. 74), "AUTHOR" (preface 1726 and elsewhere). On several occasions the poet also explicitly invokes "PROVIDENCE." Thomson's eclectic conception of the deity bears the influence of both schools of the Scottish church, old style and Moderate. His poetical representation of God certainly mellowed over the years: for example, whereas he had once described the Old Testament God's "Wrath" and "speedy Sword of Justice" ("Spring," ll. 1727–1738), his emphasis was increasingly upon a "SMILING GOD" (l. 862). His more optimistic view of God's mysterious plan not only reflected recent English intellectual trends but it was also entirely consistent with the Moderate movement within the Scottish church. At the same time, Thomson never lost sight of the traditional Calvinist deity of awe and fear, as many stern, didactic passages remaining in *The Seasons*, particularly on the sin of vanity, testify.[2] He continued to assert Joblike faith that God's justice would be executed in the afterlife. Thomson's God, like Job's, ultimately offers hope in eternal life and the grace to bear the hardships of temporal existence shown so often in *The Seasons*.

The praising role of *The Seasons*, while important, is secondary to the poem's central physicotheological purpose. Thomson, who loved the natural world and also comprehended much about its scientific laws, found physicotheology especially appealing; he came to respect it through his mentor Riccaltoun, who stressed the significance of "natural" images in the interpretation of revelation, through Professor Hamilton at Divinity College, and through his own studies of physicotheological literature, both poetry and prose. John Calvin himself had enjoined the faithful "to contemplate [God] in his works, by which he renders himself near and familiar to us and . . . communicates himself."[3] Thomson also knew such English works as Blackmore's *Creation* (1712), Ray's *Wisdom of God Manifested in the Works of the Creation* (1691), and Derham's *Physico-theology*. One recurring pattern of figurative language in *The Seasons*, complementing its physicotheological purpose, is that of nature as a book, with God as its author and the poet Thomson as translator or mediator between God and men:

> To me be Nature's Volume broad-display'd;
> And to peruse its all-instructing Page,
> Or, haply catching Inspiration thence,
> Some easy Passage, raptur'd, to translate,
> My sole Delight . . .
> ("Summer," ll. 192–196)

Thomson writes that he will "meditate the Book / Of Nature, ever open, aiming thence, / Warm from the Heart, to learn the moral Song" ("Autumn," ll. 670–672). "ALMIGHTY AUTHOR" as an appellation for God is of course highly conventional and occurs in many of Thomson's sources and analogues, among them Milton, Addison, Riccaltoun, Hutcheson, and Turnbull. In Thomson, the reference first comes in his preface to "Winter" (2nd edition, 1726), where God is author of nature itself and of descriptions of nature in Scripture; it also comes in "Spring," as "Th' informing Author in his Works appears" (l. 860). For Thomson, this conventional set of metaphors takes on personal meaning as well, illustrating his acceptance of the sacred role of poet and his identification of God's creative power with poetic inspiration; it also helps to convey the educational function of physicotheology in *The Seasons,* where nature's "book" holds emblems for religious truths, both great and small.

In *The Seasons* Thomson expresses his study of God in nature chiefly through the Christian Neoplatonic philosophy of the rising mind, a concept found in both old-style and Moderate Scottish Calvinist thought and a significant influence, through Shaftesbury, Watts, and others, on Thomson's juvenile religious poetry and that of his contemporaries. Man's active rising mind can work gradually up the parallel scale in nature, the Great Chain of Being, studying the works of Creation and learning more about the Creator in the ascent. Newtonian empiricism aids the physicotheologist in his quest for truth as it reveals the "chain"; gravity acts as a cohesive symbol in *The Seasons,* holding the chain together and representing the harmony or unity-in-variety of the poem's vision. Although reason and science cannot lead man to the ultimate goal of the rising mind, the beatific vision and God's perfect plan, they can lead some way on earth toward knowledge of the deity.

The rising mind theme figures in the works of many Scottish Calvinist writers, both old style and Moderate. Thomas Boston, for example, preached the same version of "empirical immortality," or infinitely improving intellect, as did Thomson; philosopher George Turnbull also believed that even in the afterlife the mind would continue to approach truth. Thomson referred to this idea often as an important element of his religious faith; it appears in some form in each *Season* and "Spring" is structured upon it. The poet affirmed the notion in a letter to William Cranstoun (1735): "This, I think, we may be sure of: that a future State must be better than this; and so on thro the never-ceasing Succession of future States; every one rising upon the last, an everlasting new Display of infinite Goodness!"[4] The rising mind sometimes leads the poet to heights of religious mysticism, that emotional outlet for intensely personal Calvinist introspection. Yet even as in the juvenile "Upon Happiness," Thomson's "visions" in *The Seasons* come to an end before they presume to describe the goal of the rising mind, God Himself and His truth. In "Summer" (ll. 540ff.), contemplation inspires a "sacred Terror, a severe Delight," leading the speaker "up the Mount, in airy Vision rapt"; again, he "Wakes" to return to the real world and to natural description. The "Hymn" describes another such intellectual and spiritual flight, until "I lose / Myself in HIM, in LIGHT INEFFABLE!" and "Silence" becomes the only possible response. The rising mind of man on earth is thus clearly limited; the poet's enthusiastic visions remain as yet in the realm of the irrational and imaginary, and he is careful to regain rational control, usually by resuming natural description, coming literally down to earth. Countless times in *The Seasons* Thomson asserts his awareness of the limits of the rising mind, of physicotheology and empirical science in the temporal realm, as well as his firm belief in God's wise and providential but mysterious plan: God has "fix'd us in a State / That must not yet to pure Perfection rise" ("Spring," ll. 375–376); reason cannot yet reach the "World of Spirits" where

> . . . the Cloud
> So wills ETERNAL PROVIDENCE, sits deep.
> Enough for us to know that this dark State,
>
> .   .   .
>
> This Infancy of Being, cannot prove
> The final Issue of the Works of GOD
> ("Summer," ll. 1797–1803)

Man's "bounded View" sees arbitrary "deem'd *Evil*" in God's plan, but in afterlife "*The great eternal Scheme* . . . / To Reason's Eye refin'd clears up apace" ("Winter," ll. 1066–1067, 1046–1049), "From *seeming Evil* still educing *Good*" ("Hymn," l. 114). Clergyman Patrick Murdoch confidently pronounced that Thomson's assertion of religious belief here, "the theology of [the 'Hymn'], allowance made for poetical expression, is orthodox." As Thomas Boston expressed the same belief, "Natural knowledge will be brought to perfection, by the light of glory. The web of providence . . . will appear a most beautiful mixture; so as they shall all say together, on the view of it, *he hath done all things well.*"[5]

Thomson's view of God's mysterious plan, while ultimately couched in terms of Moderate optimism, is therefore not far removed from orthodox Scottish Calvinist determinism. The poet wrote to Cranstoun in 1725 of his trust in "Providence": "ther is I'm perswaded a necessary fix'd chain of things." Like the Moderates he simply tended, for the most part, to play down the more extreme or arbitrary interpretations of this belief. In his firm insistence on the limits of reason, Thomson echoes his mentors and models Job, Milton, and the Scottish divines, both old style and Moderate. Thomson's Augustan optimism is well founded on strong religious faith that God's Providence is ultimately benevolent, yet the poet's optimism is always tempered by his Calvinist awareness of man's limits. Modern critics have thus essentially correctly defined the central paradox, indeed the unifying philosophy of *The Seasons,* as Thomson's deep desire to comprehend the natural world and its workings, together with his acknowledgment of the impossibility of attaining such comprehension in this life. The poet's conundrum, his fragmentary earthly vision itself, inspires by a sort of "negative capability" yet stronger faith in God—a God of power and wisdom, fear and love.[6]

God's mysterious scheme, good though it might ultimately be, left a vast unknown realm to intimidate the superstitious poet; Thomson's predominant religious optimism was therefore hard-won and far from exclusive. Instances of his fears of the supernatural and unknown and his corresponding attempts to qualify his superstition are numerous in *The Seasons;* they are obviously products of the irrational element of older Scottish Calvinism reinforced by the superstitious folk culture of the poet's Border youth. Examples of such supernatural incidents in *The Seasons* include "Summer"'s "Fairy People" and "yelling Ghost" (ll. 1664–1681), "Portentous" comet (ll. 1700–1729), balls of fire, thunderstorm, and lightning death of Amelia (ll. 1128ff.); "Autumn"'s battlelike aurora borealis (ll. 1115–1137); "Winter"'s "foul Shades, and frighted Ghosts" in the desecrated churchyard (ll. 409–413); "Goblin-Story" raising "superstitious Horror" (ll. 619–620); and "Demon of the Night" warning the "devoted Wretch of Woe and Death" (ll. 191–194). "Devoted" here possibly links this superstition with unenlightened religious belief, though "devoted" in the eighteenth century also meant "doomed," and Thomson may have had in mind fear grounded in guilt or predestination. Thomson himself struggled throughout his life to overcome such fears of the supernatural, which were part of his Scottish upbringing; his attempts to free himself of these fears through reason, religious optimism, and scientific knowledge were consistent with rationalistic and benevolent Moderate attitudes in the Scottish church. But Thomson, along with his fellow Scottish Calvinists and even the Moderates like Riccaltoun and later the "commonsense" philosophers, never did embrace Augustan optimism unreservedly. Their leap to faith was not an easy one.[7]

The most obvious consequence of man's limited understanding of God's predetermined scheme is the problem of evil in the world. Critical indignation over Thomson's failure to solve the problem of evil[8] is hardly justified, however. The poet sees two types of evil in the world: human sin ("real" evil, the result of the Fall and man's depravity, which he attacks with stern didacticism); and natural evil, seemingly arbitrary or unexplained natural violence ("apparent" evil, actually part of God's wise plan). Both types are amply illustrated in the complex theodicy, based in nature, of *The Seasons*.

Thomson was profoundly aware of the Fallen World. Echoing Thomas Boston's "dregs of time,"[9] he laments "these iron Times, / These Dregs of Life!" ("Spring," ll. 272–308) in a world where corrupt human passion reigns over reason and "social Feeling" is extinct. He draws from scriptural and classical sources to depict the Paradise–Golden Age and particularly from Genesis to describe the Deluge which is the result of man's fall into Original Sin (he alludes to the serpent myth elsewhere, in "Summer," ll. 897–912). Thomson always showed far greater cognizance of man's capacity for real evil than did such benevolistic optimists as Shaftesbury: this was of course the poet's Scottish Calvinist heritage. His many didactic sermons in *The Seasons,* particularly those attacking vanity and greed, address an imperfect, Fallen World, man's second or depraved spiritual state. Thomson would reconfirm his strong sense of sin in *The Castle of Indolence.*

In *The Seasons,* "Nature disturb'd" is also full of apparent evils—paradoxical in God's good Creation which the poet never ceases to praise. Of seemingly random acts of violence in the natural world, such as the destructive "Autumn" flood, the swain's death in the snow, and the death of Amelia, Thomson is profoundly aware, yet he accepts these events almost fatalistically. His explicit interpretation of them (ll. 1730ff.) refrains from directly attributing such tragedies to divine vengeance as his stern Scottish forebears might have done—David Lindsay's *Monarche,* for example, portrays evil Tullus Hostilius struck down by lightning as God's punishment. Thomson declares more tolerantly that "yet not always on the guilty Head / Descends the fated Flash" ("Summer," ll. 1170–1171). In a passage removed from "Summer" in 1730, the poet explained at great length that innocent Amelia's death was not a punishment from God. Nevertheless, he warns in that passage that the guilty man has much to fear from nature's violence; the "Atheist," for example, attempts to hide from the storm, but "The *Messenger of Justice,* glancing, comes, / With swifter Sweep behind, and trips his Heel" ("Summer," 1727). This omitted passage is intriguing, though hardly surprising, in its ambiguous attitude toward divine vengeance, as Thomson himself was constantly torn between old-style and Moderate religious influences. It is interesting to note that, however much he toned down didactic comment on such events over the years, Thomson continued to keep these passages as part of his poem.[10] In general, though, the revised *Seasons* tends toward Moderate interpretation; while always conscious of man's fallen nature, Thomson maintained that such apparent evils in nature are but "fated" parts of God's all-good, predestined plan, which will be known in the afterlife, where divine justice will ultimately be done. Thus Thomson never set out fully to explain the ways of God to men because he realized that his human limits prevented him. His failure to solve the problem of evil in man and nature was in essence the Scottish Calvinist solution of his age: in *The Seasons* he showed awareness and acceptance of the Fallen World, he assumed his duty to preach violations of and potential for earthly harmony and the ultimate goal of heavenly harmony, he professed his belief in determinism tempered with Moderate optimism, and he affirmed his genuine faith in God's benevolent master-plan.

James Thomson's code of ethics, expressed through a didactic vein in *The Seasons*, is largely an outgrowth of his religious background and beliefs and, again, strains of both old-style and Moderate Scottish Calvinism are discernible. His moral views were also influenced by Shaftesbury and particularly his Scottish disciple Hutcheson and, most of all, of course, by his close study of the book of nature, which helps to inspire virtuous sentiments and teaches the "moral Song" ("Autumn," l. 672).

From the Old Testament, mainly Job and Ecclesiastes, from the otherworldly, flesh-denying aspect of Christian Neoplatonism, and primarily from Reformation Scottish Calvinist moral rigor sounds Thomson's severe warning of the sinfulness of vanity and delusive temporal existence as he condemns pride, idleness, waste, and frivolity. This hard lesson, recalling the juvenilia, would be reiterated in *Liberty* and *The Castle*. The darker side of the book of nature itself reinforces the lesson that earthly life is unpredictable, harsh, and violent, as *The Seasons* abundantly illustrates. In his sternest didactic voice, Thomson clearly echoes the emotional, intense, and uncompromising pulpit rhetoric of his father's generation. This passage is but one of many such in the poem:

> Ah little think the gay licentious Proud,
> Whom Pleasure, Power, and Affluence surround;
> They, who their thoughtless Hours in giddy Mirth,
> And wanton, often cruel, Riot waste;
> Ah little think they, while they dance along,
> How many feel, this very moment, Death . . .
> ("Winter," ll. 322–327)

Such lines bear comparison with Scottish Calvinist tracts such as Thomas Boston's *Fourfold State* ("IV.I.Of Death"); Boston's evangelical diatribe, liberally shot with scriptural quotes, likewise resounds with the forceful rhetoric of the Presbyterian pulpit:

> Man's life is a *vain* and *empty* thing while it is: It vanisheth away; and lo! it is not, Job vii.6. *My days are vanity* . . . behold *the vanity of the world;* and of all these things in it, which men so much value and esteem, and therefore set their hearts upon. . . . But look into the grave, O man, consider and be wise; listen to the doctrine of death; and learn . . .[11]

Thomson's attack on vanity also corresponds to Blair's *Grave,* where the message of mortality as well as the manner of exclamatory direct address are strikingly similar to his own; their source in austere old-style Scottish Calvinism is the same.

The tone of Thomson's didactic passage then shifts as the poet continues,

> . . . Thought fond Man
> Of these, and all the thousand nameless Ills,
> That one incessant Struggle render Life,
> One Scene of Toil, of Suffering, and of Fate,
> Vice in his high Career would stand appall'd,
> And heedless rambling Impulse learn to think;
> The conscious Heart of Charity would warm,
> And her wide Wish Benevolence dilate;
> The social Tear would rise, the social Sigh;
> And into clear Perfection, gradual Bliss,
> Refining still, the social Passions work.
> ("Winter," ll. 348–358)

Now the rising mind has ascended to the other, more rational and positive strain of moral didacticism in *The Seasons.* A similar *Seasons* passage demonstrating the poet's carefully controlled movement from old-style to more Moderate attitudes and corresponding optimistic tones and Augustan language is in "Winter" (ll. 1028–1049). Thomson's more benevolent moral strain was influenced implicitly by the ethics of the New Testament and explicitly by contemporary interpretations of Christian Neoplatonic and empirical thought, notably by Scottish philosophers of the first generation of the Enlightenment, including Hutcheson and Turnbull who, like Thomson, came from a Scottish Calvinist background. The empirical ethics of Thomson's friend Turnbull, a founder of the commonsense school and author of *The Principles of Moral Philosophy* (1740), make a useful contemporary analogue here, as he, like the poet, was much concerned with the relationship between natural and moral laws, aesthetic and moral "sense." God's book of nature also offers instruction in this happier, benevolent vein, its natural beauties providing an atmosphere congenial to noble, generous sentiments in man; these very personal feelings in Thomson's *Seasons* have been aptly described as Hutchesonian "exaggeration" of Shaftesbury's "sensibility."[12]

Thomson's benevolistic moral theme in *The Seasons* (as in the juvenile "Upon Happiness") is built around the concept of virtue as the source of moral pleasure on earth and the closest earthly approximation to heavenly happiness. Characteristically, the Scots Calvinist poet stops short of claiming that virtue itself will earn man election to salvation but simply speaks of it as a temporal guide to heaven. The highest virtue for Thomson is love, specifically social love, or selfless benevolence, as he moves beyond Calvinist spiritual individualism and toward a more public moralistic role. Such a tendency was in line with the Moderates' emphasis on Christian conduct above rigid doctrinal concerns and also with their attempt to integrate religious with social purpose.[13] Of such social love as distinct from self-love Thomson wrote to Aaron Hill:

> The Social Love, of which you are so bright an Example,
> tho' it be the distinguishing Ornament of Humanity, yet
> there are some ill-natur'd enough to degrade it into a
> Modification of Self-love, according to them, its Original.
> Those Gentlemen, I am afraid, mingle their Tempers too much
> with their Speculations . . .[14]

In this letter of 1726, Thomson is apparently echoing Hutcheson's *An inquiry into the original of our ideas of beauty and virtue . . . In which the principles of the late Earl of Shaftesbury are explain'd and defended, against the author of the Fable of the bees . . .* (1725). Besides attacking Mandeville here, Thomson was more immediately reacting against Scotsman Archibald Campbell's current ideas on "Moral Virtue" and self-love. Campbell, a divinity student of Professor Simson at Glasgow, was involved in the contemporary ethical controversy with Hutcheson in Scotland which Thomson seems to have followed closely, so evidently Thomson knew and appreciated the work of Hutcheson very early on.[15]

Indeed, Thomson usually agrees more wholeheartedly with the benevolent ethics, the "Christian Stoicism"[16] of Francis Hutcheson than with the ethics of deist Shaftesbury himself. Hutcheson, whose Scottish enlightened pragmatic philosophy, shaped to a great extent by his Presbyterian background, restrained him from excesses of optimism and enthusiasm, held that benevolent social love and moral goodness are disinterested; that is, independent of self-interest or "natural" egocentric moral goodness. The Scottish commonsense philosophers, such as Turnbull and his pupil Thomas Reid, would also adopt this view, and Thomson himself clearly held such a philosophy. Hutcheson and Turnbull also believed that man would arrive at an idea of what social love might accomplish for the "public good" by heeding his "Moral Sense," which could be cultivated through proper exercise of empiricism and reason; Thomson likewise felt that social love or benevolence was not innate in man (as Shaftesbury might have it) but required careful cultivation. The concept of a moral sense, or higher conscience, capable of perceiving moral good or evil, was present even in older Scottish Calvinist theology. Calvin himself, and his Scottish heir Thomas Boston, both acknowledged man's moral sense but held it to be depraved, gravely damaged in the Fall. Hutcheson and Turnbull, even in their Moderate optimism, still retained much of the caution of their Calvinist forebears regarding the limited powers of man's reason to inform the moral sense. Their brand of benevolism was thus a particularly Calvinistic one; Watts and Defoe in England held comparable views. On the one hand their optimism about man's nature and potential rested on the rather negative hope that man could overcome his initial depravity through rigorous moral education. But on the other hand, their optimistic moral philosophy was founded on a firm base of explicit and orthodox Christian faith (as distinct from Shaftesbury's deism)—a faith in a providential, active, and ultimately benevolent deity. James Thomson certainly shared this Calvinist Christian moral philosophy with his fellow Scots.[17]

Thomson's idea of social love and its application in acts of unselfish public virtue necessarily raises the question of his views on the orthodox Calvinist doctrine of justification by faith alone. In truth, like most of the Moderates, Thomson had rather put aside such points of strict doctrine in favor of broader tolerance and religious optimism as well as active social concern. Also, the notion of "works" as proofs of election, while not authentic to Calvinism, had crept into Scottish and English belief, and this idea of the spiritual significance of work would give rise to the so-called work ethic which Thomson propounds, particularly in *The Castle of Indolence*. The poet evades doctrinal complexities by simply maintaining that acts of virtue are of value on earth and can give pleasure which hints of heavenly happiness; even in *The Castle* he never goes so far as to say that benevolent works can guarantee election, although they can facilitate an earthly regeneration of sorts.

Thomson's concept of virtue and its nurturing in the human spirit has many points in common with the aesthetic philosophy of the Scottish Enlightenment. Like Shaftesbury, the Scottish philosophers defined virtue or benevolence as a kind of beauty, an agreement with God's universal harmony the perception of which gives man pleasure; yet Shaftesbury's equation of beauty with benevolence is not precisely Hutcheson's or Turnbull's—or Thomson's. While Shaftesbury does not distinguish between man's sense of beauty and his moral sense, the commonsensical Scots did make that distinction and simply saw aesthetic and moral as separate systems, offering analogous rather than identical beauties.[18] Of course, any attribution of higher goodness to the beauty of sensuous aesthetic perceptions would have been rejected by austere, old-style Scottish Calvinists; Boston thus warned that "Man is never more blind than when he is looking on the objects that are most pleasing to sense." Moderate Hutcheson more mildly contrasts natural goodness of objects empirically perceived by the senses as pleasurable beauty with higher moral goodness, recognized by the cultivated moral sense in acts of public virtue or disinterested benevolence. Hutcheson's emphasis on subjective response, or a taste for beauty and goodness, is also characteristic of Thomson's sensibility; Thomson indeed demonstrates in his poetry a Hutchesonian aesthetic psychology which anticipates the Scottish Enlightenment. Thomson's more specific interest in such empirical psychology was of course the effect of the beauty of the natural world on man. While nature's beauties could not of themselves create social love or virtue, they could provide an atmosphere conducive to the cultivation of the moral sense; examples in *The Seasons* are Hagley Park's benevolent influence over the good Lyttelton and autumnal "Philosophic Melancholy"'s inspiration of virtuous impulses. The idea that the moral sense could be tutored by the aesthetic was elevated to a philosophical system by Turnbull, Reid, and the Scottish Enlightenment commonsense philosophers. Turnbull, in his *Treatise on Ancient Painting* (1740), was particularly concerned with the role of visual art, along with the art of descriptive poetry, in refining the moral sense. Thus Thomson's descriptions of "beautiful" temperate scenes were meant to help lift man's spirit outside himself in a pleasurable setting where he is not forced (as in "Summer"'s uncivilized tropics) to struggle for survival but might enjoy unselfish public virtue and promote social progress.[19]

Thomson's social love is closely linked with his deeply felt humanitarianism and concern for all creatures which informs each *Season*'s description. He did not simply borrow the idea of such generous benevolence from philosophers Shaftesbury and Hutcheson; his sympathy for man and beast is not merely abstract, Augustan public virtue but is also in a very real sense a product of the poet's rural upbringing, where man had to seek harmony with all creation in order to survive and thrive. Such cooperation was necessarily based in empiricism—on the countryman's own observations and experience. Thomson generally shows greater awareness of the harsh realities of the universe than Shaftesbury; his moral ideas, including acceptance of the Fallen World and its hard truths, ultimately derived not just from Shaftesbury nor entirely from the poet's acknowledged model Job nor even from the influence of the more fatalistic, negative side of Scottish Calvinism, but also, more directly, from the lessons taught by the book of nature in Scottish Border life.[20]

Even though his avowed purpose in *The Seasons* is a religious one, Thomson has often been criticized for failing to bring specifically Christian reference into the religious message of the poem. The poet's practice of formal religion did indeed decline over the years, and he apparently expressed certain religious doubts, although he remained a religious man; his friend George Lyttelton, who had become a Christian enthusiast, tried to convert him back to churchgoing.[21] Thomson's sole explicit reference to Christianity in *The Seasons* is pejorative ("Summer," ll. 854–855), where he describes the tropics as "The Seat of blameless *Pan*, yet undisturb'd / By christian Crimes and *Europe*'s cruel Sons." His attitude, in the historical sense, is clear: he was disillusioned by gross violations of social love committed in the name of Christianity over the centuries. He surely also had in mind Christian Scotland's long and bitter religious strife. Also, not surprisingly, almost all of the poem's scriptural allusions are to the Old Testament rather than the New; Scottish Calvinism had always been a bibliocracy which drew heavily upon Old Testament revelation, even as it prefigured the New Testament message. Even Thomson's juvenile poems, with few exceptions, had shown such Old Testament orientation despite the pervasive influence of Christian Neoplatonism, Milton, and Watts; God in the person of Christ was very rarely mentioned. Further, Thomson's scanty reference to Christ in *The Seasons* reflected the Moderate attitude generally; this reticence about Christ in the Moderates' teaching, despite their emphasis on Christian conduct, was a major factor in charges of unorthodoxy and even Arian heresy falsely leveled at them in the eighteenth century. It would be wrong to assume, however, that James Thomson himself did not believe in Jesus Christ. In his anonymous preface to Milton's *Areopagitica* (1738 edition), for example, he confidently refers to the "Kingdom of Christ" and to "our Saviour." More important, Thomson's ethical teachings themselves clearly derive from the Christian virtues, stressed by the Moderates, of benevolence and love, and the morality of *The Seasons* is perfectly congenial to Christian faith. Lyttelton said of the poet that "as to the Heart of a Christian, he always had that, in a degree of perfection beyond most Men I have known," and added, "Thomson, I hope and believe died a Christian."[22]

Thomson's public, social didacticism grows from his Christian benevolistic ethics. He rails against social crimes ("Autumn," drunken "social
Slaughter," ll. 502–609, and beehive ruined by man, ll. 1172ff.;
"Winter," penal abuses, ll. 359–375). He preaches humanitarian concern ("Winter," plea to the shepherd to be "kind" to his charges, ll.
265ff.; "Autumn," call for generosity to the poor gleaners, ll. 167–170).
Especially, he celebrates social love and life ("Spring," virtuous marriage, ll. 1113ff.; "Winter," ideal friendship, ll. 572–652; "Autumn,"
Happy Man, ll. 1235ff., who "Nor Purpose gay, / Amusement, Dance,
or Song, he sternly scorns; / For Happiness and true Philosophy / Are
of the social still, and smiling Kind"). In this last instance of the "Happy
Man," perhaps recalling convivial occasions from his native Scotland,
Thomson seems consciously to reject his austere, Scottish Calvinist
upbringing with its strictures against certain innocent social pleasures
in favor of a more tolerant, indeed sociable attitude.

In considering *The Seasons* as a religious and philosophical poem, it
is essential to recognize the strong continuity between the religious
beliefs of the young Scottish poet and his mature philosophy and
faith. Certainly, Thomson was influenced by new, more liberal trends
in religion and philosophy; he grew increasingly Moderate and optimistic in his views and avoided in *The Seasons* personal identification
with established Christianity. Still, religious purpose never ceased to
inspire the poem. The roots of Thomson's religion were firmly
planted in Scotland: in both old-style and Moderate Scottish Calvinism, in the Bible and pulpit rhetoric, and in the study of traditional
theology and moral philosophy, along with physicotheology and the
religious aspects of the new science, which were all a part of his Scottish experience and contributed to his eclectic spiritual vision. From
these same roots grew the Scottish Enlightenment itself, to which
Thomson's ethics and aesthetics are intimately related. Evidence of
these complex Scottish influences was abundant in Thomson's juvenilia, where both praising and teaching roles operate, where physicotheology reveals an immanent yet transcendent, wrathful yet loving deity, where religious enthusiasm, Neoplatonism, Christian
humanism, superstition, and reason come together. These very elements inform *The Seasons* as a religious poem. The God of *The Seasons*
is perhaps most fully manifest to Thomson in His works of nature, yet

He nonetheless shows many of the attributes of the deity of traditional Scottish Calvinism, acting through Providence according to his predetermined plan. Thomson would keep religious faith, with its foundations firmly in the teachings of the Scottish church, throughout his life. Even as old-style beliefs gave way to more Moderate views, the poet would always retain discernible old-style structures of religious thought (one example is the stern parable of regeneration, secularized and most fully worked out in *The Castle*). Allowing for strong Moderate influence and insofar as the Moderates could be counted as orthodox Christians within Scottish Presbyterianism, James Thomson's eclectic religious faith in *The Seasons* was itself, in essence, orthodox. As Patrick Murdoch affirmed, the poet's "devotion to the Supreme Being, founded on the most elevated and just conceptions of his operations and providence, shine[s] out in every page" of *The Seasons*.[23]

Even in its earliest versions, *The Seasons* displayed genuine human interest as the poem set out to explore man's relationship to God and Creation. While it is predominantly a poem about nature and a praise of its Creator, *The Seasons* is also a poem about people—their place in the natural world, their beliefs and feelings about it, and their varied responses to it. One eighteenth-century Scottish critic, James Beattie, applauded this central human concern, which gave "stability and elevation" to the religious-descriptive poem.[24] Indeed Thomson, nurtured in Scotland's democratic social and intellectual environment as well as in a freedom-loving Scottish Whig tradition, speaks eloquently for the cause of individual and national liberty in his poem. Further, Thomson was a preeminently British patriot, and his position as a Scottish, North British poet lends an unusual and intriguing dimension to his views of the contemporary social and political scene. His awareness of the place of Scotland in the larger scheme of the United Kingdom is sometimes explicit, occasionally ambivalent, but always present, informing his wider world-view. For particularly with the addition of even more descriptive and didactic material in later versions of the poem, *The Seasons* becomes a timely and far-reaching sociopolitical commentary and one which is in a significant sense a projection of James Thomson's Scottishness.

Thomson's passionate concern for the public welfare is obvious in his ethical pronouncements. He is no less concerned with the individual's—and especially the Briton's—right to freedom. Examples include his indignation at the "free-born BRITON to the Dungeon chain'd" ("Winter," l. 371) and his reference to the "cruel Trade" of slavery ("Summer," l. 1019—the Moderate Presbyterian clergy, too, had spoken out against the slave trade). Such concerns, reconfirmed in Thomson's preface to *Areopagitica* where he asserts that liberty is basic to religious belief, pursuit of truth, and practice of virtue, would culminate in the poem *Liberty* (1735–1736). Liberty, both individual and national integrity, was of course the central Whig cause; it was of special significance to a Scotsman, who had to be aware that his nation had suffered a history of political domination or intimidation at the hands of the English. Many Scots viewed the recent Union of 1707 as the final loss of Scottish liberty; however, Thomson, as a pro-Union Whig, saw it as an achievement of greater potential freedom and opportunity for Scotland as part of that powerful "deep-laid indissoluble State" ("Spring," l. 845) of Great Britain.

The central sociopolitical theme to emerge from the multitude of *Seasons* descriptions is the ongoing debate over whether primitive or progressive life is the more desirable. Thomson as a Scot found this question particularly pertinent, as he himself had moved from what many considered a very primitive culture in the Scottish Borders to the town of Edinburgh and then to the more progressive society of London and had recognized both positive and negative sides to these very different ways of life. Indeed, the very contrast between Scotland and England, Thomson's memories of one and later experience of the other, would act as an inspiration to the poet and an influence on both the meaning and the method of *The Seasons* as well as *The Castle*.[25] Both classical literature and contemporary travel literature, from which Thomson drew increasingly after 1730, also contribute to this primitivism-progress debate. The poet never does commit himself to a clear-cut solution to this problem. Even where he contrasts simple, rural amusements such as he had experienced in Scotland (story telling, folk dancing) with the "intense," "false inchanted Joy" of the progressive city (gambling, court entertainments, "Winter," ll. 617–655) he does not consistently endorse an Augustan stereotype of "country good" versus "city evil." Rather, he seems almost to delight in the court's superficial glamor. He also shows undisguised enjoyment of that urban amenity, the drama, which despite the Scottish Calvinist strictures of his youth he would help to foster in London. This element of pleasure in sophisticated urban attractions is certainly understandable after the poet's isolated youth and strict upbringing in Scotland.

At times, Thomson seems simply to imply that country life is better and more innocent than city life. These passages, like the juvenile georgic "Of a Country Life," are those most clearly influenced by Virgil and Horace. In "Spring," they include the paean to British rural industry (ll. 67ff.), pastoral Golden Age (ll. 234–271), and joyful married love set in "Retirement, rural Quiet" (ll. 1113ff.); in "Summer," the praise of Britain's rural economy (ll. 423–431); in "Autumn," the panegyric to "innocent" rural life (ll. 1235–1251); and in "Winter," the "Thrice happy Race," the peaceful Laplanders (ll. 843–886). Thomson would also refer to the happy, primitive Lapps in *Liberty* III (ll. 520–523); James Beattie imitated Thomson in depicting a similar primitivistic Lapland scene in *The Minstrel* (1771–1774). In "Autumn," the natives of the Scottish island of St. Kilda are likewise unspoiled and well-adapted examples of the natural man; Thomson's source Martin Martin described in detail their innocence, love, freedom from avarice, and "true liberty."[26] Thomson's mention of them, however, is brief and does not figure centrally in his primitivism-progress debate, perhaps because of the poet's reluctance to admit of such pure primitivism within his native Scotland, now a part of progressive Britain.

In other instances in *The Seasons,* the simple life, close to nature, is not so innocent or appealing. Most examples of unhappy primitivism occur in the less temperate *Seasons* "Winter" and "Summer," set in the arctic or tropics, where Thomson added more extreme, second-hand descriptive material to enhance the sublime effect. Incidentally, Thomas Boston, for one, termed evil, unregenerate man "natural" man, thus linking primitivism with the Scottish Calvinist conception of original sin.[27] Accordingly, the tropic dwellers in "Summer" lack social love and live in passionate violence; the Siberians in "Winter," unlike the Laplanders unable to adapt to their wintry environment, exist in primitive, uncivilized isolation.

Is "progress," then, a product of refined, civilized urban life? Not necessarily. Thomson's idea of progress is not exclusively urban, either, although he does salute the city's amenities and achievements ("Full are thy Cities with the Sons of Art; / And Trade and Joy, in every busy Street," "Summer," ll. 1457–1458). In *Liberty* the poet would offer even more extravagant praise of cities (V.701ff.). Cities do represent one standard of progress for Thomson and play a particular role in a society's development; they nurture the arts, as the poet himself had discovered, and they are centers of trade and of certain types of industry, about which the poet grew increasingly enthusiastic as the century itself progressed. Indeed his Whig party took much of the credit for such British commercial achievements.

Thomson was not blind to the fact, however, that cities also tended to encourage certain vices of over-civilization, especially vanity and greed. These were grave sins to the austere Scottish Calvinists. They were also grave offenses against the commonweal to the poet's Opposition Whig faction, who joined with the Tory gentry in promoting a patriotic, land-based "country" political ideology to counteract the corrupt influence of the Walpole Court, whose home was the city.[28]

Thomson thus recognized that another alternative exists: progress could occur in a predominantly rural society. Thomson's model Virgil had demonstrated this ideal in the *Georgics,* and Thomson's "country" Whig ideology was ultimately based on Virgilian principles. Man's control over the rural environment through careful husbandry was not less progressive than the culture, commerce, and court life of the city and was the very basis of sound national economy and international strength. In "Summer" (ll. 352–431) the poet describes a probably Scottish pastoral scene; then he anticipates Burns's "The Cotter's Saturday Night" (XIX, "From Scenes like these, old Scotia's grandeur springs . . .")[29] as he exclaims:

> A simple Scene! yet hence BRITANNIA sees
> Her solid Grandeur rise: hence she commands
> Th' exalted Stores of every brighter Clime,

The Treasures of the Sun without his Rage:
Hence, fervent all, with Culture, Toil, and Arts,
Wide glows her Land: her dreadful Thunder hence
Rides o'er the Waves sublime, and now, even now,
Impending hangs o'er *Gallia's* humbled Coast,
Hence rules the circling Deep, and awes the World.
("Summer," ll. 423–431)

Thomson and Virgil, both rural, provincial poets within a wider empire, prudently saw two sides to the primitivism-progress question; they realized that each type of society has its advantages and drawbacks, potential benefits and abuses. The most compelling interpretation of Thomson's seeming ambivalence about primitivism-progress is found, therefore, in John Chalker's comparison of Thomson's views with Virgil's own. Both poets promoted progressivism tempered with nostalgia, or so-called nostalgic progressivism, a sort of enlightened primitivism which appreciated the joys of simple, natural life but also acknowledged that man must make full use of his potential as an intellectual being, supporting the social virtues and improving nature and taking the responsibility to seek harmony with all Creation.[30] The Protestant, Scottish Calvinist work ethic constantly reinforces Thomson's Virgilian, rural progressivism; most evident in *The Seasons'* "Industry" passage ("Autumn"), it would become, in a secularized, social application of religious thought, a central theme of *The Castle of Indolence*.

Thomson's ultimate solution in bringing this Virgilian "Roman ideal" home to Britain is that which might be expected of an eighteenth-century Scot who grew up in the unimproved, isolated, and in many ways primitive Border country and who loved it, and who, too, had "progressed" to the cities of Edinburgh and London to practice his art.[31] Even by Thomson's day Edinburgh retained a rather rural ambiance, reflecting the chiefly rural character of Scotland as a whole. Even when he went south, Thomson preferred to settle in Richmond, a country village on the Thames outside London, though near enough to the city for the poet to partake of its pleasures. His literary solution of nostalgic, qualified progressivism is a corresponding compromise and in great part a product of his upbringing in Scotland, an unspoilt country life close to nature and offering much pleasure and poetic inspiration, but a life which needed, as he well knew, to be improved both culturally and economically. In the poet's mind, on some level at least, the realms of primitivism and progress looked a great deal like the Scotland of his past and the England of his present and potential. The primitivism-progress debate, which is a crucial theme not only in *The Seasons* but also in *Liberty* and *The Castle,* reveals much about Thomson's contradictory attitudes toward his native Scotland.[32] His Virgilian-Scottish idea of progress is not a simple solution but probably the best literary response to a complex issue which adds considerably to the variousness and scope of *The Seasons.*

Thomson's tempered nostalgic progressivism is, of course, closely linked with his views about national potential, his strong patriotism for "Britannia" (which "too includes our native Country, Scotland").[33] Thomson does, in fact, separate British (in "Summer," exclusively English) and Scottish ("Autumn") worthies roll calls, perhaps to acknowledge Scotland's distinct national and cultural identity despite the Union. The poet maintained an optimistic and essentially pro-Union stance in *The Seasons;* in one instance, he describes peaceful lambs, watched over by their shepherd in the Border scene, gamboling

> . . . around the Hill; the Rampart once
> Of iron War, in ancient barbarous Times,
> When disunited BRITAIN ever bled,
> Lost in eternal Broil: ere yet she grew
> To this deep-laid indissoluble State
> ("Spring," ll. 840–845)

"Broil" alludes here to the long-lived Scottish-English antagonism and Border warfare, "indissoluble State" to the United Kingdom.

Thomson saw the Union of 1707 as Scotland's opportunity for improvement or progress within Great Britain while at the same time he revealed deep feeling for its distinctive landscape and life, its national identity. He believed Britain's progress would be Scotland's progress as well; his ideal for a progressive, improved Scotland was itself considerably qualified by his nostalgia for its traditional life. "Autumn"'s key "Scottish" passage demonstrates his genuine concern for Scotland and his hopes for its future. A brief version of this passage first appeared in "Summer" along with the British worthies; Thomson moved it to "Autumn" in 1730. Autumn, a more typically Scottish and inclement season, was the poet's own favorite, inspiring that mixed emotion of "philosophic Melancholy"; he may have wanted to make the point that Scotland's distinctive culture and its poor economy were, in a sense, "fading" like the season and badly in need of regeneration and "harvest."[34] This interpretation parallels the central paradox of "Autumn," barrenness and fruition; Scottish fruits of the Union, the Scottish "harvest," were by 1730 not immediately forthcoming. Poor Scotland probably did appear to be fading and fallow to Thomson from his new perspective in prosperous London.

This Scottish segment of "Autumn" was very possibly modeled on Scots poet David Lindsay's *The Dreme* on a similar pattern. Following the prospect view of "Caledonia" where Thomson lists Scotland's many natural resources (forests, lakes, fertile valleys, rivers), he goes on, like Lindsay, to praise the Scots people themselves. His native pride is obvious; he describes "a People, in Misfortune's School / Train'd up to hardy Deeds; soon visited / By *Learning*," "A manly Race / Of unsubmitting Spirit, wise, and brave" (ll. 894–897) yet who struggled in vain, "As well unhappy WALLACE can attest" (l. 900), to keep Scotland free. Wallace, the first of Thomson's three Scottish worthies, probably appears here through the recent influence of William Hamilton of Gilbertfield's *Wallace* (1721), a Scoto-English rendering, in rhymed couplets, of Blind Hary's epic. The Scots were

> . . . of unequal Bounds
> Impatient, and by tempting Glory borne
> O'er every Land, for every Land their Life
> Has flow'd profuse, their piercing Genius plan'd,
> And swell'd the Pomp of Peace their faithful Toil.
> ("Autumn," ll. 903–907)

The poet thus extols Scottish contributions to European war and peace, culture and society. His phrase "unequal Bounds" is revealing: by it he means not merely Scotland's unfairly constricted physical, territorial boundaries but also a much broader, more significant cultural and sociopolitical limit, the invisible border between "contending Kingdoms" (ll. 713–714) Scotland and England. He is evidently referring to Scotland's situation under English political domination as well as to his country's natural limitations of harsh climate, geographical isolation, and rugged topography and likewise to its primitive life—its unimproved agriculture and industry and culture set back by the rigors of the Reformation. In other words, Thomson acknowledged that the Scots found themselves "bound" in many ways and hampered from achieving equality with neighboring, dominant England; the word "unequal" was substituted for "ignoble" (1730–1738), which had expressed even stronger nationalistic indignation at Scotland's situation. Scots had, therefore, to leave Scotland to attain their highest potential; this probably also represents a self-conscious explanation of the poet's own personal decision to go south to seek literary fortune. So even Thomson's pro-Union, British patriotism did not blind him to the inequality, poverty, and backwardness which still bound Scotland. He thus pleads:

> OH is there not some Patriot, in whose Power
> That best, that godlike Luxury is plac'd,
> Of blessing Thousands, Thousands yet unborn,
> Thro' late Posterity? some, large of Soul,
> To chear dejected Industry? to give
> A double Harvest to the pining Swain?
> And teach the labouring Hand the Sweets of Toil?
> How, by the finest Art, the native Robe
> To weave; how, white as Hyperborean Snow,
> To form the lucid Lawn; with venturous Oar,
> How to dash wide the Billow; nor look on,
> Shamefully passive, while *Batavian* Fleets
> Defraud us of the glittering finny Swarms,
> That heave our Friths, and croud upon our Shores;
> How all-enlivening Trade to rouse, and wing
> The prosperous Sail, from every growing Port,
> Uninjur'd, round the sea-incircled Globe;

> And thus, in Soul united as in Name,
> Did BRITAIN reign the Mistress of the Deep.
> ("Autumn," ll. 910–928)

Thomson's heartfelt call for leadership to develop Scotland's tremendous potential echoes the message of Lindsay's *Dreme,* where Lindsay beseeches the Scottish king, James V, to govern more wisely and well.

The Union of 1707, while vitally important, was still just a nominal union, Thomson felt, and only the awaited advancement of Scottish industries (linen and textile, trade and commerce, fisheries) and agriculture would bring the Scottish economic health which would signify true equality and unity with England. Thomson maintains his characteristic nostalgic yet progressive position here in particularly promoting the rural, mostly Lowland and Border, occupations of linen manufacturing and agriculture along with the more centralized Scottish industries. Scotland, he asserts, must learn to contribute its share to Great Britain's progress and prosperity if it wishes to reap the benefits of Union. The poet thus recognized that Scotland is full of natural and cultural resources, not least its hardy and intelligent people, but at the same time he implied that the Scots had not yet learned how best to use those resources, so Scotland's progress was still potential. While Scots had long carried their genius to other lands, "As from their own clear North, in radiant Streams, / Bright over *Europe* bursts the *Boreal Morn*" (ll. 908–909), they seemed to the poet to have done little to develop their capabilities at home. His attitude, as he chides the "shamefully Passive" Scots, cannot but recall Swift's paradoxical pride and pity, his impatience with his native Ireland. Thomson revealed his sympathetic yet critical feelings in a letter to Aaron Hill where he referred to Scotland as "that neglected Corner of the World, [of] depress'd Merit, uninform'd Beauty, and good Sense cloath'd in the Rags of Language."[35]

Thomson was not alone in his impatient concern for Scotland. Martin Martin, in *Description of the Western Islands,* described the plentiful resources of the islands and wished that they would be "improved." Union agent Daniel Defoe's poem *Caledonia* (1706) carried the theme of "Wake, Scotland, from thy long lethargic dream"; he wanted to encourage, through the Union, Scottish development of agriculture, fisheries, and trade. Allan Ramsay wrote several Scottish "improvement" poems, such as "Pleasures of Improvements in Agriculture," which shows distress over the neglectful and ignorant waste of rich Scottish land. Thomson's friend Duncan Forbes of Culloden, in *Some Considerations on the Present State of Scotland,* affirmed his love for Scotland in an eloquent, deeply felt plea for Scots to help themselves, to make the Union work. But he admitted that unless a "Miracle interpose" and "the People are brought, in spite of inveterate Prejudices, to *know* and to *pursue* their real Interests," ruin would come to Scotland. Forbes sadly saw "rooted Prejudices," "gross Ignorance," and "stupid Indifference" in his fellow-Scots. Thomson surely felt similar frustrations, yet he remained generally optimistic about Scottish potential for improvement. His concern for Scotland, where many friends and relations still dwelt, was strong and sincere. He kept well informed of the Scottish development plans of "patriots" such as the duke of Argyll and Forbes himself (the two remaining Scottish worthies of *The Seasons*) and read a great deal on the subject, collecting contemporary pamphlet literature on current Scottish schemes. He also kept apprised of the Scottish situation through friends in high places, including Forbes and his secretary George Ross and Sir Andrew Mitchell. So James Thomson's patriotism for Great Britain by no means excluded Scotland; rather, he singled out his native country for special advice and encouragement, aware as he was of Scotland's great possibilities and need for strong leadership. His optimistic interest in Scotland's progress was typical of the nascent Scottish Enlightenment "improving" spirit, and in that spirit he strove to bring Scotland into the wider British and European cultural sphere through his Anglo-Scottish poetry.[36]

Occasionally, however, a less pleasant sort of patriotism surfaces in *The Seasons,* a streak of aggressively pro-British chauvinism (such as "Autumn"'s "BRITISH THUNDER" and industry passage, for example), which seems to suggest an ambivalent attitude toward Scotland which might even be misinterpreted as anti-Scottish. When the poet protests too much, it is probably because of his subconscious insecurities and inferiority complex about being a Scot in London at a time when Scots were suffering from discrimination and Jacobitism was a threat. This overbearing tone is far more pronounced in *Liberty.* Thomson's loss of patriotic perspective and corresponding poetic lapses were really, however, a result of his original and early attempt—particularly brave for a Scot—to transcend a narrow or nationalistic English or Scottish stance and to see, through poetry, from a broader British viewpoint.[37] His conscious motives were good: he passionately hoped the Union of 1707 would realize its high expectations to the benefit of all Britain, Scotland included. He wanted the Union to work. His over-exuberant Britishness was a hyperbolic expression, under strong social and political pressures, of the progressive Whig ideology which he had espoused even as a youth in Scotland and his overweening British pride was in no way intended to be anti-Scottish. Rather, Thomson's poetry was his own public proclamation and concrete manifestation of cultural "union" between the two nations.

James Thomson's sociopolitical vision in *The Seasons* embraced human rights, individual and national liberty, nostalgic progressivism, involvement in Scottish affairs, and positive patriotism for both Scotland and Great Britain. This vision was colored to a very great degree by the poet's Scottish experience—the lessons he had learned living there about the problems and potential of a primitive society and its political realities and ideals, lessons which were continually reinforced in their very contrast with his situation in progressive England. In *The Seasons* Thomson expresses, both explicitly and implicitly, his thoughts on Scotland's past, present, and future and on Scotland itself in relation to England, united Britain, and the world; these views are constantly informed by knowledge, nostalgia, and love of his homeland. Thomson was proud of being British; nonetheless, his poetry never lets us forget that he was North British, writing from a persistently Anglo-Scottish sociopolitical perspective.

James Thomson's North British patriotism is inevitably closely linked with the final major theme of his Anglo-Scottish miscellany, *The Seasons* as neoclassical poem. For *The Seasons* is both a native georgic and an apology for the social values and virtues of Roman civilization, both Republican and Imperial. Thomson's patriotic and humanistic goals reinforce one another throughout the poem. Once again, the poetical theme is rooted in the Scottish culture of the poet's youth, in his solid classical education in the Scottish tradition of vernacular humanism as well as in the broader, prevailing Scoto-Roman ethos of his day. Critical awareness of Thomson's debt to classical literature and language—his literary sources in Virgil and other authors and his pervasively Latinate language—is certainly not new; the general subject has been fairly fully explored. However, the peculiarly Scottish character of Thomson's classicism has up until now been neglected. His works ought to be considered in the context of the classical Scottish culture which was their source.

Virgilian qualified progressivism, determined in part by Thomson's being a Scot, informs the poet's sociopolitical ideas, as previously suggested. Classical ideals shaped Thomson's political attitudes in other ways as well. Thomson consciously drew parallels between Britain and ancient Greek and particularly Roman civilizations, and this was certainly not unusual in the British Augustan Age; but his especially intimate identification with Rome first had its source in Scottish culture. Thomson's patriotism for Scotland and for Great Britain was strongly influenced by models of patriotism from the classical world and particularly from Virgilian Rome. In *The Seasons* he makes the Rome-Britain parallel explicit (and again implies the connection between himself and the poet Virgil): "Such themes as these the *rural* MARO sung / To wide-imperial *Rome*" ("Spring," ll. 55–56). Scotland is "Caledonia," the "Hyperborean," northernmost province of the empire of "Britannia" whose center, analogous to the city of Rome, is "Augusta," or London.

Thomson's Roman identification in *The Seasons* is primarily with the Roman Empire; he was proud for Scotland to be a province of the united British Empire. Anti-Union Scots, by contrast, sympathized mainly with the Roman Republic and saw independent Scotland "die" with the Union as the Roman Republic died with Caesar. The poet is pleased to report on the decline of the republic, the "purple Tyranny of *Rome*" under Julius Caesar, and recounts how, "from stooping *Rome*, / And guilty *Caesar*, LIBERTY retir'd" ("Summer," ll. 758, 952–

953). It was only natural that the Whig Thomson, of the party representing freedom and liberty, should side with the opponents of tyrant Julius Caesar and with the enlightened Augustan Age of Rome. Further, the "purple Tyranny" might also allude to Scotland under the Stuarts and the recurring threat of Jacobitism. But Thomson's Roman identification in *The Seasons* is not exclusively with the Roman Empire; there is even at this stage an element of admiration for the social "virtues" of early Republican Rome. The poet had always simultaneously embraced both Republican and Imperial ideals to some extent; this dual allegiance, as it corresponded to Thomson's complex attitudes toward Britain and toward Scotland as its "province," would become more painful later, in *Liberty* and the plays, when his loyalty shifts further toward Republicanism,[38] reflecting renewed Scottish national consciousness and also disillusionment with Augustan England.

In *The Seasons,* in addition to British and Scottish worthies, Thomson also includes a lengthy list of classical heroes and patriots ("Winter," ll. 431–554). This classical roll call first lauds Greek and Roman heroes, many represented in the "long-liv'd Volume" (l. 437), Plutarch's *Lives.* Thomson praises above all their social virtues—social love, disinterested benevolence, and particularly selfless patriotism. He recognized such virtues in heroes of both the Republic and the Empire of Rome. Among the Roman heroes are Cincinnatus and Cato; incidentally, Francis Hutcheson, in his "Inquiry Concerning Moral Good and Evil," also upheld Cato as a model of unselfish patriotism where public triumphs over private good. Thomson's roll of cultural heroes follows, including Virgil ("Fair, mild, and strong, as is a vernal Sun: / 'Tis *Phoebus'* self, or else the *Mantuan Swain!*" ll. 531–532) and Homer and their heirs the "BRITISH MUSE" Milton and Pope. Thomson, as a youth in Scotland steeped in the history and literature of the ancient world, felt close affinity with these "MIGHTY DEAD" whom he so admired.[39]

Two more key passages in *The Seasons* also illustrate classical, chiefly Roman Imperial influence on Thomson's British patriotism: the progressive "BRITANNIA" sequence ("Summer," ll. 1438–1619) and lines on "INDUSTRY" ("Autumn," ll. 43–150).[40] The "BRITANNIA" panegyric is an English georgic modeled on Virgil's praise of Italy in *Georgics* II. It is an enthusiastic and patriotic, if pompous, tribute to Britain's abundant resources and achievements, including its richest resource, "generous Youth" (l. 1467). The overall passage achieves Thomson's goal: to transplant Roman ideals to British soil.[41] This paean is followed by the roll call of exclusively English British worthies from politics, science, philosophy and literature. The passage concludes with an Augustan invocation (ll. 1602–1619) to "O THOU! by whose Almighty *Nod* the Scale / Of Empire rises, or alternate falls," to "Send forth the saving VIRTUES round the Land, / In bright Patrol: white *Peace,* and social Love . . ." Thomson thus links the rise of "Empire" and, implicitly, Britain's imperial aspirations, with both divine Providence and the presence of the social virtues, and anticipates *Liberty* in theme, tone, and benevolistic creed. "Autumn"'s "INDUSTRY" passage, a panegyric to Whig progress, is based on Lucretius, *De Rerum Natura* (V. 925–1457) and reiterates the *Georgics* premise, stiffened by the stern Scottish Calvinist work ethic, that careful husbandry can control and adapt nature and raise the laboring people from a primitive to a progressive civilization. Thomson illustrates this premise with the tale of "Palemon and Lavinia," appropriately set in a conventional classical-pastoral landscape. These two are but the most prominent of countless classical-patriotic references in *The Seasons.* Thomson was first introduced to the classical world as a youth in Scotland, and his emulation of classical concepts of nationalism and patriotism and particularly his identification of post-Union Britain with Rome were motivated to a great extent by the deep-rooted vernacular humanism of eighteenth-century Scottish culture.

Not only were Thomson's sociopolitical and patriotic attitudes shaped by the classics: classicism permeates *The Seasons,* especially in the Virgilian descriptions which make the poem in great part an Anglo-Scottish georgic.[42] Even as a boy Thomson had practiced the georgic mode; his "Of a Country Life" is partly an imitation of Gay's *Rural Sports,* itself modeled on Virgil's *Georgics* II. Young Thomson had in his "Poetical Epistle to Sir William Bennet" clearly identified himself with Virgil, the rural singer of the new Roman Empire; Thomson's and Virgil's northern provincial experiences, though centuries and lands apart, were still similar. Like Virgil, Thomson preferred to meditate on the works of nature in rural solitude; there, both poets studied the complex relationship of man to nature and expressed optimism that man could learn to improve and even to achieve fragile harmony with nature. Both *Georgics* and *Seasons* exemplify literary art controlling nature, chiefly through their realistic natural description. Much as realistic Scottish descriptive details enhanced Gavin Douglas's version of the *Eneados*, Virgilian description lends shape and substance to many of Thomson's descriptions of recollected Scottish scenes in *The Seasons*.

The impact of Virgilian description and detail on *Seasons* scenes is everywhere obvious. "Winter"'s windstorm incorporates many particulars from *Georgics* I; the description depicts the storm itself and the animals' response to it (disturbed seabirds, heifer sniffing the air) with Virgilian realism and sympathy. Virgil's feeling for animals, engaged with man in the struggle to survive nature's violence, appealed to the humanitarian Thomson; again, classicism reinforced his personal experience and instincts. The Scottish Border poet's advice to the husbandman ("Winter," ll. 265–275) also specifically echoes *Georgics* III. Another Scottish "Winter" scene, the death of the swain in the snowstorm, is a variation of Virgil's frozen cattle in *Georgics* III. Thomson's addition of more sensational, extreme seasonal material in "Winter," while partly due to Mallet's influence, was also Virgilian; Virgil, too, had introduced such foreign description to broaden the scope of the *Georgics*. Thomson's "Thrice happy Race" of Laplanders is related to Virgil's "Scythian Nations" (*Georgics* III.349–383), who have similarly adapted to the arctic environment. "Winter" closes with the Virgilian symbol of perpetual "Spring" from *Georgics* II. The other *Seasons*, too, are replete with Virgilian descriptive allusions. "Summer"'s rural hay making and sheep shearing (ll. 352–431) are Thomson's Scottish georgic adaptations of scenes recalled from youth. The "Happy Man" ("Summer," ll. 458–463) and a passage on the same theme in "Autumn" (ll. 1235–1373) echo Virgil's *Georgics* II (458–542). "Spring" is the most thoroughly Virgilian *Season* in theme, form, and language; this *Season*'s ascending love song is modeled largely upon *Georgics* III, and its very goal is the harmony of perpetual spring. Numerous descriptive details in "Spring" derive from Virgil, in scenes such as the plowing, robbed birds' nest, bees, vegetable germination, and birds' concert. "Autumn" scenes with Virgilian detailing and association include the rain and flood (ll. 311ff.), "Wild-fire," ruined bee-hive, meteors, vineyard, and hunt.

Other classical authors, to a lesser extent than Virgil, also influenced *The Seasons*' descriptions, among them Lucretius, Ovid, Juvenal, and Pliny. The multitude of classical allusions in Thomson have been carefully documented. Thomson adapted descriptive details and conventions from this classical literature he knew so well and learned to appreciate in Scotland deliberately to enhance his own first-hand—and frequently Scottish—observations. In doing so, he chose to work in a distinctive Latinate English poetic language deriving directly from his Scottish humanistic education. In the next chapter, the significance of Latin as one of Scotland's cultural languages and of Latinate English as a natural idiom for Thomson to choose for his poetry will be considered more closely. The happy result in *The Seasons* was the creation of a convincing Scottish Augustan poem of nature and society.

The Seasons, then, is many kinds of poem. It is a preaching and a teaching poem, a religious poem employing natural description, in the Scottish tradition and based on Border experience, unprecedented in English poetry in both quantity and quality. It is a personal poem and a public one. It is a moral and a meditative poem, a philosophical, patriotic, and party-political poem. It is both neoclassical and new. A survey of *The Seasons* according to its several generic aspects—descriptive, religious-didactic and philosophical, sociopolitical, and neoclassical—cannot begin to convey the complexity of Thomson's vision. Each of these aspects of the poetical miscellany cannot, in the final analysis, be treated separately without some loss of a sense of the poem's rich texture. Thomson's integration of these diverse themes was usually successful, sometimes not, giving rise to the critical question of the unity of the poem which has never been satisfactorily resolved. But while the miscellaneous mode was hardly original to Thomson, he took contemporary aesthetic values of "unity-in-variety," "beauty-in-diversity" set forth by Hutcheson and Turnbull, among others, to new heights in poetry. The most important point about these "various" themes is that each one is in some significant sense

Scottish; *The Seasons* must be reckoned with as a Scottish poem. James Thomson's abundant dynamic and realistic natural description, informed as it was by the religious, philosophical, social, political, and humanistic influences of his homeland, was the poet's particularly Scottish contribution to the poetry of Great Britain.

7 THE LANGUAGE
OF *THE SEASONS*

---ʊʊʊ---

The Seasons, inspired as it was by such amazing diversity of purpose and plan, demanded stylistic and linguistic versatility far beyond the conventions of formal Augustan poetic English. Thomson recognized this as soon as he began to write "Winter." As a Scots speaker, he also recognized the limits of his own language, yet, remarkably, he found the will to turn these formidable linguistic limitations into positive strengths and the distinctive language of *The Seasons* began to evolve.

Thomson had to find the appropriate verse form for his poem and, fortunately, for many good reasons, he chose to work in blank verse. Further, he had to create a more flexible, readily adaptable literary language for his eclectic poem, a poetic diction which would draw not only upon his familiarity with Latin, his Calvinist religion, and his knowledge of Newtonian science (all idioms of his Scottish background) but also, in more subtle ways, upon his vernacular Scots literary and linguistic heritage. Thomson's highly original language for *The Seasons* is eclectic, empirical, experimental, in the spirit of the Scottish Enlightenment. It speaks with an accent that is unmistakably Scottish.

James Thomson was a native Scots speaker, so his relative unfamiliarity with spoken English when he began *The Seasons* probably had much to do with his choice of the less-restrictive blank-verse form, which was not so heavily dependent on any standardized pronunciation as rhymed verse. Many of his contemporary Anglo-Scots such as Mallet, Armstrong, and Blair were also experimenting with blank verse. Thomson would grow more confident with rhyme later in his career after having lived in London for many years; his *Castle of Indolence* uses an intricate Spenserian verse form. When he chose blank verse for *The Seasons* he certainly had his model Milton in mind; Shaftesbury had praised Milton for casting off "the horrid Discord of jingling Rhyme" and had linked his aesthetic taste to political attitude. Milton's taste for blank verse represented liberation from neoclassical strictures and has been associated with the Whig cause of liberty which Thomson championed.[1] Thomson's assertion of "freedom" in using blank verse may thus have been, to some extent, a matter of political principle, both Whig and Scottish, as well as a practical solution to his own language limitations. Thomson's blank verse is by no means simply an imitation of Milton's or anyone else's; Dr. Johnson acknowledged its originality: "His [Thomson's] blank verse is no more the blank verse of Milton or of any other poet than the rhymes of Prior are the rhymes of Cowley . . ." Johnson also appreciated the appropriateness of Thomson's less restrictive, more open blank-verse form for *The Seasons,* allowing the greater syntactical flexibility the poet required and perfectly suited to the continuous actions and processes of nature he portrays. It is simply the most natural form for his poetry of nature.[2]

Along with his versatile blank-verse form, Thomson's poetic diction for *The Seasons* grew from his compulsion to portray in language the complex and transforming patterns of nature.[3] Formal rules of Augustan English were simply not adequate to this task, as even the juvenilia had hinted; Thomson's poetic language in *The Seasons* is no more purely Augustan English than is the variety of themes and modes he employs in the poem. It is an eclectic yet decorous literary language, organically linked to the diverse *Seasons* genres and themes themselves: neoclassical-georgic, Scottish-descriptive, religious-philosophical and homiletic, and scientific. Thomson, for whom literary English was virtually a foreign language at first, certainly found formal English an uncomfortably restrictive vehicle for his miscellaneous descriptive poem and had thus to experiment with language to create a new poetic diction for his new sort of poetry. His incentive to develop a more versatile diction perhaps had its source in his Scottish naiveté about formal English usage, but ultimately his very Scottish freedom from English aesthetic and linguistic limits, motivated by his strong empirical impulse,[4] came to produce an apt and unique poetic language. More immediately, Thomson's background as a Scots speaker actually influenced the words he chose and the sound patterns he composed. His language potential was not merely bilingual (Latin, English) but trilingual (Scots); in seeking accuracy and comprehensiveness, he succeeded in expanding English poetic diction through Latinate neo-aureation (much as his forebear Gavin Douglas had done), through exploitation of biblical and homiletic elements and scientific terms, and, most significantly, through use of Scots and northern vocabulary.

That Thomson's linguistic originality, his experimental poetic diction, was somehow especially Scottish was recognized even in his own day. English poet William Somerville, who disapproved, admonished Thomson:

> Read Philips much, consider Milton more;
> But from their dross extract the purer ore.
> To coin new words, or to restore the old,
> In southern bards is dangerous and bold;
> But rarely, very rarely, will succeed,
> When minted on the other side of Tweed.
> Let perspicuity o'er all preside—
> Soon shalt thou be the nation's joy and pride.
> ("Epistle to Mr. Thomson, on the first edition
> of his Seasons," ll. 29–36)

Fortunately, Thomson ignored Somerville's advice, continued to follow his Scottish instincts in the matter of language, and proved himself that rare Anglo-Scottish success. His poetic language followed no ready-made poetic formula, Augustan or otherwise, and while he indeed borrowed from Milton, Philips, and many others, his poetic language could never simply be called derivative. Rather, it grew naturally from his miscellaneous subject matter and sources, as in an important sense the poet applied the empirical scientific method to the synthesis of his own literary language, observing, experimenting with, and discovering the dynamic means to convey the world-in-process and man's relationship to it. In so doing, the poet also exemplified the changing aesthetic principles of his time which encouraged more varied and original, as well as more realistic, descriptive diction and imagery. Thomson's friend George Turnbull was one Scottish contemporary who took a theoretical interest in these new aesthetics of description which Thomson so "boldly" put into poetry and later Scottish Enlightenment rhetoricians would refine.[5]

One element of Thomson's linguistic experimentation was his enthusiastic coinage of new words. Most notable are his compound epithets, condensing and intensifying description. These compounds were mostly used as adjectives, joining verb with participle; for example, "gay-shifting" ("Spring," l. 191); "mute-imploring" ("Spring," l. 163); "prone-descending" ("Summer," l. 1145). He occasionally joined two nouns together, suggesting the archaic, periphrastic "kenning" (for example, "Summer-Ray," "Hymn," l. 95, with its compact connotative force; or "Forest-Walks," "Spring," l. 178). He also tried unusual "unpoetic" or colloquial words, even alongside of Latin or formal English ones, if they could convey more precisely what he intended to describe. He freely exchanged parts of speech when expedient: participles function as nouns ("Bleatings," "Spring," l. 200); intransitive verbs become transitive ("*looking* lively Gratitude," "Spring," l. 172, italics mine); and adjectives are often used with adverbial force (for example, "Man *superior* walks," "Spring," l. 170; "Earth / Is *deep* enrich'd," "Spring," l. 188; "Radiance *instantaneous* strikes," "Spring," l. 192; "Sun / Looks out, *effulgent*," "Spring," l. 190; "Shower is *scarce* to patter heard," "Spring," l. 177, italics mine). These unusual "quasi-adverbs" (as the *OED* labels them) set up a certain ambiguity as to whether they modify their nouns or whether they are simply contracted adverbs and thus refer to the verbs. In fact, while grammatically they are inverted adjectives, they also add a new dimension to the description through the tension they create, adding to the interpretation of the verb as well and drawing noun and verb into closer, active relationship. "Man superior walks," for instance, indicates that man is superior to the rest of earthly Creation and also describes his proud manner of walking and his active role as the world's overseer. "Shower is scarce to patter heard" suggests both the sparse quantity and the gentle, quiet aural quality of the falling rain. Thomson's deletion of the adverbial suffix -*ly* in many quasi-adverbs also calls to mind the typical Middle Scots contraction of certain adjectives, such as "contrair," "extraordinair," "necessair," which were likewise transposed, placed after their nouns; such variations of orthography and syntax in Thomson's poetic language give it further archaic, and Scots, flavor.

Another characteristic of Thomson's empirical adaptation of language is his use of abundant verbs and verb forms, particularly participles; he is fascinated with verbals and experiments freely with them, the better to describe in terms of action and transformation. He shares such descriptive energy with the ballads and also with the Middle Scots Makars. Thomson's Scottish trilingual heritage generally allowed for a greater flexibility of usage and syntax—since Scots and Latin syntaxes both differ from standard English—than his English contemporaries dared to attempt in poetry. Such traits as these represent what some critics have censured as "vague," indecorous, or incorrect characteristics of Thomson's diction; they should instead be recognized as examples of the subtlety, complexity, and native originality of the Scottish poet's descriptive language as he portrays the natural world-in-process.

Inevitably, in treating of a poem of *The Seasons'* length and complexity, it is inadequate to dissect the language into different categories, corresponding to its various thematic sources, just as it was inadequate to try to separate the poem's several interwoven themes. Still, certain major linguistic influences clearly predominate in *The Seasons,* each directly reflecting some aspect of James Thomson's Scottish cultural background.[6]

The most often remarked—and reproved—characteristic of Thomson's language in *The Seasons* is its pervasive Latinity. While this quality has been studied in some detail, there has been scant attention paid to its roots in the poet's Scottish culture and education. In formal Augustan English poetry, Latinisms are, of course, standard, but in invoking the Scoto-Roman ideal he so revered and directly drawing upon its classical vocabulary, Thomson added a further, Scottish dimension to the neoclassical linguistic convention of the age. Passages illustrating Thomson's Latinity abound in *The Seasons;* one such is the "Spring" shower (ll. 161–202), where many of the examples cited here occur. Much of Thomson's Latinate diction derives from Virgil, particularly in the more descriptive scenes adapted from the *Georgics;* some passages are virtually paraphrases of Virgil, while others blend Latinate with other types of language. Thomson adapted Virgilian rhetorical devices, notably periphrasis, to achieve control and precision of descriptive language. Despauter's textbook defines periphrasis as an indirect, circumlocutory way of saying something in few but meaningful words; it is based in logic and is one means of classifying or placing an element of a complicated scene into perspective. Thomson typically used the device to highlight a particular group, without describing its members individually, within the larger landscape; examples from "Spring" are "plumy People" (birds, l. 165), "umbrageous Multitude of Leaves" (l. 179), and "milky Nutriment" (lifegiving sap, l. 184).[7]

Use of strongly Latinate English was also a Miltonic trait;[8] Thomson's Latinate language in *The Seasons*, however, surpasses even Milton's in density. Most significant is Thomson's frequent use of words in their original Latin sense to achieve precision; he seems at times actually to "think" in Latin, choosing words directly from that familiar language which had not yet been filtered through literary English. Examples are "Indulge" ("Spring," l. 187) in the original sense of "yield, give up," and "Gems" ("Spring," l. 196) in the sense of "buds" as well as colorful jewels. Another instance is the revealing word "Cogenial" ("Winter," l. 6), as the poet hails the season's "Cogenial Horrors." Where one would have expected the poet to choose the standard Latinate-English "congenial," his unusual Latin "Cogenial" implies a more intimate, one-to-one relationship between himself and the well-known Scottish season; the distinction, though fine, is real. Interestingly, "cogenial" also occurs in the poems of two of Thomson's Anglo-Scottish contemporaries in the *Edinburgh Miscellany*, although the *OED* does not note its use until later in the eighteenth century.[9]

Latin had long been Scotland's second language, her formal diplomatic language; Latin had directly influenced Middle Scots, and while Scots had suffered a loss in status by the eighteenth century, Latin maintained its close kinship with Scottish literature as the ideal literary language. English as a literary medium ran a poor third until that time. After his native Scots, then, Latin was Thomson's second language at school and at university; he was less familiar even with colloquial English than he was with Latin. His classical education and cultural bias disposed him to choose words with a Latin root over Southern English words in seeking both descriptive accuracy and rich connotation.[10] Thomson's Latinate language in *The Seasons* has occasioned problems for those of a different linguistic background than his own; numerous critics from his own day to the present have insensitively charged him with obscurity and pomposity due to the strong Latinate cast of his language. But Thomson's aureation was far from a pretentious attempt merely to elevate the formal tone of the poetry; the poet drew upon Latin consciously to strengthen the expressive, descriptive power and precision of literary English. He actually added to the stock of poetical diction in English in a process eminently comparable to Gavin Douglas's enrichment of literary Middle Scots. Far from being forced or stilted, Thomson's Latinate diction came naturally and easily to him as a Lowland Scot and usually succeeded in conveying exactly what he intended. So persistent has been the classical bias in Scottish schooling that the educated Scotsman even today would have little problem with Thomson's Latinate diction.[11] The poet's Latinate linguistic facility contributes enormously to the economy and accuracy of his descriptions and constantly manifests, especially to the classically tuned reader, Thomson's Scottish humanistic heritage.

Thomson's rhetorical faults, like his strengths, are very much rooted in his Scottish formal education. These faults include his occasional tendency toward verbosity and his predilection for the grandiose rhetorical flourish or convoluted construction. Such lapses, where the sonorous effects of the words themselves obscure and overpower their sense and proportion, usually occurred in his more public and Augustan voice, where abstract ideas and bombastic pronouncements left little room for natural description. The art and science of rhetoric had become something of a Scottish preoccupation by the eighteenth century and would come into its own as a Scottish Enlightenment achievement. Professor William Hamilton's candid criticism of his pupil Thomson's florid Psalm exercise was probably fairly typical in Scotland, where students tended toward a highly wrought rhetorical style[12] and where rigorous rhetorical training, along with the strong classical emphasis in general, persisted far longer than in England. In writing descriptive poetry, Thomson was working in the classical rhetorical mode of imitation—"setting forth the nature of a 'thing' in words"— with new, more realistic focus on those "things" themselves. He was seeking to describe as fully and accurately as he could, but his rhetorical discipline was liable to fail him when he left the concrete basis of *descriptio,* or when in his enthusiasm for comprehensive expression he simply said too much and lost perspective.[13] Nonetheless, Thomson's training in rhetoric was most often an advantage in helping him to integrate and "improve" such diverse subjects and styles as his ambitious *Seasons* encompasses.

Thomson's upbringing as a son of the manse and divinity student, like his education in the humanities and classical rhetoric, had considerable impact on his poetic style. Language derived from Christian Neoplatonic philosophy and physicotheology and from the religious poetry of Milton is abundantly present in *The Seasons;* more directly, the very language of the Scriptures is there, along with the forceful rhetoric of the old-style Presbyterian pulpit. These influences were important even in the juvenilia. *The Seasons'* motivation being primarily a religious one, both devotional and didactic functions operate in the poem; the persuasive power of classical rhetoric is reinforced by the rhetoric of the Bible and the sermon. Both the rigorous homiletic tone and the "mystical" enthusiastic tone, demonstrating two sides of Thomson's deep-seated Scottish Calvinist emotional response, resound throughout *The Seasons*. Scriptural allusions in the poem are almost all from the Old Testament with few exceptions; most echo Job, Genesis, Ruth, Ecclesiastes, and the Psalms. Several passages in the poem show direct influence of the Psalms, such as the "Hymn on the Seasons" (ll. 37–99), closely based on Psalm 148 in language and structure as well as theme; it is typical of several such enthusiastic, exuberant "praising" passages in the poem. Like other "religious" passages in *The*

Seasons, the "Hymn" illustrates subtle linguistic blending, and Latin-isms abound. Alliteration is strong, enhancing imitative sound effects and forward, intensifying movement; typically, verbs and verbals are plentiful and well chosen. Natural description is inherent in the re-ligious and rhetorical purpose of this Psalm paraphrase, which shows Thomson in his happiest mode, portraying God's Creation in joyous process.

Even more significant is the influence of the traditional Scottish ser-mon, with its negative rhetoric of fear and trepidation. Thomson's stern religious-didactic "preaching" voice is heard in both manner and message of such passages as "Summer" (ll. 318–351) on "CRE-ATIVE WISDOM" and the vanity of those who disregard it ("LET no presuming impious Railer tax / CREATIVE WISDOM"). The passage concludes with a powerful parable, typical of the highly literal and concrete, image-laden Scottish sermon style:

> THICK in yon Stream of Light, a thousand Ways,
> Upward, and downward, thwarting, and convolv'd,
> The quivering Nations sport; till, Tempest-wing'd,
> Fierce Winter sweeps them from the Face of Day.
> Even so luxurious Men, unheeding, pass
> An idle Summer-Life in Fortune's Shine,
> A Season's Glitter! Thus they flutter on
> From Toy to Toy, from Vanity to Vice;
> Till, blown away by Death, Oblivion comes
> Behind, and strikes them from the Book of Life.
> ("Summer," ll. 342–351)

Here Thomson blends Latinate language ("convolv'd," "luxurious," periphrastic "quivering Nations") and his own brand of concise de-scriptive epithet ("Tempest-wing'd") with increasingly intense homi-letic language. Visual metaphors of men "fluttering" like insects in a realm of "Shine" and "Glitter," from "Toy to Toy," then "blown away" and struck from the "Book of Life" work more through cumulative force than descriptive precision: the comparison between vulnerable insects and men carries great emotional impact. The adverbial "Even so" falls heavy with didactic emphasis, clarifying the analogy and im-itating the sudden, frightening force of death's ("Fierce Winter"'s) final blow; the conventional seasonal symbol of death as winter is apt and contrasts pointedly with the summer context of the parable. Parallelism, alliteration, and repetition ("from the Face of Day," "from Toy to Toy," "from Vanity to Vice," "from the Book of Life") reinforce the message of vain man's inexorable march to death and ultimate spiritual exile ("from") into "Oblivion."

Another notable instance of homiletic rhetoric, Thomson's conclusion to "Winter" (ll. 1028–1069), has justly been compared with Blair's *Grave:*[14]

> . . . Behold, fond Man!
> See here thy pictur'd Life; pass some few Years,
> Thy flowering Spring, thy Summer's ardent Strength,
> Thy sober Autumn fading into Age,
> And pale concluding Winter comes at last,
> And shuts the Scene. Ah! whither now are fled,
> Those Dreams of Greatness? those unsolid Hopes
> Of Happiness? those Longings after Fame?
> Those restless Cares? those busy bustling Days?
> Those gay-spent, festive Nights? those veering Thoughts,
> Lost between Good and Ill, that shar'd thy Life?
> All now are vanish'd! VIRTUE sole survives . . .
>
>   . . .
>
> Ye vainly wise! ye blind Presumptuous! now,
> Confounded in the Dust, adore that POWER,
> And WISDOM oft arraign'd: see now the Cause,
> Why unassuming Worth in secret liv'd,
> And dy'd, neglected: why the good Man's Share
> In Life was Gall and Bitterness of Soul:
> Why the lone Widow, and her Orphans pin'd,
> In starving Solitude; while Luxury,
> In Palaces, lay straining her low Thought,
> To form unreal Wants: why Heaven-born Truth,
> And Moderation fair, wore the red Marks
> Of Superstition's Scourge: why licens'd Pain,
> That cruel Spoiler, that embosom'd Foe,
> Imbitter'd all our Bliss. Ye good Distrest!

> Ye noble Few! who here unbending stand
> Beneath Life's Pressure, yet bear up a While,
> And what your bounded View, which only saw
> A little Part, deem'd *Evil* is no more:
> The Storms of WINTRY TIME will quickly pass,
> And one unbounded SPRING encircle All.

Thomson's address powerfully preaches the hard lesson of *The Grave* and ultimately of Job, the message of mortality and vain earthly life (compare "Winter," ll. 322–353 on the same theme). Like Blair, Thomson holds out hope to the faithful of the afterlife, but not without grimly making it plain that life on earth is brief and difficult and death inevitable. The poet employs vivid imagery to visualize his moral message, such as the conventional metaphor comparing life with the passing of the seasons (captured in few yet accurately chosen adjectives, "flowering," "ardent," "fading," "pale") and the sentimental portraits of the Joblike "good Man" and the "lone Widow" (recalling Blair), calculated to excite sympathy. Thomson's liberal use of exclamations in direct address, typical of sermon rhetoric, is also characteristic of *The Grave*. The series of parallel, insistent questions ("Ah! whither now are fled . . .?") is another striking rhetorical device; the reply is blunt, devastating: "All now are vanish'd" (l. 1039). Three unstressed syllables imitating the rhythm of a knell, followed by the accented exclamation "van' ish'd," emphasize the finality of death. This passage in its entirety moves persuasively between severe Calvinistic harangue and Augustan optimism, concrete and abstract, concluding in resolute encouragement for the faithful as the poet draws "Winter" itself to a close with fitting seasonal symbolism.

Along with these religious and classical influences on his language, Thomson also employs the language of science, more sparingly but to good effect, in *The Seasons*. While this general topic has been the subject of study elsewhere, it is important to recall that Thomson's scientific vocabulary was to a great extent based on Newtonian concepts acquired at Edinburgh University and also later in London; such diction contributes to the didactic function of the poem as well as its description. One example is the "rainbow" passage in "Spring" (ll.

203–217), where Thomson pays explicit tribute to Newton and uses such technical terms as "refracted" and "Prism," adding realism and demonstrating his own "sage-instructed Eye," his knowledge of the laws of nature first learned in Scotland. He simultaneously portrays the swain's wonder at the beautiful phenomenon, a delight he himself never lost, lending his description double the impact.

Classical, religious, and scientific influences on Thomson's diction, while Scottish in that they were the languages of the various disciplines to which he was educated in the Borders and Edinburgh, still cannot fully account for the extraordinary immediacy and vigor of the descriptions in *The Seasons*. Thomson required a still broader, more versatile and expressive literary language, and he set out to forge it. The poet's successful and original use of language in *The Seasons* comes in large measure from his background as a Scots speaker. He retained a Scots accent and Scots expressions all his life[15] and certainly knew Scots literature and oral tradition. While this is not to say that Scotticisms and northern archaisms abound in *The Seasons,* some are there, and clearly Thomson's choice of descriptive diction owes a very great deal to his Scots habit of mind.

Perhaps the most striking stylistic quality about Thomson's poetic language coming from his Scots-speaking background is his close attention to sound effects. The poet himself, in a passage in "Summer" (ll. 1752–1757), placed "Music" before "Image," "Sentiment," and "Thought" in listing the chief characteristics of poetry, and his own "Music" sounds a pleasingly native note. Thomson's choice of descriptive language very often reflects those traits of written and spoken Scots which contribute to its acknowledged expressive power, such as abundant alliteration, which he uses especially strongly in passages describing action and process in nature, as well as assonance and consonance. He also shows a general tendency to choose onomatopoeic and imitative words, or more broadly words whose sounds enhance their meanings; Scots vocabulary itself claims a large proportion of imitative words whose very sounds evoke their sense. Such skillful use of "extended onomatopoeia" and imitative sound patterns was evident even in the juvenile poems; the poet's preoccupation with intricate and subtle sound effects can be compared in some points to Scot-

tish Gaelic poetic modes which had, in turn, influenced the Lowland
Scots literature and language he knew. Thomson was extraordinarily
sensitive to the emotional connotations or suggestive values of certain
sounds and wove in *The Seasons* delicate designs of "sound-sym-
bolism"; his sound effects are not merely decorative but organic and
help to convey his intellectual, emotional, and especially sensuous
meanings in descriptive poetry.[16]

Beyond indirect, aural influence on Thomson's use of sound effects, Scots language was a more immediate influence on his diction,
as the poet employed a number of actual Scots or northern words and
derivatives in *The Seasons*. Further, his Scots linguistic background
predisposed him to choose certain English words with close similarity
of sound and sense to Scots words and carrying their richer connotative value. Thomson's deliberate use of Scots vocabulary is perhaps the most relevant and convincing illustration in *The Seasons* of
the poet's general, instinctive "etymological" curiosity, his informed
interest in the origin and history of the meanings of words themselves. This sensitivity to the sources of language had also compelled
him to choose Latin words in their original sense and would later
influence his significant use of archaic language in *The Castle*.[17] In *The
Seasons*, Scottish linguistic influences are seen most clearly in the language of passages of most pure, energetic, and immediate natural
description, often derived from first-hand Scottish experience, where
the rare quality of race or native vitality which Dr. Johnson had
praised is its strongest. Some brief passages will illustrate that race
which is the happy result of Thomson's Scottish linguistic background.

This passage from "Autumn," demonstrating Thomson's sympathy
with animals and elaborating on a similar scene in "Of a Country
Life," describes the hunted hare's futile search for refuge from her
predators:

> Poor is the Triumph o'er the timid Hare!
> Scar'd from the Corn, and now to some lone Seat
> Retir'd: the rushy Fen; the ragged Furze,
> Stretch'd o'er the stony Heath; the Stubble chapt;

The thistly Lawn; the thick entangled Broom;
Of the same friendly Hue, the wither'd Fern;
The fallow Ground laid open to the Sun,
Concoctive; and the nodding sandy Bank,
Hung o'er the Mazes of the Mountain-Brook.
("Autumn," ll. 401–409)

Thick alliteration reinforces natural description here in Thomson's characteristic sound-sense patterning: "rushy Fen . . . ragged Furze," "friendly Hue . . . Fern . . . fallow" (Scots rolled *r* and fricative *f* alliteration imitate the rustling sounds of the hare's swift movement through the varied landscape); "Stretch'd . . . stony . . . Stubble," "thistly Lawn . . . thick" (repetition of *st* and *th* phonemes suggests friction as the hare forces its way through obstructions in the rugged terrain); "Mazes of the Mountain-Brook" (softer *m* mimics slow, gentle winding and murmur of the stream). In general, imitative alliteration facilitates the sense of rapid yet cautious forward movement of the hare's search for shelter. Thomson's individual word choices also typically enhance extended onomatopoeia ("Stubble," "ragged," "chapt," "thistly," "entangled") as their sounds contribute to the sense of difficult passage (abruptness suggested by double consonants *bb*, *gg*, *pp*; "thistly"'s fricative; multisyllabic "entangled"). Thomson further follows the practice, common in older Scottish poetry, of listing the elements of the varied landscape while simultaneously describing them with apt adjectives and effective alliteration; this concise cataloging, quickly shifting descriptive focus from point to point, also imitates the hare's frantic movements. The setting is probably Scottish: hints are "thistly" (the thistle is the Scottish national flower, though not exclusive to Scotland) and the Scotticism "chapt" ("having been dealt a blow, cut down—a variation of 'chopped,'" *Dictionary of the Older Scottish Tongue*). "O'er," which occurs frequently in the poem, is of course conventional poetical diction but also reflects current Scottish pronunciation of "over," according to James Beattie.[18] The Latinism "Concoctive" stands out amid more colloquial descriptive language: "Sun / Concoctive" is one of Thomson's "quasi-adverbs" and conveys the sun's mysterious power as well as the complex process of natural chemistry happening within the "fallow Ground." While the descriptive power of this passage has survived revision, there was perhaps some loss of race in the poet's reworking; the phrase "Scar'd from the Corn," which had been "Shook from the Corn" (1730–1738), is one example where Thomson substituted a bland word for a more "racy," imitative one.[19] Still, the revised passage remains a concise and vivid recreation of the hare's desperate search for camouflage in a rough landscape; typically, descriptive emphasis is on action and movement, with unusual yet well-chosen verb forms and modifiers and subtle sound effects.

The following passage, describing a Scottish Border scene of a river in spate, has been compared to Burns's description in "Brigs of Ayr." It likewise illustrates Thomson's skill at dynamic natural description:

> WIDE o'er the Brim, with many a Torrent swell'd,
> And the mix'd Ruin of its Banks o'erspread,
> At last the rous'd-up River pours along:
> Resistless, roaring, dreadful, down it comes,
> From the rude Mountain, and the mossy Wild,
> Tumbling thro' Rocks abrupt, and sounding far;
> Then o'er the sanded Valley floating spreads,
> Calm, sluggish, silent; till again constrain'd,
> Between two meeting Hills it bursts a Way,
> Where Rocks and Woods o'erhang the turbid Stream;
> There gathering triple Force, rapid, and deep,
> It boils, and wheels, and foams, and thunders' thro'.
> ("Winter," ll. 94–105)

This scene was original to "Winter" (1726, ll. 133–142). The Scots adjective "chapt" appeared here in early versions (1726–1738) describing the bare, rugged mountain; it was altered with "loss of race" to "rude" (l. 98) in 1744. Otherwise, the passage seems to have lost little race in revision and even to have gained in descriptive impact. The passage opens with a quasi-adverb "WIDE," describing both the river itself and its spreading action (i.e., widely). Thomson retained the most effective alliterative line, "Resistless, roaring, dreadful, down it comes," with its strong caesuras and suggestion of the northern alliterative line. To this he prefixed "At last the rous'd-up River pours along": the added *r* alliteration enhances the sense of the river's motion and sound. The *d* alliteration, with its negative sound associations,[20] suggests falling, colliding heavily, as does the *u* assonance of the phrase "Tumbling thro' Rocks abrupt." Even the rhythm of the phrase adds to its descriptive force, as the explosive, forward-moving participle "Tumbling," perhaps given the Scots pronunciation "tummling," contrasts with the contracted "abrupt," transposed to come at the end of the line, imitating the water's sudden impact with rocks. Thomson's characteristic coupling of participle with quasi-adverb ("abrupt") concisely conveys the river's action in addition to the position of the rocks themselves; "abrupt" is probably used in both the geological sense of "suddenly cropping out" (*OED*) and the original Latin sense of "breaking," that is, interrupting the river's flow. This is yet another example of Thomson's acute etymological awareness. As the river slows ("Then o'er the sanded Valley floating spreads, / Calm, sluggish, silent") sibilant *s* alliteration predominates, suggesting smoother, gentler motion and quietening; imitative words ("sluggish") also lend realism. The river regains momentum, having been "constrained" between two hills; the weighty Latinism "constrained" creates a concise image of the compacted, forceful water. Then the released river "boils, and wheels, and foams, and thunders' thro'"; this line repeats, with slight variation, the energetic caesura pattern of line 97. Thomson also catalogs the river's various actions here in verbs whose sounds reinforce their descriptive sense. Again, the poet has proven his consummate skill at describing, with a strong sense of dramatic pacing, the dynamic events of nature.

Not all of Thomson's revisions of *The Seasons* were so successful as this. Serious loss of race did result from revisions, as Dr. Johnson recognized, particularly with removal of some of the poet's more flavorful Scottish diction. Thomson's substitution of predictable, conventional words or lines for stronger, more unusual, or accurate ones was probably in deference to English taste[21] and also to avoid the possible embarrassment of Scotticisms. It was primarily, though, a result of Thomson's attempt to describe the world in process most completely and clearly, if sometimes with a little less liveliness, to a wide-ranging and largely English audience. Some of Thomson's revisions grew too verbose, and not only the original diction but also the striking sound effects became submerged. Examples are "Winter"'s "frost" sequence (ll. 695ff.) and "sea-storm" (ll. 157–175), where the vivid descriptive core is nearly swamped in excess verbiage. Further, Thomson's large-scale revisions such as his addition of geographical and sociopolitical material (especially in 1744) were not always well integrated and sometimes detracted from the poem's descriptive aims. The weight of added second-hand material and abstract comment tended to slow the flow of natural process of each *Season* and to some extent distorted the shape of the entire poem.[22] Still, the fundamental pattern of transforming natural imagery remains discernible even in the final (1746) version. Most of Thomson's small-scale revisions did no great harm and some even improved upon the original description as the poet continued to discover his own poetic voice.

Luckily, even Thomson's many careful revisions of *The Seasons* did not expunge all Scotticisms or northern archaisms. His occasional "roughness of the bothie" in diction indeed proved a very positive feature of his descriptive language. Several different types of Scotticisms or Scots analogues add race to the poem. First, there are the many words which James Beattie listed as archaic or merely "poetical" in eighteenth-century England but which were still a part of everyday speech in Scotland, including such words found in *The Seasons* as "warble," "swain," and "yon." Beattie also listed poetical words derived from Latin and Greek which occur in the poem, having come readily to the classically trained Thomson.[23] Second, a number of other words which were not strictly Scotticisms and did occur in standard English but which the poet was probably disposed to choose because of their peculiarly Scots associations of sound and sense are important in *The Seasons*. Thomson must have known, even if subconsciously, that such words could convey a richer double meaning, where Scots connotations enhanced standard English denotations. Third, and most significant, are the distinctively Scottish and northern usages themselves, some removed in revision, others allowed to remain. Not surprisingly, most of these come in "Autumn" and "Winter," Thomson's more Scottish *Seasons;* also, most are found in passages of more detailed, realistic natural description. These Scotticisms which stand out amid Thomson's English poetic diction are among his most effective and original means of describing the natural world in new ways.

J. Logie Robertson usefully pointed out many Scottish usages in his Oxford Standard Authors edition of *The Seasons* (*Works*, 1908, 1971), and especially in his important *The Seasons and The Castle of Indolence* edition of 1891. Robertson notes that "rais'd" ("Autumn," l. 702, "Round the rais'd Nations pours the Cup of Joy") is "Probably a Scotticism for 'excited by wine'" or "invigorated." He also points out that "Baffle" ("Winter," l. 266, "Now, Shepherds, to your helpless Charge be kind, / Baffle the raging Year"; and "Autumn," l. 716, "from the baffled Sense, / Sinks dark and dreary") is related to the modern Scots "baugh," meaning "dull" or with the edge worn off. "Baffle" is, however, even closer to the Scots "bauf" or "baff" ("to beat or strike," *Scottish National Dictionary*); in "Winter" it comes from Scots usage, meaning in particular "to struggle with" and especially referring to battling an illness or to animals who are "suffering uneasily" (*SND;* here, suffering from the harsh winter weather). "Baugh" is also a Scots curling term describing "dull" ice (*SND*) and the antonym of "keen," one of the poet's favorite descriptive words. He frequently uses "keen" as a standard adjective ("sharp") and occasionally in a more unusual, archaic sense as a verb ("Summer," l. 1259, meaning "ices over"; also in *The Castle*, Canto II, St. i, for "to sharpen," as well as quasi-adverbially in "Winter," 1726, replaced by "ice," meaning "to blow ice," 1730ff., l. 426). Robertson also cites "whelms" ("Winter," l. 273, "o'er the hapless Flocks . . . The billowy Tempest whelms") as a Scotticism beyond its connection with "o'er" (as in "o'erwhelms"); he relates it to the Scots "whummles" (or "whemmles," *SND*), meaning to "overturn or capsize." He also points out that "Cheek" ("Winter," l. 709, "A stronger Glow sits on the lively Cheek / Of ruddy Fire") is probably related to the Scots usage of "cheek" meaning the hearth, or side of the fireplace. The onomatopoeic participial adjective "bickering" ("Winter," l. 725, "Arrests the bickering Stream") is thought by Robertson to have come from the Celtic, meaning "skirmishing"; both he and Morel refer to Professor Walter Skeat for this note. "Bicker" is also found in *The Castle*, Canto I, St. iii. In Scottish and Northern English dialects, "bicker" also means to move noisily and quickly (*SND*). As a noun, "bicker" is defined as a "short, rapid run" as well as an encounter with missiles or rocks in Scots and northern usage (*OED*). So by subtly combining the various English and Scots definitions and connotations of "bicker," Thomson succeeded in suggesting both sound and movement of the "bickering Stream" and added a new dimension to the descriptive value of the term. Robertson finally notes that Thomson's use of "Friends" ("Winter," l. 310) might be in the Scottish sense of "relatives," as Beattie in *Scoticisms* defines it.[24]

These Scotticisms discovered by editor Robertson are by no means the only Scottish usages in *The Seasons*. "Ken" ("Summer," l. 178, "Angel's purer Ken") is of course an archaic English poetical word as well as a Scotticism, but Beattie in *Scoticisms* warns of "ken" as a word to be avoided as it might betray one's Scottish origins. "Ken" may first have come to Thomson's mind in the Scots sense of "knowledge" (*OED*); he probably felt that its poetical use, meaning "vision" or "view," was acceptable and therefore retained it in *The Seasons*. The adjective "tedded" ("Summer," l. 361, "Wide flies the tedded Grain") is usually defined as "spread out to dry," but an unusual, particularly Scottish usage seems to have meant "scattered," as Thomson used it in this context (*OED* finds "ted" with its unusual meaning of "to scatter" in Alexander Scott's *Poems*; *SND* calls its use in the *Edinburgh Evening Courant*, 1787, for "scattered" an "erroneous" usage). The imitative verb "flounce" ("Winter," l. 285; "Spring," l. 824; and again *The Castle*, Canto II, St. xliii) is probably related to the Scots "flounge" ("to plunge wildly, to flounder," *SND*) and was also found in the poet's juvenile manuscript in "Of a Country Life" and "Psalm 104." "Chapt," noted above ("Autumn," l. 404) is also a Scotticism (*Dictionary of the Older Scottish Tongue*), as is "clammy" ("Spring," l. 116; *SND*). "Lass," meaning "young girl" ("Autumn," l. 154) is of course chiefly a Scottish and Northern English dialect usage. The adverbial "Mean-time" ("Winter," ll. 54, 617; "Spring," l. 203) for "meanwhile" occurs three times in *The Seasons* and more frequently in *The Castle* and in *Liberty;* it is an expression often heard in modern Scottish speech, and Thomson uses it in *The Seasons* mostly to make transitions into passages of natural description. The verb "recks" ("Winter," l. 92, "And much he laughs, nor recks the Storm that blows") derives from "reckon," which Beattie lists as a Scotticism and meaning in standard English "to pay heed to"; Scots "reck" is also "to matter" (*SND; OED*). The onomatopoeic standard English descriptive adjective "grumbling" ("Winter," l. 76, "Woods, / That grumbling wave below. Th' unsightly Plain / Lies a brown Deluge") is probably related to the Scots "grummle" (*SND*), which has the double meaning, exploited by the poet here, of "to grumble at" (from "grum" or "grumlie," grim, sullen) and also "to make muddy, turbid" (as in the juxtaposed muddy, "deluged" plain which Thomson describes as the result of the flood). Here sound reinforces sense, and Scots connotations add to the standard English definition of "grumble." A similar onomatopoeic adjective is "brawling" ("Winter," l. 69, "brawling Brook"). Like "bicker," "brawling" combines sound (meaning "to quarrel," it comes from Middle English and is used in standard English) with movement (its Scots definition is "to gallop," *SND*) to describe the brook. "Taste" (meaning "smell," "Spring," l. 107 and creating a synaesthetic effect) is also a northern usage. "Freakt" ("Winter," l. 814) is recorded in Johnson's *Dictionary* as a Scotticism. Thomson's coinage "friskful" ("Spring," l. 837, "Lambs, / . . . in friskful Glee") was possibly suggested to him by the Scots "frisksome" ("sportive," *SND*); he had used a variation, "friskish," in his 1726 preface to "Winter."[25]

While these Scotticisms and northern usages stayed even after several careful revisions of *The Seasons,* many more were removed over the years, often resulting in loss of race. For example, the weaker English expletive "Ah" replaced Scots exclamation "Ay" ("Spring," 1728–1738, l. 1086) in 1744. "Bootless" ("Summer," 1727–1738, l. 236, describing dogs who "bootless snap" at the wasp; that is, to no avail) occurs in both English and Scots, but its archaic use as a quasi-adverb, as Thomson used it, might have been more particular to Scotland or retained there longer in common use (in addition to Shakespeare, *OED* cites such a usage in James I's *Kingis Quair* lxx and Walter Scott's *Triermain* III.1). "Bootless" is again used as a quasi-adverb in *Liberty* IV.644. For the description of the sky "begreying" with clouds ("Summer," 1727, l. 1648) Thomson substituted "All ether sadening" (1730–1738), then "All Ether softening" (1744ff.). "Begreying," apart from its pseudo-archaic sense of "growing grey," also carried the connotation of the Scots "begratten" or "begrutten" ("tearstained, lamenting," *SND; DOST* gives "begrett, begroutin," from the verb "grete," "to weep") with its suggestion of mood similar to the rejected "sadening" and with the added comparison of tears with rain. "Softening," the poet's final choice, sadly weakens the descriptive impact here. Similarly, "glomerating" ("Autumn," 1730–1738, "glomerating tempest grows," l. 333) was rejected in 1744 in favor of "mingling" ("mingling Tempest weaves its Gloom"). The participial adjective "glomerating," building up or gathering, comes from the Latin root "glomus" (ball) and also carries the modern Scots connotation of "to grow dusky" (*SND*) from "glom" or "gloam," meaning "gloom," related to the familiar "gloaming." Thus, "glomerating" would have expressed for Thomson the meaning not only of the storm's accumulation of clouds, but also of its darkness, its gloomy mood. Again, there is loss of race. The apt and alliterative "louring" ("Winter," 1726–1738, "Late, in the louring Sky," l. 120), meaning to become overcast, was also removed in 1744. "Louring" is found in both English and Scots, though its English usage is chiefly poetical-archaic. In *The Roxburghshire Word-Book* it is given as "loory." Thomson replaced "louring" with the adjective "palid," a tame and indeed pallid substitute. One further Scotticism (this one accidental) should also be mentioned: the Scots metathesis of "thatched," "thacht," which occurs only in the first edition of "Winter" (March 1726, l. 182). This may simply have been a printer's error (the printer of this edition was Archibald Campbell, a Scotsman in London), but it might have been the poet's own misspelling; similar orthography occurs in Thomson's juvenilia and early letters. The error was removed with the second edition of 1726.[26]

Even though so many Scotticisms and racy English words bearing Scottish connotations had been excised from *The Seasons*, the fact that Thomson kept so many more proves that he had hardly abandoned his Scots linguistic heritage; on the contrary, he sensed that Scots words—their sounds and meanings—were a vital force in his poetic expression. Over years of revisions he made the effort to eliminate Scotticisms and northern or local usages which might not have been as clear or resonant to English as to Scottish readers, but he still allowed some to remain, as if he could not bear to part with such expressive, evocative, and, to him, accurate descriptive language, especially where Scots associations could enhance standard English definitions. With these, he still further expanded and enriched English poetic diction.

James Thomson's use of language in *The Seasons* was daring indeed for a Scottish poet in eighteenth-century England, as William Somerville had warned. But Thomson's bold Anglo-Scottish experimentation proved surprisingly successful. He discovered the natural flexibility and flow of blank verse for a poetry describing the processes of nature. Sensitivity to the sounds of words and their infinitely varied patterns, too, seemed to come naturally to him; he was already attuned to the descriptive possibilities of such northern sound effects as alliteration, which he used skillfully to compose subtle imitative patterns capturing the music and movement as well as the moods of the natural world. In the Enlightenment spirit of empiricism, Thomson tried new words and new usages for old words. He adapted Latinate English and even Latin words themselves to his comprehensive descriptive purpose. He borrowed both from the traditional language of the Bible and the Scottish sermon and from the fresh-minted language of contemporary philosophy and science. Most especially, he invoked the strength of his native Scots speech to intensify emotional response and at the same time to sharpen descriptive precision in his complex poem. Thomson accomplished the Virgilian ideal of progressive adaptation which inspires *The Seasons* generally by applying it to language, transforming conventional, formal literary English to meet his own descriptive needs and to "control" and ultimately improve nature through poetic art. Thus did Thomson create his highly original and genuinely Anglo-Scottish poetic idiom in the cause of natural description.

8 LIFE, *LIBERTY*, AND THE PLAYS: THE SCOTTISH POET IN LONDON

The Seasons followed so closely upon James Thomson's own Scottish life and experience that of all his works it most immediately and directly reflects native influences on his language, thought, subject matter, and style. Nonetheless, in each of the several major works which succeeded Thomson's Anglo-Scottish masterpiece Scottish influences can be clearly traced. Continuity with the early Thomson—his juvenile poems and *The Seasons*—can still be seen in the plays and in *Liberty* and especially in *The Castle of Indolence*. Further, the poet deliberately created for himself in London a distinctively Scottish ambiance, surrounding himself with trusted Scots friends and colleagues, keeping abreast of Scottish affairs, and maintaining certain Scottish-born attitudes and interests which he had brought with him from home. He accomplished this in the face of enormous prejudice against Scots in eighteenth-century England and pressures on them to disavow or disguise their national identity. The crucial biographical fact that Thomson came down to London a Scot, and a good Scot he was determined to remain, has not been taken very seriously by his otherwise conscientious biographers. A brief review of Thomson's life in London, along with the works of his mid career, the plays and *Liberty*, will therefore take a closer look at the specifically Scottish implications of those years, such as the poet's complicated ideas of nationalism and patriotism, and the continuing fruitful relationship between his personal life as an Anglo-Scot and his poetic art.

When Thomson arrived in London in the spring of 1725, he was poor and lonely and at once sought out his Scottish friends who had gone there before him. Early on, he visited Duncan Forbes, then a Member of Parliament, who recalled his juvenile poems favorably, and though he probably did not offer monetary aid, took a sincere interest in the young poet's projected literary career. Forbes introduced Thomson to many influential people in London, including Pope and Gay, powerful public figures the duke of Argyll and Robert Walpole, and also, if the poet had not in fact already met him in Scotland, artist William Aikman. Forbes, a shrewd leader, was also a kind and sociable man who loved and patronized the arts; he proved an invaluable advocate to Thomson at this time. Statesman and young poet grew to be close friends, and when Thomson came to write his *Seasons* Forbes gave him considerable help and advice; the two spent many an evening together preparing the poem for the press.[1]

Thomson also looked up fellow-student David Mallet. Mallet, too, was initially very helpful to the newcomer. In mid 1725, Thomson was appointed tutor to Scotsman Lord Binning's eldest son Thomas, the future seventh earl of Haddington, age five, at East Barnet. Mallet, who was tutor to the sons of the duke of Montrose, possibly influenced Lord Binning through his own employer to secure Thomson's post. Lord Binning was an amateur pastoral poet; he was married to Rachel, daughter of Grisell and George Baillie of Jerviswood. Lady Grisell herself, a cousin of Thomson's mother, may have had even more to do with Thomson's appointment than Mallet. Whatever Mallet's part in helping Thomson find work, he was a true ally to Thomson in his critical first year in the city; only later did he earn his deserved reputation as an unscrupulous literary opportunist. Mallet even canvassed London booksellers to find a publisher for "Winter" and generally gave Thomson great encouragement in his literary efforts.[2]

Thomson found a different teaching post in May 1726, one probably better suited to his interests. He became a private tutor to a "young Gentleman" at a school thus advertised:

'At the Academy in Little Tower-street is to be learned every Qualification necessary for business or Accomplishment, after a peculiar and approved Method; there being retain'd several Professors, capable to answer for their respective Trusts, to teach Writing, Arithmetick, and Merchants Accounts; all Parts of Mathematicks; and to give Courses of Experimental Philosophy, also the Classicks and Modern Languages; and to Foreigners and others, not well inform'd therein, the English Language, Drawing, Dancing, Etc. . . .'

Its proprietors, Thomas and William Watts, were respected scientists and mathematicians who professed the Newtonian philosophy. Their name suggests that they may have been Scotsmen. Among the teachers at the academy was James Stirling, F.R.S., a learned Scots mathematician forced to retire from Oxford in 1715 for Jacobitical involvement and friend and correspondent of Newton himself. Watts' Academy, with its learned staff and advertised programs of study, was evidently a London center for the study of Newtonianism. There Thomson's early enthusiasm for Newtonian science, first sparked at Edinburgh University, was rekindled. Mr. Stirling might even have introduced Thomson to the aged Newton himself, accounting for the sense of personal grief which pervades the poet's "A Poem Sacred to the Memory of Sir Isaac Newton" (1727). Thomson probably also met mathematician John Gray at this time; Gray, also a disciple of Newton, is said by Murdoch to have advised Thomson on the Newtonian principles celebrated in that famous elegy. Gray, who later served as rector of Marischal College, Aberdeen (1764–1769), was a longstanding member of Thomson's Scottish circle of friends in London.[3]

Even while he was teaching at Watts' Academy, Thomson had not forgotten why he had come to London. He kept assiduously at his writing and somehow found the time, by 1730, to complete his *Seasons*. During this period he also wrote the first of his plays, *Sophonisba* (1730). For his dramatic subject he looked back to the classical Roman world where he felt at home. *Sophonisba*, modeled on French neoclassical drama, is the true history of the queen of Carthage who dies rather than submitting to Rome and who herself embodies the chief Roman social virtue of patriotism. Her story was treated in Roman histories and also occurs in Petrarch's *Trionfi*, which Thomson may have known in Scot William Fowler's translation. The story had already been the subject of many dramatic interpretations; the prologue to Thomson's play, by Pope and Mallet, especially acknowledges his debt to Trissino and Corneille. While perhaps not directly influenced by Trissino, Thomson did own a copy of Trissino's version, a favorite in Scotland since the days of James VI.[4] There were also English versions, notably by John Marston (1606) and Nathaniel Lee (1676). A Scot, David Murray of Gorthy, who styled himself "Scoto-Britainne," also wrote an early poetic version of the tale. Murray's dramatic poem *Sophonisba* (1611) invented upon the plays of Trissino and Marston.[5] Thomson himself drew upon a variety of sources for his *Sophonisba*. He knew of the historical Sophonisba from Livy and other historians, and he attempted to keep closer to historical fact than had some of the previous dramatists of the story. In his important preface to the play he reveals his overall aims for the drama, pledging simplicity, truth to history, and truth to life.[6]

Thomson's *Sophonisba* shares these qualities, to some extent, with Murray's Scottish *Sophonisba*, which he probably knew. Both Murray and Thomson draw the apt parallel of Sophonisba with Dido, both victims of love who desire death (in Thomson, II.ii; III, 33); this allusion does not occur in Trissino but originates in the *Trionfi*. Both Scots playwrights reveal a highly rhetorical bias. Murray's verse tragedy simplifies the story into just two soliloquies, first the queen's lover Massinissa's, then Sophonisba's; Thomson's plot is also much simplified and concentrates on the speeches rather than on dramatic action. While both Murray's and Thomson's characters remain flat, they share a strong element of psychological truth, particularly in their portrayal of Massinissa's mental torment. Murray's character is "swoolne with griefe and rage," "halfe mad, distraught, confus'dly doth hee write," representing a very early realistic psychological portrait in Scottish poetry.[7] Thomson powerfully dramatizes Massinissa's "passions . . . unconfin'd, and mad" using much imagery from nature, and especially of storms, for "All deaths, all tortures, in one pang combin'd / Are gentle to the tempest of the mind" (I.v; III, 24).

Thomson, along with other contemporary Scottish playwrights, deemed it prudent to clothe his views of current Hanoverian policy in neoclassical, historical guise. Though *Sophonisba* is less markedly political than some of Thomson's later dramas, it is dedicated to Queen Caroline and has been seen as a plea for her to eschew French influ-

ence.[8] More important, the play also bears a Scottish political interpretation: the heroine's self-sacrifice in the face of Rome's superior
power parallels Scotland's sacrifice of her national identity in the recent Union with the dominant English nation. As in *The Seasons,* Roman and British imperial ambitions can again be equated, although
Thomson's growing ambivalence toward Rome and for what it stood,
also seen in *Liberty,* appears in *Sophonisba.* Thomson clearly admires
Roman Republican social virtue as well as strength; the magnanimous
Roman leader Scipio triumphs, and Sophonisba is paid the ultimate
posthumous compliment: "She had a *Roman* soul; for every one / Who
loves, like her, his country, is a *Roman*" (V.ix; III, 101)—just as the
highest honor for many an Anglo-Scot would be to have a "British
soul." Yet Thomson also expresses, through Sophonisba herself, disgust with Roman Imperial oppression and "slavery"; she and her
country, like Scotland, represent admirable independence of spirit, an
ideal of individualistic liberty for which the poet shows great sympathy. This pattern of identification with the smaller, weaker nation,
even alongside of predominant admiration for Rome, is also a central
theme of Thomson's last play, *Coriolanus.*

Massinissa was born a Carthaginian but chose to join the Romans,
seeking a sort of union with the dominant power; his contribution to
their cause is his potential strength of character, for he was trained in
the "wintry blasts" of "misfortune's school." This directly echoes
Thomson's description of the brave and hardy Scots in "Autumn" (ll.
894–895), "a People in Misfortune's School / Train'd up to hardy
Deeds" (see also *Liberty* V. 73–74). Massinissa, however, proves too
emotional when he is ultimately caught between two strong loyalties,
patriotism for Rome and love for Sophonisba of Carthage. Likewise,
Thomson's own inner conflicts emerge as he tries to reconcile his love
for Scotland with his strong British patriotism. Thomson finally
makes the Roman/British parallel explicit, as "'warm with freedom
under frozen skies, / In farthest *Britain Romans* yet may rise.'" (V.ix;
III, 102). The moral of the tragedy, predictable in this period of the
poet's career ca. 1730, when he was most concerned with social reform, is that Hutchesonian social love, which stresses public good over

private, for " 'such is / The spirit that has rais'd Imperial *Rome.*' " (V.ii; III, 89).

Sophonisba was an immediate success with the public, enjoying a ten-night run at Drury Lane, the London theater of Whig affiliation. But the play was not without its faults, particularly its turgid, twisted language as the classical plot labors for elegance and elevation. A contemporary pamphlet by one "T.B.," *A Criticism of the New Sophonisba*, jealously attributed the play's success at Drury Lane to the large and loud Scottish contingent in the audience, " '*Scotchmen* with tuneful Hands and merry Feet.' " The pamphleteer also remarked with crude wit on the faults of the play. The dialogue is not natural, for Thomson's rhetorical bias, reinforced by the homiletic influence of his religious background, readily led him to such declamatory excess. Without the empirical inspiration of natural description, Thomson sometimes loses rhetorical control. The characters in *Sophonisba* are flat; Syphax, for example, is all evil, Sophonisba all patriotism, Massinissa all passion. Yet despite its problems, *Sophonisba* was popular because it voiced some stirring rhetoric (such as the heroine's fiery anti-Roman speeches, I.i, III.iii, V.vi), it told a moving and patriotic tale, it was well acted, it commented on contemporary politics, and, not least, it contained some passages of fine heroic poetry.[9]

Thomson felt that the drama was a "powerful School of humane polite Morality"[10] and upheld its serious, civilizing function, "Dashing Corruption down through every worthless Age" (*Castle*, I.xxxii.9). His dramas served mostly as vehicles for his social and political views, and, as in *Liberty*, sociopolitical and didactic aims rather than religious, descriptive, or indeed artistic aims predominate. The dramas, like *Liberty*, are heavily indebted to classical and neoclassical models; there is very little natural description. But more significant than the merits or faults of the individual plays are the attitudes they reveal about the poet's Anglo-Scottish allegiances in the 1730s and 1740s and especially the role they play in the revival of the moribund Scottish tradition of serious drama.

Thomson's main focus as a dramatist is on his characters, or actually their elevated, highly rhetorical speeches, rather than on description or setting. The poet had tremendous difficulty giving life—convincing action and dialogue—to his characters drawn from literature and history, and they mostly act as mouthpieces for various sides of some abstract debate. Thomson's inability to bring characters alive was first glimpsed in *The Seasons,* where human figures tended to be conventional or caricatured; exceptions in "Spring" were the mourning lovers, whose plight was so similar to Thomson's own. Only *Tancred and Sigismunda* approaches such realism, and this psychological accuracy, as in "Spring," grew from Thomson's own unhappy love for Elizabeth Young. In general, Thomson had little poetic sense of human—as opposed to natural or elemental—drama; his control of the human scene in the dramatic genre cannot compare with his sensitive staging of the dynamic natural scene in descriptive poetry. Like most northerners writing plays in London in the mid eighteenth century, Thomson chose to work in tragedy; like them, he was absorbed with the language of his characters in this highest form of dramatic art, which tended toward formal rhetoric rather than emotional realism.[11] Nonetheless, there are some fine passages of blank verse in the dramas, as Thomson typically delights in innovative language and sound effects. Thomson's dramatic efforts enjoyed considerable success in their day, but the vogue for such declamatory tragedy soon passed, and they are largely, if unjustly, neglected now.[12]

Thomson's limited skill as a dramatist can be attributed partly to the absence of a well-developed dramatic tradition in his native Scotland. Medieval Scottish drama had thrived, but this is mostly lost now and was lost even by Thomson's time. There was some dramatic activity in seventeenth-century Scotland; George Buchanan, for instance, wrote Latin biblical plays modeled on classical drama which, like Thomson's plays, commented on current political issues; his *Baptistes,* on the theme of liberty, was translated into English prose by Milton (1642). Sir William Alexander's *Monarchicke Tragedies* (1607) were, like Buchanan's plays, preoccupied with language and were written to be read rather than acted; they, too, held contemporary political relevance. Thomson probably knew Buchanan's and Alexander's highly rhetorical dramas; he was certainly working within their tradition of Scottish neoclassical rhetoric. Thomson was also familiar with those pedantic Latin school plays, the only other dramatic form to survive the rigors of Reformation in Scotland. The Scottish Kirk vigorously censured drama for its own entertaining sake, and Kirk opposition and effective prohibition continued in force through the mid eighteenth century.[13]

There was almost no drama being performed in the Scotland of Thomson's youth, and even if there were he, as a divinity student, would surely have been forbidden to attend it. So it is no wonder that Thomson, who eagerly read classical and Scottish and English neo-classical plays as well as Shakespeare at an early age and who later admired French and Italian plays, came to write tragedies of such a highly literary and rhetorical rather than dramatic or stage bias. It is no wonder that he was unable to animate characters with convincing action and dialogue; his early contacts with live theater were virtually nonexistent. It is no wonder, too, that when he arrived in London he behaved as one starved of dramatic diversion and hungrily snatched the opportunity to attend many plays at Drury Lane within his first weeks in the city; he specifically mentioned seeing *Oroonoko, The Constant Couple,* Addison's *Cato,* and *Hamlet,* among others. He wrote even then to Cranstoun, "a tragedy I think or a fine charecter [*sic*] in a comedy gives greater pleasure read than acted" (April 3, 1725).[14] So his essentially literary bias persisted, and his own plays were necessarily highly derivative of sources outside Scottish literature: the classics, English Renaissance drama, and Continental tragedy. The positive result of Thomson's literary dramatic inclination is the genuine poetry which elevates some few passages of the dramatic blank verse.

As Scottish Reformation strictures began to ease and a more liberal attitude prevailed, Scots at home and in London again began to write plays, but at first these were almost all comedies, either satire or light pastoral. A real tradition of "poetic tragedy" had thus far been a missing link in the development of Scottish literature, an important stage by which (according to Edwin Muir) a nation's poetry "matures." James Thomson himself, the foremost figure in the mid eighteenth-century shift of Scottish dramatists from comedy to tragedy,[15] would be the catalyst of this essential maturation process. With *Sophonisba* he initiated the revival of serious Scottish drama after its long suppression by the Scottish church. This, then, is Thomson's chief accomplishment as a Scottish dramatist.

Thomson's earlier dramatic attempts, like *Sophonisba,* were traditional neoclassical tragedies similar to Addison's *Cato,* but the empiricist Thomson soon moved away from strict neoclassical rules to experiment with new styles and themes in his plays, placing increasing emphasis on the sentimental or "romantic" element and considerably loosening the form. Some critics saw his rhetorical influence as detrimental to the development of British drama as a whole. Walter Scott, for one, felt that Thomson's "wordy and declamatory system of composition, contributed rather to sink than to exalt the character of the stage"; such "wordy and declamatory" style was of course a product of the Scottish rhetorical—and dramatic, such as it was—influence on Thomson. Others feared that the themes of romantic melodrama which Thomson and his followers began to introduce lacked substance and would cause the theater lasting harm. In truth, the various dramatic "concessions" which Thomson and his imitators allowed themselves to make, such as modifying classical unities, adapting historical truth to the contemporary political situation, and exploiting more "romantic" elements, corresponded to the empirically evolving aesthetic tastes of the Scottish literati.[16] Again, one finds Thomson practicing Scottish Enlightenment sensibility while his compatriots were busy articulating its theory. Thomson's blank-verse tragedies are not entirely successful, yet they are good of their kind and period and they are of interest as expressions of the poet's aesthetic, ethical, and sociopolitical ideals. More importantly, they have a significant place in Scottish literature, as they represent a continuation of the literary tradition of vernacular humanism and especially a rebirth of serious Scottish drama.

Thomson remained at Watts' Academy working on *The Seasons* and *Sophonisba* until autumn 1730, when his patron, Charles Talbot, Baron Talbot of Hensol, asked him to accompany his son Charles Richard on the Grand Tour. With the complete *Seasons* and also *Sophonisba* lately in print and proving highly popular, Thomson eagerly took the opportunity to travel to the Continent and particularly to the land of his hero Virgil:

> Travelling has long been my fondest wish for the very purpose you recommend: the storing one's Imagination with Ideas of all-beautiful, all-great, and all-perfect Nature. . . . I long to see the feilds [*sic*] whence Virgil gathered his immortal honey, and to tread the same ground where men have thought and acted so greatly! If it does not give, it must at least awaken some what of the same Spirit. . . .[17]

Early in his tour, Thomson had begun to envision his poem *Liberty* as "a *poetical* landscape of countries, mixed with moral observations on their governments and people . . . the *Portrait-painting of Nature*." Thomson at this stage wrote that "I shall return no worse Englishman than I came away"; this curiously ambiguous remark, where he associates himself patriotically with the dominant English culture, is intriguing and hints at tensions about national identity which the young Scottish poet was certainly experiencing in the 1730s.[18]

The Grand Tour generally sharpened Thomson's political awareness and fired his British patriotism and at every step he compared unfavorably the countries he visited with Britain. The poet and his party first traveled through France, whose absolute monarchy he abhorred. From France they traveled to the Republic of Switzerland. Thomson the Scottish Presbyterian was more impressed with Geneva, where he felt comfortable with both the Calvinist religious climate and the progressive political ideals and delighted in the sublime Alpine scenery.[19] When Thomson at last reached Italy, the land of Virgil and of the ancient Roman ideals he held so dear, he was deeply disillusioned. He saw only poverty and ruins, the remains of the once-great Roman civilization so revered by his countrymen. Italy's "bad Government," under the influence of the Catholic church, had "even disfigured Nature herself," and "human Arts and Industry" were scarcely to be seen in the desolate landscape. On viewing the city of Rome, he could only exclaim, "Behold an Empire dead!"

The poet's melancholy mood at this stage of the journey was aggra-

vated by two unhappy events. First, while in Italy Thomson learned of
the deaths of William Aikman and his son Jocky in 1731. Aikman had
been a good friend to Thomson in his early years in London, had
painted several portraits of him, and had no doubt also sparked in the
poet his lifelong interest in fine art. Thomson wrote his moving elegy
["On the Death of Mr. William Aikman, the Painter"] in Italy and
posted the verses to Lady Hertford. In a second sad incident, Thomson met with George and Grisell Baillie in Rome, along with the poet's
former employer Lord Binning, who was gravely ill. He had come to
Italy to try to restore his health but was beyond recovery and died
soon after this meeting with Thomson. Understandably, Thomson,
saddened by the death of the Aikmans and the encounter with dying
Lord Binning, now longed to return to Britain.[20]

When Thomson arrived back in Britain in late 1732, he immediately set about recording his impressions of the Grand Tour in *Liberty.*
Now began the period of about a decade (1732–1742) of the poet's
most intense political involvement as well as his most aggressively
British patriotism, fraught with personal Anglo-Scottish insecurities
and ambivalent nationalistic impulses. In addition to *Liberty,* Thomson
was also at work on the politically allusive tragedy *Agamemnon,* followed by *Edward and Eleanora,* during this time. He resolved to take
more direct action to help preserve Britain's precious liberty, which he
better appreciated since his sojourn abroad, and he now allied himself
openly with Prince Frederick's Opposition Whig faction against Walpole's corrupt administration and dangerous "peace-at-any-price" foreign policy. Walpole was anti-Scottish in his policies, too, and extremely unpopular with Scotsmen, so Thomson's Opposition stance,
in company with such Opposition Whigs as Duncan Forbes, the dukes
of Argyll and Roxburghe, Sir William Bennet, and other Scottish no-
bles also represented pro-Scottish support. In 1733 Thomson's benefactor Charles Talbot, now solicitor general, found the poet a government sinecure as his secretary of the briefs, a post which he would
hold until 1737. Thomson's heightened political consciousness during
this decade was most openly expressed in his writings of the period, in
the political plays, possibly in anonymous contributions to periodicals,
and, particularly, in *Liberty.*

The poem *Liberty* (1735–1736) was directly inspired (or rather uninspired) by Thomson's experiences on the Grand Tour. As he wrote to Dodington from Rome (November 28, 1731), "I belive [*sic*] she [his muse] did not cross the channel with me." He had planned "the description of the different face of Nature, in different countries . . . the *Portrait-painting of Nature,*" a sort of poetical Grand Tour, when he first conceived *Liberty.* Unfortunately the poet abandoned these early aims and adopted a primarily sociopolitical and didactic purpose: the projected poem of personal observation and natural description became instead a far more ambitious public proclamation, an allegorical dream vision following the Goddess of Liberty through the history of civilizations to her present home, Great Britain, and there celebrating Whig progress and potential. As he had increasingly done in *The Seasons,* Thomson in *Liberty* sought "the secular but spiritual meaning of history, . . . the transformation of Providence into Progress." Although this historical quest was intellectually challenging, it proved too vast for the poet, who had already betrayed a weakness in handling such public, abstract expressions in several *Seasons* passages; he should never have departed from his original subject of nature. *Liberty* was, from the first, a poetical failure.[21]

Yet at the same time Thomson now saw it as his duty publicly to defend British freedom. Where before he had taken his role to be a primarily religious one, in *Liberty* he assumed the role of sociopolitical bard in order to proclaim to Britons the Goddess of Liberty's commands. Later in the eighteenth century, the eleventh earl of Buchan would praise the poet lavishly for the libertarian ideals he expressed in *Liberty:* "the highest encomium of Thomson is to be given him on account of his attachment to the cause of political and civil liberty." Lord Buchan had in mind particularly Scottish ideals of freedom, which he felt had been compromised in the Union with England: "Of [Dr. Samuel] Johnson's criticism on the Poem of Thomson, entitled Liberty, I shall say nothing; but I will take the liberty to say that Britain knows nothing of the liberty that Thomson celebrates!" While *Liberty* is not wholly successful as a poem, it does reveal a great deal about Thomson's political views, particularly on nationalism and patriotism, in the 1730s. It elaborates many of the poet's ideas formed in Scotland, variations on themes seen in *The Seasons* and juvenilia and recurring in *The Castle*. There are even a few felicitous passages of poetry to be found in *Liberty*.[22]

Liberty combines the same basic ingredients which make up *The Seasons,* but here Thomson drastically altered their proportions. Where *The Seasons* was above all a religious-descriptive poem, *Liberty* is primarily a public, patriotic, and sociopolitical work with natural description at a minimum and religious thought only implicitly expressed. Both poems are didactic, but *Liberty* is far more heavily, relentlessly so. *Liberty* is more strictly neoclassical than *The Seasons* in form, theme, and language; Thomson evidently first envisioned it as an "epic," following upon *The Seasons* as Virgil's epic *Aeneid* followed upon his *Georgics* and *Eclogues*. The epic plan encompassed a survey in five books of the rise and fall of civilizations, concluding with an optimistic vision of Liberty's triumphant reign in Britain (Part I is "Ancient and Modern Italy Compared," II is "Greece," III "Rome," IV "Britain," and V "The Prospect"). The neoclassical poem is rhetorically elevated throughout, and the convoluted language is oppressively Latinate. Here Thomson had assumed the Scottish rhetorical voice with ponderous, tedious decorum, unskilled as he was in treating large abstract topics. In fact, though the epic framework is discernible, *Liberty* never achieved true epic status as he had planned it.[23]

Thomson, having seen the "dead" Roman Empire first-hand, had by this time grown disillusioned with the fallen classical world and was impatient to establish Liberty's reign in the north, in Great Britain. His admiration for Rome and Roman social virtues such as selfless patriotism and cultural progress, first learned in Scotland, is abundantly obvious in *Liberty,* especially in I and II. But at this stage of the poet's career there is an important change in his attitude toward Rome already hinted at in *Sophonisba* and even more striking here in *Liberty.* Whereas in *The Seasons* and even in the juvenilia Thomson proudly identified the Roman Empire with the ascendant British Empire, in *Liberty* he shows deep disgust with the Roman Empire and focuses far more on the early Roman Republic as the model for good government and public virtue. The goddess angrily remarks:

> WHAT tho' the first smooth CÆSARS Arts caress'd,
> Merit, and Virtue, simulating ME?
> Severely tender! cruelly humane!
> The Chain to clinch, and make it softer sit
> On the new-broken still ferocious State.
> From the dark *Third,* succeeding, I beheld
> Th' Imperial Monsters all.—A Race on Earth
> Vindictive sent, the Scourge of Human-kind!
> (*Liberty* III.484–491)

Where Imperial and Republican values coexisted harmoniously in *The Seasons,* they come into open conflict in *Liberty.*[24] This unresolved conflict almost certainly reflects a corresponding disillusionment with Augustan Britain, once the national ideal for ambitious Anglo-Scots like Thomson. By the mid 1730s the poet had grown more and more deeply disturbed by Walpole's tyranny, strong control over the monarchy, and unwise peace policy; Augustan enlightenment had begun to resemble despotism and foreign depredations continued to threaten the age of peace. Further, Thomson had by now come to know first-hand the weaknesses of the Augustan English system of literary patronage; Walpole himself had not time for men of letters and neither did his followers, nor even the king himself. Also, Thomson was all too aware of Walpole's anti-Scottish policies, as the prime minister shamelessly exploited and subjugated "North Britain." These Scottish abuses were at their worst in the 1730s, the period when Thomson's attitudes to nationalism and empire altered most dramatically. In short, the promise of a new Augustan Age transplanted to post-Union Great Britain which had seemed so bright to the young Scottish poet had by this time grown dim. His increasing emphasis on pre-Empire, early Roman Republican sociopolitical and cultural ideals in *Liberty* and the plays thus might well represent symbolically the poet's delayed reaction against the Union and stronger nostalgia for Scottish national ideals of independence, strength, and native integrity. North Britain had not become an equal partner in the Union with "South Britain," and the Union was proving in many ways a huge disappointment to one who had so eagerly embraced the hopes of the patriotic Athenian Society. Thomson knew now that true British liberty had yet to be achieved.[25]

In *Liberty*, as in *Sophonisba*, Rome is not the sole custodian of true freedom and national pride; another side also gains the poet's sympathy. Thomson's inheritance of traditional ideas of liberty was in fact twofold. In addition to those adopted Roman values, as a Scot the poet also held deep respect for so-called Northern liberty, a concept first glimpsed in *The Seasons* and made much more explicit in *Liberty*. He sees Northern liberty as a fresh burst of freedom nurtured in the harsh, cold north which ultimately supplanted the fallen glory of the dead Roman Empire (III). Barbarian invasions from the north (IV) carried positive "Gothic" virtues, first into Italy and from there to Switzerland, Germany, Scandinavia, and, finally, Britain. Thomson as a Scot especially closely identified with the Swiss (IV.337–338ff.) as Calvinists of an efficient, progressive republic; he also admired their thrilling mountain scenery, which may have reminded him of his own mountainous Borders. In praising the Scandinavians, he no doubt recalled their important role in Scottish history and their influence on Scottish culture. He calls the Swedes the "manly Race" (IV.372), as in "Autumn" he had called the Scots a "manly Race," and he obviously thought of his compatriots, too, as bearers of the same Northern liberty and strength.[26]

When Northern liberty finally reaches Britain, Thomson's deep-rooted conflicts of national allegiance again surface. In *Liberty* Thomson by no means concealed his Scottish national pride. The idea of historic Caledonian freedom greatly appealed to the Scottish poet, and Gothic northern virtues also had certain Celtic associations at the time. The Scots were those brave northerners who resisted the spread of the corrupt Roman empire in Britain:

> The *North* remain'd untouch'd, where those who scorn'd
> To stoop retir'd; and, to their keen Effort
> Yielding at last, recoil'd the *Roman* Power.
> In vain, unable to sustain the Shock,
> From Sea to Sea desponding Legions rais'd
> The Wall immense, and yet, on Summer's Eve,

> While sport his Lambkins round, the Shepherd's Gaze.
> Continual o'er it burst the *Northern Storm* . . .
> (IV.647–654)

Thomson shows more sympathy for the Scots than for the Romans here, similar to his admiration for Sophonisba and her brave Carthaginians. The Romans at last withdrew from Britain; the "Wall immense" is, of course, Hadrian's Wall near Thomson's native Borders or, as Thomson explains, "The Wall of *Severus,* built upon *Adrian's* Rampart, which ran for eighty Miles quite cross the Country from the Mouth of the *Tine* to *Solway* Frith." Thomson further notes that the "*Northern Storm*" refers to "Irruptions of the *Scots* and *Picts*" over the wall. There are several more specific references to Scotland in *Liberty,* such as this tribute (echoing "Autumn," ll. 894–909) to

> ". . . the lofty SCOT,
> To Hardship tam'd, active in Arts and Arms,
> Fir'd with a restless an impatient Flame,
> That leads him raptur'd where Ambition calls . . .
> (V.73–76)

"Ambition" had thus called Thomson himself to England.[27]

Even with these expressions of Scottish national pride, however, *Liberty* is overwhelmingly British. It represents Thomson's most enthusiastic, aggressive, even chauvinistic statement of wider British patriotism (particularly in IV and V), greatly inflating the Opposition Whig encomium, the bombast of his verse "Britannia" (1729). In *Liberty,* too, Thomson takes great pains to dissociate himself from any taint of Jacobitism; in his survey of British history, he launches a vituperative attack against the Stuart reigns (IV), never once mentioning that the Stuarts were Scots but making it clear, nonetheless, that it was Scots, the army under Alexander Leslie which invaded England in 1640 in defense of Scottish Presbyterianism, who first sparked the civil war which led to the Stuarts' downfall:

> . . . instant from the keen resentive *North,*
> By *long Oppression* by *Religion* rous'd,
> The *Guardian Army* came . . .

> . . . There a Flame
> Broke out, that clear'd, consum'd, renew'd the Land.
> (IV.1016–1021)

Thompson's exaggerated, offensively pro-British patriotism which largely sets the tone for *Liberty* can be explained—if not excused—by his Scottishness. So anxious was the poet to defend himself against prevailing prejudice against Scots and evidently so filled with paradoxical pride and shame at being a Scot that he put himself in jeopardy of being seen as anti-Scottish in *Liberty*. Party-political motives, too, were responsible for his aggressive stance. Thomson had begun to take a more public Opposition Whig position at this time, and even while he was involved in narrow Whig "Party-Rage" (V.162) and faction, he was still especially concerned to show his support for the broader Whig aim of British progress.

Liberty leaves no doubt as to Thomson's stand on that primitivism versus progress debate first posed in *The Seasons*. While he acknowledges the humble rural origins of Liberty (II.3ff.), his vision of Great Britain's future is of "PUBLIC WORKS," bustling cities, "improved" landscapes and waterways, lively trade; that is, Whig progress. The conclusion to Part V rejoices in this prospect:

> "AUGUST, around, what PUBLIC WORKS I see!
> Lo! stately *Streets,* lo! *Squares* that court the
> Breeze.
>
> .   .   .
>
> See! long *Canals,* and *deepen'd Rivers* join
> Each Part with each, and with the circling Main
> The whole enliven'd Isle. . . .
> (V.701–702, 709–711)

Lines from this passage were chosen by Thomson's nephew, architect James Craig, to crown his Plan of the New Town of Edinburgh (1767). The poet's neoclassical, orderly, and optimistic vision of Britain's future described here is, like Craig's plan itself, highly representative of the cultural ideals, the expansive cosmopolitan concept of civilization so dear to the Scottish literati of the next generation.[28] Again, Thomson can be seen to anticipate, aesthetically and philosophically, the Scottish Enlightenment.

Liberty is predominately a didactic poem, preaching the lessons of progress and public morality first heard in *The Seasons*. Again, as even in the early "Upon Happiness," "VIRTUE" (V.237) is the key, now to the public, sociopolitical goals of "real Joy" (V. 239) and *"universal Love"* (V. 245) of freedom in progressive civilization. The Goddess of Liberty proclaims, "On VIRTUE *can alone* MY KINGDOM *stand,* / *On* PUBLIC VIRTUE, EVERY VIRTUE JOIN'D" (V.93–94); the three main virtues necessary for British freedom are "INDEPENDENT LIFE; / INTEGRITY IN OFFICE; and, o'er all / Supreme, A PASSION FOR THE COMMON-WEAL." (V.121–123). The juvenilia had dwelt mostly on private, individual moral virtue, and *The Seasons* had taught the need to practice both private and public virtue; in *Liberty*, the poet's emphasis is on unselfish public virtue, or social love, and his concern is increasingly with man as a social being. *Liberty* is based on that Shaftesburyian, or more accurately Hutchesonian, benevolism seen in *The Seasons*, where active social love is independent of and superior to self-interested virtue: " 'TIS not enough, from *Self* right understood / Reflected, that ['noblest Passion's'] Rays inflame the Heart" for "FROM *sordid Self* shoot up no shining Deeds" (V. 235–236, 262). Thomson's word "Deeds" here conveys the same emphasis on active social concern, the Hutchesonian ethic of benevolent "Christian Stoicism," which would motivate the Moderate clergy and their secular counterparts in Enlightenment Scotland.[29] The poet goes on to describe this active and selfless benevolence with a Newtonian image, *"moral Gravitation"* (V.257). He had previously used the gravity image to represent the attractive force linking the Chain of Being as well as the goal of spiritual harmony of the individual rising mind (*Seasons*, "Upon Happiness"). In *Liberty*, overriding concern for the *"public Good"* (V.258) is the cohesive gravitational force which binds Thomson's ethical and historical systems and achieves the ideal of social harmony.[30]

Liberty expounds its public morality in an allegorical dream vision, recalling a similar Scottish allegory (which might also have influenced *The Seasons*), David Lindsay's *The Dreme*. Like *Liberty*, *The Dreme*, which deals specifically with Scotland's potential, treats of such sociopolitical themes as justice, patriotism, and good government. *Liberty,* the five-part historical journey led by the Goddess of Liberty, even more strongly resembles Lindsay's *The Monarche* (ca. 1552–1554), which Thomson probably knew.[31] *The Monarche,* in four books, likewise surveys the rise and fall of ancient civilizations—Assyria, Persia, Greece, and Rome. Like *Liberty, The Monarche* sets up the ideal of a limited monarchy, and both poems outline the duties of a good king (in *Liberty,* IV.1161 ff.). *The Monarche* is directed at Scottish reform, civil and mainly religious; Thomson's attacks on the medieval Roman church (IV.48–99) and on the Stuart monarchy (IV.957–1115) are similar in both theme and tone. While *The Monarche* is more explicitly religious in purpose, *Liberty* carries Thomson's implicit religious message in its broader sociopolitical and moral philosophy. Most importantly, both poems sound a strong warning against the abuse of the nation's greatest gift, freedom.

As a religious poem, *Liberty,* like *The Seasons,* shows the dual influence of the poet's old-style Scottish Calvinist and Moderate views. In general the poem's "improving" spirit, extolling progressive commercial enterprise, represents conventional Scottish Calvinist attitudes toward work and wealth. Moderate influence, informing Thomson's primary social concerns in the poem, naturally predominates: characteristic of a Moderate approach, the poet seeks to integrate religious and moral with social purposes here.[32] He pays homage to his orthodox Christian God, even within the neoclassical framework of *Liberty,* as he praises:

> . . . the whole-moving, all-informing GOD,
> The *Sun* of Beings! beaming unconfin'd
> Light, Life, and Love, and ever-active Power:
> Whom nought can image, and who best approves
> The silent Worship of the moral Heart,
> That joys in bounteous Heaven, and spreads the Joy.
> (III.49–54)

Thomson's benevolistic "beaming" deity clearly reflects optimistic Moderate views, but at the same time the poet affirms God's providential omnipotence and omnipresence, His orthodox, nondeistical attributes. In another passage, Thomson characterizes God in his favorite way as "KING OF NATURE, in full Blaze," and within a conventional Neoplatonic image of the bright beatific vision as the goal of the rising mind (III.556ff.).

Scriptural influence is also found in *Liberty,* and to an even greater degree the rhetoric of the pulpit resounds throughout the didactic poem, as Thomson roundly condemns the enemies of public virtue and of the Scottish Calvinist-Puritan work ethic, vanity, sloth, and idle wealth. Vanity is portrayed in the familiar insect parable (recalling "Winter," ll. 644–645, and "Summer," ll. 342–351, and recurring in *The Castle* I.li): "'vain Insects fluttering in the Blaze / Of Court and Ball and Play; those venal Souls . . .'" (V.593–594). Sloth, or indolence, the opposite of progressive "social LABOUR" (III.121–135; V.620ff.), is shown to have caused the downfall of both Greece and Rome (II.398; III.383). Calvinists and Puritans, while they were not opposed to wealth itself (indeed honest profit from work well done could be seen as a mark of God's favor), generally condemned the abuse of wealth, which could distract man from the ways of righteousness.[33] The poet accordingly attacks luxury or idle wealth, with especially graphic, potent homiletic rhetoric laced with Augustan indignation:

> Lo! damn'd to Wealth, at what a gross Expence,
> They purchase Disappointment, Pain and Shame.
> Instead of hearty hospitable Chear,
> See! how the Hall with brutal Riot flows;
> While in the foaming Flood, fermenting, steep'd,
> The Country maddens into Party-Rage.
> Mark! those disgraceful Piles of Wood and Stone;
> Those Parks and Gardens, where, his Haunts betrimm'd,
> And *Nature* by presumptuous *Art* oppress'd,
> The *woodland Genius* mourns. See! the full Board
> That steams Disgust, and Bowls that give no Joy:
> No *Truth* invited there, to feed the Mind;
> Nor *Wit,* the Wine rejoicing Reason quaffs.

> Hark! how the Dome with *Insolence* resounds,
> With those retain'd by *Vanity* to scare
> Repose and Friends. To tyrant *Fashion* mark!
> The costly Worship paid, to the broad Gaze
> Of Fools. From still delusive Day to Day,
> Led an eternal Round of Lying Hope,
> See! self-abandon'd, how they roam adrift,
> Dash'd o'er the Town, a miserable Wreck!
> (V.157–177)

Abuse of wealth thus fosters the sins of vanity and indolence (echoing the message of the juvenile "Upon Happiness"); these sins assume wider social importance here and ultimately undermine the common-weal, destroying a civilization. The wealthy become "A wandering, tasteless, gaily-wretched Train, / Tho' rich, are Beggars, and tho' noble, Slaves" (V.155–156). Thomson would treat of these themes most fully and coherently in the allegorical *Castle of Indolence,* where, similarly, individual religious morality is secularized and transformed to a broader social scale.

Liberty, as a sociopolitical and didactic poem, is so full of abstract ideas that it leaves very little room for any natural description. Unfortunately, the poem's theme was not at all congenial to Thomson's most valuable Scottish literary legacy, his genius for poetry of natural description, and when the poet strayed from nature his muse faltered. There is some description in the poem, but much of it is highly generalized, such as the several "cataloging" prospect views, including a remote Hebridean scene, "the Western Main, / Where Storms at large resound, and Tides immense: / From *Caledonia's* dim *Cærulean* Coast" (III.227–229). Such stylized and fanciful prospects have limited visual truth; they are often borrowed from literary or travelogue sources (for instance, this and the other Hebridean scenes in Thomson, compare "Autumn," ll. 862–865, *Castle* I.xxx, and "Britannia," ll. 84–89, derive from Martin Martin and from lines in Milton's *Lycidas*). Familiar Thomsonian patterns of borrowed imagery recur in *Liberty:* Neoplatonic light imagery and the rising mind; Newtonian imagery from both *Principia* and *Optics* (the sun/Rome as attractive force, I.103–106; "*moral Gravita-*

tion," V.257; color and prismatic imagery, II.223–225, V.13–14; re-fraction, IV.592); pastoral-Virgilian imagery; and scriptural imagery. Another sort of descriptive borrowing also occurs in the poet's descriptions of ancient sculpture (IV.134–214). Thomson probably saw these very works of art on the Grand Tour; he brought back prints and drawings of them and perhaps wrote this passage with these as models. Further, this motif probably reflects his association with George Turnbull, whose *A Treatise on Ancient Painting* (1740) shares similar didactic moral and aesthetic purposes with *Liberty;* the two friends almost certainly influenced one another. Thomson's representations of works of art within poetry look forward to his descriptions of paintings by Lorrain, Rosa, and Poussin in *The Castle.*

By far the best parts of the poem are the rare, realistic first-hand descriptions. These happy exceptions are mostly based on Thomson's observations on the Grand Tour, and the poet delights in them for their own sake. One such scene is the often-cited, sublime Alpine prospect (IV.344–362), more "amazing" even than the rugged mountains of Thomson's native Scottish Borders. The scene is dramatic, continually transforming in the shifting light; clouds and fog swirl, the stream tumbles into the lake. This is the very sort of dynamic scene Thomson captures most accurately, controlling the action and pace of the elements and recreating the subtle effects of light and atmosphere. The imagery is sensuous, energetic, and imaginative ("hollow-winding" stream, "flitting Cloud," "broken Scene," "vapour-wing'd" tempest, "gemmy Shower," "solemn-sounding Pine," mountain top which "Licks . . . the Snows") in marked contrast to the ponderous abstractions which comprise the bulk of the poem. Many of Thomson's stylistic and linguistic traits noted in *The Seasons* recur here; typically, his sound-sense patterns are most intricately woven in such passages of natural description. He again employs abundant imitative and onomatopoeic language, creative compounds, many participles, strong alliteration, deliberate assonance and consonance, and, of course, Latinate diction in such passages of directly observed description.

Except in those few descriptive passages, where Latinisms are less dense, the language of *Liberty* is heavily Latinate, pompous, and frequently so convoluted as to obscure its sense. In using such Latinate English the poet was of course working within the Scottish neo-classical tradition as well as conforming to epic convention, but in the vast and abstract *Liberty*, his rhetoric often grows monotonous or over-wrought. So, too, the blank verse, while it is surely the appropriate meter for "liberty," free from the restraint of rhyme, tends to lack the freshness and flexibility of the descriptive blank verse of *The Seasons*. Significantly lacking in *Liberty* is Thomson's expressive use of Scot-ticisms and colloquial derivatives; he clearly considered them inde-corous in his neoclassical "epic." In *The Seasons*, such diction had proved to be one of his best descriptive tools, but as *Liberty* largely abandons description, it also discards this lively and original diction. The few Scotticisms or northern archaisms which do occur include "mean time" (I.386 and elsewhere), "lowrs" (lours) (IV.160), "bootless" (as quasi-adverb, IV.644), "baffled" (V.716), "throng'd" (I.50, V.190, as "crowded," variation of Scots "thrang," *Chambers Scots Dictionary*), and "wither'd" (V. 195, possibly in the Scottish sense of trembling with cold in "wintry Winds"). Notably, these words occur mostly in Parts IV and V (1736), presumably when Thomson was hurrying to complete the work and perhaps not so meticulous about the decorum of his diction. These, too, are the parts of the poem where are found the majority of the British and Scottish descriptive scenes.

Even though *Liberty* is more formally neoclassical and decorous and carries a rather more coherent message than *The Seasons*, the poem was never popular. In *Liberty* Thomson had attempted to alter dras-tically the proportions of the basic (and in a basic sense Scottish) in-gredients of his poetry—neoclassicism, sociopolitical idealism, moral and implicitly religious didacticism, and natural description—and the epic experiment failed. This was surely because in *Liberty* the most distinctively Scottish of those ingredients, the ones which were Thom-son's most original contribution to English poetry, were so weak. His realistic, native natural description based on experience and observa-tion, expressed in a creative poetic language subtly influenced by Scots, turned out to be the least important elements in the epic con-ception of the poem. This weakness was a serious problem in the plays, too, and only later, in *The Castle of Indolence*, would Thomson fully restore those familiar Scottish ingredients to a prominent place in his poetry.

Liberty was published in 1735–1736, and although it was not as well-received as *The Seasons* had been, James Thomson was by this time a well-established and successful figure on the London literary scene. He was working on another play, *Agamemnon*, when in 1737 his friend and patron, Charles Talbot, who had appointed him to the position of secretary of the briefs, died. The grieving, apathetic Thomson neglected to reapply for the post, to the great distress of his friends.[34] The poet did not gain another government sinecure until 1744, when George Lyttelton had him appointed surveyor general, or chief customs officer, of the Leeward Islands. Thomson deputized that post to his friend, playwright William Paterson, who went to the Barbados while he himself remained in London to write.

The year 1737 was difficult for Thomson in other ways as well. In that year the Walpole government passed the notorious Stage Licensing Act, whereby stage plays had to obtain a permit from the official censor, the Lord Chamberlain, before they could be produced. This measure was designed to curb the rash of blatantly antigovernment political allusion in contemporary drama. Thomson, who had by now openly espoused the Opposition Whig cause and fully intended to express his opinions in his plays, was evidently deeply disturbed by the act. Andrew Millar published in January 1738 a new edition of Milton's defense of freedom of the press, *Areopagitica*, with an anonymous preface attributed to Thomson. Eloquently responding to the licensing act, Thomson vehemently condemned censorship of the press. Thomson, like Milton, saw literary censorship as a threat to all British liberty—the term "liberty" frequently recurs—akin to the horror of "Slavery." With passionate indignation he pleads, "because wicked things are publish'd, must there be no publishing? . . . Let no True Briton therefore be deceived. . . ."[35]

In view of the Licensing Act, it is a wonder that Thomson's next play, clearly and defiantly political, ever appeared on the stage. Yet *Agamemnon* (1738), Thomson's second classical tragedy, was licensed; probably, at this stage, government ministers did not want to call special attention to its political implications.[36] Like *Sophonisba, Agamem-*

non proved popular, particularly in its printed version; Millar had to print a second edition only three days after publication to meet public demand. The play's political message, along with some impressive descriptive poetry, certainly contributed to its success.

Again, Thomson drew from several sources for his tragedy; the plot borrows much from Seneca's and Aeschylus's versions and the character Melisander was added by the poet after Nestor's account of Aegisthus in Homer's *Odyssey.* Unfortunately, Thomson's distortion of the classical plot and characters to fit the current political situation severely weakened the dramatic effect. Generally, the wicked usurper Egisthus seems to represent Walpole; Clytemnestra, the misled Queen Caroline; Agamemnon, weak King George II; and threatened Orestes, Frederick, Prince of Wales. But again, Thomson's play lends itself to an alternative, Scottish political interpretation.[37] The usurpation theme suggests that he may also have had in mind the topical Jacobite threat; the Old Pretender, like Agamemnon, returns to his land hoping to regain a lost throne. Thomson's complex of ambivalent nationalistic feelings might well have disposed him at once to do his patriotic Whig duty—warning against the dangers of usurpation by external Jacobite force as well as internal ministerial corruption—while at the same time, perhaps, to show an element of sympathy or "sentimental Jacobitism" for the weak, defeated King Agamemnon and his son Orestes, possibly representing the exiled Pretender James VIII & III and his son, young Prince Charles Edward Stuart.

Agamemnon is less "classical" and more "romantic" than *Sophonisba.*[38] With so much passion there is again little action, and the dialogue consists of highly rhetorical speeches; nonetheless, there are a number of passages of very effective and original descriptive poetry. One such is Melisander's moving speech describing his exile on a desert island (III.i; III, 156–157). There is more than a little of Thomson himself, lover of nature, humanitarian, and religious-minded poet, in the character Melisander, who lives in harmony with all creation:

> In my own breast, a world within myself,
> In streams, in groves, in sunny hill, and shade;
> In all that blooms with vegetable life,

Or joys with kindred animal sensation;
In the full-peopled round of azure heaven;
Whene'er I, studious, look'd, I found companions.
But chief, the muses lent their soft'ning aid.

.   .   .

. . . and oft, in hymns
And rapturous thought, even with the gods convers'd,
That not disdain sometimes the walks of man.
(III.i; III, 156–157)

This scene, which recalls the shipwrecked sailor in early versions of "Summer" and also the familiar "Happy Man" theme, might also have been suggested by Scotsman Alexander Selkirk's island adventure, described by Defoe in *Robinson Crusoe* (1719). Other striking descriptions in the play are the prophecies of Cassandra; graphic and gruesome, they recall the elements of the grotesque and supernatural so important in Scottish literature and folklore. Such descriptions illustrate many of the poet's deliberate linguistic devices, noted in *The Seasons,* including the imitative language, attention to sound effects, and apt use of verbals and modifiers, especially quasi-adverbs. Thomson's sensitivity to poetic sound patterns, particularly in dynamic descriptive passages, can be detected here as in all the dramatic works. So in those rare scenes where Thomson indulges in his Scottish mode of accurate, detailed, and evocative description in his plays, poetry again prevails.[39]

Thomson's next play, *Edward and Eleanora* (1739) was not so fortunate as *Agamemnon.* It did not escape the censor's notice and was banned by the Lord Chamberlain due to a ministerial change of policy, the government having grown more strict since the success of *Agamemnon* and subsequent glut of Opposition Whig plays, including David Mallet's *Mustapha.* Dr. Johnson paraphrased one ministerial writer's remark that in *Edward* Thomson "'had taken a *Liberty* which was not agreeable to *Britannia* in any *Season.*'" Another ministerial paper, the *Hyp-Doctor* (June 5, 1739), in a scathing attack on *Edward,* blamed Thomson's views on his Scottishness: "'I should be apt to suspect that Mr. T . . . n was a Scot, for the Scots killed most of their Kings: And Captain Porteous was a pretty Fellow in his Time.'"[40]

Thomson and his friends feigned ignorance of the reasons for the ban, and in truth *Edward,* based on the apocryphal story of Edward I's crusade to the Holy Land, was less boldly controversial than *Agamemnon.* The play is mainly a praise of Frederick, Prince of Wales, leader of the Opposition Whigs; Edward and Eleanora clearly represent the Prince and Princess of Wales, and Gloster expounds Thomson's own patriotic ideals. The plot alludes to a ministerial threat to the English throne, obviously Walpole.[41]

Beyond general political parallels, the play is another experiment on Thomson's part in moving further away from neoclassical tragedy to a more sentimental, romantic theme. There is some modeling on Euripides' *Alcestis* (which George Buchanan, for one, had translated from Greek to Latin), but the play is not itself a tragedy. It is rather a melodramatic love story; its unlikely plot and impossibly virtuous characters come to a happy ending.[42] *Edward* shows Thomson again concerned with individual passions, with personal as well as public values, a concern even more fully realized in *Tancred and Sigismunda* and in *The Castle.* The play is didactic not only about social and political issues but also about the poet's early moral themes of private "virtue" and "vanity," as sermonlike rhetoric stresses:

> "What is vain life? an idle flight of days,
> A still delusive round of sickly joys.
> A scene of little cares and trifling passions,
> If not ennobled by such deeds of virtue . . ."
> (III.i; IV, 41)

Edward is most emphatically didactic on the issue of religious toleration, demonstrating Moderate influence on Thomson's ethical views as he preaches against sectarian prejudice; the poet surely had in mind recent traumas caused by religious bigotry in Britain and particularly in his native Scotland. The Arab Selim's criticism of the crusaders for their intolerance and religious persecution (V.i; IV, 74–75) recalls Thomson's comment on "christian Crimes" in *The Seasons* ("Summer," l. 855) and anticipates his criticism of wars waged by "Christian Kings" (*Castle,* I.lv.4). Some party writers attacked *Edward*'s alleged "deism," accusing Thomson of avoiding references to the

Christian God, but such attacks were mainly disguised attempts further to discredit the political views of the play. Though critical of certain attitudes and practices of the established Christian religion, the play, like all of Thomson's works, rests on a foundation of religious faith. Thomson's experimental "romantic" drama *Edward and Eleanora,* so heavily weighted with preaching and pious moralizing, lacks dramatic conflict. Nevertheless, its general political implications, with the added interest piqued by its prohibition, made it a highly successful published work in its day.[43]

Alfred, A Masque was a collaboration between Thomson and David Mallet and was performed on August 1, 1740, at Cliveden to celebrate the birthday of Prince Frederick's daughter Augusta. After *Edward,* Thomson's dramatic works became less obviously controversial;[44] the English historical and musical pageant *Alfred,* though it pointedly omits any reference to the current monarch, George II, is less an Opposition Whig propaganda statement than a broader Whig panegyric. *Alfred* requires little comment here, except that it mostly reiterates the ostentatiously patriotic themes of *Liberty,* such as the optimistic Whig vision of Britain's progress and glorious future and another attack on the Stuart monarchy. *Alfred* is remembered mainly for the Bard's concluding ode, "Rule, Britannia," which family tradition and abundant evidence attribute to Thomson; in truth, however, the song is memorable more for Thomas Arne's music than for Thomson's lyrics.[45] *Alfred* was revived at Drury Lane in 1745, possibly in part to stir patriotic feeling against the Jacobites. After Thomson's death, Mallet considerably revised the masque, including "Rule, Britannia," which he then claimed as his own in his collected *Works* (1759).

This period of the 1740s was a difficult time for Scots in London. Far from home, hypersensitive about their Scottishness, they were often treated as foreigners and set apart by their speech (Thomson himself kept a broad Scottish accent throughout his life); they tended to behave as foreigners, banding together and helping one another. Their national self-consciousness was frequently heightened by English ridicule and enmity. Apart from English scorn of the Scots' provincial ways, there was in the 1730s and particularly in the 1740s the very real fear of Jacobitism; this theme seems to have been an undercurrent in several of Thomson's plays of the period. Paranoia ran rampant, as even Scots who were avowed Whigs were regarded with suspicion. Andrew Mitchell, under secretary of state for Scotland and Thomson's close friend, wrote to Duncan Forbes in Scotland that in London around 1745 every Scotsman was " 'looked on as a traitor, as one secretly inclined to the Pretender and waiting but an opportunity to declare.' " Opposition Whigs were not infrequently accused of Jacobitism by establishment Whigs.[46] Thomson, as a committed Opposition Whig, would have been one of those Scots held suspect, despite his very vocal British patriotism, publicly proclaimed in *The Seasons, Liberty,* "Britannia," and *Alfred.* Indeed, the poet's overweening, aggressive pro-British patriotism at this time carried a certain tone of defensiveness, conscious or unconscious, countering any such suspicions. Officially Thomson left no record of his reaction to the Jacobite threat other than some strongly anti-Stuart historical passages in *Liberty* IV and an attack on the Stuart reign in *Alfred.* It is interesting to speculate, however, that he very possibly attacked the Jacobites anonymously in one of the many political periodicals of the time.

Perhaps the most likely of these was Henry Fielding's *True Patriot;* it aimed to support the Whig administration and to alert the citizenry to the dangers of Jacobitism to British liberty. Fielding was a friend of Thomson's; both novelist and poet enjoyed the patronage of Lyttelton and Dodington. In the *Patriot's* opening number (Tuesday, November 5, 1745) the anonymous editor (Fielding himself) gives clues as to his identity: he is a "Gentleman," an author and wit, a zealous Protestant, and "of no Party," thus,

> From some, or all of these Reasons, I am very likely Mr. W[in-ningto]n, Mr. D[odingto]n, Mr. L[yttelto]n, Mr. Mr. [*sic*] F[ield-in]g, T[homso]n, or indeed any other Person who hath ever distinguished himself in the Republic of Letters.
>
> This at least is very probable, that some of these Gentlemen may contribute a Share of their Abilities to the carrying on this Work. . . .[47]

Since Thomson is mentioned here, it seems very probable that he did contribute to the *True Patriot.* One entry worth noting is a letter from

"Gravis" (no. 11, Tuesday, January 14, 1746) condemning the laziness, sloth, and "Luxury" (such as brought Rome's fall) which are presently corrupting Britain; this echoes *Liberty's* theme and tone and anticipates the message of *The Castle.* Indeed, the *True Patriot's* more general purpose, to rouse apathetic Britain to action, corresponds to the sociopolitical goal of the Knight of Arts and Industry in *The Castle,* which Thomson was working on at this time. More importantly, the *Patriot* pleads strongly for tolerance toward loyal Scotsmen, urging the English not to condemn all Scots people for the offenses of the Jacobite rebels. Loyal Hanoverian Thomson himself had no doubt been the victim of such wholesale anti-Scottish prejudice. He may also have suggested or collaborated on another entry, "Observations on the Present Rebellion"; the author of "Observations" attacks the "indiscriminate Censure" in "this Season" of the whole "Scottish Nation" and highly praises the courage and patriotism of the Moderate "Scotch Clergy" as well as the honest, long-suffering "common People of the Lowlands." If Thomson did not actually write this piece, he certainly wholeheartedly shared its views. The *Patriot* also advocates mercy for the conquered Highlanders, reflecting the tolerant sentiments of editor Fielding and of concerned Scots such as Duncan Forbes and Thomson himself.[48]

The *True Patriot* was published not by Fielding's usual publisher Andrew Millar, who was also Thomson's publisher, but instead by Mrs. Mary Cooper. Millar, a Scot, probably felt it wise to avoid identification with the *Patriot's* attacks on his fellow-Scotsmen.[49] Millar's attitude—firmly anti-Jacobite yet not wishing to appear anti-Scottish and therefore declining to take a public stand against the Jacobites—was surely Thomson's own. Despite his staunch Whig allegiance and anti-Jacobitism, though, Thomson may have found that the Jacobite rising of 1745 rekindled his "nostalgic" Scottish patriotism, just as the "'15" rebellion had raised his national pride when he was a student in Edinburgh under Allan Ramsay's influence; such feeling among young Thomson and his contemporaries, it will be recalled, inspired the Anglo-Scottish patriotism celebrated in *The Edinburgh Miscellany.* So while he publicly continued to channel his Scottish nationalistic sentiment into broader, British patriotism, Thomson could never disclaim his North British roots nor deny how much they meant to him.

Back in Scotland in 1745, Edinburgh and the Borders were again under siege; the Moderate clergy of the Scottish church expressed a dual allegiance similar to Thomson's but in a more active way. They actually prepared to join the militia to protect Edinburgh with military force, and while preaching their patriotic Hanoverian loyalty they also proclaimed their strong Scottish national pride. They were outspoken in their criticism of the British government for failing to provide adequate militia to guard the Lowlands since 1603. These Moderates saw the '45 rising in religious and moral as well as political terms. They felt that the Jacobite rebellion was a providential punishment visited by a wrathful God upon a corrupt Great Britain and recognized the need for a cleansing "regeneration" of society, a regeneration such as Thomson's religious and sociopolitical allegory *The Castle of Indolence* would project in poetry.[50]

All Scots, even the most ardent Whigs and Hanoverians, could not but be saddened by the effects of the '45 on their native land and people. Lady Grisell Baillie, Thomson's kinswoman living in London, found the rebellion "a great affliction to her; the distress of her country and friends went near her heart, and made great impression on her health and spirits."[51] Duncan Forbes of Culloden, now Lord President of Session, tried valiantly to minimize violence in the Highlands during the rebellion; after the uprising, as he had also done in 1715, he counseled mercy in dealing with his rebellious countrymen and consequently was himself under strong suspicion of Jacobitism and treason. Thomson's attitude, too, was surely that he wanted, above all, what was best for Scotland: he still had family and friends there and would have felt deep concern for them. He said nothing publicly about his uncomfortable position so as not to incur undue suspicion, yet his very silence is eloquent: he would not compromise his Scottishness in voicing even anti-Jacobite sentiments lest they be taken as anti-Scottish as well.

An interesting if improbable legend survives that Thomson did in fact compose a "Jacobite" lyric. The poet's garrulous barber William Taylor, interviewed in 1791, swore that "'Shepherd, who formerly kept the Castle inn, showed me a book of Thomson's writing, which was about the rebellion in 1745, and set to music, but I think he told me not published.'" The interviewer added, "I mentioned this to Mr. [Dr. William] Robertson, but he thought Taylor had made a small mistake; perhaps it might be some of the patriotic songs in the Masque of Alfred."[52] If Thomson had indeed written such a piece he would wisely have suppressed it, though his Scottish circle of intimate friends would have enjoyed a Jacobite satire; it is difficult to imagine a Scottish work being confused with the ultra-English *Alfred*.

Thomson's play *Tancred and Sigismunda*, published in 1745, carefully makes no very explicit reference to the current Jacobite unrest. The most obvious contemporary political allusion in *Tancred* is the reconciliatory gesture,

> "I here renounce those errors and divisions
> That have so long disturb'd our peace, and seem'd
> Fermenting still, to threaten new commotions—
> By time instructed, let us not disdain
> To quit mistakes . . ."
> (II.iv; IV, 124)

This, according to Benjamin Victor, was a pronouncement of the current Opposition Whig position: in 1742 Walpole's administration had finally fallen and the Opposition Whigs, the party of "liberty," had prevailed. This liberation from Opposition party-political purpose now freed Thomson to develop plot, characters, and philosophy with far greater fullness and imagination. Yet political reference (contrary to conventional readings of the play) remains an important, if subtle, element in *Tancred* and again the play has certain Scottish associations. For *Tancred* is a conscious and cautious attempt on Thomson's part to placate the restless Jacobites in that crucial year of 1745 while at the same time satisfy the Hanoverians of the poet's continued loyalty. As John Loftis persuasively argues, the play's themes of rival dynastic claims, fear of civil war, and desire to reconcile two feuding royal families could well apply to the current situation in Britain; a number of the speeches could be interpreted to favor either the Hanoverians or the Jacobites equally, yet many do have an undeniably Jacobite ring to them. Tancred, for example, proclaims his loyalty to a "prince in Sicily" who represents the true line of royal succession; he prophesies a rally of "loyal Hearts" to his cause (I.iv), and the emphasis is clearly on ancient lineal descent (such as the Stuarts claimed), though the Sicilian prince could also be identified with Frederick, Prince of Wales, or his father, George II.[53] Why did Thomson deliberately sustain such clever ambiguity of political interpretation throughout *Tancred*? To avoid censorship, of course, and also to appeal to the widest possible theater-going audience. But also (as he had done in *Agamemnon*), surely to signify that despite his strong Hanoverian allegiance he was a Scot in London in 1745, feeling once again that insistent strain of Scottish sentiment for the Stuart cause, or at least sympathy for his fellow-Scots who embraced that cause.

While contemporary political allusions in *Tancred* are implicit, am-biguous, even obscure, other familiar Thomsonian themes are treated more directly. The didactic strains of public morality and social benev-olence recur; further, the play represents Thomson's return to in-creasing emphasis on personal moral concerns. The weighing of uni-versal against individual values here has been termed "Hutchesonian" and corresponds to the poet's more subjective expression and roman-tic focus on personal feelings in the dramas. Such renewed concern with individual and more subjective values, and specifically the secu-larized virtue of industry as the root of social love, would culminate in *The Castle of Indolence*. Social love was indeed the Moderates' antidote to the grave ills of British society which brought God's wrath in 1745.[54] Tancred insists (voicing the views of Hutcheson and Thom-son) that " 'There is, / Can be no public without private virtue' " (II.viii; IV, 136). Thomson reaffirms his religious faith in the play; Tancred's prayer, for example, is addressed to an ever-active, pro-vidential, nondeistical deity: " 'O wonder-working Hand / That, in majestic silence, sways at will / The mighty movements of unbounded nature' " (I.iv; IV, 109).

Tancred had to be much shortened for the stage. Thomson's friend, statesman Andrew Mitchell, probably referring to the abridged *Tan-cred,* later remarked to James Boswell that " 'the Drama was not [Thomson's] province. He was too descriptive. When a sentiment pleased him he used to extend it with rich luxuriance. His friends used to prune very freely, and poor Thomson used to suffer.' "[55] This candid comment recalls that youthful poetic "luxuriance" which Professor William Hamilton was obliged to reprimand; the poet's rhetorical over-enthusiasm was never entirely subdued.

In *Tancred* Thomson finally achieved Voltaire's ideal of the drama, wherein the time-honored classical unities are combined with freer, more romantic, and experimental interpretations of plot and character. The now-familiar theme of selfless patriotism, or "reason," as represented by the stern father Siffredi's sacrifice, is central to the play and is again set in conflict with the love of hero and heroine, their "passion," as in *Edward and Eleanora.* For the first time, however, patriotism now takes second place to romance; Thomson's sympathy is wholly with the tragic lovers and he asserts that passion can be right, reason wrong.[56] The love story of *Tancred and Sigismunda* holds a strongly subjective element which gives life and psychological realism to the drama. The depth of emotion in this play, portraying unfortunate lovers (compare "Spring") was inspired by the poet's own troubled love for Elizabeth Young. The theme of parental oppression, represented by Siffredi, may also be a comment on Miss Young's cruel mother, who opposed a marriage between her daughter and Thomson.[57] Grieving Siffredi finally cautions parents, " 'who from nature stray, / And the great ties of social life betray; / Ne'er with your children act a tyrant's part . . .' " (V.viii; IV, 200). It was in the fateful year of 1745, the year *Tancred* appeared, that Thomson made his last attempt to woo Miss Young and was rejected.

Tancred and Sigismunda never achieves wholly natural portrayal of action, character, dialogue, and emotion; there is still that characteristic distance resulting from the formal language and themes of Thomson's chosen form, the tragedy. He continues, typically and verbosely, to elevate philosophical abstractions such as passion versus reason and public versus private good above psychological truth.[58] Nonetheless, *Tancred* is certainly Thomson's most carefully constructed plot, his most readable and "human" play, his one "genuine tragedy."[59] It was widely popular from the first and enjoyed numerous revivals in the eighteenth and nineteenth centuries. It was especially successful in Scotland, being one of the rare plays by a Scot which played in Edinburgh beyond one season; with *The Gentle Shep-*

herd and Home's *Douglas,* it became a repertory favorite in the north.[60] In *Tancred and Sigismunda,* as in *The Seasons,* Thomson's bold experimentation, fortified with a liberal dose of personal, subjective experience (along with some finely gauged pro-Hanoverian and at the same time pro-Scottish political comment) had at last earned him a substantial and long-lived triumph in dramatic tragedy.

Thomson's final play was *Coriolanus* (written 1746–1747). Thomson did not live to see it produced in January 1749; it had been delayed by a dispute between actors David Garrick (Tullus) and Quin (Coriolanus). The 1749 performance was staged partly to benefit the late poet's sisters in Scotland. For his plot, Thomson characteristically synthesized several different sources. He certainly knew Shakespeare's version and also its source, Plutarch; Thomson's adaptation is in some ways more original and stageworthy than Shakespeare's.[61] Whereas much of Shakespeare's action occurs in the Roman political arena itself, Thomson's *Coriolanus,* largely encompassing Shakespeare's acts IV and V, is better balanced, simpler, and more concentrated; much of Thomson's play is set in the Volscians' camp and his plot is presented more from their viewpoint. Again, the pattern seen in *Sophonisba,* of Thomson's ambivalence toward Roman values and of a degree of sympathy for the integrity of the smaller nation, emerges: are the Romans models of social virtue, or are they oppressors? Heroes or tyrants? Thomson seems never to have resolved this dilemma to his own satisfaction but, corresponding to his own British and Scottish conflicts, his ambivalence appears to generate a certain creativity, a "negative capability," in his handling of the themes of nationalism and patriotism in the dramas.

Significantly, the central contemporary political allusion in *Coriolanus* seems to be a conscious reference to the Jacobite crisis. Prince Charles Edward Stuart and his army advanced on London in late 1745, arousing the fearful panic of Londoners. But after reaching Derby, the prince inexplicably retreated and the tide turned in favor of the Hanoverians. The history of Coriolanus—a noble, rebellious leader camping outside his own capital, then withdrawing—closely parallels the Jacobites' abortive London campaign. *Coriolanus* probably celebrates the Whig poet Thomson's relief as well as gratification at this turn of events.[62] Again the persistent Rome/Britain parallel implicitly reasserts itself: the city of Rome is clearly linked with London as capitals of nations under threat. The poet certainly shows some sympathy with the brave, warlike Volscians, perhaps representing the Scots, hinting at, if not a "sentimental Jacobite" strain, at least a concern and respect for his countrymen. The Anglo-Scottish poet is still obviously ambivalent about his national allegiance. The pacifist character Galesus, invented by Thomson, might speak for those such as Duncan Forbes who would urge mercy toward the Jacobite rebels. But Coriolanus, and Scottish Jacobite hopes, were killed; both leaders had been proud "traitors" to their nations, Rome and Great Britain. While it is very likely that Thomson had the complex Scottish situation in mind here, his final moral, " 'Then be this truth the star by which we steer, / *Above* ourselves *our COUNTRY should be dear'* " (V.iv; IV, 286) ultimately refers to his united *"COUNTRY"* of Great Britain.

For the first time in Thomson's dramas there is no love theme in *Coriolanus;* the poet was despondent over the loss of his beloved Elizabeth Young when he wrote the play and clearly sought to avoid any trace of the romantic so important in his previous plays. Writing to Mallet, he claimed to be "pretty much indifferent whether he [*Coriolanus*] appear upon the Stage or no." The poet, numb with grief, returned to the solid and admired yet remote classical world for his plot and there reiterated his public values and virtues, once again steering clear of private concerns. He accordingly chose to portray a hero conspicuously deficient in emotion and particularly love. [63]

As a tragedy, *Coriolanus* seems to have suffered from Thomson's own broken heart; his attempt to renounce passion and return to reason resulted in an unsympathetic, hollow hero, a spiritless play. The poet's relentlessly elevated rhetoric, his public preaching on patriotism and on Pythagorean philosophy and pacifism is abstract and empty. There is little enlivening emotion or human interest to provoke dramatic conflict. *Coriolanus*, like that "failed epic" *Liberty*, lacks the vital, empirical ingredients of Thomson's best work—natural description and subjective experience—to leaven the weight of ideas. So despite a few passages of noble blank verse, *Coriolanus* largely lacks poetry.[64] Happily, however, *Coriolanus* did not signal a final decline in James Thomson's poetic powers. He was able to overcome his personal sorrow to complete in 1748 the imaginative and finely crafted poem *The Castle of Indolence*.

Throughout his life in London, while writing his poems and plays, James Thomson conscientiously kept up many fruitful contacts with Scotland, both public and private. He kept abreast of Scottish affairs and especially schemes for Scottish improvement through Duncan Forbes (who conceived of many such schemes) and through Forbes's agent in Edinburgh, George Ross, friend and correspondent of the poet and his circle. Through Forbes Thomson also met John Campbell, duke of Argyll, who virtually ruled Scotland for much of the century and was considered by many Scots in London a link with "home." Especially, his knowledge of Scottish affairs was supplied by his good friend and member of the Scottish circle Andrew Mitchell (1708–1771). Mitchell, under secretary of state for Scotland under Tweeddale (1743–1747), worked closely with Forbes on Scottish tax reforms and other improvements, and as a Scotsman with intimate understanding of the clans on settling the '45 with justice and mercy toward the Highlanders. After 1747, when the office of Scottish secretary temporarily lapsed, Mitchell became Member of Parliament for Aberdeenshire and acted as consultant to the government on Scottish affairs. He later served as envoy to the court of Frederick the Great at Berlin.[65]

The wealth of James Thomson's valuable "public" ties with Scotland is recorded in the list of subscribers to *The Seasons* (1730) and also the *Works* (1762, Murdoch's Memorial Edition); the high proportion of Scots, some representing institutions and many in high places, is impressive. Among *Seasons* (1730) subscribers were the duke of Argyll; earl of Bute; King's College Library, Aberdeen; William Aikman; Sir William Bennet of Grubbet; the Hon. Hugh Dalrymple; Robert Dundas of Arnistoun; Edinburgh University Library; several of the Border Elliots, including Lord Minto; Duncan Forbes (five books): Rt. Hon. Patrick Lindsay (Lord Provost of Edinburgh, ten books); former Lord Provost George Drummond; the duke of Roxburghe; John Clerk of Penicuik; Allan Ramsay; Simon, Lord Lovat; Lord Jedburgh; and many other Scottish noblemen and friends. Thomson's brother

John ordered four books; other subscribers were the poet's friends Dr. William Cranstoun, David Mallet, Lord Binning, Patrick Murdoch, William Paterson, Hugh Warrender, Thomas and William Watts, John Gray, George Ross, Andrew Mitchell, Robert Symmer, and Joseph Mitchell, to name but a few. Scotsmen were again generous in subscribing to the *Works* of 1762, and included Dr. John Armstrong; James Boswell, Jr.; James Craig (Thomson's nephew and Edinburgh New Town architect); the Kelso Library; Andrew Mitchell; and many, many more. The strength of Scottish support for Thomson's literary achievements illustrates not merely poetical appreciation but also a Scottish solidarity, a show of national loyalty. Thomson represented successful Anglo-Scottish, North British poetic ambition and was thus the object of legitimate Scottish national pride.

In private life, too, Thomson took care to maintain connections, especially family connections, with Scotland. Though he apologized for being a poor correspondent, he kept in touch with his relatives, particularly with his sisters in Edinburgh, Elizabeth ("Lisy") and Jean, and took an active interest in their affairs. He sent them what money he could through friends the Rev. Mr. Gusthart and Baillie Gavin Hamilton there and helped his sisters set up a milliner's shop, arranging for it to be stocked through his friend in London, draper John Sargent. He rejoiced in their marriages: Lisy to Mr. Robert Bell, minister of Strathaven, and Jean to Robert Thomson, master of Lanark Grammar School.[66] Thomson's eldest sister, Mary Craig, wife of Edinburgh merchant William Craig, was the mother of architect James Craig; she was executrix (in absentia) of the poet's estate. Thomson's younger brother John came to London to live with him for a time in the early 1730s and served as his amanuensis. John became ill with consumption, however, and returned to Scotland in 1735, where to Thomson's deep sorrow he soon died. Two of the poet's distant relations, the brothers Gilbert and Thomas Thomson, came to work as the poet's gardeners at Richmond.[67]

Thomson pursued many of the same interests in England that he had acquired as a youth in Scotland, such as horticulture, art history and appreciation, an avocation given new impetus by his Grand Tour and opportunity to collect prints and drawings, and, of course, avid reading of classical, historical, and geographical literature. Around 1735 Thomson settled in a comfortable home with a pleasant garden in the London suburb of Richmond; there he led a casual life, keeping eccentric hours, and his home atmosphere was warm and genial. He welcomed friends, and especially his Scottish circle, to the cottage in Kew Lane and kept his cellar well stocked with "Scotch ale."[68]

Among the poet's closest friends during his London years were both Scotsmen and Englishmen, for despite his deep-rooted conflicts of national and personal identity Thomson was an amiable, good-natured, and tolerant man. He was one of the few Scottish authors to find favor and friendship with many of the London literati, including Pope, Aaron Hill, and Shenstone; Englishmen George Bubb Dodington and George Lyttelton were among his most concerned and generous patrons. When asked whether Thomson was "national in his affections?" the poet's friend and neighbor in Richmond, Dr. William Robertson, replied that "He had no prejudices whatever.—He was the most liberal of men in all his sentiments."[69]

Still, typical of Scots in eighteenth-century London, Thomson's circle of most intimate friends was largely made up of Scots. It is significant that Thomson found himself at the center of an established Scottish circle of loyal friends, many of whom he had known since student days in Edinburgh. He kept in contact with Duncan Forbes, but the busy Lord President was frequently away in Scotland, so they probably did not see one another often. Forbes's son John, or "Jock," however, came to be one of the poet's dearest friends and an important member of the Scottish circle. Jock served in the army (ca. 1738–1749); he is the "joyous Youth" of *The Castle* (I.lxii–lxiv) who arrives occasionally to disturb the circle's peaceful indolence with his excess of energy and good humor. Patrick Murdoch, before he was ordained, was Jock's tutor on the Grand Tour (ca. 1729–1732); the two probably met up with Thomson and Talbot at some point on the Continent. Duncan Forbes was very concerned about his son's education and welfare; Murdoch wrote to the worried father (June 24, 1730) about Jock's antics in Europe:

the apprehension your Lordship has been under, that [Jock's] head might suffer by some civilities he met with on the road will be over, when I assure you that any vanity of that sort is not his foible. . . . he is ever ready, in very good earnest, to own the necessity of redeeming the time he has lost, and to enter into resolutions and schemes for that purpose.

Jock's high spirits did eventually cause him trouble; he became a chronic spender, perpetually in debt, which greatly disturbed the elder Forbes as well as the boy's friends. Andrew Millar, for one, lent him large sums while lamenting his wastefulness. Still, Jock was much loved. After his father's death in 1749 he settled in Suffolk near Murdoch. Thomson called Jock "the dearest, truest, heartiest Youth that treads on Scottish Ground." He is frequently and affectionately mentioned in the correspondence of Scottish circle members Andrew Mitchell, John Armstrong, Andrew Millar, and especially Patrick Murdoch.[70]

Patrick ("Peter," "Petie," or "Patie") Murdoch, Thomson's fellow divinity student, was a long-standing member of the Scottish circle and kept in close contact with the poet throughout his life. He became a minister of the Church of England and settled as rector of Stradishall, Suffolk. Thomson wrote to George Ross of Murdoch's ordination:

Pe[t]ie came here two three Days ago. I have not yet seen the round Man of God, to be. He is to be Parsonifyed, a few Days hence. How a Gown and Cassock will become him! And with what a bold Leer he will edify the devout Females! There is no Doubt of his having a Call; for he is immediately to enter upon a tolerable Living—God grant him more, and as fat as himself. It rejoices me to see one worthy honest excellent Man raised, at least, to an Independency.

Murdoch is the "little, round, fat, oily Man of God" with the "roguish Twinkle in his Eye" of *The Castle* (I.lxix). He was also a respected mathematician and especially well versed in Newtonian science; he edited Colin McLaurin's *An Account of Sir Isaac Newton's Philosophical Discoveries* (1748) and wrote a memoir of his teacher McLaurin as well as a number of other scientific works. Murdoch edited Thomson's *Works* of 1762, wisely correcting Lord Lyttelton's liberal emendations to *The Seasons* and insisting upon returning to the poet's own text.[71]

Statesman Andrew Mitchell, a son of the manse, was born in Edinburgh and went to England in 1729; he had been at Edinburgh University with Thomson and remained the poet's faithful friend. Writing to Jock Forbes, Patrick Murdoch recalled of Mitchell:

> His honesty and superior talents for business are acknowledged and admired—and what he is in private life you and I best know—Has he not been as a father to us both? the Same to McLaurin's family—to Thomson, and of late to [Hugh] Warrender? and to many others that we never heard of? And all with a narrow fortune, and moving in an inferior Sphere.

Mitchell, with Lyttelton, was an executor of Thomson's estate. Murdoch praised Mitchell as "a gentleman equally noted for the truth and constancy of his private friendships, and for his address and spirit as a public minister."[72]

Hugh Warrender, mentioned above, was another Edinburgh classmate who remained Thomson's friend in England. Like Murdoch, he was eventually ordained in the Church of England; he became rector of Aston, Yorkshire. Also in the Scottish circle was Robert Symmer, who knew Thomson in Edinburgh and contributed to the *Edinburgh Miscellany*. Symmer seems to have gone to work as a tutor to children of nobility.[73]

William Paterson, still another university-fellow of Thomson's, also stayed a close friend. He worked as a clerk in London and also acted as Thomson's amanuensis for a time. Like Thomson, Paterson, too, tried his hand at tragedy: Murdoch recounts that Paterson's Germanic tragedy *Arminius* (1740) was banned by the Lord Chamberlain soon after Thomson's own *Edward and Eleanora* was prohibited simply because it was in the same handwriting as Thomson's politically sensitive play. *Arminius*, which shows the influence of Thomson's *Liberty*, was, however, far more controversial than *Edward* and was perhaps more deservedly banned.[74] In 1744 Thomson made Paterson his joint-patentee or deputy when the poet was appointed surveyor general of the Leeward Islands. Paterson succeeded Thomson in the surveyor generalship in 1746; Thomson probably recognized that his friend would be better at handling the practical, fiscal duties of the post than he himself. Paterson went to live in Bridgetown, Barbados, and from there continued to correspond with Thomson, supplying the poet with first-hand descriptions of tropical life which would influence revisions of "Summer." Paterson, a quiet, modest man, is thought to be *The Castle*'s "Night-pensioner" (I.lvii–lix), ". . . a Man of special grave Remark: / A certain tender Gloom o'erspred his Face, / Pensive not sad, in Thought involv'd not dark." An incurable dreamer, "Ten thousand glorious Systems would he build, / Ten thousand great Ideas fill'd his Mind."[75]

It is just possible, though, that *The Castle*'s thoughtful "Night-pensioner" might have been another Scottish circle member, George Turnbull (1698–1748), moral philosopher and art historian:

> As soot this Man could sing as Morning-Lark,
> And teach the noblest Morals of the Heart:
> But These his Talents were ybury'd stark;
> Of the fine Stores he Nothing would impart,
> Which or boon Nature gave, or Nature-painting Art.
> (*Castle*, I.lvii.5–8)

Turnbull, a contemporary of Thomson's at Edinburgh University (1717–1721), was a prolific author; his most important works were *The Principles of Moral Philosophy* and *A Treatise of Ancient Painting* (both published by Andrew Millar, 1740). He can hardly be said to have been "ybury'd stark" or to have "left no Tracet behind" (I.lix.9) in the world of letters; still, Turnbull was never widely appreciated and his works faded fast from public notice. Turnbull, a son of the manse, was an enthusiastic Newtonian and taught philosophy at Marischal College, Aberdeen; his most famous pupil was philosopher Thomas Reid. He then went to England, where in the 1730s he associated with the literati, including Thomson. In his preface to *Moral Philosophy* Turnbull expressed the wish that some poet—evidently Thomson— would versify the beauties and laws of the universe which Newton had systematized. He hoped "a certain poet, who is universally confessed to have shown a most extraordinary genius for descriptive poetry in some of his works, and in all of them a heart deeply impregnated with the warmest love of virtue and mankind," and who was also his good friend, would take up his challenge as a labor of love. Turnbull and Thomson, having come from the same Scottish background, shared the same early Scottish Enlightenment views on both ethics and aesthetics; Thomson expressed them in poetry, Turnbull in prose. Turnbull's *Moral Philosophy* probably influenced Thomson's moral ideas (see Chapter 6). *Liberty* almost certainly suggested the subject and plan of *Ancient Painting* ("On the Rise, Progress and Decline of that Art amongst the Greeks and Romans") to which Thomson and the Scottish circle subscribed and which in turn influenced the passages on descriptive painting in *The Castle*. A deeply religious man and committed Christian, Turnbull ultimately entered the ministry of the Church of England and served in Drumachose, Northern Ireland.[76]

The remaining Scottish circle member to be honored with a place in *The Castle* was Dr. John Armstrong (1709–1779), "One shyer still, who quite detested Talk: / Oft, stung by Spleen" (I.lx). Armstrong was the author of "Winter," that verse in imitation of Shakespeare which may have influenced Thomson's "Winter." Not very successful as a physician in London, Armstrong pursued his poetical career, specializing in didactic works such as *The Œconomy of Love* (1736) and blank-verse *Art of Preserving Health* (1744). He was known for his gloomy and taciturn nature; Thomson wrote to Paterson that "there is a certain Kind of Spleen that is both humane and agreeable. . . ." Armstrong composed the four concluding stanzas to Canto I of *The Castle*, describing in grotesque detail the physical consequences of indolence. Despite his splenetic disposition, Armstrong was a loyal friend to Thomson, and with the poet's neighbor Dr. William Robertson attended him at his deathbed.[77]

Another regular member of the Scottish circle was publisher and bookseller Andrew Millar (1707–1768), son of Robert Millar, minister of Paisley. He served his apprenticeship in printing in Edinburgh and may have first met Thomson there. He went to London in 1728 or 1729, eventually setting up at Tonson's old shop, the Shakespeare's Head, which he patriotically renamed Buchanan's Head. Millar was known for his special generosity to Scottish authors. He published, in addition to Thomson's *Seasons* and collected *Works,* a number of Ramsay's and Mallet's works, Hume's and Robertson's histories, Turnbull's treatises, Armstrong's didactic poems, and Colin McLaurin's *Account of Sir Isaac Newton's Philosophy* edited by Murdoch. He is also said to have published some of Sir William Bennet of Grubbet's Latin poems, brought from Edinburgh with the unsold sheets of Archibald Pitcairne's *Poemata*. Millar was described by Dr. William Robertson, also a Scottish circle intimate, as "a good-natured fellow, and not an unpleasant companion, but he was a little contracted by his business; had the dross of a bookseller about him." Nonetheless, Millar remained not only Thomson's fair and generous publisher but also his true friend; he donated the profits from Murdoch's 1762 edition of Thomson's *Works* toward a monument to the poet in Westminster Abbey.[78]

One lifelong friend and compatriot of Thomson's who stayed on the outer fringes of the Scottish circle itself was David Mallet. Mallet was not well liked even by fellow Scotsmen in London: as Dr. Johnson recalled, "it was remarked of him that he was the only Scot whom Scotchmen did not commend." But Mallet and Thomson, who had been classmates at university, remained close. The two were very different in disposition and demeanor—Mallet dapper, smooth, unscrupulous and Thomson corpulent, unkempt, but sincere and good-hearted. Mallet may have been the more self-interested party in maintaining the friendship with Thomson, who became the more talented and famous poet. Thomson's other friends found it difficult to understand their relationship; Dr. William Robertson observed that "Sir, [Mallet] had not Thomson's heart.—He was not sound at the core; he made a cat's paw of Thomson, and I did not like the man on that account." Yet Thomson was genuinely fond of Mallet, who had been so helpful to him in his early months in London.[79]

Mallet was in many instances more explicitly Scottish in his writings than Thomson; always the literary opportunist, he tended to exploit his Scottishness when expedient and also to suppress it as he did his Scots accent when it seemed more prudent. Some saw his play *Eurydice* (1731) as pro-Jacobite; the political parallels were set forth by an anonymous pamphleteer. If in fact Mallet's neo-Greek tragedy could be interpreted as an instance of "sentimental Jacobitism,"[80] then the underlying patterns of thought and feeling in Thomson's own neo-classical dramas can certainly be seen to correspond, indirectly, to his perceptions of current Scottish-English relations. Thomson, however, was far more cautious in his expressions of Scottish nationalistic sympathy. He by no means concealed his love for Scotland, but neither did he draw attention to it for literary effect; rather, as a true North Briton he continued sincerely to try to reconcile his loyalties to Scotland with his strong British patriotism. Thus his nationalistic conflicts and insecurities, while certainly present, were less conspicuous than those of such Scots as Ramsay, Mallet, and Boswell. Mallet frequently followed Thomson's poetic lead, exaggerating or expanding Thomson's ideas and descriptions; *The Excursion* was thus much influenced by *The Seasons*. Mallet's tragic poem *Amyntor and Theodora* (1747) is another of his specifically Scottish works; set in St. Kilda, it echoes Thomson's tribute in "Autumn" to the unspoilt islanders and is likewise based on Martin Martin. Here Mallet elaborates Thomson's pre-Romantic conceptions of the Highlands and islands which anticipate Ossianic literature. As they had when they were fellow-members of the Grotesque Club in Edinburgh, Mallet and Thomson would continue throughout their careers to take an active interest in one another's literary productions while struggling, each in his own way, to meet the challenge of surviving as Scots in London.

Joseph Mitchell, poet and dramatist who had encouraged both Thomson and Mallet to make their poetic debut in Edinburgh, was one London Scot who failed to gain entry into Thomson's congenial Scottish circle. This was largely due to his ill-tempered remark, when presented by the author with a copy of "Winter," that " 'Beauties and faults so thick lye scattered here, / Those I could read, if these were not so near,' " to which Thomson replied extempore,

> "Why not all faults, injurious Mitchell; why
> Appears one beauty to thy blasted eye;
> Damnation worse than thine, if worse can be,
> Is all I ask, and all I want from thee."

Whether or not the testy, mercurial Mitchell was jesting, Thomson seems never to have forgiven his insult. Further, Mitchell was a supporter of Walpole, deeply offending Thomson's political principles. The less successful poet Mitchell probably also resented his protégé Thomson as a rival. Mitchell did, however, pay Thomson a genuine compliment in his "To Mr. Thomson, the Author of Winter" (1729), which alludes to their early association on the *Edinburgh Miscellany:*

> I prophesy'd of Thee; nor blush to own
> The Joy I feel, in making THOMSON known,
> Thy first Attempts, to me, a promise made:
> That Promise is, by this Performance, paid.

Mitchell's mock-heroic "The Charms of Indolence" (1729) may have helped suggest to Thomson the theme of his *The Castle of Indolence.*[81]

One more significant Scottish connection in Thomson's London life meant perhaps the most to the poet: the love of his life, Elizabeth Young ("Amanda"). She was a Scotswoman from Gulyhill, Dumfriesshire. John Ramsay of Ochtertyre described her as a "gentle-mannered, elegant-minded woman," even though her mother was reputedly coarse and ill-mannered. Another writer, however, called her "as regular a red-haired, 'rump-fed ronyon' as ever startled the passing traveller into wondering whether she were man or woman." Yet another source portrayed Miss Young as a woman " 'violent and harsh in expression' " who spoke with a broad Scots accent, yet despite her faults possessing " 'as strong humanity as any woman I ever was acquainted with' " and having many " 'good qualities.' " Miss Young was the sister-in-law of Thomson's neighbor in Richmond, Dr. William Robertson; the poet met her at Robertson's home about 1742 and fell deeply in love. His letters to her of 1743–1745 reveal his sensitive and passionate nature and the pathetic persistence of his unrequited feelings for her. He wrote (March 10, 1743): "Not even Friendship and the Study of Nature will be able to maintain any Charms for me. I care not where I am if I am not with you: I care not what I am if I live not for you . . ."

The poet's obsession with Miss Young directly affected his beneficial 1743–1744 revisions of the love poem "Spring," as also the romantic-tragic plot of *Tancred and Sigismunda,* written in 1745, the year she finally rejected him. Her rude mother is said to have vehemently opposed her daughter's marriage to the aging, overweight poet, who perhaps, Dr. Robertson felt, "was never wealthy enough to marry." Miss Young instead married a Scots seaman, John Campbell, son of the minister of Kirkbean, Dumfriesshire, who later became an admiral. Poor Thomson succumbed to a fever not long afterward; Dr. Robertson, who attended him, reported that "He seemed to me to be desirous not to live; and I had reason to think that my sister-in-law was the occasion of this.—He could not bear the thoughts of her being married to another." Thomson, grieving for his lost love, had written to his sister Jean that he had sadly resigned himself to being "too far advanced in Life for such youthful Undertakings" as romance and marriage.[82]

James Thomson was never to return to his native Scotland, though he certainly wished to do so. He wrote to his sister in 1747 of a proposed "Visit to Scotland (which I have some Thoughts of doing soon)." But instead he remained at Richmond, trying to forget "Amanda" and busily working on *The Castle of Indolence* and *Coriolanus.* Perhaps he would have gone home had he lived longer, but he died very suddenly at age forty-seven on August 27, 1748. At his death, of a fever caught while boating on the Thames, his friends and especially the Scottish circle were grief-stricken. Andrew Mitchell wrote to Murdoch to inform him of Thomson's death, closing with " 'I am almost sunk w^t this last stroke.' " Mitchell and Lyttelton were the poet's executors on behalf of his sister Mary Craig. A monument to Thomson, paid for thanks to Murdoch's and Millar's generosity with subscriptions to the 1762 *Works,* was placed in the Poets' Corner of Westminster Abbey in 1762. Appropriately, the monument was sculpted after a design by Scotland's foremost architect, Robert Adam.[83]

James Thomson's London years, 1725 to 1748, show that he adapted admirably to life in England. He weathered well strong anti-Scottish pressures and prejudices and even managed to make a great many English friends with his affable, easy-going manner and hearty British patriotic spirit. The Scottish poet indeed thrived in the milder English cultural climate, where he was free to cultivate his poetical pursuits and to nurture his deeply held literary and classical ideals. There he could also continue actively to defend his lifelong Whig

principles of freedom and progress through Opposition Whig involvement as well as through his poetry and plays. The English religious climate, too, was milder than that of his native Scotland and
proved congenial to his Moderate Presbyterian faith, though as *The
Castle*'s religious message would sharply demonstrate, the more bracing currents of older Scottish Calvinism in his religious belief never
completely diminished. Thomson was generally comfortable in England but certainly not complacent—about nationalism, religious belief, or literary art. He never compromised his Scottish values, and in
all those years in England he lived as a Scot, among Scots, at the center of his loyal Scottish circle. His enthusiastic British patriotism did
not preclude his sincere Scottish allegiance, for, after all, Scotland was
that corner of Great Britain he knew and loved best.

Of course, the middle works of this period, *Liberty* and the plays, do
not appear as Scottish on the surface as do either *The Seasons* or *The
Castle of Indolence*. They contain little nature poetry and even less direct Scottish literary influence. Yet at the same time they could not
have been what they are had not their author been a Scot. Both negative and positive Scottish influences were at work here. The weaknesses of *Liberty* and the plays, including their over-rhetorical and un-
der-dramatic qualities, were rooted in Scotland's peculiar literary
history: rhetoric was praised, and drama proscribed. Thomson's bombastic, chauvinistic strain was the voice, oftentimes, of a Scot on the
defensive in a foreign land and a Scottish Whig opposing the English
court establishment. His occasionally oppressive Latinate language
was not unnatural coming from a Scottish student of vernacular humanism. Even with their faults, *Liberty* and the plays give glimpses of
Thomson's true poetical talent, his skill at description and his innovative use of language, and, more particularly, provide intriguing insights into the contemporary sociopolitical situation in Britain and
Thomson's response to it from his perspective as an Anglo-Scot.

Liberty celebrates the social virtues of freedom and patriotism the
poet was raised in Scotland to respect as well as the dual traditions of
Roman and northern liberty to which he was heir. Even in its excess of
pro-British fervor, and even in its implied anti-Jacobitism, *Liberty* is in
no way anti-Scottish; on the contrary, *Liberty*'s pro-British patriotism

was but one manifestation of the poet's pro-Union, pro-Scottish senti-ment. In the poem he takes pains to praise his native land while trying to come to terms with his personal and national identity crisis. Though the "epic" *Liberty* was not a literary success like the Anglo-Scottish "georgic" *The Seasons* which preceded it, the poem's neo-classical mode was a direct product of the humanistic world-view of Thomson's Scottish youth; the social, political, and patriotic ideals of that ancient classical tradition were impressed on him at an early age.

Thomson's plays represent a resurgence of serious Scottish drama after a long silence; they signal the revival of true Scottish tragedy, an essential step toward the maturity of the Scottish literary tradition itself. The plays parallel the contemporary political situation from the Opposition viewpoint and, in some instances, as in *Sophonisba* and *Cor-iolanus*, comment indirectly on current Scottish-English relations as well in the guise of "Roman" history. The plays celebrate patriotism, but their patriotism is not so simplistic as *Liberty*'s; they reveal a com-plex of sometimes contradictory motives as Thomson grew disen-chanted with "Empire" and increasingly nostalgic for "Republican"—and Scottish—native virtue and national integrity. Further, some of the plays preach Thomson's Moderate Christianity and his human-itarian social concern while also reasserting an element of Calvinistic individual moral accountability. Along with their public, didactic mes-sages, the plays also reflect the poet's personal feelings during the period as certain romantic themes become more important; this em-phasis on emotions, as in *Tancred and Sigismunda*, corresponds to Thomson's renewed interest in more subjective, individual moral and artistic criteria generally in line with Scottish Enlightenment intellec-tual and aesthetic views. He would succeed in striking a balance be-tween subjective and objective ethical and aesthetic standards in *The Castle*.

So even though Thomson left his homeland in 1725 never to re-turn, the Scottishness of the poet would continue to exert its dis-tinctive—and mostly positive—influence on his works throughout his career. In all of Thomson's later works, *Liberty* and the dramas as well as *The Castle*, one can trace to varying degrees the essential continuity of the major cultural influences, attitudes, and expectations—literary, linguistic, neoclassical, social, political and patriotic, religious and philosophical—which the poet carried with him from Scotland and which would remain powerful determinants, guiding and sustaining him in his public and private life in London. As a Scot in England, James Thomson was writing "out of context"; yet, rediscovering and reaffirming his Scottish strengths from the security of his Scottish circle, this poet of extraordinary talent and imagination was able to create a *new* context where his unique Anglo-Scottish poetry could flourish. From these Scottish strengths he would go on to write a second Anglo-Scottish masterpiece, *The Castle of Indolence.*

9 THE CASTLE OF INDOLENCE: AN ANGLO-SCOTTISH ALLEGORY

The making of *The Castle of Indolence* (1748), like that of *The Seasons,* is an Anglo-Scottish success story. Though the two poems are very different, they share the same Scottish ingredients, all too rare in *Liberty* and the plays, which characterize James Thomson's finest work. *The Castle* proclaims Thomson's auspicious return to his most congenial mode, the poetry of natural description with profound religious purpose. This return to description corresponds to his return to a more varied, creative poetic language, this time within the discipline of confident strict form. Further, *The Castle*'s religious message signifies a return to a more stringent ethical stance, rooted once more in individual, private morality. *The Castle* is an allegory, adapting a modified Spenserian framework and borrowing from the Scottish allegorical tradition, in particular from the works of Gavin Douglas; the poem thus also signals the poet's return to specifically Scottish literary sources for his inspiration. *The Castle of Indolence* ranks with *The Seasons* as a true Anglo-Scottish triumph.

The Castle was written over a period of about fifteen years. According to Murdoch, "It was, at first, little more than a few detached stanzas, in the way of raillery on himself, and on some of his friends, who would reproach him with indolence; while he thought them, at least, as indolent as himself. But he saw very soon, that the subject deserved to be treated more seriously, and in a form fitted to convey one of the most important moral lessons." The poem thus became a Christian sermon on the work ethic,[1] a religious-didactic allegory preaching the stern Scottish Calvinist doctrine of regeneration, or spiritual and moral recovery on an individual basis, the effects of which would, Thomson hoped, extend to effect a wider regeneration of British society itself, especially after the evils of the '45. Therefore *The Castle* is both a religious and sociopolitical allegory; Thomson achieves full integration of religious and moral with social goals—the aim of those Moderates who were in the intellectual vanguard of the Scottish Enlightenment. Along with their spiritual, social, and moral significance, indolence and industry also carry important aesthetic values in the poem. As Thomson's most compact and formally controlled poem, *The Castle* practices as well as preaches the lesson of art improving upon nature. Thomson, like his Knight of Arts and Industry, "polish'd Nature with a finer Hand" (II.xxviii.2), and *The Castle* is of course his most consistently artistic work. *The Castle of Indolence* is, then, an entertaining allegory in the Spenserian manner and far more. Thomson's persona, the "indolent Bard," lives within the Castle, reporting from personal experience, and he also views it critically from without, pronouncing the poem's serious moral message; the poem is at once public and private, objective and subjective.[2] It is the poet's own final reworking of the significant and Scottish themes which had figured in his poetry from the start.

Thomson's return to natural description is most refreshing after the drily abstract *Liberty* and dramas. The poem's central moral conflict of industry versus indolence, or of action versus stagnation, is itself drawn in terms of the natural world in lines from the Bard's Song which also demonstrate Thomson's special skill at describing dynamic nature-in-process; the "November-Fogs" described here are reminiscent of "Autumn"'s Scottish fog scene:

> "Is not the Field, with lively Culture green,
> A Sight more joyous than the dead Morass?
> Do not the Skies, with active Ether clean,
> And fan'd by sprightly Zephyrs, far surpass
> The foul November-Fogs, and slumbrous Mass,
> With which sad Nature veils her drooping Face?

>Does not the Mountain-Stream, as clear as Glass,
>Gay-dancing on, the putrid Pool disgrace?
>The same in All holds true, but chief in Human Race.
>(II.xlix)

Description in *The Castle* is not precisely the same sort of realistic natural description which predominated in *The Seasons,* however. While based on observation and employing much vivid natural imagery and authentic detail, it usually goes beyond realistic representation to a realm removed from, transcending, the natural world to the extremes of supernatural description. Thomson's choice of the Spenserian supernatural itself owed something to the poet's Scottish background: as a Scot brought up on folk tales and Border ballads, Thomson would naturally have been attracted to such fantastic themes as he found in his model *The Faerie Queene*—and not only happy fairy tales but also the more sinister supernatural.[3] Both types of supernatural description color nature in *The Castle*'s vision. First, there is a wealth of highly idealized, fanciful description, as befits a fairy story; this delicately sensuous, atmospheric scene painting includes indoor scenes, many showing Spenserian influence, as well as pastoral-conventional scenes and selective prospect views. Second, at the other extreme of supernatural description, is Thomson's introduction of the more typically Scottish element of the grotesque, mildly-to-wildly exaggerated description which tends to outdo even Spenser.[4] This grotesque or surreal strain plays a crucial role in the allegory, intensifying Spenserian descriptions, and can be traced to the influence of Scottish folklore and Middle Scots poetry on Thomson. The central irony of *The Castle,* which governs most of its descriptions, is that the idealized "appearance" of indolence is deceptively luxurious and attractive while its "reality" is ugly, thus graphically illustrating the poet's hard lesson that indolence is a sin. As the poem is subjective to a great extent, this irony is partly self-directed; Thomson himself, as a Castle inmate, is sorely torn between indolence and virtuous industry. Between the two poles of idealized and grotesque description, he frequently makes startling contrasts (as in II.lxvii, where the appearance drops sharply away to reveal the harsh reality), representing deeper moral contrasts. Such an abrupt visual effect recalls the Scottish ballads, where sudden shifts of focus are an important dramatic device.

Among the many idealized descriptions in the poem is the natural setting of the Castle itself (I.ii–vii). This pastoral scene, couched in "Images of Rest" and set in a surreal "Season atween June and May," affords an example of that skillful, impressionistic mood painting which especially characterizes Canto I. Typical of much of the description in the poem, the atmosphere is created not merely with visual imagery but with abundant imagery of sound and movement as well. While the overall scene is generalized and owes something to *The Faerie Queene*'s Bower of Blisse and House of Morpheus,[5] Thomson characteristically adds accurate and realistic details:

> Was nought around but Images of Rest:
> Sleep-soothing Groves, and quiet Lawns between;
> And flowery Beds that slumbrous Influence kest,
> From Poppies breath'd; and Beds of pleasant Green,
> Where never yet was creeping Creature seen.
> Mean time unnumber'd glittering Streamlets play'd,
> And hurled every-where their Waters sheen;
> That, as they bicker'd through the sunny Glade,
> Though restless still themselves, a lulling Murmur made.
> (I.iii)

Thomson's versatile, original use of language, which gave race to *The Seasons,* again animates many such descriptive passages of *The Castle.* Realistic touches within the stylized "sunny Glade" are drawn with effective and well-chosen diction. Thomson typically employs abundant verb forms (such as the alliterative compound epithet "Sleep-soothing," archaic "kest," "breath'd," "creeping," "glittering," "play'd," "hurled," "bicker'd," quasi-adverb "restless still" with its added suggestion of oxymoron, and "lulling Murmur made") to recreate action and process; fanciful and thoroughgoing personification ("Poppies breath'd," "Streamlets play'd") to give the landscape a vigorous, imaginative life of its own; carefully woven patterns of sound effects or extended onomatopoeia, with imitative alliteration and assonance; and the occasional Latinate polysyllable ("Influence," "unnumber'd") to vary pace and control tone. Notable, too, is the poet's use of extensive "negative" rhetoric ("nought . . . but," "never yet," "unnumber'd"); such negative rhetoric is especially prevalent in Canto I,[6] and is calculated to reinforce the negative message underlying the superficially positive idealized scenes here.

While the "lowly Dale, fast by a River's Side, / With woody Hill o'er Hill encompass'd round" (I.ii.1–2) where the Castle lies is generalized and imaginary, it also resembles the poet's idealized recollection of his hilly, stream-fed Scottish Borders. Indeed, one of the diversions of the Castle's inmates, including Thomson and his fellow-Scots, was

> . . . To retrace our boyish Plays,
> Our easy Bliss, when each Thing Joy supply'd:
> The Woods, the Mountains, and the warbling Maze
> Of the wild Brooks—
> (I.xlviii.5–8)

Here the poet's memories of a pure and wholesome Teviotdale youth are deliberately invoked to counteract the vices and vanities of his indolent adulthood as a sort of saving spell against deceptive and dangerous sloth. A. D. McKillop has termed Thomson's recourse to a youthful ideal of virtue in defense against the sin of indolence a "regeneration." His use of the word "regeneration" is intriguing: the Scottish Calvinist concept of spiritual regeneration, which cannot come entirely from within but must be initiated from without through divine grace,[7] parallels the mission of the Knight in Canto II and is a scheme which can very usefully be applied to the interpretation of the entire allegory, as shall be seen. Significantly, then, Thomson's recollections of childhood went beyond the memory of the Scottish Border landscape to represent the spiritual values of his Scottish Calvinist upbringing, discernible even as early in *The Castle* as this passage. The only sinister note in this idyllic scene is the description of "blackening Pines, ay waving to and fro" which "Sent forth a sleepy Horror through the Blood" (I.v.6–7), hinting at the Castle's grotesque reality and the spiritual depravity for which it stands.

The description of the interior of the Castle of Indolence (I.xxxiii–xliv), like that of its external setting, maintains a subtle balance between vivid, sensuous detail and atmospheric impression. Thomson deliberately idealizes the Spenserian scene,[8] much as the inmates' dreams call up an artificial, supernatural fantasy world, "a World of gayer Tinct and Grace; / . . . And shed a roseate Smile on Nature's Face" (I.xliv.2, 5). Multisensuous images—textures and tastes, sounds and sights—subtly blend in this vivid mood picture, where all is soft, well padded against the outside world ("Soft Quilts on Quilts, on Carpets Carpets spread," I.xxxiii.6), and a perpetual rich and exotic banquet is offered (I.xxxiv). Visual images portray "art within art": tapestries of pastoral and biblical scenes and landscape paintings by Claude Lorrain, Salvator Rosa, and Nicholas Poussin (I.xxxvi–xxxviii).[9]

The metaphor of art within the Castle is a central one as the poet seeks to explore the relationship between art and nature, the role of art in imitating, controlling, and enhancing nature. The Knight of Arts and Industry himself embodies Virgilian rural progressivism as he creates and "improves" his own landscape in Deva's Vale. Thomson's lifelong fascination with the art of landscape gardening, cultivated in Scotland, has already been noted; it clearly determined his conception and execution of descriptive poetry, his way of seeing and describing, as he, too, created and "improved" the landscapes of his poetry in an artistic role analogous to the Knight's.[10] The idealized, evocative paintings of the classical landscape by artists such as Lorrain, Poussin, and Rosa particularly appealed to Thomson and others who, like him, appreciated the new style of freer, more imaginative and fanciful landscaping; the poet pays specific tribute to these artists who inspired him (I.xxxviii). Thomson's taste for landscape painting as for gardening grew from associations of youth, such as his friendship with artist William Aikman. He also viewed many masterpieces and collected prints of them on his Grand Tour. He was knowledgeable about artistic theory and history and owned a number of works on these subjects, including his friend George Turnbull's *Treatise on Ancient Painting*. Thomson had evidently influenced Turnbull's *Ancient Painting*, where the author refers to *Liberty* and treats of similar classical, aesthetic, and didactic themes. The commonsense empiricist Turnbull saw art as a moral force and one "language," of which poetry is another, for educating youth in virtue. Turnbull expressed keen appreciation for the paintings of Rosa and Poussin, whom Thomson in turn praises in *The Castle*, especially as they captured the human emotion, the passion of the scenes they portrayed. Turnbull was no doubt a model for Thomson in these artistic passages of *The Castle*.[11] Thomson's accurate, enthusiastic interpretations of landscape paintings in *The Castle* reveal not only his trained critical eye but also his strong sensibility to such works of visual art:

> Sometimes the Pencil, in cool airy Halls,
> Bade the gay Bloom of Vernal Landskips rise,
> Or Autumn's vary'd Shades imbrown the Walls:
> Now the black Tempest strikes the astonish'd Eyes;
> Now down the Steep the flashing Torrent flies;
> The trembling Sun now plays o'er Ocean blue,
> And now rude Mountains frown amid the Skies;
> Whate'er *Lorrain* light-touch'd with softening Hue,
> Or savage *Rosa* dash'd, or learned *Poussin* drew.
> (I.xxxviii)

Thus in *The Castle* Thomson skillfully exploits the ongoing, creative tension, the interplay between art and nature, to enhance the reader's perceptions of both.[12]

Aural imagery is also important in *The Castle* and helps set the gentle, languid atmosphere of indolence in Canto I. The poem's opening stanzas describing the Castle's setting (such as the "Images of Rest" passage above) blend sounds in Thomson's characteristic, carefully worked sound-sense patterns to create a rare hypnotic effect. Stanzas xxxix–xli, set inside the Castle, further develop imitative aural imagery. Thomson refers here to a contemporary musical novelty, the aeolian harp (*"Harp of Æolus"*), revived and made popular by a Scots musician and composer of the poet's acquaintance, James Oswald. Oswald, who came to London from Edinburgh in 1741, was a friend of Allan Ramsay. He wrote classical sonatas inspired by Scottish folk music and collected folk tunes; he set some of Thomson's love lyrics to music and also composed in 1755 a work apparently inspired by *The Seasons* called "Airs for the Four Seasons." The aeolian harp is an instrument which is placed in an open window to catch the breeze and emit pleasing vibrations: "Ah me! what Hand can touch the Strings so fine? / . . . Such sweet, such sad, such solemn Airs divine" (I.xli.1, 3). Again, art and nature work in harmony, nature ultimately transcending art to express the full scale of human feelings: "Wild warbling Nature all, above the Reach of Art!" (I.xli.9).[13]

Eventually, the sumptuous interior of the Castle of Indolence, colored by the inmates' rosy-hued dreams, proves so very falsely idealized that the poet of nature cannot describe it:

> No, fair Illusions! artful Phantoms, no!
> My Muse will not attempt your Fairy-Land:
> She has no Colours that like you can glow;
> To catch your vivid Scenes too gross her Hand.
> (I.xlv.1–4)

Of the idealized external landscapes in the poem, one famous scene is the specifically Scottish description of the solitary "Shepherd of the *Hebrid-Isles*" (I.xxx). Versions of this remote, romantic setting, which echoes *Lycidas,* occur in "Autumn" (ll. 862–865), "Britannia" (ll. 88–89), and *Liberty* (II.227–229). Although Thomson had never visited the Hebrides, his nostalgia for Scotland, his homesickness or *heimweh,* surely inspired the idealized scene. In *The Castle*'s variation, the shepherd experiences a vision of the "second sight." Thomson's interest in the second sight may have been suggested by Martin Martin; the superstitious Border poet certainly knew of such phenomena in local Scottish folklore as well. Significantly, he appears even to make allowance for the possible truth of this supernatural experience: "(Whether it be, lone Fancy him beguiles; / Or that aerial Beings sometimes deign / To stand, embodied, to our Senses plain)" (I.xxx.3–5).[14]

Another idealized landscape description deserving mention occurs in Canto II; this is Thomson's conception of the retreat of the Knight of Arts and Industry in Deva's Vale (II.xxv–xxviii). Here the poet brings the familiar, classical "Happy Man" theme to "Britain-Land" (II.xxiv.1) and illustrates the Virgilian ideal of rural improvement or progress which figured significantly in *The Seasons*' vision. Again, he blends broad literary convention with realistic, freshly described detail:

> Nor, from his deep Retirement, banish'd was
> Th' amusing Cares of Rural Industry.
> Still, as with grateful Change the Seasons pass,

> New Scenes arise, new Landskips strike the Eye,
> And all th' enliven'd Country beautify:
> Gay Plains extend where Marshes slept before;
> O'er recent Meads th' exulting Streamlets fly;
> Dark frowning Heaths grow bright with *Ceres'* Store,
> And Woods imbrown the Steep, or wave along the Shore.
> (II.xxvii)

Notable here are the Latinate diction, with allusion to Ceres, in keeping with the Virgilian theme and the energetic personification animating the "enliven'd Country." Thomson's setting of the scene in Deva's Vale is intriguing. Critics have discovered no particular reason for his use of this place-name, apart from a remote allusion to the Dee in *Lycidas;* Thomson seems not to have known the English Dee Valley, and his description of the Knight's retreat does not resemble that sandy estuary. There are, however, two rivers Dee in Scotland as well as the ancient locale near Aberdeen, mentioned in Ptolemy, called Devana (Devanha). Thomson may have had his homeland in mind when he named the remote, idealized Deva's Vale; in conventional pastoral poetry, after all, the poet is traditionally identified with a river close to his place of birth.[15]

In sharp contrast to such idealized, stylized, and literary-conventional descriptions as these are Thomson's grotesque descriptions in *The Castle*. These scenes, while more immediately Spenserian, have deeper roots in the Middle Scots descriptive tradition. The caricatures of the poet himself and his friends in Canto I are part of this exaggerating tendency; while they are mildly distorting portraits, rather burlesque than truly grotesque (like "Autumn"'s caricatures of the hunters), they are not without an edge of satirical truth and realism. The caricatures are part of *The Castle*'s subjective vision and demonstrate Thomson's genial wit. They provide pleasant relief from the passage which precedes them, the "Mirror of Vanity," an ironic view of corruption in the real Fallen World outside the Castle (I.xlix–lvi). Thomson affectionately caricatures William Paterson (or possibly Turnbull, lvii–lix), Dr. John Armstrong (lx), John Forbes (lxii–lxiii), George Lyttelton (lxv–lxvi), James Quin the actor (lxvii), and Patrick Murdoch (lxix). Thomson himself, with his reputation for a seemingly indolent, casual lifestyle of "nightly Days" (I.xxxi), was drawn (probably by Lyttelton from line 2 on) thus:

> A Bard here dwelt, more fat than Bard beseems;
> Who void of Envy, Guile, and Lust of Gain,
> On Virtue still, and Nature's pleasing Themes,
> Pour'd forth his unpremeditated Strain,
> The World forsaking with a calm Disdain:
> Here laugh'd he careless in his easy Seat,
> Here quaff'd encircled with the joyous Train;
> Oft moralizing sage; his Ditty sweet
> He loathed much to write, ne cared to repeat.
> (I.lxviii)

Here again is that "chearfull presence" singing to the "circling swains," the poet who had entertained his Edinburgh friends in youth (in the juvenile "A Pastoral betwixt Thirsis and Corydon upon the death of Damon"), now mature and at the center of his faithful Scottish circle, immortalized in *The Castle*.

More extreme, truly grotesque description darkens the poem as early as Canto I (xlvi–xlvii) with the first glimpse of the Castle's ugly reality, its private hell on earth, concealed at this stage from the deceived followers of the Wizard Archimago. The "Fiends, whom Blood and Broils delight," the "foul Demons" are not yet allowed to disturb the Castle's false peace. The poet describes the terrible scene, ". . . as if to Hell outright, / Down down black Gulphs, where sullen Waters sleep, / Or hold him clambering all the fearful Night / On beetling Cliffs, or pent in Ruins deep" (I.xlvi.6–8). This "hellish" scene owes much to such conventional literary influences as Spenser,[16] Dante, and Milton and probably also to another Scottish source—Gavin Douglas's *Eneados*. Douglas portrays the "deidly golf" of hell as "A hiddus hoill, deip gapand and grisly, / All ful of cragis . . . / With a fowle layk, als blak as ony craw" (Book VI.iv.4–7). Thomson's description, like Douglas's, goes beyond literary allusion to convey an element of horrible realism, appropriate to its symbolic function in the poem, representing the gruesome "truth" about indolence. In general, there is a stronger strain of descriptive realism in these grotesque scenes of *The Castle*, however exaggerated, than in the poem's more idealized scenes. Middle Scots poetry as well as old-style Scottish sermon rhetoric, where descriptions of hell were particularly vivid, replete with powerful, concrete imagery, were undoubtedly influences. The various "Hags of Hell," "Fiends," "Demons," and "Spirits" which appear in the poem's grotesque descriptions were also a part of Scottish folklore and were, in a sense, very real to the superstitious poet from the Borders.

Another grotesque description occurs at the conclusion to Canto I (lxxiv–lxxvii) in the repulsive personifications of the illnesses which result from indolence, those "Diseas'd, and loathsome" inmates of the Castle's private hell: "Fierce Fiends, and Hags of Hell, their only Nurses were." These stanzas of the allegory, much revised by Thomson, were contributed by Dr. John Armstrong, author of *The Art of Preserving Health*, with graphic physiological detail and a Scottish delight in wild hyperbole recalling Middle Scots poetry such as Dunbar's "The Dance of the Sevin Deidly Synnis." Armstrong probably also had immediately in mind Allan Ramsay's poem "Health" (1724), with its personification of "Lethargus," the "lazy Lubbard," when he wrote these verses.[17]

Grotesque description in *The Castle* intensifies in the more serious didactic Canto II. The Knight of Arts and Industry waves his "anti-magic" "Wand," "Truth from illusive Falshood to command," and the hideous reality within the Castle is shockingly revealed:

> Sudden, the Landskip sinks on every Hand;
> The pure quick Streams are marshy Puddles found;
> On baleful Heaths the Groves all blacken'd stand;
> And, o'er the weedy foul abhorred Ground,
> Snakes, Adders, Toads, each loathly Creature crawls around.

> And here and there, on Trees by Lightning scath'd,
> Unhappy Wights who loathed Life yhung;
> Or, in fresh Gore and recent Murder bath'd,
> They weltering lay; or else, infuriate flung
> Into the gloomy Flood, while Ravens sung
> The funeral Dirge, they down the Torrent rowl'd:
> These, by distemper'd Blood to Madness stung,

Had doom'd themselves; whence oft, when Night controul'd
The World, returning hither their sad Spirits howl'd.
(II.lxvii–lxviii)

Beyond Spenserian influence here,[18] Thomson's graphic concretizing
of moral corruption cannot help but call to mind similar startling and
surreal scenes in Middle Scots poetry, particularly descriptions of the
netherworld in Gavin Douglas's *Eneados* and also his hell-like landscapes in the allegorical dream vision *The Palice of Honour*. Prefiguring
Thomson, Douglas in *The Palice* thus described the dreamer's vision of
the sudden transformation of a beautiful garden into this horrible
wilderness:

> In that desert dispers in sonder skatterit
> Wer bewis bair quhome rane and wind on batterit.
> The water stank, the feild was odious,
> Quhair dragouns, lessertis, askis, edders swatterit,
> With mouthis gapand, forkit taillis tatterit,
> With mony a stang and spoutis vennemous
> Corrupting Air be rewme contagious.
> Maist gros and vile enpoysonit cludis clatterit,
> Reikand like hellis smoke sulfurious.
> (*Palice,* Part I, ll. 346–354)

In Thomson's vision of "Hell," imagery of wetness predominates:
"marshy Puddles" full of "loathly" reptiles and other beasts, "fresh
Gore," Stygian "gloomy Flood," "Torrent," "distemper'd Blood." Hellish description goes on (II.lxxvii–lxxx) with the gruesome "Desert
wild" of "Gibbets, Bones, and Carcases defil'd" contrasted with yet
another inclement, wet, and cold landscape:

> . . . a joyless Land of Bogs,
> The sadden'd Country a grey Waste appear'd;
> Where Nought but putrid Streams and noisome Fogs
> For ever hung on drizzly *Auster*'s Beard;
> Or else the Ground by piercing *Caurus* sear'd,
> Was jagg'd with Frost, or heap'd with glazed Snow.
> (II.lxxviii.1–6)

There is a brief sketch of such a scene in *The Faerie Queene* (I.iv.36.7–9),[19] and Douglas in *The Palice* depicted at greater length a similar hell of extremes of desert and wintry bog:

> My rauist spreit in that desert terribill
> Approchit neir that vglie flude horribill,
> Like till Cochyte the riuer Infernall,
> With vile water quhilk maid a hiddious trubil,
> Rinnand ouirheid, blude reid, and Impossibill
> That it had bene a riuer naturall;
> With brayis bair, raif Rochis like to fall,
> Quhairon na gers nor herbis wer visibill
> Bot swappis brint with blastis boriall.
>
> (*Palice*, Part I, ll. 136–144)

Douglas's description continues in this vein, with emphasis on the damp, cold, and uncomfortable Scottish climatic details; his *Eneados*, too, describes a northern hell of chilly, foggy atmosphere—a scene straight from the Scottish winter descriptive tradition and also characteristic of conceptions of hell in Scottish folklore; for example, the ballad "The Daemon Lover."[20] Much of Thomson's portrayal of the Castle's private hell, too, falls within this Scottish tradition of winter descriptive poetry. Elsewhere in *The Castle,* Thomson explicitly compares the sin of indolence with "Snows pil'd on Snows" which "in wintry Torpor lie"; he describes those who repented of their indolence with the metaphor of a thaw: " 'Th' awaken'd Heaps, in Streamlets from on high, / Rous'd into Action, lively leap away, / Glad-warbling through the Vales, in their new Being gay' " (II.lxiv.7–9). He also personifies the allegorical figure of *"Scorn"* in northern winter alliterative terms: "his Eye / Was cold, and keen, like blast from boreal Snow" (II. lxxx.6–7). Such hyperbolic winter scenes, like the other grotesque descriptions in the poem, incorporate a strong element of realism and accurately observed nature.

All of the grotesque descriptions in *The Castle,* while highly imaginative, exaggerated, and even surreal, are rooted in realistic descriptive detail and play a vital role in the allegory, conveying Thomson's conception of the horrors of the sin of indolence. They rival or surpass in sheer grotesqueness such descriptions in Thomson's immediate model *The Faerie Queene* and also derive to a very great extent from the poet's Scottish heritage of literature and folklore.

In the absurd, seriocomic concluding scene of *The Castle* (II.lxxxi), the unrepentant indolent are pictured as a "Herd of brisly Swine" being driven through the mire of Brentford Town. The muddy market town of Brentford, neighbor to salubrious Richmond, had the reputation of being so dirty that it was something of a joke in Thomson's day and much maligned in poetry of the period.[21] Besides its general allusion to *Comus,* this unsavory scene also calls to mind Dunbar's characterization of indolence or sloth in the "Sevin Deidly Synnis," "lyk a sow out of a midding." Indeed, the metaphor of the unregenerate driven like a filthy herd also figures significantly in Scottish Calvinistic writings, which may also have influenced Thomson in this allegory of sin and regeneration. The dirty description literally brings the poem down to earth and back to British mud from its allegorical extremes of idealized and grotesque description.

Through these various vivid and imaginative supernatural descriptions, both ideal and grotesque, within the allegorical framework, Thomson graphically illustrates the serious didactic message of *The Castle.* The poem is a secularized moral injunction issuing directly from the poet's Scottish Calvinist religious background and represents his most fully realized integration of religious with social, private with public aims in poetry. While Thomson had apparently long since given up the formal practice of religion, in this, his last major work, he reaffirms his strong Christian faith, which still characteristically bears the influence of both old-style and Moderate beliefs. Some have even seen *The Castle* as evidence of Thomson's "new orthodoxy"; what is new is the force with which the poet reasserts that religious faith he had never really lost. Thomson reiterates his fundamental religious philosophy in the song of the poem's Bard, Philomelus:[22]

> . . . "Ye hapless Race,
> Dire-labouring here to smother Reason's Ray,
> That lights our Maker's Image in our Face,
> And gives us wide o'er Earth unquestion'd Sway;
> What is th' ador'd supreme Perfection, say?
> What, but eternal never-resting Soul,

Almighty Power, and all-directing Day;
By whom each Atom stirs, the Planets roll;
Who fills, surrounds, informs, and agitates the Whole?

"Come, to the beaming GOD your Hearts unfold!
Draw from its Fountain Life! 'Tis thence, alone,
We can excel. Up from unfeeling Mold,
To seraphs burning round th' ALMIGHTY'S Throne,
Life rising still on Life, in higher Tone,
Perfection forms, and with Perfection Bliss.
In Universal Nature This clear shewn,
Not needeth Proof; To prove it were, I wis,
To prove the beauteous World excels the brute Abyss.
(II.xlvii–xlviii)

Here the God of *The Seasons*—His "panergism" or ever-active, omnipresent, and omnipotent Providence—again shows His "beaming," benevolent face. The Neoplatonic rising mind, leading up through "beauteous" Creation to divine perfection, again informs the poet's optimistic faith. Thomson's God here, as in *The Seasons,* is the conventional Moderate Christian deity as well as the God of nature. The Knight of Arts and Industry bids his companion the Bard to "'thy heavenly Fire impart; / Touch Soul with Soul, till forth the latent Spirit start'" (II.xlv.8–9), making the Bard his spokesman for explicit religious doctrine; thus, significantly, Thomson again proclaims his acceptance of the poet's role as a sacred calling. Appropriately, the Bard Philomelus is a "Druid"; druids, religious leaders of the ancient Celtic Britons, were in Thomson's day regarded as the poet-priests of nature.[23] William Collins would honor Thomson himself as a "Druid" in his elegy "Ode on the Death of Mr. Thomson" (1749).

Even while Thomson portrays the Moderates' benevolent deity here, the basic religious message of hard regeneration which he preaches in *The Castle* and which motivates the allegory as a whole still shows the very powerful stamp of the poet's earliest religious experience of stern, old-style Scottish Calvinism; again, comparisons with Thomas Boston prove illuminating. Thomson had begun with a Scottish Calvinist structure of thought, and in the didactic *Castle* gave it a broader, secularized moral and social message to bear. The primary lesson of *The Castle* is addressed to the private soul, the introspective, individualistic side of the Calvinist spirit: Thomson yet again teaches that "Virtue" is the key to true "Human Bliss" (II.xxxvi.ff.), and he particularly stringently condemns vanity, especially as it is manifested in sloth or indolence. In Canto II he powerfully repudiates the attractive, sensuous trappings of indolence, as Scottish Calvinism itself had sought to reject such sinful worldly pleasures and impose its moral rigors on the Scottish soul.

So despite its benevolistic doctrinal aspects, as the Bard sings them, Thomson's moral stance in *The Castle* proves in many ways just as strict as the Calvinism he knew in youth. *The Castle* is certainly much less brightly optimistic in its philosophy than even *The Seasons;* Thomson seems more concerned than ever now with the value, indeed the necessity, of suffering[24] to attain individual sanctification. He makes this clear in Canto II.lxxii–lxxiii, where the Knight exhorts his followers to " 'Then patient bear the Sufferings you have earn'd, / And by these Sufferings purify the Mind' " (II.lxxii.1–2). Throughout the poem Thomson is frank, too, about his belief in hell and damnation and the need for penance, repentance, and acceptance of divine grace.[25] He likewise shows a much more explicit awareness of personal sin in *The Castle* than anywhere else in his mature poetry. Much as Gavin Douglas had portrayed the "sleuthfull" in *The Palice of Honour,* suffering in the "laithlie deip" of hell's pit, Thomson in the more heavily didactic Canto II portrays the indolent not merely as lazy, amusing characters but as unregenerate sinners deserving of terrible punishment. He clearly recognizes the repercussions of indolence on both individual and society in the Fallen World.

The grim opening lines of *The Castle*—with their homiletic tone, heavy didacticism, archaic style—pronounce the poem's Scottish Calvinist moral of the work ethic: "O MORTAL MAN, who livest here by Toil, / Do not complain of this thy hard Estate" (I.i.1–2). The so-called Calvinist work ethic, while not authentic to Calvin's religious teachings, developed in English and Scottish Calvinism with the growth of commerce in the seventeenth century. Protestants in general continued to maintain that salvation by works was impossible and that faith alone could save; as Thomas Boston expressed it, "Sinner, I would have thee believe that thy working will never effect [recovery, or regeneration]. *Work,* and do thy best; thou shalt never be able to work thyself out of this state of *corruption* and *wrath.*" But at the same time they placed increasing importance on the value of work (this attitude is found, for instance, in Spenser's House of Pride, *FQ*). Calvinists came to regard tangible success at one's work as a proof of election and salvation; further, good works done in the state of grace would count toward the "glory" of the elected one, or saint, at the Last Judgment: "it is Christ's stamp on good works, that puts a value on them, in the eye of a gracious God." Thus Boston, for example, exhorts his congregation to

> Dispatch the work of your day and generation, with speed and diligence. . . . God has allotted us certain pieces of work, of this kind, which ought to be dispatched, before the time of working be over. . . . Wherefore, whatever is incumbent upon thee to do for God's honour, and the good of others, either as the duty of thy *station,* or by special *opportunity* put into thy hand, perform it *seasonably,* if thou wouldst die *comfortably.* [26]

So while good works could not actually earn salvation, it was nonetheless accepted as the Scottish Calvinist's duty to work hard and well at his calling; his success at material endeavors could signify his election to eternal happiness and also give glory to God. Thomson, too, cautiously stops short of preaching that good works will merit eternal salvation; like his orthodox Scottish Calvinist teachers he focuses on the more immediate social benefits of work well done, ultimately toward the good of the wider community of faithful. Yet as *The Castle* amply illustrates, "For tho' good works do not merit salvation, yet evil works merit damnation" (Boston). Boston's warning reflects a typical Scottish Calvinist negative ethic, emphasizing the dire results of the sin of failure to work (that is, indolence) more strongly than the rewards of work itself. To Scottish Calvinists and indeed all Puritans waste of time was the gravest of sins; Thomson in *The Castle* obviously shares this mistrust of idleness, this abhorrence of time misused, with his model Spenser as well as with his Calvinist forefathers. From such moral rigor grew that so-called work ethic which is the secularized, social application of Calvinist religious thought. Whether or not such attitudes toward work themselves gave rise to a capitalist economy has been the subject of much controversy, but it seems true that Calvinist respect for work well done and its outward signs of material success did help create a favorable atmosphere for the growth of capitalism. While the Scottish church officially preached the dangers of accumulated wealth, its latent "spirit of capitalism" coupled with more liberal, Moderate trends generally, prepared the way for wider acceptance of the new economic order. The Scottish Calvinist work ethic, its negative attitude toward indolence and its positive view of successful effort, directly inspired Thomson's *Castle;* indirectly it fostered that spirit of capitalism so congenial to his own Whig vision for the material progress and prosperity of Great Britain.[27]

Thomson's contemporaries, the first generation of Moderates of the Scottish church, like the poet himself in *The Castle*, extended the work ethic into areas of both Christian social concern and aesthetics. Individual good works, carried out in the spirit of selfless benevolence, could clearly benefit society as a whole. The reward for such works of social love was the pleasure perceived by the cultivated moral sense, as Francis Hutcheson and George Turnbull, for instance, explained. Turnbull termed this responsibility and reward the "law of industry." Hutcheson further discerned an element of pure aesthetic pleasure which is the God-given reward for rational endeavor or empirical thought beyond its merely practical results. Such intellectual beauty as Hutcheson recognized can conceivably extend to an aesthetic gratification deriving from any labor well done, and this is how Thomson literally interprets it in *The Castle*, to make the apt contrast between the improved, idealized beauty which is the result of industry, exemplified in the retreat of the Knight in Deva's Vale, and the ugly, aesthetically revolting reality of the sin of indolence. The poet clearly equates hard work, in addition to beauty, with virtue, health, and godliness, though he gives no guarantee of eternal salvation; the Knight of Arts and Industry himself personifies the dynamic of the Calvinist work ethic, the individual moral force leading a virtuous and progressive society.[28]

In the religious-didactic *Castle,* a number of cleverly reworked scriptural allusions operate to reinforce the moral lesson of the work ethic. The Wizard's overall stratagem in Canto I recalls the Old Testament theme of the Temptation and Fall of man. His beguiling speech (I.ix–x) is a subtle parody of Christ's Sermon on the Mount; the Wizard, modeled on Spenser's Archimago, is portrayed as a very convincing anti-Christ, the antithesis of the Knight. Biblical parody generally strengthens the more prominent Spenserian structure of the whole of Canto I. Stanza xi, for example, echoes Genesis 3:[29]

> "Outcast of Nature, Man! the wretched Thrall
> Of bitter-dropping Sweat, of sweltry Pain,
> Of Cares that eat away thy Heart with Gall,
> And of the Vices, an inhuman Train,
> That all proceed from savage Thirst of Gain:
> For when hard-hearted *Interest* first began
> To poison Earth, *Astræa* left the Plain;
> Guile, Violence, and Murder seiz'd on Man;
> And, for soft milky Streams, with Blood the Rivers ran.
> (I.xi)

Echoes of Ecclesiastes and Psalms also occur in the poem (I.xix); the line "their scorned Day of Grace was past" (II.lxxvii.1) especially recalls the *Scots Paraphrase,* X.[30] In addition to direct scriptural influence, the rhetoric of the pulpit also influenced the exposition of the Scottish Calvinist "sermon" of *The Castle.* Much of the Bard's Song in Canto II resembles a rhetorically persuasive homily, characteristically building in religious enthusiasm as the Bard ascends the familiar rising spiritual scale (II.lxiii) and demonstrating Thomson's effective use of rhetorical questions, parallel and antithesis, exclamations, and accurate and vivid imagery. The Knight himself adds force to the didactic lesson of Canto II with his striking "anti-magic" (II.lxvii.3) views of the horrors of hell, recalling the graphic imagery Scottish preachers had traditionally reserved especially for describing hell and human depravity. Waving his wand, the Knight reveals the appalling truth about indolence; "'Ye impious Wretches! (quoth the Knight, in Wrath) / Your Happiness behold!'" (II.lxvii.1–2):

> "For you (resum'd the Knight, with sterner Tone)
> Whose hard dry Hearts th' obdurate Demon sears,
> That Villain's Gifts will cost you many a Groan;
> In dolorous Mansion long you must bemoan
> His fatal Charms, and weep your Stains away
> (II.lxxiii.2–6)

Generally, the Bard teaches a more Moderate lesson than the sterner Knight, who is sometimes "gentle" (II.lxxi) and compassionate but also capable of anger and hard justice; each character reflects an aspect of the dual Scottish religious inheritance of Thomson himself.

The Knight of Arts and Industry can be seen, to some extent, as a sort of secularized Christ figure, foil to that charismatic anti-Christ, the Wizard of Canto I. The *Castle* allegory has been compared to the Christian salvation myth as a whole,[31] which is rather overstating the case, yet strong parallels with the orthodox Christian redemption myth are certainly there, secularized to a great degree within the broader social purpose of the poem. Thomson very likely had in mind in *The Castle*, not exactly the wider salvation tradition itself, but more specifically the regeneration doctrine of Calvinism: "begun Recovery," the earthly process of Fallen Man's return to holiness through grace. The Knight, whom Thomson had originally named the "Knight of Resolution," leads his repentant followers out of the Castle, not immediately to perfect happiness in heaven, but to a pious, dutiful life on earth, "a Life more happy and refin'd" (II.lxxii.5). Ultimately their faith in the saving Knight, their pledge of union with him, rather than their good works has earned their sanctification.[32]

The private hell within the Castle is likewise an earthly state; accordingly, Boston preached, "As a gracious state is a state of glory in the bud: so a graceless state is hell in the bud, which, if it continue, will come to perfection at length." Boston employed the graphic scriptural metaphor of stagnation to describe the unregenerate, depraved spiritual condition, with grace as the saving "stream":

When the spring is stopt, the mud lies in the well unmoved: But when once the spring is cleared, the waters springing up, will work away the mud by degrees. Even so, while a man continues in an unregenerate state, sin lies at ease in the heart: but as soon as the Lord strikes the rocky heart, with the *rod of his strength,* in the day of conversion; grace is *in him a well of water, springing up into everlasting life,* John iv.14. working away natural corruption, and gradually *purifying the heart,* Acts xv.9.[33]

Thomson draws this same vivid metaphor from nature in the Bard's Song: "'Does not the Mountain-Stream, as clear as Glass, / Gay-dancing on, the putrid Pool disgrace?'"(II.xlix.7–8; see p. 255); he also refers to the "hard dry Hearts" of the sinners (II.lxxiii.2). Boston's phrase "work away" to describe the water's regenerative effect is suggestive, as it implies a connection with the work ethic. Thomson's verb "disgrace" is also interesting, evoking the idea of grace itself and its loss. Thomson in *The Castle* makes frequent and explicit reference to grace; grace, in Calvinist doctrine, is the gift Christ offers in the process of regeneration, which, if accepted with faith, brings man sanctification:

But ah! their scorned Day of Grace was past
(II.lxxvii.1)

It [the vision of the "goodly Hospital"] was a worthy edifying Sight,
And gives to Human-Kind *peculiar* Grace,
To see kind Hands attending Day and Night
(II. lxxv.1–3)

". . . soft and pure as Infant-Goodness grown,
    You feel a perfect Change: then, who can say,
What Grace may yet shine forth in Heaven's eternal Day?"
(II.lxxiii.7–9)

"Grace be to Those who can, and will, repent;
    But Penance long, and dreary, to the Slave,
Who must in Floods of Fire his gross foul Spirit lave."
(II.xxxix.7–9)

Thus the Knight of Arts and Industry, Christlike, offers grace to those who will accept it, repent, and follow him with resolution out of the Castle. As for those who fail to repent, Thomson depicts them driven like a herd of "filthy" swine through muddy Brentford Town (II.lxx-xi). Boston, too, used similar concrete imagery, describing sinners as "unclean," "filthy" beasts ("the wicked are *driven* away in *their wickedness* at death"; "What a multitude of the devil's *goats*, do now take place among Christ's *sheep!*" and so on).[34] So while *The Castle of Indolence* should not be seen solely as a doctrinal parable of regeneration, it is certainly likely that such a Scottish Calvinist concept did form the basis of much of the poem's uncompromising moral, didactic theme of earthly recovery as well as of its manner of exposition—its allegorical framework, its colorful and concrete figurative language, its reverberating biblical and homiletic rhetoric.

Only when the rigorous private morality of the individual work ethic and the potential for spiritual regeneration have been so established can Thomson's wider social goals as set forth in *The Castle* be realized and the Moderate ideal of union of religious with social concerns be achieved. Public is founded upon private good, as the poet had professed in *The Seasons* and in the late play *Tancred and Sigismunda*. The public good as Thomson envisions it in *The Castle* encompasses the familiar abstract themes of Virgilian improvement, Whig progress, British patriotism, and cultivation of true liberty. The goals of the Knight of Arts and Industry are the same sociopolitical ideals Thomson had set forth in *The Seasons*, in the dramas, and especially in *Liberty*. Now, too, the regeneration is seen as a necessary recovery of British society itself following the ills of the Jacobite rising of 1745. Such a quest, penance, and recovery as *The Castle* presents poetically is the very lesson the Scottish Moderate clergy such as Adam Ferguson and Hugh Blair were preaching; they, too, saw the need for a national regeneration after God's wrath had punished both Scottish and English "indolence" and corruption in the '45.[35] The tale of the Knight's several missions (II.xiv–xviii), culminating in his British crusade, is also a reworking of *Liberty*'s theme of the cyclical history of civilizations. The Knight thus plays two mutually reinforcing roles in the poem: that of Christ-figure or savior in the regeneration parable, and that of the personified Whig ideal of selfless public service in the parallel, secular social myth.[36]

The primitivism-progress debate is associated with these themes and recurs in *The Castle* as part of the secularized social allegory; again, the Scottish poet is seemingly ambivalent. The alluring world of the Castle itself is one sort of primitivistic idyll, but it proves false, and Thomson obviously condemns this; a parallel in Scottish Calvinism is set forth by Thomas Boston, who uses the terms "unregenerate" man and "natural" man synonymously, imposing strongly negative moral and spiritual connotations on primitivism.[37] So the very word "natural" for Thomson, the poet of nature, would have had rather ambiguous meaning in this "supernatural" context. It is especially revealing to recall here that most of the Castle's identifiable "unregenerate" inmates were in fact Scotsmen—the poet and his friends. They were natives of a primitive land, a land which had as yet done little to improve itself, a land about which Thomson had in *The Seasons* expressed not only his affection but also his exasperation. The Castle's natural, unimproved landscape in Canto I, too, is a Border landscape idealized. Thomson was surely commenting consciously here both on his dangerously cozy life within the Scottish circle and the idealizing, rose-tinted nostalgia he felt for his homeland and on the real primitive, indolent Scotland he could not help but see. *The Castle*'s primitivism-progress theme thus reflects the contrast between Scotland and England as well as Thomson's contradictory response to it. The Knight of Arts and Industry, who ultimately triumphs over indolence, is apparently English and leads the way for those Scots who are willing to unite with him and move toward progress and Enlightenment; for Thomson, therefore, active and committed union with Great Britain could prove to be Scotland's salvation from primitivism.[38]

As much as he admires Britain, however, Thomson does not miss the opportunity to comment satirically on the real world of contemporary British society outside the imaginary, insulated Castle; he describes this society in the "Mirror of Vanity" passage (I.xlix–lv) as an essentially urban, progressive society. This clever Augustan social satire is partly self-ironic: Thomson and his fellow (mostly Scottish) inmates mock the corruption they witness outside the Castle walls while they remain for the time being blissfully unaware of the depth of corruption within. Thomson's "mirror" view of British society here resembles Spenser's "Merlin's Globe" (*FQ,* III.ii.18–20).[39] Further, it recalls Gavin Douglas's use of the "Mirrour" symbol in *The Palice of Honour* (III, ll. 1476ff.), where the "Mirrour of Venus" reveals a harsh panorama of biblical and classical history with all its sin, cruelty, and pain, culminating in ". . . the Feind fast folkis to vices tyst, / And all the cumming of the Antechrist." In Thomson's vision, witty self-irony reflects particularly upon authors:

> Why, Authors, all this Scrawl and Scribbling sore?
> To lose the present, gain the future Age,
> Praised to be when you can hear no more,
> And much enrich'd with Fame when useless worldly Store.
> (I.lii.6–9)

This sentiment is echoed in his more serious complaint on the poet's plight in Canto II ("They praised are alone, and starve right merrily," II.ii.9). Thomson's reference to "puzzling Sons of Party" (I.liv) alludes to perennial party-political controversy and his own Opposition Whig involvement. He also attacks city greed and debauchery, sounding a very Scottish Calvinistic censorious note. The poet's comment on wars is deadly serious: "Christian Kings, inflam'd by black Desire" (I.lv) (echoing "Summer," l. 855, and *Edward and Eleanora,* V.i) voices his disillusionment with abuses in a progressive, so-called Christian society, and those "Christian Kings" might also be an ironic reference to the Stuart monarchs and their European allies. As Thomson makes clear in the "Mirror of Vanity" passage, then, British "progress" is certainly not immune to abuse and corruption, particularly in an urban society like his contemporary London.

So once again Thomson's stance is neither simply progressive nor primitivistic; again, he harks back to the "classical" compromise. His Virgilian attitude of nostalgic progressivism, expressed in *The Seasons,* is most fully worked out in *The Castle,* where the Knight's, and Britain's, sociopolitical goal of progress encompasses urban development, trade, and cultural refinement and is at the same time rooted in healthy rural industry. The Bard's Song (II.lv–lvi) celebrates the classical-conventional "Happy Man" theme which was a favorite of the poet's. The Bard explicitly acknowledges "MARO" (II.lii); Douglas's

Palice, too, had paid explicit tribute to Virgil (I, l. 283; II, ll. 898, 1225). The Knight of Arts and Industry himself retires to a country home in Deva's Vale, but his rural retreat is not primitive or deceptively over-idealized like the Scotland of Thomson's memory; rather, it is improved and cultivated in the Virgilian ideal, representing true beauty in contrast to the false charms of the Castle. Even so, the Knight must leave his home to take a more active, public stand against corruption in contemporary Britain. So while Thomson's ideal of progress is based in rural life, it is by no means exclusively rural. The Bard accompanies the Knight out of idyllic Deva's Vale to play his public "*British* Harp"; the Bard's—and ultimately the poet Thomson's—role is not just religious but sociopolitical as well. It becomes clear that Thomson's own solution is once again a qualified, rural "nostalgic progressivism," with the emphasis on "progressivism," and that the tension between indolence and industry in many ways parallels the original primitivism versus progress dilemma. The parallel also points up Thomson's own ambivalence over nationalistic loyalties and the deeply felt contrast between the Scotland he loved and left and the England he admired and adopted. Thomson would therefore take the most practical and appropriate solution for an Anglo-Scot, hoping that on the firm foundation of individual industry Great Britain—including Scotland—would achieve genuine progress.[40]

Along with the general sociopolitical views Thomson propounds in *The Castle of Indolence,* he also comments indirectly on a more immediate and specific situation in British politics. The Jacobite crisis was at its most intense when Thomson was writing *The Castle,* and Thomson and his Scottish circle surely had mixed feelings about the issue; while anti-Jacobite and pro-Hanoverian, they were reluctant to appear anti-Scottish, so they for the most part kept silent. So in this particular situation, too, Thomson identified himself and the other members of the Scottish circle with those indolent inmates of the Castle, content at first to remain comfortably sheltered from the real-life fray rather than committing themselves to anti-Jacobite action. The poet clearly condemns this attitude of noninvolvement, of course, despite his own lingering insecurities. The Knight represents, in one sense, the Whig-Hanoverian leadership, and Thomson and his fellow-inmates eventually rally to his call to action. Thomson had in *Liberty* IV characterized the Stuart kings, with their overweening divine right, as sort of wicked "anti-Christ" figures; here, in *The Castle,* the Stuarts can be associated with the anti-Christ Wizard Archimago. The Jacobites would be among those deceived followers of the Catholic, Stuart "Christian Kings, inflam'd by black Desire" (I.lv); Thomson sees them as enemies of the virtuous and progressive society which is the goal of the consummately Whig, Hanoverian, and Protestant British Knight. He therefore suggests in *The Castle* that while it would seem more prudent and pleasant for a Scot in London, particularly in the 1740s, to keep aloof from current political strife, in truth it is his duty to profess his own—and his fellow-Scots'—loyal allegiance to the Hanoverian government and to work toward the greater good of united Britain.

Thomson's own anti-Jacobite "action" took the form of his writings—*The Castle* itself, patriotic poetry, and possibly also anonymous contributions to such periodicals as the *True Patriot.* His stance had much in common with that of the Moderate Whig clergy in Scotland, though they took an even more active, even militaristic position against the Jacobites. Both Thomson and the Moderates expressed their British patriotism in a peculiarly Scottish way; they were pro-British and pro-Scottish alike.[41] Both Thomson and the Moderates further recognized the moral and spiritual dimensions of the Jacobite crisis, and Thomson's allegory of regeneration sought to propose a cure, not only for the social and political ills but also for the moral evils which had brought God's vengeance upon Britain in 1745.

Allegory is Thomson's chosen genre for *The Castle of Indolence;* the poet succeeds here in combining the traditional personal or "psychological" allegory with its dominant narrative device of the individual knightly quest (bearing the religious-didactic message of regeneration and possibility of salvation) with public, sociopolitical, and satirical purpose. The private, inner quest has innumerable literary antecedents; Thomson's juvenile "Upon Happiness" as well as a passage in *Tancred and Sigismunda* (the "Course of Honour") portray similar spiritual pilgrimages.[42] Thomson's immediate model for *The Castle* was, of course, Spenser's *Faerie Queene,* built around twelve knightly quests in pursuit of "virtues." Thomson had evidently read Spenser at an early age and owned his works in John Hughes's 1715 edition, whose glossary supplied many of the archaic words for *The Castle*. *The Faerie Queene* would have appealed to Thomson as a Scot in its supernatural themes and its archaic English language, which bears such close kinship with Scots vernacular and especially literary Middle Scots. Indeed, eighteenth-century Spenserian imitation was particularly associated with Scottish poets, who, like Thomson, seemed to be drawn to the archaic mode.[43] Thomson carries out the strict Spenserian form of *The Castle*, nine-line stanzas in the *a b a b b c b c c* rhyme scheme, with discrimination and decorum; he was by this stage so self-assured in handling literary English usage that he could work well within the limits of complex strict form and delight in it. He now shared this skill with his forebears the Middle Scots Makars and also with the Gaelic poets, who prided themselves on their mastery of formal intricacy. Happily, the discipline of strict form encouraged Thomson to avoid the rhetorical excesses which had weakened so much of his work in blank verse; that he was able to maintain this discipline in a poem of length and depth while at the same time inventing upon the Spenserian style and making it his own demonstrates his mature, "improving" poetic art.

Beyond the Spenserian model, Thomson also drew from a wide variety of other sources for the descriptions and symbols of his allegory. The poem's central symbol of the castle is highly conventional and of course figures in *The Faerie Queene*. For Thomson and his fellow Scottish inmates of the Castle of Indolence, a castle had long been a literal presence in their lives as well.[44] Thomson, Murdoch, Paterson, Armstrong, and Forbes had all dwelt in Edinburgh, where the fortress castle dominates the townscape and evokes rich, romantic, yet often cruel history as well as awesome power, or perhaps the empty, deceptive appearance of power, since by Thomson's day the center of Scottish government was no longer Edinburgh but London; the appearance versus reality theme is central to the poem. As has been mentioned, Scotland and indolence were surely associated in the poet's mind as well, perhaps suggesting the castle motif. There are many Scottish literary castles. Alexander Barclay translated in the sixteenth century Pierre Gringore's poem *The Castell of Laboure*, the opening of which resembles Thomson's *Castle*. Barclay's own *Fourth Eclogue* included a description of the tower of virtue and honor.[45] The Middle Scots moral allegory *King Hart* (attributed to Gavin Douglas, though its authorship is unknown) is built around two symbolic castles, those of King Hart himself, representing the human heart, and Dame Pleasance. While Thomson probably would not have known *King Hart* itself, as there were no early printed texts, the poem has much in common with his *Castle:* themes of spiritual struggle and imprisonment and release, self-directed satire, homiletic influence, and physiological imagery of bodily illness representing ills of the soul.[46] *King Hart* possibly influenced Thomson indirectly, nonetheless, through Spenser, since *King Hart* may have influenced both the manner and the matter of *The Faerie Queene*.[47]

Thomson almost certainly knew the other works of Gavin Douglas, particularly his *Palice of Honour* (London, ca. 1553; Edinburgh, 1579). As has been suggested, there are many similarities in descriptive imagery between Thomson's *Castle* and Douglas's Middle Scots allegory of religious knightly quest; there are also significant thematic and linguistic affinities. In the lengthy, ambitious *Palice* Douglas debates ethical and aesthetic questions within a rich allegory, much as Thomson does in *The Castle*. Both Thomson's and Douglas's central, symbolic "castles" are depicted with extravagant idealism and aureation and are ultimately inexpressibly beautiful. This, of course, is the point of Thomson's irony—the beauty of indolence is unreal. Douglas's "Honour" is identified with God himself, and Thomson likewise portrays his Knight of Arts and Industry as a sort of Christ figure, though both poems also embody a strong secular element along with their fundamental religious-didactic purpose in a Christian context of sin and redemption. Thomson, perhaps more so than Douglas, intended a social, secular purpose to run parallel to and mutually reinforce his religious and moral allegory of regeneration; his key concept of "Virtue," like Douglas's "Honour," carries both religious and secular meanings, such as integrity, courage, and progressive worldly improving activity as well as moral and spiritual goodness. Thomson's poem shares with Douglas's a strong strain of self-directed humor.[48] The poems also have in common a peculiarly northern fantastic imagination,[49] coloring their vivid supernatural descriptions. Lastly, both *The Castle* and *The Palice* place the poet as a central figure in the allegory itself. Douglas's poet figure is subjective; he is the dreamer of the dream vision and acquires a moral education through his quest.[50] Thomson's *Castle* is actually home to two poets, the subjective "Bard . . . more fat than Bard beseems"—Thomson himself, inmate of the Castle (I.lxviii)—and the Bard Philomelus, the more objective teacher and companion of the Knight. The inhabitants of Thomson's Castle, including the portly poet himself, also obtain an education in ethics and social activism and, implicitly, religious truth. It is significant to consider that Gavin Douglas's allegorical method so strikingly resembles Spenser that Douglas himself may even have been Spenser's teacher; indeed, Douglas's great reputation in England at the time makes it highly likely that Spenser knew him.[51] So Thomson, in closely imitating Spenser, was already an indirect heir to a Scottish tradition of allegory. He almost certainly came by this Scottish tradition more directly as well through the immediate influence of Gavin Douglas and *The Palice of Honour.*

In addition to Douglas's *Palice* with its central castle symbol, the Middle Scots allegorical tradition is rich in religious-didactic and moral works, such as Alexander Montgomerie's *The Cherry and the Slae,* which Thomson surely knew, and which advises, "Quoth Reason, then let us remove, / And sleep no more in Sleuth." Scottish literary tradition also embraces sociopolitical allegory; frequently the two purposes were combined, as in David Lindsay's satirical moral allegories[52] *The Dreme, The Monarche,* and *Ane Satyre of the Thrie Estaitis.* Thomson's *Castle* similarly joins its primary religious-didactic purpose with sociopolitical goals. In addition to his major source *The Faerie Queene* and the Scottish allegories, Thomson also drew from broader European literary sources for *The Castle.* Descriptions of the Castle's hell-like reality, for example, owe something not only to Spenser and Gavin Douglas but also to Virgil's *Aeneid* and Douglas's Scots translation of it, Milton's *Paradise Lost,* and Dante's *Inferno.* Certain more romantic episodes of *The Castle* derive from Tasso's *Gerusalemme Liberata,* which Thomson also knew. The Italian influences on Thomson's *Castle* demonstrate the truly international scope, in the Scottish tradition, of the poet's diverse cultural experience.[53] French influences are also discernible: Rabelaisian hyperbole, for example, enriches the Spenserian luxury of the Castle's sumptuous decor. The Castle's "One great Rule for All; / To-wit, That each should work his own Desire" (I.xxxv.5–6) recalls Rabelais's Abbey of Theleme in *Gargantua and Pantagruel* (translated by a Scot, Sir Thomas Urquhart), where the cardinal rule is "DO WHAT THOU WILT" and residents dwell in languid and lazy freedom.[54]

Beyond his debt to a long tradition of European, including Scottish, allegory in *The Castle,* Thomson was also influenced by other strains of Scottish literature. Middle Scots descriptive poetry, and especially Scottish ballads and folklore, almost certainly colored the descriptions, and particularly the more grotesque and supernatural descriptions, of *The Castle.* The knightly quest was, of course, a favorite ballad motif. Similarity has been seen, too, between Thomson's Knight's call to action (II.xxxi) and the summons of Lord Hardyknute in the eighteenth-century ballad imitation by Lady Wardlaw, "Hardyknute";[55] Thomson would certainly have known this "ballad," published by James Watson (1719) and also by Ramsay in *The Ever Green. The Castle of Indolence* thus represents Thomson's rich and complex reworking of a great variety of literary sources and conventions, not least his native Scottish literary heritage, to achieve his own artistic goals.

More conscious and complex linguistic artistry, too, characterizes *The Castle of Indolence.* The poem's language makes a fascinating subject for the study of Thomson's influences and innovations. The elements of Thomson's original *Seasons* diction appear here in new ways, to new aims, and again the influence of Scottish language is strong.[56] A good deal of the poet's familiar Latinate English recurs in *The Castle,* but here it is better balanced and integrated; weighty Latinisms tend to occur more frequently in the more serious, didactic Canto II.[57] Thomson again uses many creative compound words in the poem as well as unusual and resonant quasi-adverbs. The poet's skillful handling of subtle and suggestive sound patterns, particularly alliteration, assonance, and internal rhyme, is at its best in this poem of conscious formal artistry. Significantly, these artistic devices increased in frequency and intricacy with Thomson's return to poetry of natural description.

The most striking feature of the poetic language of *The Castle* is

Thomson's use of Spenserian archaisms. He found many of these words in John Hughes's "Glossary Explaining the Old and Obscure Words in Spenser's Works," from Hughes's 1715 edition of Spenser's *Works*, which he owned. But Thomson's archaisms in *The Castle* are by no means exclusively or strictly Spenserian; most of Spenser's archaisms have their immediate roots in Middle English, which is also the basis of vernacular Scots. Gavin Douglas, for example, chose to use archaic diction for both the *Palice* and the *Eneados*, especially in his verb forms; this tendency probably owed much to Chaucer but resulted in a poetic effect far closer to Spenser, prior to that English poet's writings. Archaisms and archaic forms are also important in the works of Dunbar, Lindsay, and Bellenden.[58] While Thomson did derive many of his *Castle* archaisms from Hughes's Spenserian glossary, he almost certainly used additional sources as well, probably contemporary glossaries of Scots such as Ramsay's for *The Ever Green;* for this, Ramsay had in turn drawn heavily upon Thomas Ruddiman's extensive glossary for Douglas's *Eneados* (published 1710), which Thomson would also have known. A brief survey of Thomson's Spenserian archaisms in *The Castle* reveals that many of these also occur in Ramsay's glossary,[59] including such so-called Spenserian archaisms as "depaynt," "ene," "keist" (Thomson uses "kest"), "eith" (Thomson gives "eath"), "mot," "schene" (Thomson gives "Sheen"), "mell," "noy," "wene" or "wein" (Thomson uses "ween"), and "wist" (in Thomson, "wis"). Both archaic Spenserian and Scots diction would have had poetic appeal to eighteenth-century readers for their novelty as well as for their peculiar remote, romantic connotative force. Furthermore, a fair number of words archaic even in Spenser's day were still current in Scots and northern dialects in Thomson's day, and some can even now be found in modern Scots; such words would have had special expressive appeal beyond mere literary antiquarianism for the Scots-speaker Thomson.

Spenserian archaisms in *The Castle* which also have or had Scottish or northern dialect usage include "moil" (I.i.3, II.ii.4, Thomson defines it to "labour"; not in Hughes's glossary, it occurs in *Chambers Scots Dictionary* and *English Dialect Dictionary*); "sweltry" (I.xi.2, Thomson glosses it as "sultry"; *OED* notes its dialect usage; *Scottish National Dictionary* defines it as "oppressively hot"); "Stounds" (I.xiii.2, Thomson defines it "misfortune, pang"; *OED* notes its "chiefly northern" usage for "pang"; *SND* gives "Stunning blow"; *Chambers* gives "ache, pain . . . pang"); "inly" (I.xxviii.1, *Dictionary of the Older Scottish Tongue* traces derivation from Old English for "inwardly"; by Thomson's day it was not considered a Spenserianism; *OED* calls it obsolete in English and it is apparently obsolete also in modern Scots); "weet" (I.xxv.2, Thomson gives "To know; to weet, to wit"; from Middle English; *SND* says it is obsolete in English but occurs in modern Scots; also cited in *Roxburghshire Word-Book*); "Losel" (I.xxiii.7 and II.lvi.9, Thomson gives "loose, idle fellow"; found in Hughes, it is now chiefly dialect English, but occurs in modern Scots, according to *Chambers*); "swink" (II.ii.4, Thomson defines it "to labour," as does *Chambers; SND* records its chiefly literary usage now in English and Scots); "breme" (II.vii.9, occurs in Hughes's glossary; *DOST* traces it from Middle English, "furious"; *SND* defines "breem" as "keen . . . fierce . . . violent," now obsolete in English except dialect; *Chambers* also gives "keen, fierce, violent, bleak"; occurs in Ramsay's *Ever Green* glossary as "brim"); "Wonne" (II.viii.7 and II.xxxvii.5, found in Hughes; Thomson glosses it "dwelling"; *SND* traces it from Old Norse, through OE and OS to ME and Scots; *Roxburghshire* has "wonning" or "chief house on a farm"; verb "won," "to dwell," is listed in Ramsay's *Ever Green* glossary); "throng'd" (II.xliii.1, meaning "crowded"; Thomson's version of Scots "thrang"; *SND* and *OED* cite this usage as current in Scottish and northern dialects); "felly" (II.xliii.9, Spenserian usage in *FQ* for "cruelly"; *DOST* gives "fierce"; *OED* and *SND* record it as obsolete in both English and Scots; James Beattie's eighteenth-century list of current Scottish usages, by his day merely poetical or archaic in England, includes "fell"); "spill" (II.lix.3, "To spoil," found in Ramsay's *Ever Green* glossary; *OED* calls it obsolete in English, *SND* says it is also obsolete in modern Scots, yet J. Logie Robertson notes it was in Scots use until early nineteenth century); "unkempt" (I.lxi.7, "Uncombed," from Scots "unkaim'd, rude," according to Robertson; Thomson defines it as "unadorned," noting its derivation from Latin *incomptus; OED* cites Thomson's use in *Castle* as earliest example in the sense of "Having the hair uncombed or dishevelled"; *SND* and *Chambers* give its Scots equivalent as meaning "not combed," and Thomson surely had Scots "unkaim'd" in mind; Ramsay's *Ever Green* glossary lists "kemd" for "combed"); and "Tract" (first edition, May 1748, I.lix.9, meaning "track"; *OED* gives "Course, path, way, route" now rare or obsolete, and gives a late example from Alexander Smith's *A Summer in Skye*, 1865; found in *Chambers* as "a track, a path"; either Thomson, his printer or George Lyttelton Anglicized it to "trace" for the second edition, September 1748, and this usage survives in modern editions).[60]

Other "archaisms" in *The Castle* are in more general Scottish use. These include "louting" (I.xiii.3, occurs in Hughes and in Ramsay's *Ever Green* glossary; Thomson defines it as "bowing, bending"; *OED* holds it archaic in English; *DOST* and *SND* cite its current Scots usage; *Roxburghshire*'s variation is "loutherin'"); "Lubbard" (I.lxxiv.4, Scots variant of English "lubber," compare "Autumn," l.562; *DOST* traces ME root; Armstrong's use here is probably based on Ramsay's poem "Health," where "Lethargus" is a "lazy lubbard"); "muchel" (II.vii.2, Thomson gives "much, great"; in general use in Scots, as cited in *SND*—compare also "mickel," "meikle," "muckle"; Ramsay uses "mekle" or "meikle"); "Rabblement" (II.xlv.3, Robertson gives "Mob. From the noise of their chattering. Lowland Scots 'raible,' to chatter [Burns]"; occurs in *FQ* I.xii as *OED* notes but "rare" in English; in use in modern Scots; *SND* cites example from Jamieson, 1887, of "rabblement" as "noisy mob"; also found in *Chambers*); "sicker" (II.xxxix.1, Thomson glosses it as "sure, surely"; not in Hughes, but found in the *Ever Green* glossary; *OED* says the usage, common in ME, is now limited to Scots and northern dialects; *SND* cites "sicker" and also "siccar" as "safe, secure" and "sure"). In *The Castle* Thomson also uses some of his favorite rather idiosyncratic, imitative, or onomatopoeic descriptive words which had previously occurred in the juvenilia and *The Seasons*, such as "flounce" (II.xliii.7), "bicker" (I.iii.8), and "keen" (as a verb, II.lxxx.3). Expressions common in Scottish speech, "ay," "for aye," and "mean time," also frequently recur. Other, more subtle Scotticisms appear in *The Castle* as well, such as Thomson's use of "Tradesman" (I.xiv.6) in the Scottish sense, listed in Beattie's *Scoticisms*, of "one who works with his hands at a trade" rather than in the English sense of "shopkeeper."[61]

The noun "Glaive"(II.xxxix.6) is an unusual and revealing usage: Thomson defines it as "sword, coming from the French" and ultimately from the Latin "gladius"; "glaive" also occurs in Ruddiman's glossary to Douglas's *Eneados,* where Ruddiman cites both French and Latin antecedents. The word is not found in Hughes's glossary. *OED* gives examples of its archaic use in both English and Scots; in *FQ* (V.xi.58) it means "halbert" or "long-handled weapon." "Glaive" also appears in Blind Hary's *Wallace* (X.367), Douglas's *Eneados* (III.viii, and Ruddiman's glossary), Ramsay's *Ever Green* glossary (as "glave"), and in Burns, Byron, and Scott. *OED* speculates that in the earlier Scottish instances it possibly represented a corruption of the Gaelic *claidheamh,* which became "glaymore" or "claymore." In general, "glaive" seems to have lingered longer in Scottish than in English use, hence Thomson's choice of the uncommon word. Other words in *The Castle* of Gaelic origin and not particularly associated with Spenser are "Glen" (II.lv.4, also in the *Ever Green* glossary) and "Bard" (II.xxxiii.1 and elsewhere). The noun "Coil" (I.iv.8), describing the insects' noise, is of uncertain origin according to J. A. H. Murray (*OED*), but Robertson believes it is related to the Celtic "goil." Several of the more striking descriptive words in *The Castle,* while they do occur in Spenser, are not exclusively Spenserian and in some instances might have come to Thomson through the Middle Scots aureate tradition, such as "burnish'd" (I.lxiv.1), which recurs in Douglas's *Palice,* and "enamel'd" (I.li.3), which appears notably in Douglas and in Dunbar and (as "enamilit") is also listed in the *Ever Green* glossary.[62]

In its originality and flexibility, the diction of Thomson's *Castle* equals that of *The Seasons* and enjoys the added linguistic freedom sanctioned by the poem's archaic genre, allowing the poet to draw even more liberally from his Scots literary and language sources. Thomson's return to the poetry of description certainly inspired his innovative verbal skill yet again. This time, though, the language is even more polished, accurately chosen, and better balanced by virtue of the artistic discipline demanded of the poem's strict form.

In *The Castle of Indolence* one discovers the mature genius of the poet of *The Seasons.* In *The Castle* Thomson again reworked the very themes—descriptive, religious-didactic and philosophical, sociopolitical, and Virgilian classical—which had motivated the miscellaneous *Seasons*. Especially welcome is Thomson's return to the poetry of natural description in *The Castle*. So there is a discernible continuity between the two works, yet there is creativity as well: *The Castle* is an imaginative and carefully crafted poem in strict Spenserian form, and while it may lack something of *The Seasons'* refreshing spontaneity, it proves Thomson's versatility, his formal poetic control, his growth as a literary artist. Most of all, *The Castle* shows Thomson again synthesizing his Scottish cultural and literary resources and putting them to best possible use.

The poet again delights in vivid description, both natural and supernatural, rooted in affectionate observation of the natural world and yet also bold enough to explore the imaginative extremes of the Castle's domain in descriptions of the ideal and the grotesque. *The Castle*, like *The Seasons,* thus deserves its place in the Scottish tradition of descriptive poetry. Also based on Thomson's Scottish background and experience is the poem's moral allegory and stern religious didacticism, preaching of sin (especially the sin of sloth), the work ethic, and the potential for recovery or regeneration corresponding to old-style Scottish Calvinist structures of thought as well as Moderate interpretations. Here, too, is the familiar Scoto-Roman sociopolitical ideal of Virgilian improvement, reinforcing the poet's North British patriotism in a period of strained Scottish-English relations. Thomson's deep-seated allegiance to his native Scotland takes fascinating forms in *The Castle:* he writes the poem from his safe, secure place within the Scottish circle, at once wishing to continue in passive indolence, and also actively to attack the national (and especially Scottish) "sin" of indolence, and, more specifically, to act against the threat of Jacobitism. *The Castle* is a complex response to Thomson's Anglo-Scottish anxieties and his attempt to safeguard his personal sentiments for Scotland while also following the Knight of Arts and Industry, representing united Britain, in public support of the Whig-Hanoverian regime. The poem's projected regeneration would thus be social, political, and patriotic as well as moral and spiritual and would, Thomson hoped, particularly help Scotland to recover from both her indolence and her Jacobite arrogance. Thomson's attitude is, of course, progressive yet still nostalgic for the Scotland he loved and left. Most significantly, this nostalgia and respect for Scotland was reflected in the poet's literary and linguistic models for *The Castle*. The literary form as well as the language of the poem are not simply Spenserian but draw a great deal from distinctively Scottish sources—chiefly the allegories of Gavin Douglas and both written and spoken Scots vernacular. Thomson adapted all of these Scottish elements in new and artistic ways in *The Castle*. After *Liberty* and the plays, *The Castle* represents Thomson's return to those rich Scottish resources which had made *The Seasons* strong to create another delightful, successful, and thoroughly Anglo-Scottish poem. In his last poem *The Castle of Indolence* James Thomson "comes home" again to his Scottish heritage.

EPILOGUE

---·ʊʊʊ·---

This study of James Thomson's life and art has aimed to illustrate how the poet's Scottishness—literary and broadly cultural—had a fundamental and far-reaching influence on his work. Thomson's upbringing as a son of the manse, his life in the Border landscape, his humanistic schooling at Jedburgh Grammar School, his classical, philosophical, and theological education at Edinburgh University, his interest in Scottish literature and involvement in Scottish cultural life of the early eighteenth century (a critical period for the establishment of the identity of post-Union Scotland), and his enduring links with Scotland even while he lived in London all helped to shape his poetry. These influences also worked to define his ideals of poetry and the poet's role, his eclectic subject matter, and his original language and style. More directly, and to an appreciable extent, Scottish literature, folklore, and language had enormous impact on his poetry. These Scottish influences are perhaps best seen in *The Seasons*, written just after Thomson left Scotland, but are nonetheless an integral part of his other works— from the juvenilia, to *Liberty* and the plays, and particularly to *The Castle of Indolence*. Behind all of these more specific influences of upbringing and education lies the very fact of Thomson's Scottishness itself, which profoundly affected the way he saw himself and his art. As John Clive has suggested, the eighteenth-century Scotsman's "provincialism," his especially complex "image of the world and of himself," was not necessarily a bad thing. It could serve to "shake the mind from the roots of habit and tradition. It led men to the interstices of common thought where they found new views and new approaches to the old."[1] Such a sense of Scottishness released the restless intellectual energy of the Scottish Enlightenment. In James Thomson himself, the very precarious provincial identity which came from his being Scottish surely shook his imagination into creating original Anglo-Scottish poetry. Thomson was courageous enough to attempt a "new approach" to poetry in English, bringing the many distinctive qualities of his Scottish literary culture together with those of Augustan England; he was genius enough to succeed, becoming by far the best and most influential Anglo-Scottish poet of his age. Thomson truly brought Anglo-Scottish poetry into its own as one of the legitimate native literatures, along with Scots and Gaelic, of Scotland. It is enlightening to consider that Thomson, whom many had criticized for "selling out" his Scottish origins, abandoning his native land and language to write English poetry in England, would have a profound influence on the Scottish poets who came after him, on their broader conceptions of poetry as well as on their individual style and language, themes and modes.

James Thomson was a great inspiration to his fellow Scottish Augustans in the eighteenth century. They emulated his accurate and loving natural description, they echoed his religious-didactic and philosophical voice, they followed his lead in Spenserian imitation, they eagerly took up his themes of superstition and the supernatural, and they celebrated his Whig sociopolitical ideals of liberty, in poetry and also in dramatic tragedy. Such major Anglo-Scottish poets as James Beattie, Robert Blair, and James Macpherson, with a host of minor disciples, came under his immediate influence. Early on, Thomson innovated and put into practice the literary aesthetics of the Scottish Enlightenment itself, which Anglo-Scottish rhetoricians, who came from the same cultural background as he, would soon methodize. Like Thomson's poetry itself, their theories were firmly rooted in Scottish vernacular humanism yet also allowed for greater sensibility of subjective response, thus preparing the way for the revolution of Romanticism. Besides his influence on these Anglo-Scots, Thomson also had a significant impact on poets who wrote in vernacular Scots, foremost among them Robert Burns, who himself gratefully acknowledged his debt to Thomson in both style and subject matter.[2] Scottish

Gaelic poets of the eighteenth century, too, such as Alexander Macdonald and Duncan ban McIntyre, admired Thomson's poetry of natural description and adopted his seasonal theme.[3]

The Romantic period saw Thomson's especially Scottish themes—
nature (and particularly wild, sublime nature), Northern liberty, and
northern mystery and superstition—achieve preeminence not only in
Scottish poetry but in all Western literatures. Thomas Campbell, Walter Scott, and Lord Byron were but the most famous of the many
Scottish Romantics who showed unmistakable Thomsonian influence.
In the Victorian age, Thomson's direct poetical influence waned in
Scotland and elsewhere as Augustan literature generally fell out of
favor. Even so, clear echoes of Thomson could still be heard in the
verse of such Scottish Victorians as Alexander Smith and the poet's
namesake James Thomson ("B.V."), author of "The Lord of the Castle
of Indolence." By this time, of course, Thomson's pervasive influence,
particularly on the poetry of natural description, had become assimilated into the wider British poetic tradition. Scottish authors of both
poetry and prose continued to pay tribute to the Thomsonian vision
in their way of seeing the natural world and man within it. Such long-
lived imitation and emulation of James Thomson by the poets of his
homeland is one very positive measure of his success as a genuinely
North British, Scottish poet.

In this century, while Thomson's direct influence can no longer be
presumed, Scottish poets still show kinship with the eighteenth-century Anglo-Scot and return to the very themes he introduced and
explored. These twentieth-century poets represent all three languages of Scottish literature—Gaelic, Scots, and English—as well as
poetic modes ranging from intricate strict form to free verse. Scottish
poetry of closely observed natural description, and along with it the
consideration of man's relationship to the natural and frequently
harsh Scottish environment, has remained a major preoccupation of
such poets as Norman MacCaig, Sorley MacLean, George Bruce,
George Mackay Brown, Iain Crichton Smith, and Sydney Goodsir
Smith as well as the many younger poets who regard nature with
Thomson's acute sensibility. Natural description is but one element of
the extraordinarily varied, complex poetry of Hugh MacDiarmid; he

likewise treats of science and philosophy, religion and society, with a bold empirical spirit akin to Thomson's own. Dr. Johnson's fulsome praise of Thomson's eclectic genius, his "eye that distinguishes in every thing presented to its view whatever there is on which imagination can delight to be detained, and . . . a mind that at once comprehends the vast, and attends to the minute . . ."[4] might equally well apply to MacDiarmid, Scotland's chief poet of this century. Modern poets besides MacDiarmid who, like Thomson did, make outspoken political pronouncements and show profound concern for Scotland's situation include Edwin Muir and more recently Edwin Morgan and Alexander Scott. Satire on human vanity, a favorite target of Thomson's, is the province of witty Robert Garioch. Scottish vernacular humanism, the traditional Scottish classical mindset, has been both a formal and a philosophical inspiration for both Garioch and MacCaig. Themes of religion and metaphysical enquiry, the motivation for much of Thomson's poetry, remain viable themes in modern Scottish poetry, notably in the work of Muir and his disciple George Mackay Brown. It is heartening to be reminded that today's Scottish poets, and especially the Anglo-Scots, continue to proclaim James Thomson's poetic priorities—God and nature, man and society—and to aspire to his high standards for a true Scottish poetry which can speak not only to Scotland but to the world.

The present century has witnessed a healthy resurgence of nationalism in Scotland. The so-called Scottish Renaissance movement has again focused attention on the need to cultivate a native Scottish national literature. This focus has sometimes, however, tended to grow too narrow: as in the eighteenth century, the definition of "native" Scottish poetry has too often in recent years been limited to that which is written in Scots. What of Anglo-Scottish poetry, not to mention the Scottish Gaelic? The lesson which the poetry of James Thomson holds for twentieth-century literary nationalists must be that the Anglo-Scots, too, can bring much that is distinctively and positively Scottish to poetry written in the English language. Their contributions must not be neglected, for they are one essential element of Scottish literature itself.

This study of James Thomson's Anglo-Scottish poetry has set out to restore the poet to his rightful cultural context, shedding some light on the significance of his Scottish experience to his art. It is hoped that so doing will also have expanded the very definition of literary Scottishness, ultimately to benefit future studies of both Scottish, and eighteenth-century British, literatures.

APPENDIX 1

"A WINTER'S DAY,"

BY [ROBERT RICCALTOUN]

———————————ひひひ———————————

A Winter's Day. Written by a Scotch Clergyman.
Corrected by an eminent Hand.

Now, gloomy soul! look out—now comes thy turn;
With thee, behold all ravag'd nature mourn.
Hail the dim empire of thy darling night,
That spreads, slow-shadowing, o'er the vanquish'd light.
  Look out, with joy; the Ruler of the day,
Faint, as thy hopes, emits a glimm'ring ray:
Already exil'd to the utmost sky,
Hither, oblique, he turns his clouded eye.
Lo! from the limits of the wintry pole,
Mountainous clouds, in rude confusion, roll: 10
In dismal pomp, now, hov'ring on their way,
To a sick twilight they reduce the day.
And hark! imprison'd winds, broke loose, arise,
And roar their haughty triumph thro the skies.
While the driv'n clouds, o'ercharg'd with floods of rain,
And mingled lightning, burst upon the plain.
Now see sad earth—like thine, her alter'd state,
Like thee, she mourns her sad reverse of fate!
Her smiles, her wanton looks,—where are they now?

Faded her face! and wrap'd in clouds her brow!   20
No more, th' ungrateful verdure of the plain;
No more the wealth-crown'd labours of the swain;
These scenes of bliss, no more upbraid my fate,
Torture my pining thought, and rouze my hate.
The leaf-clad forest, and the tufted grove,
Ere while, the safe retreats of happy love,
Stript of their honours, naked, now appear;
This is, my soul! the winter of their year!
The little, noisy songsters of the wing,
All, shiv'ring on the bough, forget to sing.   30
Hail, rev'rend silence! with thy awful brow!
Be musick's voice for ever mute—as now:
Let no intrusive joy my dead repose
Disturb—no pleasure disconcert my woes.
In this moss-cover'd cavern, hopeless laid,
On the cold clift I'll lean my aking head,
And, pleas'd with winter's waste, unpitying, see
All nature in an agony with me!
Rough, rugged rocks, wet marshes, ruin'd tow'rs,
Bare trees, brown brakes, bleak heaths, and rushy moors,   40
Dead floods, huge cataracts, to my pleased eyes
(Now I can smile!) in wild disorder rise:
And now, the various dreadfulness combin'd,
Black melancholy comes to doze my mind.
See! night's wish'd-shades rise, spreading through the air,
And the lone, hollow gloom, for me prepare!
Hail! solitary ruler of the grave!
Parent of terrors! from thy dreary cave!
Let thy dumb silence midnight all the ground,
And spread a welcome horror all around.   50
But hark!—a sudden howl invades my ear!
The phantoms of the dreadful hour are near.
Shadows, from each dark cavern, now combine
And stalk around, and mix their yells with mine.

Stop, flying time! repose thy restless wing;
Fix here—nor hasten to restore the spring:
   Fix'd my ill fate, so fix'd let winter be,
Let never wanton season laugh at me!

From *The Gentleman's Magazine* 10 (1740): 256.

APPENDIX 2

"IMITATION OF SHAKESPEARE" ("WINTER"), BY JOHN ARMSTRONG

Now Summer with her wanton court is gone
To revel on the south side of the world,
And flaunt and frolic out the live-long day.
While Winter rising pale from northern seas
Shakes from his hoary locks the drizzling rheum.
A blast so shrewd makes the tall-bodied pines
Unsinew'd bend, and heavy-paced bears
Sends growling to their savage tenements.

Now blows the surly north, and chills throughout
The stiffening regions; while, by stronger charms   10
Than Circe o'er fell Medea brew'd,
Each brook that wont to prattle to its banks
Lies all bestill'd and wedg'd betwixt its banks,
Nor moves the wither'd reeds: and the rash flood
That from the mountains held its headstrong course,
Buried in livid sheets of vaulting ice,
Seen thro' the shameful breaches, idly creeps
To pay a scanty tribute to the ocean.
What wonder? when the floating wilderness
That scorns our miles, and calls Geography   20
A shallow pryer; from whose unsteady mirrour
The high-hung pole surveys his dancing locks;
When this still-raving deep lies mute and dead,

Nor heaves its swelling bosom to the winds.
The surges, baited by the fierce north-east
Tossing with fretful spleen their angry heads
To roar and rush together,
Even in the foam of all their madness struck
To monumental ice, stand all astride
The rocks they washed so late. Such execution,   30
So stern, so sudden, wrought the grisly aspect
Of terrible Medusa, ere young Perseus
With his keen sabre cropt her horrid head,
And laid her serpents rowling on the dust;
When wandering thro' the woods she frown'd to stone
Their savage tenants: just as the foaming lion
Sprung furious on his prey, her speedier power
Outrun his haste; no time to languish in,
But fix'd in that fierce attitude he stands
Like Rage in marble.—Now portly Argosies   40
Lie wedg'd 'twixt Neptune's ribs. The bridg'd abysm
Has chang'd our ships to horses; the swift bark
Yields to the heavy waggon and the cart,
That now from isle to isle maintain the trade;
And where the surface-haunting Dolphin led
Her sportive young, is now an area fit
For the wild school-boy's pastime.

   Meantime the evening skies, crusted with ice,
Shifting from red to black their weighty skirts,
Hang mournful o'er the hills; and stealing night   50
Rides the bleak puffing winds, that seem to spit
Their foam sparse thro' the welkin, which is nothing
If not beheld. Anon the burden'd heaven
Shakes from its ample sieve the boulted snow;
That fluttering down besprinkles the sad trees
In mockery of leaves; piles up the hills
To monstrous altitude, and choaks to the lips
The deep impervious vales that yawn as low

As to the centre, Nature's vastly breaches.
While all the pride of men and mortal things   60
Lies whelm'd in heaven's white ruins.—

   The shivering clown digs his obstructed way
Thro' the snow-barricadoed cottage door;
And muffled in his home-spun plaid encounters
With livid cheeks and rheum-distilling nose
The morning's sharp and scourging breath; to count
His starving flock whose number's all too short
To make the goodly sum of yester-night:
Part deep ingurgitated, part yet struggling
With their last pantings melt themselves a grave   70
In Winter's bosom; which yields not to the touch
Of the pale languid crescet of this world,
That now with lean and churlish husbandry
Yields heartlessly the remnants of his prime;
And like most spendthrifts starves his latter days
For former rankness. He with bleary eye
Blazons his own disgrace; the harness'd waste
Rebellious to his blunt defeated shafts;
And idly strikes the chalky mountains tops
That rise to kiss the Welkin's ruddy lips;   80
Where all the rash young bullies of the air
Mount their quick slender penetrating wings,
Whipping the frost-burnt villagers to the bones;
And growing with their motion mad and furious,
'Till swoln to tempests they out-rage the thunder;
Winnow the chaffy snow, and mock the skies
Even with their own artillery retorted;
Tear up and throw th' accumulated hills
Into the vallies. And as rude hurricanes,
Discharged from the wind-swoln cheeks of heaven,   90
Buoy up the swilling skirts of Araby's
Inhospitable wilds,
And roll the dusty desart thro' the skies,

Choaking the liberal air, and smothering
Whole caravans at once; such havock spreads
This war of heaven and earth, such sudden ruin
Visits their houseless citizens, that shrink
In the false shelter of the hills together,
And hear the tempest howling o'er their heads
That by and by o'erwhelms them. The very birds,   100
Those few that troop'd not with the chimeing tribe
Of amorous Summer, quit their ruffian element;
And with domestic tameness hop and flutter
Within the roofs of persecuting man,
(Grown hospitable by like sense of sufferance;)
Whither the hinds, the debt o' the day discharg'd,
From kiln or barn repairing, shut the door
On surly Winter; croud the clean-swept hearth
And chearful shining fire; and doff the time,
The whilst the maids their twirling spindles ply,   110
With musty legends and ear-pathing tales;
Of giants, and black necromantic bards,
Of air-built castles, feats of madcap knights,
And every hollow fiction of romance.
And, as their rambling humour leads them, talk
Of prodigies, and things of dreadful utterance;
That set them all agape, rouse up their hair,
And make the ideot drops start from their eyes;
Of church-yards belching flames at dead of night,
Of walking statues, ghosts unaffable,   120
Haunting the dark waste tower or airless dungeon;
Then of the elves that deftly trip the green,
Drinking the summer's moonlight from the flowers;
And all the toys that phantasy pranks up
T' amuse her fools withal.—Thus they lash on
The snail-pac'd Hyperborean nights, till heaven
Hangs with a juster poize: when the murk clouds
Roll'd up in heavy wreathes low-bellying, seem
To kiss the ground, and all the waste of snow
Looks blue beneath 'em; till plump'd with bloating dropsy,   130

Beyond the bounds and stretch of continence,
They burst at once; down pours the hoarded rain,
Washing the slippery winter from the hills,
And floating all the vallies. The fading scene
Melts like a lost enchantment or vain phantasm
That can no more abuse. Nature resumes
Her old substantial shape; while from the waste
Of undistinguishing calamity,
Forests, and by their sides wide-skirted plains,
Houses and trees arise; and waters flow,   140
That from their dark confinements bursting, spurn
Their brittle chains; huge sheets of loosen'd ice
Float on their bosoms to the deep, and jarr
And clatter as they pass; th' o'erjutting banks,
As long unpractic'd to so steep a view,
Seem to look dizzy on the moving pomp.

   Now ev'ry petty brook that crawl'd along,
Railing its pebbles, mocks the river's rage,
Like the proud frog i' the fable. The huge Danube,
While melting mountains rush into its tide,   150
Rolls with such headstrong and unreined course,
As it would choak the Euxine's gulphy maw,
Bursting his chrystal cerements. The breathing time
Of peace expir'd, that hush'd the deafning scenes
Of clam'rous indignation, ruffian War
Rebels, and Nature stands at odds again:
When the rous'd Furies of the fighting winds
Torment the main; that swells its angry sides,
And churns the foam betwixt its flinty jaws;
While thro' the savage dungeon of the night   160
The horrid thunder growls. Th' ambitious waves
Assault the skies, and from the bursting clouds
Drink the glib lightening; as if the seas
Wou'd quench the ever-burning fires of heaven.
Strait from their slipp'ry pomp they madly plunge
And kiss the lowest pebbles. Wretched they

That 'midst such rude vexation of the deep
Guide a frail vessel! Better ice-bound still,
Than mock'd with liberty thus be resign'd
To the rough fortune of the froward time;   170
When Navigation all a-tiptoe stands
On such unsteady footing. Now they mount
On the tall billow's top, and seem to jowl
Against the stars; whence (dreadful eminence!)
They see with swimming eyes (enough to hurry round
In endless vertigo the dizzy brain)
A gulph that swallows vision, with wide mouth
Steep-yawning to receive them; down they duck
To the rugged bottom of the main, and view
The adamantine gates of vaulted hell: 180
Thence toss'd to light again; till borne adrift
Against some icy mountains bulging sides
They reel, and are no more.—Nor less by land
Ravage the winds, that in their wayward rage
Howl thro' the wide unhospitable glens;
That rock the stable-planted towers, and shake
The hoary monuments of ancient time
Down to their flinty bases; that engage
As they would tear the monuments from their roots,
And brush the high heavens with their woody heads;   190
Making the stout oaks bow.—But I forget
That sprightly Ver trips on old Winter's heel:
Cease we these notes too tragic for the time,
Nor jar against great Nature's symphony;
When even the blustrous elements grow tuneful,
Or listen to the concert. Hark! how loud
The cuckoo wakes the solitary wood!
Soft sigh the winds as o'er the greens they stray,
And murmuring brooks within their channels play.

From John Armstrong, *Miscellanies* (London, 1770), vol. 1, pp. 146–159.

NOTES

───────────── ʊʊʊ ─────────────

INTRODUCTION

1. MacQueen, *Progress and Poetry,* vol. 1, p. 7.
2. Scott, "Observations," p. 9.
3. Smith, *Scottish Literature,* pp. 276–277.
4. Sher, *Church and University,* pp. 9–10, so defines the general Scottish context.
5. Cohen, *Art,* p. 381.
6. Home, *Elements of Criticism,* vol. 2, pp. 197–198; Beattie, "On Poetry and Music," in *Essays on Poetry and Music,* pp. 29–30, 53; Blair, *Lectures on Rhetoric and Belles Lettres,* pp. 518–519.
7. Thomson, *Works,* ed. Murdoch, vol. 1, pp. i–xx; [Shiels], "James Thomson," vol. 5, pp. 190–218; John Aikin, "An Essay on the Plan and Character of Thomson's 'Seasons,'" in *The Seasons* (Leipzig, 1781), pp. iii–xxix; Robert Heron, "A Critical Essay on *The Seasons,*" in *The Seasons* (Perth, 1793); Scott, *Critical Essays;* Pinkerton, *Letters of Literature;* Warton, *Essay on the Genius,* vol. 1.
8. McDiarmid, ed., *Poems of Robert Fergusson,* vol. 1, p. 55. In the eighteenth century "Mr. Thomson's anniversary has been celebrated in Scotland by so many others since [the earl of Buchan's gatherings at Ednam], that it would be impertinent to take farther notice of them," letter from "A Friend to Thomson and to Justice," *The Bee* 7 (February 1792): 237.
9. Burns, "Address, To the Shade of Thomson, on crowning his Bust, at Ednam, Roxburgh-shire, with Bays" (St. 5), and "Extempore—on some Commemorations of Thomson" (St. 1), in *Burns: Poems and Songs,* ed. Kinsley, pp. 458–459; Burns was invited to attend the fetes organized by the eleventh earl of Buchan to honor Thomson but declined.
10. Erskine, *Essays on the Lives.* One of the earl's Thomsonian fetes is described in detail in "Fete at Dryburgh Abbey," *Kelso Mail* (August 17, 1812), National Library of Scotland MS 9848; the earl erected a "Temple of the Muses" crowned with Thom-

son's bust which still stands near Dryburgh Abbey. See Cohen, *Art*, p. 271; Somerville, *My Own Life and Times*, p. 42n; *The Bee*, ed. Anderson, 5, 6 (1791), 7, 8 (1792), 18 (1793).

11. [Wilson], "Winter Rhapsody," Fytte I, p. 877.

12. Cohen has identified John More as the Rev. John Moir, a clergyman in England; Cohen, *Art*, appendix 2, "The Identification of a Critic," pp. 508–512, 290; More, *Strictures*, pp. 17–18.

13. Bate, *Samuel Johnson*, p. 526.

14. Johnson, "Thomson," in *Lives of the English Poets*, ed. Hill, vol. 3, pp. 282–283, 298–301; Cohen, *Art*, pp. 39–40.

15. Thomson, *James Thomson: Poetical Works*, ed. Robertson, pp. v–vi.

16. Eleventh earl of Buchan, "Eulogy of Thomson the Poet, delivered by the Earl of Buchan on Ednam Hill, when he crowned the first Edition of the Seasons with A Wreath of Bays, on the 22d of September 1791," *The Bee* 5 (1791): 200–203. The earl chose to interpret Dr. Johnson's negative criticisms as slurs on Thomson's national origins.

17. Hazlitt, "On Thomson and Cowper," pp. 164–200; Thomson, *Poetical Works*, ed. Nicolas; Campbell, "Thomson," in *Specimens*, vol. 5, pp. 215–219.

18. Cohen, *Art*, pp. 394–395.

19. Bulwer-Lytton, "The New Phaedo," vol. 2, p. 295. See Cohen, *Art*, p. 419.

20. [Wilson], "Winter Rhapsody," Fytte I, p. 877; Cohen, *Art*, pp. 408–409.

21. Brooke, *Naturalism*, p. 41; Bayne, *James Thomson*, pp. 9ff.; Wittig, *Scottish Tradition*, pp. 5–6, 107–112, 135ff., 197–198; Thomson, "Gaelic Writers," pp. 37–38. See Cohen, *Art*, p. 221.

22. Brooke, *Naturalism*, p. 46.

23. Shairp, *On Poetic Interpretation*; Smith, *Scottish Literature*, pp. 167–169; Miller, *First Impressions*, pp. 111–112; Aubin, *Topographical Poetry*, pp. 56–59; Veitch, *Feeling*, vol. 2, pp. 44, etc.

24. Morel, *James Thomson*, pp. 424–425, 487, 649–650; Cohen, *Art*, pp. 347–349; Veitch, *Feeling*, vol. 2, 50–51; Graham, *Scottish Men of Letters*, p. 297.

25. Smith, *Scottish Literature*, p. 55; Thomson, *The Seasons and The Castle of Indolence*, ed. Robertson; Thomson, *Poetical Works*, ed. Robertson, p. xiii.

26. Macaulay, *James Thomson*; Bayne, *James Thomson*.

27. Thomson, *Poetical Works*, ed. Robertson, pp. xiii–xiv, quoting James Thomson, "To David Mallet," [August 21–27, 1726]; in Thomson, *Letters and Documents*, ed. McKillop, p. 48.

28. Grant, *James Thomson*; Campbell, *James Thomson*; Cohen, *Art* and *Unfolding*; in a letter to the present author from Professor Cohen (September 28, 1976), he is also noncommittal as to whether Thomson's Scottishness matters to the poetry. He makes only vague reference to the poet's rather negative mixture of nostalgia, alienation, and anxiety at being a Scot in London and efforts to suppress evidence of his Scottish origins, and also comments generally on the poet's Scottish experiences

of winter and rural life and their influence on *Seasons* descriptions. These topics are not treated in Cohen's books. Thomson, *The Plays*, ed. Adams; McKillop, *Background of Thomson's 'Seasons'* and *Background of Thomson's 'Liberty'*; Thomson, *Letters and Documents* and *The Castle of Indolence and Other Poems*, both ed. McKillop, and many more articles and notes; Thomson, *The Seasons* and *Liberty*, both ed. Sambrook.

Among recent studies of eighteenth-century literature which attempt to place Thomson in a social and historical context but which take little or no account of his Scottish roots are Barrell, *English Literature;* Rothstein, *Restoration;* Sitter, *Literary Loneliness;* Speck, *Society and Literature.*

29. Spacks, *The Varied God*, and *Poetry of Vision;* Fairchild, *Religious Trends*, vol. 1; Nicolson, *Newton Demands the Muse;* Drennon, "James Thomson's Contact," pp. 71–80; Lindsay, *History of Scottish Literature;* Mackenzie, *Scottish Literature to 1714;* de Haas, *Nature in English Poetry;* Wittig, *Scottish Tradition;* Speirs, *Scots Literary Tradition;* Butt, *Augustan Age;* Oliver, "The Scottish Augustans," pp. 119–149; Golden, *The Self Observed*, pp. 17–25; Tobin, *Plays by Scots;* MacQueen, *Progress and Poetry.*

30. Smith, "Thomson and Burns," pp. 180–193; and in Smith's *Some Observations;* Butt, *Augustan Age;* Lindsay, *History of Scottish Literature.*

1 SCOTTISH NATURE AND NURTURE

1. Grant, *James Thomson*, p. 15; Thomson, *Poetical Works*, ed. Nicolas, vol. 1, p. viin. Scots traditionally showed particular skill at gardening, and many went to England to practice their art: see Graham, *Social Life of Scotland*, pp. 513–514; Smith, "Some Eighteenth-Century Ideas," p. 110. For background on Scottish gardening styles in Thomson's day, see Tait, *The Landscape Garden;* Somerville, *My Own Life and Times*, pp. 330–331; Reid, *The Scots Gard'ner.* For background on Thomson's views of landscape gardening, see Isabel Chase, *Horace Walpole, Gardenist* (Princeton, 1943), pp. 109–115; Hunt, *The Figure;* Barrell, *The Idea of Landscape.* Thomson had two relations (possibly nephews or cousins) who lived near him in Richmond: "One of them was formerly gardner to Lord Bute, now a nursery-man at Milend near London, the other is full brother to this man, and is at present gardner to squire Bouverie," letter from "Friend to Thomson and to Justice," *The Bee* 7 (1792): 236–237.

2. Thomson, *Works*, ed. Murdoch, vol. 1, p. ii.

3. Graham, *Scottish Men of Letters*, p. 283; Fairchild, *Religious Trends*, vol. 1, p. 510; Burleigh, *Ednam*, p. 86; Thomson, *Letters and Documents*, ed. McKillop, pp. 3n, 5n. Among Thomas Thomson's friends were Alexander Colden and Gabriel Wilson, close associates of the evangelical Thomas Boston of Ettrick.

4. Watson, "Rev. Thomas Thomson," pp. 177–178; Thomson, *Letters and Documents*, ed. McKillop, p. 5n; Macaulay, *James Thomson*, p. 5; Burleigh, *Ednam*, p. 161. Thomas Boston of Ettrick records a severe epidemic of fever, January–April 1716

in the Borders, following unusually bad snowstorms which killed many people; Boston, *The Complete Works*, vol. 12, pp. 276–279.

5. Graham, *Social Life of Scotland*, pp. 404–405; Jack, *Scottish Prose*, p. 25.

6. Grant, *James Thomson*, pp. 7–9; Thomson, *Works*, ed. Murdoch, vol. 1, p. iv; Fairchild, *Religious Trends*, vol. 1, p. 510.

7. Jeffrey, *History and Antiquities*, vol. I, pp. 16–17; Somerville, *My Own Life and Times*, pp. 202, 304–305; Rev. William Scott, "Southdean," in *First Statistical Account of Scotland* 12 (1794): 72.

8. Grant, *James Thomson*, pp. 9–10; Wittig, *Scottish Tradition*, pp. 144–145n.

9. Taylor, "James Thomson," p. 4; More, *Strictures*, pp. 172–173.

10. Bayne, *James Thomson*, p. 28.

11. This was suggested by Prof. John MacQueen; see Harvey, ed., *The Oxford Companion*, p. 447, speculating that the "romantic" element of Virgil's feeling for nature in the *Aeneid* derives from his Celtic background.

12. Smith, *Specimens*, pp. xlvi–xlvii; Jack, *Scottish Prose*, p. 25.

13. Law, *Education in Edinburgh*, pp. 33, 195–196; also, Dr. Law, interview with Mary Jane W. Scott, February 9, 1976. Such textbooks based on the Shorter Catechism were very common in the eighteenth century.

14. Watson, *History of Jedburgh*, p. 7, citing his source, *Historical Notices of the Superstitions of Teviotdale*, p. 535. There are several references to Brown in minutes of the Jedburgh Town Council, vol. 1 (1715–1735), Scottish Record Office MS B.38/7/1. fol. 28; Brown's successor was appointed in March 1721.

15. Despauterius, *Ninivitae Gramaticae*. Despauter was supplanted as the standard text in Scotland by Ruddiman's *Rudiments of the Latin Tongue* (1714ff.), which taught Latin and English in parallel; see Duncan, *Thomas Ruddiman*, p. 89n. Thomas Watt's *Grammar Made Easie* (1704, 1708, 1714ff.) was a forerunner of Ruddiman in this parallel-text method.

16. Duncan, *Thomas Ruddiman*, pp. 149–151, 154. Buchanan's *Opera Omnia* is listed in "A Catalogue of all the Genuine Houshold [*sic*] Furniture, Plate, China, Prints and Drawings, Etc. of Mr. James Thomson, (Author of the *Seasons*), Deceased . . ."; original MS in Mitchell Library, Glasgow; printed in Munby, ed., *Sale Catalogues*, vol. 1, pp. 45–66, hereafter referred to as *Catalogue*.

17. See Scotland, *Education*, vol. 1, pp. 82–83, 86, 73; Grant, *History of the Burgh*, vol. 1, pp. 159, 90–92.

18. Scotland, *Education*, vol. 1, pp. 84–85; the range of school plays broadened considerably by the mid-eighteenth century to include Shakespeare and contemporary English plays as well as Scottish works such as the popular *Gentle Shepherd;* see Tobin, "School Plays," p. 49.

19. The Wideopen lands were part of the Bennet estate before 1700 and later became so again; see Jeffrey, *History and Antiquities*, vol. 3, pp. 303–306. Letter from Dr. A. A. Tait, professor of fine art, Glasgow University, to M. J. W. Scott (April 23, 1981); Thomson, letter to Wm. Bennet (April 22, 1725), "Three New Letters," ed. Bell, p. 368.

20. Tait, *Border Church*, p. 34.

21. Andrew Millar (Thomson's publisher in London and personal friend) published some of Bennet's Latin poems; see Ramsay, *Works*, ed. Kinghorn and Law, vol. 6, pp. 214–215; John Ramsay, *Scotland and Scotsmen*, vol. 1, p. 39n. Several Latin poems are dedicated to Bennet in *Selecta Poemata Archi. Pitcairnii* (Edinburgh, 1727), and a supplement to this volume, *Poems on the Royal-Company of Archers* (Edinburgh, 1727) contains two of Bennet's poems in English.

22. Ramsay, *Works*, ed. Kinghorn and Law, vol. 4, p. 172; Ramsay, *Works*, ed. Martin and Oliver, vol. 1, p. 227 ("To Sir William Bennet of Grubbet, Bar!"); Ramsay, *Works*, ed. Kinghorn and Law, vol. 3, pp. 316–317, 325 ("To Sir William Bennet of Marlefield"; "Spoken to Aeolus, in the House of Marlefield, on the Night of a violent Wind"; "A Poem in Honour of the Return of the Sons of Sir William Bennet of Marlefield").

23. John Ramsay, *Scotland and Scotsmen*, vol. 1, p. 39n; Somerville, *My Own Life and Times*, pp. 29–30; Jeffrey, *History and Antiquities*, vol. 3, p. 339; Tait, *Border Church*, p. 39.

24. Grant, *James Thomson*, pp. 14–15. Thomson's family continued to maintain a close relationship with the Elliots; Elizabeth Bell, a descendant of Thomson's family, referred to her emotional ties with Minto, where she was an occasional visitor, in a letter "To Mrs. Stewart," January 20, 1829, Edinburgh University Library MS. Dc.6.111, fol. 146 v.

25. Grant, *James Thomson*, p. 13; Thomson, *Works*, ed. Murdoch, vol. 1, p. ii; [Shiels], "James Thomson," vol. 5, p. 190; Somerville, *My Own Life and Times*, pp. 128–129; Robert Riccaltoun, "Letter to William Hogg, merchant of Edinburgh," in "A.B.G." [Grosart?], "Memorials," p. 369.

26. Thomson, "To William Cranstoun," [ca. October 1, 1725], *Letters and Documents*, ed. McKillop, p. 17; see Appendix 1. Riccaltoun, *Works;* other works by Riccaltoun, listed in Hew Scott, *Fasti Ecclesiae Scoticanae* (Edinburgh, 1917), vol. 2, p. 119, are: *The Politick Disputant* (Edinburgh, 1722); *A Sober Enquiry into the Grounds of the present Differences in the Church of Scotland* (n.p., 1723); "Letters to a Friend," *Edinburgh Christian Instructor* 6 (n.d.); *An Enquiry Into the Spirit and Tendency of [Sandeman's] Letters on [Hervey's] Theron and Aspasio, with a View of the Law of Nature and an Enquiry into [Sandeman's] Letters on the Law of Nature* (anon., London, 1762); Poem, "A Winter's Day," *Savage's Miscellany* (1726), and *Gentleman's Magazine* (May 1740).

27. Riccaltoun believed Hume helped rather than hurt the cause of Christianity and said, "If Hume would but declare himself a Christian, he [Riccaltoun] would undertake to vindicate his opinions and defend his orthodoxy against all his antagonists, at the bar of the General Assembly," Somerville, *My Own Life and Times*, p. 128; Riccaltoun, "Of the Human Constitution, and Capacity arising upon the proper improvement of it," *Works*, vol. 1, pp. 31–34.

28. Riccaltoun, "Of Human Knowledge, its nature, extent, and use," *Works*, vol. 1, pp. 143ff.

29. Riccaltoun, "Of Human Knowledge," *Works*, vol. 1, pp. 157–162; Fairchild, *Religious Trends*, vol. 1, p. 510.

30. Riccaltoun, "Certain truths current in the world, which could never have entered but by Revelation, and the Creator's testimony," and "The Original State of Mankind," *Works*, vol. 1, pp. 203–238; "The Original and Progress of Knowledge," *Works*, vol. 1, p. 174.

31. Somerville, *My Own Life and Times*, p. 128; John Hutchinson (b. Yorkshire) was a fundamentalist who studied the earth to seek confirmation of Revelation but strongly opposed natural theology and deism and even rejected Newton's discoveries as not being authorized by Scripture. His principle work was *Moses's Principia* (Part I, 1724; Part II, 1727). The anonymous *An Abstract from the Works of John Hutchinson, Esq.* (Edinburgh, 1753) is a useful summary of his twelve volumes of works and clarifies his somewhat obscure notions. On Forbes and Hutchinson, see Menary, *Life and Letters*, p. 93.

32. Riccaltoun, "Certain truths," *Works*, vol. 1, pp. 203–204; "Reconciliation," *Works*, vol. 1, pp. 380–381.

33. Riccaltoun, "Revelation founded on Fact," *Works*, vol. 2, pp. 19–21; "The Spirit and Inspiration," *Works*, vol. 1, pp. 422ff.

34. Cohen, *Unfolding*, p. 3, on Spacks, *Poetry of Vision*, pp. 19ff.

2   EDINBURGH YEARS

1. Taylor, "James Thomson," p. 309.

2. Thomson, *Works*, ed. Murdoch, vol. 1, pp. iii–iv; William Gusthart was called to Edinburgh's Tolbooth Kirk in 1721; Grant, *James Thomson*, pp. 19–21, 27, 282n; Beatrix Trotter (Thomson), "Testament," June 17, 1725, Register of Testaments, MS CC8/8/90, Scottish Record Office, Register House, Edinburgh: her estate was valued at £18. 16s. 5d Sterling (£225. 17s. Scots).

3. George Watson cites Thomas Somerville, on authority of [John] Cranstoun of Ancrum, as his source; Watson, "Rev. Thomas Thomson," p. 177.

4. Thomson, "To William Cranstoun," December 11, 1724, *Letters and Documents*, ed. McKillop, pp. 1–2; Fairchild, *Religious Trends*, vol. 1, p. 511; Thomson, *Letters and Documents*, ed. McKillop, p. 3n. Somerville, *My Own Life and Times*, p. 44, feared such "tavern adjournments" harmed the characters of some divinity students.

5. Grant, *Story of the University*, vol. 1, p. 270, vol. 2, pp. 322–323, 328; Drummond later taught Hume, whose scepticism might have been a reaction against Drummond's old-fashioned views. Grant, *James Thomson*, pp. 17, 22; Matriculation Rolls, Edinburgh University Library.

6. Drennon, "James Thomson's Contact," p. 73n; Grant, *James Thomson*, p. 23; Taylor, "James Thomson," pp. 9–10n. Bower, *History of the University*, vol. 2, pp. 81–82, says David Gregory, who was made professor of mathematics in 1683, lectured on Newton's *Principia* at Edinburgh University and became Savilian Professor of As-

tronomy at Oxford in 1691. Gregory impressed his Scottish students with Newtonianism; one was Edinburgh native John Keill, who also went on to Oxford to
practice Newtonian experiments: "Thus Gregory in Scotland, and Keill in England, were the first public lecturers on the 'Principia,' and both issued from the
same school." See Grant, *Story of the University*, vol. 1, p. 271.

7. McCosh, *Scottish Philosophy*, p. 103; Turnbull, *Principles;* Turnbull, *Treatise*.

8. Taylor, "James Thomson," pp. 5, 10n; Grant, *Story of the University*, vol. 1, p. 272,
lists Stewart's curriculum for 1741, which included Newton's *Of Colours* and David
Gregory's *Optics;* Drennon, "James Thomson's Contact," p. 71; Thomson, *Liberty*,
ed. Sambrook, pp. 4–5.

9. MacQueen, *Progress and Poetry*, p. 57.

10. Turnbull, *Principles*, pp. xii–xiii; McKillop, *Background of 'Seasons'*, pp. 31–39; Nicolson, *Newton*, p. 99. Also see Ketcham, "Scientific," pp. 33–50.

11. McKillop, *Background of 'Seasons'*, pp. 64–66, 28; the description of the "meteor" is
in a letter from Edinburgh by William Whiston, *An Account of a Surprizing Meteor
Seen in the Air, March the 6th (1715–16)*. Thomson also knew contemporary scientific
accounts of the aurora, notably Edmund Halley's.

12. Grant, *Story of the University*, vol. 1, pp. 264–265, vol. 2, p. 367; Grant, *James Thomson*, p. 23.

13. Fairchild, *Religious Trends*, vol. 1, pp. 510–511. Use of the term "Moderate" in discussing the religious views of certain elements of the Scottish church in Thomson's
day is something of an anachronism, but I use it for want of a more satisfying
alternative. The Moderates did not become a coherent "party" until the 1750s, but
the liberalizing theological and intellectual trend they represented was evident in
the Scottish church much earlier, even in Thomson's youth; the moderating process began long before the party itself was formed.

14. Fairchild, *Religious Trends*, vol. 1, pp. 545–546, 539–540; Morel, *James Thomson*, p.
252.

15. Robert Blair, letter "To Dr. Philip Doddridge," February 25, 1741–42, in Blair, *The
Grave*, ed. Means, p. i; Blair, "To Philip Doddridge," July 11, 1743, in ibid., p. ii.

16. Macaulay, *James Thomson*, pp. 139–140.

17. Adams, *Graces of Harmony*, p. 137.

18. Graham, *Social Life of Scotland*, p. 352; Grant, *Story of the University*, vol. 1, pp. 335–
337, vol. 2, pp. 307–308.

19. John Ramsay, *Scotland and Scotsmen*, vol. 1, pp. 227–228; Thomson, *Works*, ed. Murdoch, vol. 1, p. v; [Shiels], "James Thomson," vol. 5, p. 192.

20. Scott, *Fasti*, vol. 1, pp. 11, 146. William Hamilton (1669–1732) was educated at
Edinburgh University and came to Divinity College as professor from Cramond
Parish; he was professor from 1709–1732. Hamilton was moderator of the general
assembly in 1712, 1716, 1720, 1727, and 1730. He wrote *The Truth and Excellency of
the Christian Religion* (Edinburgh, 1732). See "J. O.," "Scotch Professors," pp. 524–
528. Drummond and Bulloch, *Scottish Church*, p. 23 say "his teaching, while

guarded and orthodox, left a different impression," and quote Wodrow, *Analecta*, vol. 3, p. 139, vol. 2, p. 360.

21. John Ramsay, *Scotland and Scotsmen*, vol. 1, p. 228.

22. Thomson, *Works*, ed. Murdoch, pp. v–vi; Thomson, *Liberty*, ed. Sambrook, p. 398n.

23. [Shiels], "James Thomson," vol. 5, p. 193; Wodrow, *Analecta*, vol. 3, p. 432, reported: "Mr. Walter Steuart, lately come from Holland . . . tells me Mr. James Thomson, so famed at London for his poems, Winter and Summer, and some others, was a student at Edinburgh, and of his acquaintance. His genius led him to poetry when at Professor Hamilton's lessons, and his reputation was good . . ." (1727). Grant, *James Thomson*, p. 34, has conjectured that this overly poetical exercise was based on Psalm 98; Macaulay, *James Thomson*, p. 8, and Smith, "Thomson and Burns," p. 183, suggest it was based on Psalm 119. The blank-verse exercise was possibly the germ of the juvenile poem ["Works and Wonders of the Almighty Power"] (published in *The Plain Dealer* in 1724), discovered to be a paraphrase of Shaftesbury.

24. Professor William Hamilton, "Notebook (1707–1727)," including divinity class lists and a theological library list, Reid Bequest (uncataloged), fol. 28, Edinburgh University Library. The "Notebook" records James Thomson from "Merse" as being recommended to the course by Mr. W. Douglas (probably the Rev. Mr. Walter Douglas of the Parish of Linton in Teviotdale) and by Mr. Simson (probably the Rev. Mr. John Simson, M.A., of the Parish of Morebattle and Mow, a Roxburghshire native); see Scott, *Fasti*, vol. 2, pp. 76, 81.

25. Although Hamilton carefully listed all the assignments of his students over the years, it is difficult to determine exactly which ones were completed by the poet Thomson, as another "James Thomson," from "Fiffe," entered Divinity Hall in 1721. Thereafter, Hamilton distinguishes between "Junior" and "Senior" James Thomsons; the James Thomson in Group 4 of the class societies is thence designated "Junior," so this is probably the poet. James Thomson "Senior" appears in the notebook entries only for 1721–23. Under "Prescribed-Exercises to be Delivered," Hamilton lists:

    1720:   Jan. 9 Mr. Ja. Thomson the Addition
    1721:   Dec. 9 Mr. Ja. Thomson the Addition
    1723:   Jan. 13 Mr. Ja. Thomson Jun., a homily Matth.10.29.30.31
    1723:   Mar. 2 Mr. Ja. Thomson Sen., the lecture Ps. 98
    1724:   Mar. 28 Mr. Ja. Thomson the Homily Matth.26.29

Under a different set of "Exercises they had in the Hall," James Thomson from "Merse" is listed as having performed in February 1720, February 1722, and May 1724.

26. Hamilton, "Notebook," library list; Taylor, "James Thomson," pp. 14–15.

27. Daiches, *Paradox*, p. 12.

28. Nicholas T. Phillipson, "Sir John Clerk in his Time," lecture delivered to symposium "A Treasure of Learning and Good Taste—Sir John Clerk of Penicuik," Edinburgh University, May 15–16, 1976.

29. For instance, witness the shift in tone of the Opposition Whig periodical *The Crafts-man* by "Caleb D'Anvers" [Nicholas Amhurst or Amherst], which reminded its readers of the Jacobite threat, no. 70 (November 4, 1727). This article moved from a confident, cocky stance in the face of the puny "Weakness" and "Impotence" of the Pretender's cause (p. 275), to bitter invective against the corrupt and treacherous "outlaw" Jacobites (p. 278), to righteous indignation felt by the Opposition Whigs (like Thomson) who were often labeled "Jacobites" for daring to oppose Walpole (pp. 279–280), to a solemn warning of the real, ongoing Jacobite threat. See *The Craftsman*, 4th edition for 1726–27 (London, 1728), vol. 2, pp. 269–283.

30. Duncan, *Thomas Ruddiman*, pp. 150ff., 21–22; Daiches, *Scotland and the Union*, pp. 186–187; McElroy, "Literary Clubs," pp. 64–65, 75.

31. Thomson, "To David Mallet," [August 2, 1726], *Letters and Documents*, ed. McKillop, pp. 41, 43n.

32. Daiches, *Paradox*, p. 22, and many others have taken the motives of the Anglicizers as a sort of misdirected patriotism. Hugh Haliburton [J. Logie Robertson], "James Thomson: A Poet of the Woods," *Good Words* 34 (1893): 476–477, saw the more positive patriotic motives of Anglicizers like Thomson. Sher, *Church and University*, p. 324, describes the Moderates' "cosmopolitan" nationalism, which is comparable to Thomson's attitude in many ways.

33. Somerville, *My Own Life and Times*, pp. 29–30; John Ramsay, *Scotland and Scotsmen*, vol. 1, p. 39n; Jeffrey, *History and Antiquities*, vol. 3, p. 339. Also, Dr. Alexander Law, interview.

34. Elizabeth Bell (descendant of Thomson's sister, probably a daughter of the poet's nephew the Rev. Mr. James Bell of Coldstream), letter "To Mrs. Stewart," January 20, 1829, Edinburgh University Library; Martin, "Allan Ramsay," vol. 1, p. 194n, lists the articles debating authorship of *The Gentle Shepherd*. Mr. Bell, the poet's nephew, may have been encouraged in his claim that Thomson authored the pastoral by Thomson enthusiast the eleventh earl of Buchan, with whom he corresponded.

35. Thomson, *Works*, ed. Murdoch, vol. 1, pp. v–vi.

36. Original sketch in Edinburgh University Library; reproduced in Grant, *James Thomson*. Also see [Taylor], "James Thomson," pp. 421, 429; Taylor dates the portrait ca. 1725. But a note with the drawing in the Edinburgh University Library "Quarto Seasons" dates it ca. 1720, and "A.B.G." [Grosart?], "Memorials," p. 371 agrees. Murdoch reports that the poet was indeed "thought handsome" in youth, Thomson, *Works*, ed. Murdoch, vol. 1, p. xvi. However, Sambrook (in Thomson, *Liberty*, ed. Sambrook, p. 417n) says it is doubtful that the sketch is of Thomson at all, as Lord Buchan had claimed.

37. Thomson, "To Sir John Clerk," [January 18, 1728], *Letters and Documents*, ed. McKillop, pp. 58–60.

38. See, for instance, Thomson's "To William Cranstoun" (Edinburgh, December 11, 1724), in ibid., pp. 1–2, which is full of irregular and colloquial forms. The typical Scots metathesis confusing *tch* with *cth* as in "macthless" or "cacth" occurs often

early on, as do such Scots idioms as "hear storied," "com'd," "lugs." Thomson, *Liberty*, ed. Sambrook, points out a number of Scottish rhymes in the juvenilia.

39. John Ramsay, *Scotland and Scotsmen*, vol. 1, p. 8; McElroy, "Literary Clubs," p. 570; Mallet, "To John Ker," (June 1726), in Thomson, *Letters and Documents*, ed. McKillop, pp. 34–35.

40. Craig, *Scottish Literature*, pp. 54–55; McElroy, "Literary Clubs," p. 572; Thomson, *Works*, ed. Murdoch, vol. 1, p. v.

41. McElroy, *Age of Improvement*, p. 21; Dr. Nicholas T. Phillipson, interview with M. J. W. Scott, May 25, 1976, Edinburgh, suggests that "Fergus Bruce" might be Ramsay himself.

42. "Fergus Bruce," letter to *The Plain Dealer* 46 (August 28, 1724), in [Hill and Bond], eds., *The Plain Dealer*, vol. 1, pp. 393–394. Hill had also recently published Mallet's ballad "William and Margaret."

43. Johnson, "David Mallet," in *Lives*, vol. 3, p. 402 and n. Also Boswell, *Life of Johnson*, p. 229, quoting Johnson: "Johnson. 'I never catched Mallet in a Scotch accent; and yet Mallet, I suppose, was past five-and-twenty before he came to London'"; Anderson, "David Mallet," in *Scottish Nation*, vol. 3, p. 100; John Ramsay, *Scotland and Scotsmen*, vol. 1, pp. 22–25.

44. McElroy, *Age of Improvement*, p. 20; John Ramsay, *Scotland and Scotsmen*, vol. 1, p. 22n; Alexander Law, interview; Thomson, *Letters and Documents*, ed. McKillop, pp. 52–53n; Thomson, "To David Mallet," [August 21–27, 1726], in ibid., p. 50; "J.C." [John Callender or Calendar of Craigforth], "Epistle to Mr. M[itchel]l," in *The Edinburgh Miscellany*, pp. 116–118; Fairchild, *Religious Trends*, vol. 1, pp. 412–419.

45. John Ramsay, *Scotland and Scotsmen*, vol. 1, pp. 21–22n; four of the epistles were by Scots, including Mitchell. While no longer extant, the *Scots Miscellany* is apparently not a "bibliographical ghost"; it is clearly referred to in the preface to the *Edinburgh Miscellany*.

46. Mitchell and Calendar, *Lugubres Cantus*. *Lugubres* is almost certainly the volume recalled by John Ramsay, *Scotland and Scotsmen*, vol. 1, p. 22n, "by that class of people [the Athenians]. I remember neither the title nor contents, but I was struck with many verses by the author of the 'Night Thoughts,' to these juvenile poets, praising them for their generous attempt to introduce the English muses into Scotland . . ."

47. A. [Ambrose] Philips, "To the Author of the First Part of the Lugubres Cantus," *Lugubres*, n.p.; Philips, "A Winter-Piece," *Tatler* 12 (May 7, 1709); Thomson, *Seasons*, ed. Sambrook, p. 394n. E. [Edward] Young, "To Mr. Mitchell," in *Lugubres*, n.p.

48. The *Edinburgh Miscellany* was printed by James McEuen and Co., Edinburgh. McEuen also had a shop in London; he was a Whig, and for a time published the *Edinburgh Evening Courant*. He was also a bookseller and heir to Allan Ramsay's circulating library; see Couper, *Edinburgh Periodical Press*, vol. 2, pp. 19, 24–25. The *Courant* gave notice of the publication of the *Edinburgh Miscellany* in no. 165 (December 29–31, 1719): 990 and no. 166 (December 31–January 4, 1719–20): 996.

No. 165 announced: "N.B. at the said Mr. James M'Euen's Shop will be published next Monday the Edinburgh Miscellany Volume first. . . ." A second volume seems never to have been published; see Thomson, *Liberty*, ed. Sambrook, p. 227n. The "W.C." who wrote the preface to the *Edinburgh Miscellany* has not been identified. The initials might stand for "Worthy Club" and its representative—clearly an elder man of letters, who is rather patronizing toward the novice exercises in the volume. Might this writer have been Allan Ramsay himself?

49. "J. C." [John Callender], "An Address to the Masters in the University of Edinburgh," ll. 47–50, *Edinburgh Miscellany*, p. 122; "A." [probably James Arbuckle, friend of Ramsay and a student at Glasgow], "Holy Ode," pp. 91–93; Thomas Boyd, "A Poem Upon the Young-Company of Archers," pp. 39–41.

50. Attribution of poems to Blair in *New Cambridge Bibliography of English Literature*, ed. George Watson, vol. 2 (1660–1800), col. 537. Tytler, *Memoirs*, vol. 1, p. 71, reported that Lord Hailes was his source; "Mr. Hume"'s poems were "On a Certain dull Beau at the Play-house," *Edinburgh Miscellany*, pp. 103–104; "Ode xxiii of Anacreon, English'd," pp. 104–105; "A Song," pp. 105–106; "To a very Poring and Speculative Gentleman," pp. 102–103.

51. Taylor, "James Thomson," pp. 57–58; Thomson, "To William Cranstoun," April 3, 1725, *Letters and Documents*, ed. McKillop, pp. 6–8; Thomson, "To William Cranstoun," [February 1725], ibid., pp. 5–6; Fairchild, *Religious Trends*, vol. 1, p. 514, quoting Morel, *James Thomson*, p. 34; Thomson *Letters and Documents*, ed. McKillop, pp. 8–9n.

52. Thomson, letter to William Bennet (April 10, 1729), "Three New Letters," ed. Bell, p. 369; Taylor, "James Thomson," p. 58; [Shiels,] "James Thomson," vol. 5, p. 194.

53. Thomson, *Works*, ed. Murdoch, vol. 1, p. vi; Grant, *James Thomson*, pp. 37–39; Thomson, "To William Cranstoun," [ca. February 1725 (1)], *Letters and Documents*, ed. McKillop, p. 4; Thomson, "To William Cranstoun," [February 1725 (2)], ibid., p. 5; Thomson's poem "On his Mother's Death," in Thomson, *Liberty*, ed. Sambrook, pp. 278–280, describes that night of the poet's sailing.

3 THE JUVENILE POEMS

1. Craig, *Scottish Literature*, p. 265, applies this generally to Anglo-Scots of the period.

2. McKillop, *Background of 'Seasons'*, p. 7; Fairchild, *Religious Trends*, vol. 1, p. 514.

3. My primary source for the juvenile poems, unless otherwise noted, is *Liberty, The Castle of Indolence and Other Poems*, ed. Sambrook. I have also consulted the photostat copy of Thomson's holograph "Newberry MS," Newberry Library, Chicago. The original MS, twenty-six folio pages and severely damaged, has unfortunately been lost since 1970; the photostat was also missing but was rediscovered in 1978. The photostat is not entirely legible. Early published versions of the juvenile poems are found in William Goodhugh, ed., *The English Gentleman's Library Manual* (1827); Harris Nicolas, ed., *The Poetical Works of James Thomson*, Aldine Edition (1830, 1847);

and *Thomson: Poetical Works,* ed. J. Logie Robertson. Other important scholarly references are Schmidt-Wartenberg, "Das Newberry Manuskript," pp. 129–152; and McKillop, "First Works," pp. 13–23. Also see Scott and Scott, "Scots Elegy," pp. 135–144.

4. Schmidt-Wartenberg, "Das Newberry Manuskript," p. 137, dates the juvenile MS ca. 1719; McKillop, "First Works," pp. 18, 20, dates the MS ca. 1720 or earlier. Sambrook, ed. (Thomson, *Liberty*), p. 228, prefers a ca. 1718–1719 compilation date. Sambrook traces the history of the Newberry MS in Thomson, *Liberty,* ed. Sambrook, pp. 224–228. He places two Thomson poems conventionally considered juvenilia under "Miscellaneous Poems," as their dates are uncertain: "Lisy's parting with her cat" and ["The Works and Wonders of Almighty Power"].

5. See Scott and Scott, "Scots Elegy," and McKillop, "First Works," pp. 15, 19.

6. Bayne, "Thomson and Allan Ramsay," p. 72.

7. "I have always been of Opinion that none make better Wives than the Ladies of Scotland. . . . You see I am beginning to make Interest already with the Scots Ladies," wrote Thomson, "To Mrs. Jean Thomson" (his sister), October 4, 1747, *Letters and Documents,* ed. McKillop, p. 191.

8. See Wittig, *Scottish Tradition,* pp. 101ff.

9. MacQueen, *Robert Henryson,* pp. 153–156, 100–101ff.

10. Thomson, *The Seasons and The Castle of Indolence,* ed. Robertson, pp. 4–5, notes resemblance to "Leader-Haughs"; [Robert Crawford?], "Leader-Haughs and Yarrow," published by Allan Ramsay in *The Tea-Table Miscellany* (1723).

11. Marlefield is mentioned in William Hamilton of Bangour's poetical catalog of Scottish estates in his "Horace. Book I. Ode VII to the Earl of Stair," *Poems on Several Occasions,* pp. 130–132. Hamilton was a contemporary of Thomson's in Edinburgh and a close friend of William Bennet.

12. See Watts, "Asking Leave to Sing," in *Horae Lyricae,* p. 3; in its opening lines on the poet-mentor relationship, Watts's verse also resembles John Callender's "Epistle to Mr. M[itchel]l," *Edinburgh Miscellany,* p. 116.

13. "Verses on receiving a Flower from his Mistress," in *The Edinburgh Miscellany,* pp. 203–204, in Thomson, *Liberty,* ed. Sambrook, p. 264.

14. See John Gay, *Trivia* (1716); Jonathan Swift, "Description of a City Shower" and "Description of Morning," *The Tatler* (1709).

15. Thomson, *Liberty,* ed. Sambrook, includes "Lisy's parting with her cat" under "Miscellaneous Poems," pp. 275–276, rather than "Juvenilia." Thomson, *Poetical Works,* ed. Robertson, pp. 511–513, notes that "a copy of these boyish verses was written out by Thomson for Lord George Graham," whose sons were tutored in London by David Mallet. Thomson possibly transcribed the poem from memory—perhaps an improving memory—ca. 1726. See Thomson, *Liberty,* ed. Sambrook, p. 405n. The poem was first published by Harris Nicolas in 1830.

16. Drummond, *Poetical Works,* vol. 2, pp. 141–145; Ruddiman's edition of Drummond was Edinburgh, 1711; Masson, *Drummond of Hawthornden,* pp. 472–473. Compare,

for instance, Watts's line, "And bid the brook, that still runs warbling by, / Move silent on, and weep his useless channel dry" ("To the Memory of my Honoured Friend, Thomas Gunston, Esq.," ll. 246–247, *Horae Lyricae*, p. 276) with Thomson's "Ye gliding brooks O weep your channells dry," l. 51.

17. Wells, "James Thomson and Milton," p. 60; Thomson, *The Seasons and The Castle of Indolence*, ed. Robertson, p. 8; Ramsay, *Works*, ed. Kinghorn and Law, vol. 4, pp. 90–92, on Ramsay's "domestication" of the classical pastoral.

18. "Of a Country Life," in *Edinburgh Miscellany*, pp. 193–197, in Thomson, *Liberty*, ed. Sambrook, pp. 269–272.

19. Adams, *Graces of Harmony*, supplies many of the critical terms for the study of language here, such as "extended onomatopoeia," sound metaphors, and "imitative" language; also see Chapter 7 and Scott, "Scottish Language," pp. 370–385.

20. Fairchild, *Religious Trends*, vol. 1, p. 511.

21. Drummond, *Poetical Works*, vol. 2, pp. 10–11; Watts, *Horae Lyricae*, pp. 14–16.

22. McKillop, *Background of 'Seasons'*, p. 11; Watts, "Two Happy Rivals: Devotion and the Muse," *Horae Lyricae*, pp. 98–102; Stock, *The Holy and the Daemonic*, p. 179, points out the similarity of ideas of religious poetry as well as tone between Watts's preface to *Horae Lyricae* and Thomson's 1726 preface to "Winter."

23. Some Scottish versions of Psalm 104 are Murray of Gorthy, *A Paraphrase;* Mackenzie of Rosehaugh, *Works,* vol. 1, pp. 16–20; King James VI & I [and Sir William Alexander], *The Psalmes of King David* (London, 1631). The later volume *Poetarum Scotorum Musae Sacrae* (Edinburgh, 1739) collected many Scottish Latinist versions of Psalm 104, including those by George Buchanan, George Eglisham, Arthur Johnston, Thomas Hope of Craighall, David Hume, Thomas Reid, William Stuart of Ochiltree, Henry Henderson of Elphinstone, Ninian Paterson, and Archibald Pitcairne. In the volume, Buchanan's and Eglisham's Psalm 104 renderings were compared in a poetical "duel," which of course Buchanan "won." The *Catalogue* of Thomson's effects indicated that he owned this volume. For more on Scottish and English versions of Psalm 104, see Rothstein, *Restoration and Eighteenth Century Poetry*, p. 152; Rothstein cites Thomas Blacklock as a later Scottish "Thomsonian" poet who adopted Psalm 104 as a subject. See Thomson, *Liberty*, ed. Sambrook, pp. 398–399n.

24. Grant, *James Thomson*, pp. 32–33; [Shiels], "James Thomson," vol. 5, p. 194; Thomson, *Liberty*, ed. Sambrook, p. 398n. English critic and patron William Benson (who was later involved in the controversy over the relative merits of Buchanan's and Johnston's Latin Psalms and supported Johnston's in opposition to Thomas Ruddiman; see Duncan, *Thomas Ruddiman*, p. 116) praised young Thomson's "Psalm 104." He "admired the full diction and distinctive thought of these verses, which, despite faults and occasional lapses, rise far above a literary exercise." While much of the language of "Psalm 104" is Thomson's own, the verse is also partly derivative of English Augustan poetry (as are all the juvenile poems); Reisner, "Dryden's 'Metamorphoses,'" p. 31, for example, points out that Thomson's ll. 19–20 are

taken almost verbatim from Dryden's version of Ovid's "Metamorphoses" (1693), ll. 421–422.

25. ["Works and Wonders"] in *The Plain Dealer*, no. 46 (1724); 2nd edition, vol. 1, pp. 394–395; [Hill and Bond, eds.], *Plain Dealer*, vol. 1, pp. 394–395; and in Thomson, *Liberty*, ed. Sambrook, pp. 277–278 under "Miscellaneous Poems."

26. Drennon, "The Source," p. 34.

27. [Shiels], "James Thomson," vol. 5, pp. 192–193. Thomson, *Letters and Documents*, ed. McKillop, p. 3, notes that Thomson's numeral "4" is easily misread as a "9" or a "1." See Chapter 2, especially note 23.

28. Fairchild, *Religious Trends*, vol. 1, pp. 511–512.

29. "Upon Happiness," in *Edinburgh Miscellany*, pp. 197–203; the poem occurs in less polished form in the Newberry MS; in Thomson, *Liberty*, ed. Sambrook, pp. 264–269.

30. Norris of Bemerton, "An Idea of Happiness," pp. 317–354; McKillop, "First Works," p. 20, cites Herbert Drennon, "James Thomson and Newtonianism," Ph.D. dissertation, University of Chicago, 1928.

31. Grove's essays for *The Spectator* were nos. 588, 601, 626, and 635 (vol. 8, 1714); he was also a poet and contributed to Dryden's *Miscellany* (vol. 6, 1706) and other collections. See Linck, "Benevolism," p. 201.

32. Riccaltoun, "Of Happiness and Perfection in general, absolute and limited," *Works*, vol. 1, pp. 1–31; McCosh, *Scottish Philosophy*, p. 110, regards Boston as a representative figure of old-style, early eighteenth-century Scottish Calvinism; Boston, *Human Nature*, pp. 439–445. McKillop, *Background to 'Seasons'*, p. 22, uses the term "empirical immortality" to describe the poet's conception of the rising mind. Examples in *The Seasons* are "Spring," ll. 556ff.; "Summer," ll. 1803–1805; "Winter," ll. 606–608; "Hymn," ll. 100ff. See Chapter 6.

33. Florentius Volusenus (Florence Wilson), "Ode," trans. Robert Blair, in Wilson, ed., *Poets and Poetry*, half-vol. 1, pp. 43–44. His Neoplatonic essay *De Animi Tranquillitate*, where this ode and other poems occur, was published by Ruddiman (Edinburgh, 1707); it was a favorite of Principal Wishart and the Moderate Presbyterians; see Duncan, *Thomas Ruddiman*, pp. 45–47.

34. Blackmore, "Happiness Discover'd," pp. 413–418; 1st publ. 1696; McKillop, "First Works," p. 20.

35. Taylor, "James Thomson," p. 36; Wells, "Thomson and Milton," p. 60; Morel, *James Thomson*, pp. 489–490. The poem's incident of the fairies dancing recalls the story of Thomson's schoolmaster Mr. Brown (see Chapter 1). Brown must have died about the time this poem was written, though perhaps a year or two later. Thomson may also have been influenced by *Spectator*, no. 419 (July 1, 1712) by Addison, which argued the value of the supernatural as a poetic theme.

36. Ramsay, "Content: A Poem," in *Works*, ed. Martin and Oliver, vol. 1, pp. 90–105; also worth noting is Hamilton of Bangour's poem in this vein, "Contemplation, or the Triumph of Love" (probably written later than Thomson's "Upon Happiness").

Hamilton's poem could almost be a parody of Thomson's serious poem; in it, the speaker fails to attain the happy heights of Contemplation, but nevertheless finds bliss by succumbing to earthly love: Hamilton of Bangour, *Poems on Several Occasions*, pp. 4–23.

4 SCOTTISH BACKGROUND OF *THE SEASONS*

1. Burrow, *A Reading*, p. 35; Prof. John MacQueen pointed out this strain of vivid winter description in English alliterative verse, particularly *Gawain*, which established certain descriptive conventions inherited by Scottish poets such as Henryson. Two examples of Scottish alliterative verse which include "winter" settings are *Rauf Coilyear* and *The Awntyrs of Arthure*. See MacQueen, *Robert Henryson*, pp. 57, 161; Wittig, *Scottish Tradition*, pp. 108–109.

2. On the alleged "Celtic" strain in Scottish descriptive poetry, see Brooke, *Naturalism*, p. 41; Bayne, *Thomson*, pp. 9–11; Cohen, *Art*, p. 221.

3. Wittig, *Scottish Tradition*, pp. 5–6; Thomson, "Gaelic Writers," pp. 37–46.

4. Thomson could have known both Henryson's *Testament* and his fables. See Wittig, *Scottish Tradition*, p. 37; Speirs, *Scots Literary Tradition*, pp. 39–40; Kinsley, "The Mediaeval Makars," in *Scottish Poetry*, ed. Kinsley, p. 20. MacQueen, *Robert Henryson*, pp. 160–161, qualifies this view, asserting that there is also much conventional imagery in "Wynter" as well as some realistic detail in "Somer," "Harvest," and "Ver."

5. Speirs, *Scots Literary Tradition*, pp. 69–76, 165–197; MacQueen, preface, *Twelve Modern Scottish Poets*, p. 11.

6. Speirs, *Scots Literary Tradition*, pp. 71, 74, 185–186; Wittig, *Scottish Tradition*, p. 79, notes that even Douglas's milder, Mediterranean scenes might have some Scottish connotations and perhaps have their source in Scottish seasonal songs.

7. The episode portrayed by Collins of the drowned cottager, St. 7–8, was probably suggested by a Scottish scene in Thomson's "Autumn," the cottager lost in the swamp. James VI published his *Daemonologia* in 1597; among other popular Scottish works on the spirit world were George Sinclair's *Satan's Invisible World Discover'd* (1685) and Gaelic scholar Robert Kirk's *The Secret Commonwealth of Elves, Fauns and Fairies* (1691), which expressed sincere belief in the supernatural world. Kirk's book in particular treated the subject of the supernatural as "at least potentially as much the subject of scientific investigation as any of those proposed in England by the recently founded Royal Society . . . ," MacQueen, *Progress and Poetry*, p. 33.

8. James VI & I, *The Essayes*.

9. Wittig, *Scottish Tradition*, pp. 148–149, and quoting E. K. Wells, *The Ballad Tree: A Study of British and American Ballads* (1950), p. 75; Speirs, *Scots Literary Tradition*, p. 171.

10. Allan Ramsay, preface to *The Ever Green*, in Ramsay, *Works*, ed. Kinghorn and Law, vol. 4, p. 236.

11. Thomson, "To William Cranstoun," [ca. October 1, 1725], *Letters and Documents*, ed. McKillop, p. 17; see Appendix 1, "A Winter's Day," *Gentleman's Magazine* 10 (1740): 256; Thomson, *Letters and Documents*, ed. McKillop, p. 18n, refers to Mallet's letters published in *European Magazine* 24 [1793]: 258; see "A.B.G." [Grosart?], "Memorials," pp. 366–369.

12. Somerville, *My Own Life and Times*, p. 129; the Rev. John Richmond of Southdean (1812) also assumed that there must have been two different "Winter" poems by Riccaltoun—Thomson, *Letters and Documents*, ed. McKillop, p. 18n. Recently, however, Robert Inglesfield has argued that "A Winter's Day" is indeed the poem by Riccaltoun which influenced Thomson's "Winter": Inglesfield, "Thomson," pp. 27–29.

13. Thomson, *'Seasons': Critical*, ed. Zippel, pp. xxxii–xl, traces in detail the influences of Riccaltoun's "A Winter's Day" on Thomson: "Autumn," (1730), ll. 919–920 influenced by Riccaltoun's ll. 29, 20; "Winter" (1730), ll. 45–50 influenced by Riccaltoun's ll. 5–8; "Winter" (March 1726), ll. 216–220 influenced by Riccaltoun's ll. 9–12.

14. Appendix 2: John Armstrong, "Winter," *Miscellanies* (London, 1770), vol. 1, pp. 147–158; "Advertisement from the Publisher," in Armstrong, *Miscellanies*, vol. 1, n.p.; on the tradition that Thomson saw Armstrong's MS after the first edition of "Winter" had appeared, see Cohen, *Art*, p. 19; Grant, *James Thomson*, p. 163; Thomson, *'Seasons': Critical*, ed. Zippel, p. xxxviii. (N.B. Zippel holds that the 2nd edition of Thomson's "Winter," June 1726, was influenced by Armstrong's MS poem but makes no reference to the first edition, March 1726.)

15. Taylor, "James Thomson," pp. 84–86, notes influence of *Macbeth* I.vii on Thomson's ll. 112–113 and *Measure for Measure* III.i.124 on Thomson's ll. 150–154.

16. Macaulay, *James Thomson*, p. 152; Thomson, *'Seasons': Critical*, ed. Zippel, pp. xxxii–xl, points out a substantial number of influences of Armstrong's poem on the 2nd edition of Thomson's "Winter" and later editions.

17. Mallet, *The Excursion;* Thomson, *Letters and Documents*, ed. McKillop, cites three letters from Thomson to Mallet on "sublimity": (1) [August 2, 1726], pp. 40–41; (2) August 11, 1726, pp. 44–46; (3) [August 21–27, 1726], pp. 48–50; two more letters were apparently lost. McKillop, *Background of 'Seasons'*, pp. 68–70, treats of Mallet's influence; Zippel lists parallels with Mallet in *'Seasons': Critical*, p. xxxv ("Summer") and pp. xxxix–xl ("Winter").

18. Thomson, preface to "Winter" (2nd edition, June 1726), in *Seasons*, ed. Sambrook, pp. 303–307.

19. Nicolson, *Newton*, p. 109, cites parallel with Addison's "Pleasures of the Imagination" *Spectator* essays; Francis Hutcheson treats of "beauty-in-variety" in *An inquiry* (1725); Thomson, "To William Cranstoun," [ca. October 1, 1725], *Letters and Documents*, ed. McKillop, p. 16.

20. Thomson probably did not read Hebrew, at least with any facility. Menary, *Life and Letters*, pp. 92–93, notes that Forbes's *A Letter to a Bishop concerning some important*

discoveries in Philosophy and Theology (1732) tried to prove that the Hebrew Scriptures had been badly, "falsely" translated and were in need of a new, "true" translation; Thomson's words "mangling Translation" reflect the opinion of his mentor Forbes, who was a Hebrew scholar.

5   *THE SEASONS* AS A POEM OF NATURAL DESCRIPTION

1. Smith, "Thomson and Burns," p. 182.
2. Thomson, "To William Cranstoun," [ca. October 1, 1725], *Letters and Documents*, ed. McKillop, p. 16.
3. This and subsequent quotations from *The Seasons* will be taken from James Sambrook's edition of *The Seasons* (1981) unless otherwise noted.
4. Cohen, *Unfolding*, pp. 93–94; letter to M. J. W. Scott, September 28, 1976.
5. Cohen, *Unfolding*, pp. 38–39, 155–156, 94–95, etc. on Thomson's so-called illusive allusion (reworking of convention) and also his "transforming" imagery; Taylor, "James Thomson," p. 5.
6. Thomson, *The Seasons and the Castle of Indolence*, ed. Robertson, p. 358n.
7. Oliver, "Scottish Augustans," p. 127.
8. Thomson, *The Seasons and The Castle of Indolence*, ed. Robertson, p. 359n; also Snyder, "Notes," p. 309, points out the similarity of this Thomson passage to Burns's description of the river in spate in "Brigs of Ayr."
9. Thomson, "To William Cranstoun," [ca. October 1, 1725], *Letters and Documents*, ed. McKillop, p. 16; Graham, *Men of Letters*, pp. 285–286, quoting Moore's *Life of Smollett*, p. 104, reports that "when Thomson heard of an epic written by a poet who lived all his life in London, he pronounced it impossible. 'Why, the man never saw a mountain!'"; Martin, *A Description*, p. 86.
10. McKillop, *Background of 'Seasons'*, p. 43, citing Defoe [*Review* 6 (July 26, 1709), no. 49], and Smollett [*Humphry Clinker*]: both Defoe and Smollett blame the animals' hardship in winter on the negligence of Scottish farmers; Scott, *Critical Essays*, p. 383; More, *Strictures*, p. 48. Thomson's experience of winter was an especially harsh one, as all Europe in the late seventeenth-early eighteenth centuries was suffering unusually severe cold weather, a mini ice age associated with low solar activity.
11. Smith, "Thomson and Burns," p. 182.
12. Sources of Scottish wolf lore include Leslie of Ross, *History of Scotland*, vol. 1, p. 29, first publ. 1578, repr. 1675; the *Orkneyinga Saga*, describing wolves as gravediggers; Prof. Ritchie's "The Influence of Man on Animal Life in Scotland" corroborating that belief; and various local traditions. The last wolf in Scotland is said to have been killed by MacQueen of Pall-a-chrocain, stalker to the laird of MacKintosh, in 1743. Wolves were so numerous in the Highlands in the sixteenth century that a man risked his life traveling through Lochaber or Rannoch; many of these wolves may also have been rabid.

Pope in his *Pastorals* "'informs us in a note, that he judiciously omitted the following verse, "And list'ning wolves grow milder as they hear" on account of the absurdity, which Spenser overlooked, of introducing wolves into England,'" de Haas, *Nature in English Poetry*, p. 32; such a reference would not, however, have been "absurd" in a Scottish poem of the early eighteenth century such as *The Seasons*. Hamilton of Bangour, in "Horace. Book I.Ode XXII," also writes of a wolf in a poem set specifically in Scotland; Hamilton of Bangour, *Poems on Several Occasions*, pp. 134–135.

The wolf has long been a literary symbol for the devil or evil men, especially in Scriptures and religious literature. David Lindsay, in *The Dreme*, I.31 (which may have influenced *The Seasons*), uses wolves figuratively to characterize Scotland's oppressors, whom negligent leaders allowed to ravage the "flock." The wolf was also an important metaphor in Scottish Calvinist writings; Boston, in *Fourfold State*, for example describes cruel and violent men as wolves. Thomson himself used the wolf metaphor, meaning evil men, in *Liberty* III, 370, in describing the decline of Rome.

13. Thomson, *The Seasons and The Castle of Indolence*, ed. Robertson, p. 380n.

14. Ibid., p. 392n.

15. The concluding passage echoes Pope's "Winter" pastoral; Oliver, "Scottish Augustans," p. 140.

16. Thomson, *The Seasons and The Castle of Indolence*, ed. Robertson, p. 278n.

17. Nicolson, *Newton*, pp. 51, 114; Thomson, "A Poem Sacred to the Memory of Sir Isaac Newton"; Thomson, *Liberty*, ed. Sambrook, pp. 1–14; MacQueen, *Progress and Poetry*, p. 57; Ketcham, "Scientific," shows how Thomson illuminates the relationship between the unifying scientific imagination and the expansive poetic vision in his "Newton" elegy.

18. McKillop, *Background of 'Seasons'*, pp. 150–151ff., and Thomson, *Letters and Documents*, ed. McKillop, pp. 198–199n; Thomson, "To William Paterson," [ca. mid-April 1748], ibid., pp. 194–198. Thomson's "tropical" descriptions are not necessarily unrelated to Scottish experience: on plague, see Smout, *A History*, pp. 150–153; on sandstorms, see [Leslie], *Manual of Antiquities*, pp. 69–75, who notes that Boethius described devastating sandstorms ca. 1100; Fordun's *Scotochronicon* (Chapter 50, Bk. 7); and Henderson, *The Findhorn*, pp. 153–165, who reports that a 1694 sandstorm in Morayshire was seen by many as God's punishment. Henderson says the Culbin Sands on the Moray coast, "a miniature Sahara," marked a "crushing defeat of Man by Nature" and that the destructive seventeenth-century storm still lingers in the memory of the people there, where it buried cottages, farms, and whole villages.

19. Thomson, *Seasons*, ed. Sambrook, pp. 356–357n; Thomson owned prints of both "The Judgement of Paris" and "Susanna and the Elders," *Catalogue*, nos. 1 and 15, p. 18; Thomson, *The Seasons and The Castle of Indolence*, ed. Robertson, p. 300n cites *Gentle Shepherd*; "Song CV" in *Tea-Table Miscellany*, ed. Ramsay, repr. 14th ed.

(Glasgow, 1871), vol. 2, pp. 102–103 (in first collected edition, 1740, pp. 311–312—Thomson revised the tale in 1744).

20. Cohen, *Art*, pp. 291–297; also see Thomson, *Castle*, ed. McKillop, p. 44.

21. Thomson, *The Seasons and The Castle of Indolence*, ed. Robertson, pp. 303–304n; MacQueen, *Progress and Poetry*, p. 63.

22. McKillop, *Background of 'Seasons'*, p. 67, holds that the 1744 revision was influenced by the appearance of a "conspicuous comet" in December 1743, reaching its perihelion in March 1744; he cites W. T. Lynn, *Notes & Queries*, ser. 8, no. 9 (1896): 443–444. However, the comet which appeared over London and Edinburgh in early 1742 was just as likely to have influenced Thomson's revision of the passage. See John M. Gray, ed., *Memoirs of the Life of Sir John Clerk of Penicuik, Baronet of the Exchequer, Extracted by Himself from His Own Journals 1676–1755*, Scottish History Society (1st ser.) 13 (Edinburgh, 1892), pp. 164, 166–168. Notice of the 1742 comet was given in *Scots Magazine* 4 (1742): 94; the 1744 comet was also reported in the *Scots Magazine* 5 (1744): 573.

23. McKillop, *Background of 'Seasons'*, p. 36; Turnbull, *Moral Philosophy*, p. 190; Cohen, *Unfolding*, p. 93.

24. Thomson knew Bradley's *General Treatise of Husbandry and Gardening* (1724), *New Improvements of Planting and Gardening* (1717–18), and many more such works on agriculture; McKillop, *Background of 'Seasons'*, pp. 45–46.

25. Boston, *Fourfold State*, p. 34; McKillop, *Background of 'Seasons'*, pp. 97–98; *Abstract from Hutchinson*, pp. 18–21 (on *Moses's Principia*, Part I, *Works*, 1724): Hutchinson describes the earth's shell all cracked, the "elements in confusion," the waters "pressed up"; after the calm, the earth showed and continues to show the effects of this devastation, representing a new order, a sort of "second Creation." Hutchinson was also attacking contemporary physicotheologists in his commentary on the flood here.

26. Thomson, *The Seasons and The Castle of Indolence*, ed. Robertson, p. 256n; Thomson, *Seasons*, ed. Sambrook, p. 331n.

27. McKillop, *Background of 'Seasons'*, pp. 132–133, gives sources for the "eagle" as Pliny, *Natural History* X.3, and Lucan, *Pharsalia* IX.902–906; Thomson's revised version was also influenced by Martin's *A Late Voyage* and *A Description*.

28. Thomson, *Seasons*, ed. Sambrook, p. 335n, identifies Southdean Law; Miller, *First Impressions*, pp. 97–98, 111–112.

29. Thomson, "To Elizabeth Young," August 29, 1743, *Letters and Documents*, ed. McKillop, p. 165.

30. Thomson, *Works*, ed. Murdoch, vol. 1, p. xvii; and see Thomson, "To George Lyttelton," July 14, 1743, *Letters and Documents*, ed. McKillop, p. 163, and "To William Cranstoun," [ca. October 1, 1725], ibid., p. 16.

31. Johnson, "Thomson," *Lives*, vol. 3, p. 290n, quoting H. D. Best, *Memorials*, p. 266.

32. Thomson, *Seasons*, ed. Sambrook, p. 366n; Thomson also owned a print of "The

Harvest" by Maratti, which possibly suggested the scene's composition: *Catalogue,* no. 82, p. 20.

33. Thomson's line "The big round Tears run down his dappled Face," l. 454, echoes Shakespeare, *As You Like It* II.i, ". . . and the big round tears / Coursed down his innocent nose / In piteous chase," Thomson, *The Seasons and The Castle of Indolence,* ed. Robertson, p. 326n; Thomson's lines would influence Anglo-Scot Thomas Campbell's description of a wounded deer in "Lines on Leaving a Scene in Bavaria," in *Poetical Works,* pp. 278–283. Bishop John Leslie's *History of Scotland,* S.T.S., vol. 1 p. 21, records hunting with hounds in the Borders in the sixteenth century. Arnot, *History of Edinburgh,* wrote that hunting had been popular around Edinburgh ever since the Restoration. English fox-hunting aficionado "Nimrod" [Charles James Apperley] in his *Nimrod's Northern Tour* (London, 1838) reported that the Merse and Berwickshire, near Roxburghshire, "struck me, taking it all in all, as being the best country for hounds I saw in Scotland"; he added, "It appears Berwickshire has been hunted beyond the memory of man," and mentioned men of whom he had heard who had been avid hunters there in the early eighteenth century.

34. Even in Thomson's day, fox hunting had become associated with the Tory gentry, and the crude literary stereotype had developed which Whig Thomson was exploiting here as he satirized the drunken hunters; see Speck, *Society and Literature,* pp. 1–13.

35. Thomas Somerville, "Jedburgh," in Sinclair, ed., *Statistical Account,* vol. 1, p. 11, describes Jedburgh's pear orchards in the eighteenth century. McKillop, *Background of 'Seasons',* p. 77, quotes C. V. Deane, *Aspects of Eighteenth-Century Nature Poetry* (Oxford, 1935), pp. 97–99, on this Scottish scene; the scene also recalls Thomas Somerville's description of the ridge of hills, "contiguous to the English Border," and with many rivers and streams, in "Jedburgh," Sinclair, ed., *Statistical Account,* vol. 1, p. 4. Ruberslaw (the mountain said to have been depicted in Riccaltoun's lost winter verse) has a "dark serrated top"; near Jedburgh, Dunian Hill is described as "conical" and very tall: Jeffrey, *History and Antiquities,* vol. 1, pp. 21–22.

36. Thomson, *The Seasons and The Castle of Indolence,* ed. Robertson, p. 333n, says this phenomenon "is not uncommon in the Scottish Highlands and uplands in misty weather"; he refers to the shepherd here as the "Cheviot shepherd."

37. Lindsay, *The Dreme,* in *Works,* vol. 1, pp. 28–31 ("Of the Realme of Scotland"); Lindsay's works were readily available to Thomson. In this passage, Thomson mentions two of the three northernmost points of Scotland given in Camden's *Britannia,* Orcas (Orca) or Howburn, and Berubium (Betubium) or Urdehead; the third is Virvedrum or Duncansbay; McKillop, *Background of 'Seasons',* p. 134. See Thomson, "To William Cranstoun," [ca. October 1, 1725], *Letters and Documents,* ed. McKillop, p. 16, and Chapter 4.

38. Thomson, "To William Cranstoun," [ca. October 1, 1725], *Letters and Documents,* ed. McKillop. p. 16.

39. See Chapter 2 and Chapter 2, note 11; McKillop, *Background of 'Seasons'*, pp. 64–66, cites Whiston's *Account of a Surprizing Meteor* and other sources; Thomson, *Seasons*, ed. Sambrook, p. 379n, says a similar comet was sighted over northern Europe on October 19, 1726.

6 *THE SEASONS* AS AN ANGLO-SCOTTISH MISCELLANY

1. Wendel, *Calvin*, pp. 169–170, 175.
2. Stock, *Holy and Daemonic*, pp. 177–188, comments on Thomson's eclectic beliefs and on his "aesthetic of awe and terror"; he insists that "it would be foolish to ransack the poem for a coherent theology," whether deistic or Calvinistic.
2. John Calvin, *The Institutes of the Christian Religion*, vol. 1, 5.9, quoted by Wendel, *Calvin*, p. 162.
4. McKillop, *Background of 'Seasons'*, pp. 31, 36, 22ff.; see Chapter 3 on "Upon Happiness"; Thomson, "To William Cranstoun," [October 20, 1735], *Letters and Documents*, ed. McKillop, p. 100; also Thomson, "To Elizabeth Young," January 21, 1743–4, ibid., p. 170, on the death of Miss Stanley, the philosophy of which is reiterated in the elegiac passage to Stanley in "Summer," ll. 564ff.
5. Macaulay, *James Thomson*, p. 76, quotes Patrick Murdoch, "To Andrew Millar," n.d.; Boston, *Fourfold State*, pp. 444–445.
6. Thomson, "To William Cranstoun," April 3, 1725, *Letters and Documents*, ed. McKillop, p. 7; Spacks, *Poetry of Vision*, p. 38; Cohen, *Unfolding*, pp. 3, 6, etc. (Cohen, however, tends to take this useful interpretation of Thomson's "fragmented vision" to the extreme of imitative fallacy; i.e., he excuses certain real stylistic faults in *The Seasons* such as poor transitions or lack of integration of added material by claiming that even these are a "functional" part of Thomson's world-view of "inevitable fragmentation of man's knowledge. . . .") Barrell, *English Literature*, pp. 56, 74, 77–78, feels that such an idea of Thomson's vision is "naive" and indeed finds no real "unifying vision" in *The Seasons* apart from the poet's trust in "co-operative labour" to unify a divided society.
7. Stock, *Holy and Daemonic*, pp. 177–188, treats of the element of fear and superstition in Thomson's poetry, though he attributes this more to the influence of Watts than to that of Scottish Calvinism or Scottish folklore.
8. For example, Spacks, *Varied God*, pp. 34–37, feels that Thomson simply rejects the "paradox" of evil in the world instead of trying to solve it.
9. Boston, *Fourfold State*, p. 1.
10. David Lindsay was a Roman Catholic but a stern critic of the Roman church who held rigorous proto-Reformation views. For the full twenty-four-line passage from "Summer" (1727), see Thomson, *Seasons*, ed. Sambrook, Appendix A, pp. 290–291; Stock, *Holy and Daemonic*, p. 186.
11. Boston, *Fourfold State*, pp. 302ff.

12. Turnbull, *Moral Philosophy;* Linck, "Benevolism," p. 248.

13. Drummond and Bulloch, *Scottish Church*, p. 106; Chitnis, *Scottish Enlightenment*, pp. 59ff.; see Sher, *Church and University,* pp. 40ff.

14. Thomson, "To Aaron Hill," April 18, 1726, *Letters and Documents,* ed. McKillop, pp. 25–26.

15. Archibald Campbell wrote *An Enquiry into the Original of Moral Virtue,* which he sent to his Scots friend in London, Alexander Innes, D.D., to have published; Innes, however, published the first edition in his own name (Tothill Field, January 20, 1727–1728) and was offered a living on the basis of this stolen work. Campbell soon exposed the theft; Innes later returned to Scotland to become professor of ecclesiastical history at St. Andrews: [Campbell], *ARETE-LOGIA.* See McCosh, *Scottish Philosophy,* pp. 89–90; Mathieson, *Scotland and the Union,* pp. 253, 261–262; McKillop, *Background of 'Liberty',* p. 107n, says that this remark of Thomson's seems too early to have been influenced by Hutcheson; however, he does acknowledge that Hutchesonian influence on Thomson is significant; see also Linck, "Benevolism," on Thomson and Hutcheson.

16. Sher, *Church and University,* pp. 176–177, on Hutcheson's "Christian stoicism."

17. Hutcheson, Treatise II, "Concerning Moral Good and Evil," in *An Inquiry,* (1729), pp. 104ff., 199ff.; Turnbull, *Moral Philosophy,* pp. 107–141ff. and *Ancient Painting,* pp. 138ff.; Wendel, *Calvin,* p. 206; Boston, *Fourfold State,* pp. 97–98. Also see Speck, *Society and Literature,* p. 92; Sher, *Church and University,* pp. 43–44 and 176–177; Norton, *David Hume,* pp. 87–90, 169–171, 153n.

18. Drummond and Bulloch, *Scottish Church,* p. 47; Fowler, *Shaftesbury,* pp. 125, 127; Turnbull, *Moral Philosophy,* Chapter 4, Part I, pp. 115–120ff. and *Ancient Painting,* pp. 138ff.

19. Boston, *Fourfold State,* p. 40; Hutcheson, Treatise II, "Concerning Moral Good and Evil," *Inquiry,* (1729), pp. 112–113ff.; Linck, "Benevolism," pp. 292–293.

20. Spacks, *Varied God,* p. 51; Cohen, *Unfolding,* pp. 265–267.

21. Grant, *James Thomson,* pp. 248–249, 270: Lyttelton gave Thomson a copy of his treatise, *Observations on the Conversion of St. Paul* (1746); Fairchild, *Religious Trends,* vol. 1, p. 515; George Lyttelton, "To Philip Doddridge," November 7, 1748, Thomson, *Letters and Documents,* ed. McKillop, p. 210.

22. Drummond and Bulloch, *Scottish Church,* pp. 107, 90, 56–57; [James Thomson], preface, *Areopagitica,* John Milton (London: A. Millar, 1738), p. vi; George Lyttelton, "To Philip Doddridge," November 7, 1748, Thomson, *Letters,* p. 210.

23. Bayne, *James Thomson,* p. 41, asserted that "[Thomson's] religious faith was, upon the whole, perfectly orthodox"; Thomson, *Works,* ed. Murdoch, vol. 1, p. xix.

24. Beattie, *Poetry and Music,* p. 34; Spacks, *Varied God,* pp. 43ff., 64, 143ff., 29ff., holds that Thomson increasingly failed to integrate successfully man within his natural environment as he revised his *Seasons;* she feels Thomson betrayed his original natural-religious ideals, his "vision," when he continued to introduce more moral and sociopolitical themes, placing man and his actions to the fore. Ralph Cohen,

however, rightly claims that Spacks's "nature" criterion is too limited and fails to take into account the fundamental presence of man, who "walks superior" in the poem even in its early versions; Cohen, *Art,* pp. 127–128.

25. MacQueen, *Progress and Poetry,* p. 65.

26. McKillop, *Background of 'Seasons',* pp. 113–114; Beattie, *The Minstrel* (McKillop cites 1784 edition); Martin, *St. Kilda,* vol. 2, pp. 65–66.

27. Boston, *Fourfold State,* pp. 23ff.

28. Speck, *Society and Literature,* pp. 35–37.

29. Snyder, "Notes on Burns and Thomson," p. 316.

30. Chalker, "Thomson's *Seasons,*" p. 53; the term "nostalgic progressivism" is Chalker's. Also see Barrell, *English Literature,* on Thomson's "contradictory" visions of history and society and his prescription of "labour" or industry as a unifying force.

31. Havens, "Primitivism," pp. 51–52; similar ambivalence over primitivism versus progress occurs in Anglo-Scot James Beattie's *The Minstrel.*

32. MacQueen, *Progress and Poetry,* pp. 124, 63–67ff.

33. Thomson, "To David Mallet," [August 21–27, 1726], *Letters and Documents,* ed. McKillop, p. 48.

34. Cohen, *Unfolding,* p. 283.

35. Thomson, "To Aaron Hill," October 20, 1726, *Letters and Documents,* ed. McKillop, p. 54.

36. Martin, *Western Islands,* pp. 336–342; McElroy, *Age of Improvement,* p. 5, citing Daniel Defoe, *Caledonia, a Poem in honour of Scotland, and the Scots Nation,* in 3 parts (Edinburgh, 1706); Ramsay, *Works,* ed. Kinghorn and Law, vol. 4, 18–19; Ramsay, "Pleasures of Improvement in Agriculture," in ibid., vol. 3, pp. 171–172; Forbes, *Some Considerations,* pp. 1–2ff.; McKillop, *Background of 'Seasons',* p. 136n, lists a number of books and pamphlets, dated 1727 and after, such as Thomson probably studied regarding Scottish "improvement"; see *Seasons,* ed. Sambrook, p. 374n.

37. MacQueen, *Progress and Poetry,* pp. 59, 67.

38. Duncan, *Thomas Ruddiman,* pp. 150–151; McKillop, *Background of 'Liberty',* p. 9.

39. Hutcheson, Treatise II, "Concerning Moral Good and Evil," *Inquiry,* (1729), p. 124; David Mallet's "A Fragment" (date unknown) contains a similar "high converse" with the dead, listing Sages and Poets (it has not been determined which poet influenced the other in this), Thomson, *The Seasons and The Castle of Indolence,* ed. Robertson, p. 369n.

40. Thomson, *Seasons,* ed. Sambrook, pp. 358–359n, 365n. For a more comprehensive study of Thomson's classical sources and analogues, refer to the annotated editions of *The Seasons,* especially Zippel, Robertson (1908/1971 and especially the useful 1891), and the most up to date, Sambrook (1972 and especially 1981); also see Chalker on Thomson and Virgil.

41. One small example of Thomson's transplanting of "Roman ideals" to Britain is his early use of the term "villa" for country house ("Summer," l. 1454); this Roman term was beginning to be used in Scotland in Thomson's day with the Palladian

revival in architecture. Sir John Clerk of Penicuik's Scottish "villa" at Mavisbank (ca. 1724) was perhaps the first use of the term "villa" in Britain, according to James Simpson, "A Judge of Architectory," lecture to symposium "A Treasure of Learning and Good Taste—Sir John Clerk of Penicuik Tercentenary," Edinburgh University, May 15–16, 1976.

42. John Ramsay, *Scotland and Scotsmen,* vol. 1, pp. 25–26, lamented that Thomson had not followed Allan Ramsay's lead in vernacular poetry and "supplemented" *The Seasons* with "Scottish Georgics"; yet *The Seasons* is no less a Scottish georgic for its English literary language.

7 THE LANGUAGE OF *THE SEASONS*

1. Butt, *Augustan Age,* p. 93, quoting Shaftesbury's "Advice to an Author" (1710), II.i; Kliger, "Whig Aesthetics," pp. 150, 135, 139, citing Richard Hurd, "On the Idea of Universal Poetry," *Works* (London, 1811), p. 2, and pointing out that this Whig taste for "freedom" also included the taste for freer, more natural landscape gardening in that period; Thomson's preface to *Areopagitica* (1738), pp. iii–viii, praises Milton's libertarian sentiments; also see Sitter, *Literary Loneliness,* pp. 176ff.

2. Johnson, "Thomson," *Lives,* vol. 3, pp. 298–299.

3. Spacks, *Poetry of Vision,* p. 39.

4. Cohen, *Unfolding,* pp. 7ff., and *Art,* pp. 11ff.

5. William Somervile [Somerville], "Epistle to Mr. Thomson, on the first edition of his Seasons," ll. 29–36, quoted by Oliver, "Scottish Augustans," p. 131; Cohen, *Art,* pp. 150ff.; Cohen cites Turnbull's *Observations,* pp. 427–428.

6. Scott, "Scottish Language."

7. Butt, *Augustan Age,* pp. 93–94; see introduction; also see Thomson, *Seasons,* ed. Sambrook, p. 328n.

8. Havens, *Influence of Milton,* p. 134.

9. "Cogenial" occurs in John Callender's "The Elevation," *Edinburgh Miscellany* (1720): 271, and also in "Lucifer's Speech" by "R.," p. 72.

10. Butt, *Augustan Age,* pp. 93–94; Murray, *Dialect,* pp. 60–61; Smith, *Scottish Literature,* pp. 94–96; Grant, *James Thomson,* p. 114.

11. Smith, "Thomson and Burns," p. 184.

12. Spacks, *Varied God,* p. 23; Smith, "Thomson and Burns," p. 183.

13. Cohen, *Art,* pp. 131–136; Oliver, "Scottish Augustans," pp. 128, 130.

14. Oliver, "Scottish Augustans," p. 140.

15. Morel, *James Thomson,* pp. 649–650 (Appendix IV, "The Pronunciation of Thomson"); Morel, however, says Scotticisms are "absent" from *The Seasons.*

16. Adams, *Graces,* pp. 118–135, 23ff.; M[asson], "Sound in Poetry," pp. 784–790. See also Chapter 3 on "Of a Country Life" and Chapter 4 on Scots bilingual influence.

17. Rothstein, *Restoration,* p. 57.

18. Beattie, *Poetry and Music,* p. 222.

19. Thomson, *Poetical Works*, ed. Robertson, p. vi.

20. Adams, *Graces*, pp. 29, 31, says the *d* sound has a negative emotional effect (as in dread, dulness, darkness, death); he cites J. R. Firth's definition of such phones-themes (i.e., certain sounds or clusters of sounds which carry conventional associations of meaning and are shared by a group of words).

21. Thomson, *Poetical Works*, ed. Robertson, p. vi, refers specifically to Pope and Lyttelton here.

22. Spacks, *Varied God*, p. 42.

23. Beattie, *Poetry and Music*, pp. 220–221.

24. "Raised": Thomson, *The Seasons and The Castle of Indolence*, ed. Robertson, p. 333n and *Poetical Works*, ed. Robertson, p. 182n; "baffle": Thomson, *The Seasons and The Castle of Indolence*, ed. Robertson, p. 364n; "whelms": ibid.; "Cheek": ibid., p. 384n; "bicker": ibid., pp. 384–385n, and Morel, *James Thomson*, pp. 424–425 (Professor Skeat defines "bicker" as "to keep pecking at"); "Friends": Thomson, *The Seasons and The Castle of Indolence*, ed. Robertson, p. 365n, and Beattie, *Scoticisms*, p. 35.

25. "Ken," "recks": Beattie, *Scoticisms*, pp. 49, 76; "taste": Thomson, *Seasons*, ed. Sambrook, p. 327; "freakt": ibid., p. 392, citing Dr. Johnson.

26. "Louring": Watson, *Roxburghshire Word-Book*, p. 203.

8 LIFE, *LIBERTY,* AND THE PLAYS

1. Margaret Forbes (daughter of Duncan Forbes), letter to eleventh earl of Buchan, June 14, [1791], MS Laing II.330, fol. 1, Edinburgh University Library, reported that Thomson and her father spent many evenings "closeted" together, "correcting for the press." Also, Anon., "A Biographical Memoir," p. 654; Grant, *James Thomson,* pp. 41–42.

2. Thomson, "To William Cranstoun," July 20, 1725, *Letters and Documents,* ed. McKillop, p. 12; Grant, *James Thomson,* pp. 41–48, 64; Thomson, *Letters and Documents,* ed. McKillop, p. 14n.

3. Thomson, "To Aaron Hill," May 24, 1726, *Letters and Documents,* ed. McKillop, p. 30; Grant, *James Thomson,* pp. 56–58, 71–72, quoting advertisement for Watts's Academy which appeared in *The Post-Boy* (April 28–30, 1726). James Stirling (1692–1770), b. Garden, Stirlingshire, was a mathematician educated at Glasgow University; he spent some time in Venice, where he learned the secrets of the glass-makers, and was thence called "The Venetian." He published several mathematical and scientific works; after teaching at Watts's Academy for ten years, he returned to Scotland to become manager of the Scots Mining Company at Leadhills. In 1746 Stirling applied for the chair of mathematics at Edinburgh University (to succeed Colin McLaurin) but his Jacobite principles prevented his appointment. Thomson, *Works,* ed. Murdoch, vol. 1, p. ix, on John Gray.

4. Jack, *Italian Influence,* p. 184; Thomson probably read Italian.

5. Murray of Gorthy, *Tragicall Death,* n.p.; Jack, *Italian Influence,* pp. 108–109, 113.

6. James Thomson, author's preface, *Sophonisba*, III, p. [vi]. References to Thomson's plays will be to the following edition: *The Works of James Thomson*, 4 vols. in 2 (Edinburgh: J. Robertson, for W. Anderson, 1768), [III–IV]. Short references will be given as act.scene; vol., page no. Percy G. Adams's recent edition of the *Plays* (1979) simply reproduces a different Edinburgh edition of 1768 with no particular textual authority (see James Sambrook, review of Adams's edition of the *Plays*, in *The Library*, 6th ser., vol. 3 [September 1981]: 257–260). A critical edition of the plays is much needed.

7. Jack, *Italian Influence*, pp. 111–112.

8. Tobin, *Plays by Scots*, p. 134.

9. Ibid., pp. 134–135; Grant, *James Thomson*, pp. 85ff., 91–92; Grant cites "T.B.," *A Criticism*. Benjamin Martyn's *Timoleon* was produced a few weeks prior to *Sophonisba*; the pamphlet was probably written by one of Martyn's supporters, "inspired by literary jealousy." Another pamphlet, Anon., *A Defence of the New Sophonisba*, redressed the balance.

10. Thomson, "To Aaron Hill," August 23, 1735, *Letters and Documents*, ed. McKillop, pp. 97–98.

11. Tobin, *Plays by Scots*, p. 159.

12. Thomson, *Plays*, ed. Adams, pp. v–xxxvii.

13. Tobin, *Plays by Scots*, pp. 1–4; Macmillan, *George Buchanan*, p. 83; [Buchanan], *Tyrannical-Government Anatomized; Baptistes*, listed in the National Library of Scotland as "probably" translated from Latin by John Milton; mentioned in Macmillan, *Buchanan*, pp. 83–87; see Tobin, "School Plays," and Chapter 1 on Thomson's schooling. One notable late example of the Scottish church's negative attitude to drama was the uproar over clergyman John Home's attendance of a play in Edinburgh in the 1740s; Home was the author of *Douglas*.

14. Thomson, "To William Cranstoun," April 3, 1725, *Letters and Documents*, ed. McKillop, pp. 7–8, mentions "five visits" to Drury Lane in early spring, 1725; ibid., p. 9n, has identified four of these.

15. Tobin, *Plays by Scots*, pp. 131–132; he mentions Archibald Pitcairne's satire *The Assembly* (1692), Ramsay's pastoral *The Gentle Shepherd* (1725), and Joseph Mitchell's comedy *The Highland Fair* (1731); Muir, *Scott and Scotland*, pp. 77–78.

16. [Scott], "Drama," vol. 3, pp. 629–671; Bayne, *James Thomson*, p. 144, citing Scott's essay; Tobin, *Plays by Scots*, pp. 143, 159–160.

17. Thomson, "To George Dodington," [October 24, 1730], *Letters and Documents*, ed. McKillop, pp. 73–74.

18. Thomson, "To George Dodington," December 27, 1730, ibid., p. 78.

19. Grant, *James Thomson*, p. 123.

20. Thomson, "To Lady Hertford," October 10, 1732, *Letters and Documents*, ed. McKillop, pp. 81–82; ibid., p. 84n. Also see Thomson, "To George Dodington," November 28, 1731, ibid., pp. 80–81n.

21. Edition of *Liberty* used here is Thomson, *Liberty*, ed. Sambrook; Thomson, "To George Dodington," November 28, 1731, *Letters and Documents*, ed. McKillop, pp.

79–80; Thomson, "To George Dodington," December 27, 1730, ibid., p. 78; Sitter, *Literary Loneliness*, pp. 158, 180ff.; McKillop, *Background of 'Liberty'*, pp. 4, 100.

22. Eleventh earl of Buchan, "Thomson," *Essays*, pp. 214, 259.

23. McKillop, *Background of 'Liberty'*, pp. 9, 59–60; Taylor, "James Thomson," p. 161.

24. McKillop, *Background of 'Liberty'*, p. 9.

25. Grant, *James Thomson*, p. 137; Ferguson, *Scotland 1689 to the Present*, p. 143; Daiches, *Union*, p. 191.

26. McKillop, *Background of 'Liberty'*, p. 74; McKillop, "Local Attachment and Cosmopolitanism," pp. 191–218. McKillop discusses the "Swiss sickness" which Thomson portrays in *Liberty*, "Heimweh" or homesickness, but he feels that Thomson himself did not dramatize his own "Heimweh" or nostalgia for Scotland explicitly in his works; the present writer disagrees and feels that the poet's homesickness was an important motivating influence on his works, particularly *The Seasons* (see Smith, "Thomson and Burns"). Thomson's own sentiments would have disposed him to sympathize with the "Swiss sickness"; McKillop holds that Thomson was the first British poet to make significant use of this concept. Later, such feelings were frequently directly transferred to Scottish literature, and particularly literature about the Highlands, referring to nostalgia for a similar, mountainous landscape; McKillop cites several Scottish examples ("Local Attachment," p. 206).

27. McKillop, *Background of 'Liberty'*, p. 82; Kliger, "The 'Goths' in England," p. 115; Thomson, *Liberty*, ed. Sambrook, p. 108 (author's notes).

28. Daiches, *Paradox*, pp. 69–71.

29. Sher, *Church and University*, pp. 175ff., refers specifically to Adam Ferguson, John Drysdale, William Robertson, and Hugh Blair.

30. Fairchild, *Religious Trends*, vol. 1, p. 528; McKillop, *Background of 'Seasons'*, pp. 36ff., 39.

31. MacQueen, *Progress and Poetry*, p. 35.

32. Marshall, *Presbyteries and Profits*, treats convincingly of Scottish Calvinistic views of wealth and the work ethic; Chitnis, *Scottish Enlightenment*, p. 59; also see Sher on the Moderates' social goals.

33. Weber, *Protestant Ethic*, p. 157; see also Marshall, *Presbyteries and Profits*.

34. Thomson, *Works*, ed. Murdoch, vol. 1, p. xi.

35. [Thomson], preface to *Areopagitica*, pp. iii–viii; see McKillop, "Licensers," p. 448; Loftis, *Politics of Drama*, p. 143. The lord chamberlain was relieved of his duty as censor in 1967.

36. McKillop, "Licensers," p. 448.

37. Taylor, "James Thomson," p. 231; Grant, *James Thomson*, pp. 178–180; Macaulay, *James Thomson*, pp. 225–226. A play by William Shirley, *Electra* (1745) is, like Thomson's *Agamemnon*, based on Aeschylus, but its "Jacobite" implications were more obvious and ill-timed than Thomson's; it was not produced until 1763, long after the immediate Jacobite threat had passed; Loftis, "Thomson's *Tancred and Sigismunda*," pp. 51–52.

38. Taylor, "James Thomson," p. 232; Tobin, *Plays by Scots*, p. 136.

39. Grant, *James Thomson*, pp. 182–183; Thomson, *Plays*, ed. Adams, pp. xivff.

40. McKillop, "Licensers," pp. 449–452; Johnson, "Thomson," *Lives*, vol. 3, p. 292; Dr. Johnson's source was the *Daily Gazeteer*, April 12, 1739.

41. Grant, *James Thomson*, pp. 188–189, cites Thomson's disclaimer from the *London Evening News*, April 12–14, 1739; Thomson, *Works*, ed. Murdoch, vol. 1, p. xii, also makes a "naive" disclaimer on behalf of his friend Thomson; Loftis, *Politics*, pp. 150–151; Tobin, *Plays by Scots*, pp. 137–138.

42. Tobin, *Plays by Scots*, p. 138; Taylor, "James Thomson," p. 234; Grant, *James Thomson*, p. 191.

43. Taylor, "James Thomson," pp. 235–236; McKillop, "Licensers," pp. 451–452.

44. McKillop, "Licensers," p. 452.

45. Elizabeth Bell, letter to Mrs. Stewart, January 20, 1829: "I do think the Song itself ['Rule, Britannia'] completely Thomson's both in language and turn of thought— particularly in the elevation and nobleness of sentiment . . ." Miss Bell heard from a "near relation of Thomson's": "I had his answer yesterday, expressing great surprise that there should be a doubt of Thomson's having written Rule Britannia, as it always had been considered in his family as completely his as The Seasons themselves, and that he never once before had heard the thing even called in question." See Thomson, *Castle and Other Poems*, ed. McKillop, p. 178; Tobin, *Plays by Scots*, pp. 139–140.

46. Smith, "Some Eighteenth-Century Ideas," pp. 108, 110; Oliver, "Scottish Augustans," p. 120; Menary, *Life and Letters*, p. 232, citing *Culloden Papers*, p. 472.

47. [Fielding], *The True Patriot*, no. 1 (Tuesday, November 5, 1745), in *The True Patriot*, pp. [35], 43–44n; Jarvis, ed., *Collected Papers*, vol. 2, p. 192. Both editors of Fielding have completed the blanks in the author's statement, including Thomson's name, based on good grounds; see also Cross, *History*, vol. 2, p. 20.

48. "Gravis," letter to *The True Patriot*, no. 11(Tuesday, January 14, 1746), in [Fielding], *The True Patriot*, pp. [116–117]; Anon., "Observations on the Present Rebellion," in *The True Patriot*, no. 1 (Tuesday, November 5, 1745), no. 2 (Tuesday, November 12, 1745), and no. 3 (Tuesday, November 19, 1745), in ibid., pp. [38, 50, 56], 43–44n; see Jarvis, ed., *Collected Papers*, p. 210.

49. [Fielding], *The True Patriot*, pp. 14–15; Locke cites J. Paul de Castro, "The Printing of Fielding's Works," *Library*, 4th ser., no. 1 (1920–21), pp. 256–270.

50. Sher, *Church and University*, pp. 37–40, 43–44.

51. Murray of Stanhope, *Memoirs*, part 2, p. 97.

52. "G. H. I.," "Letter, enclosing Interview with Mr. William Taylor, James Thomson's Barber, Given September, 1791," [interviewer may have been eleventh earl of Buchan, or perhaps Thomas Parke], in Hone, ed., *The Table-Book*, [2], p. 590.

53. Taylor, "James Thomson," p. 243; Benjamin Victor, "Letter to the *Daily-Post*," April 26, 1745, quoted in Thomson, *Letters and Documents*, ed. McKillop, pp. 178–80; Loftis, "*Tancred and Sigismunda*," pp. 34–52. Loftis cites an earlier "Jacobite" reading of *Tancred*: John Doran's *London in the Jacobite Times* (1877).

54. Linck, "Benevolism," p. 281; see Sher, *Church and University*, pp. 44ff.

55. Grant, *James Thomson*, p. 235, quoting Boswell, *Private Papers*, iii, p. 37.

56. Bayne, *James Thomson*, pp. 150–151; Tobin, *Plays by Scots*, p. 239.

57. Tobin, *Plays by Scots*, p. 142, citing Bonamy Dobrée, "English Literature of the Early Eighteenth Century (1700–1740)," in *Oxford History of English Literature* (Oxford, 1959), vol. 7, pp. 252–253; Taylor, "James Thomson," p. 242.

58. Tobin, *Plays by Scots*, p. 142; Taylor, "James Thomson," p. 244.

59. Thomson, *Plays*, ed. Adams, p. xviii.

60. Tobin, *Plays by Scots*, p. 140. Also see Armstrong, "The Edinburgh Stage," vol. 3, p. 72: in Edinburgh, 1715–1820, only one of Thomson's plays, *Tancred and Sigismunda*, was produced, but this enjoyed numerous performances over the years.

61. Tobin, *Plays by Scots*, p. 142; Thomson, "To William Paterson," [mid April 1748], *Letters and Documents*, ed. McKillop, pp. 196–197, on the actors' dispute; Thomson, *Plays*, ed. Adams, pp. xx–xxi; Grant, *James Thomson*, pp. 246–247.

62. Taylor, "James Thomson," p. 245.

63. Ibid., p. 244; Thomson, "To David Mallet," [March 31, 1747], *Letters and Documents*, ed. McKillop, p. 188.

64. Taylor, "James Thomson," p. 246; Grant, *James Thomson*, pp. 246–247; Thomson, *Plays*, ed. Adams, pp. xx–xxi, nevertheless praises the simple, stageworthy plot and "fine blank verse" of *Coriolanus*.

65. Menary, *Life and Letters*, pp. 352, 244. Andrew Mitchell was born in Edinburgh in 1708 of an Aberdeen family; he was the son of the minister of St. Giles, William Mitchell. In 1747 he became Whig M.P. for Aberdeenshire; in 1755–1761 he served as M.P. for Elgin Burghs and was appointed (1756) envoy to Frederick the Great at Berlin, where he died in 1771.

66. Thomson, "To Jean Thomson," April 24, 1742, *Letters and Documents*, ed. McKillop, pp. 134–135; Thomson, "To George Ross," November 6, 1736, ibid., pp. 107–108; p. 72n; Thomson, "To Jean Thomson," [1740], ibid., pp. 131–132; Grant, *James Thomson*, pp. 253–256. James Boswell's two nephews studied under Robert Thomson at Lanark; Johnson, *Lives*, vol. 3, p. 297n.

67. Thomson, "To William Cranstoun," August 7, 1735 and [October 20, 1735], *Letters and Documents*, ed. McKillop, pp. 94–95, 99–101; Grant, *James Thomson*, pp. 150–151, 158; "A Friend to Thomson and to Justice," Letter to *The Bee* 7 (1792): 236, says the brother-gardeners took advantage of the poet's genial nature and rather lived "upon him" than with him; Thomson, "To William Paterson," [mid April 1748], *Letters and Documents*, ed. McKillop, p. 196, wrote: "With Regard to the Brother-Gardiners; you ought to know, that, as they are half Vegetables, the Animal Part of them will never have Spirit enough to consent to the Transplanting of the Vegetable into distant dangerous Climates. They, happily for themselves, have no other Idea, but to dig on here, eat, drink, sleep, and mow their wives."

68. Macaulay, *Thomson*, p. 74; *Catalogue*, nos. 6 and 7, p. 8, lists sixty-six bottles of "Edinburgh ale" and ninety bottles of "Dunbar ale" in the poet's cellar.

69. "T. P." [Thomas Parke], "Gleanings of Biography," interview with Dr. William Robertson of Richmond, *The Bee* 6 (1791): 283.

70. Menary, *Life and Letters*, p. 85, citing *Culloden Papers*, pp. 147, 334, 337–341: Jock's father "spared neither expense nor effort to secure for the youth a liberal education, and watched with a keen paternal eye the progress made, not only in his studies but, strangely enough, in his prowess as a golfer!" Jock became a lieutenant in the Blues, or Royal Regiment of Horse Guards, of which the duke of Argyll was captain; he was never promoted, however, as his father refused to pull strings to advance him. Andrew Millar, "To John Forbes," April 24, 1760, Culloden Papers, MS 2968, fol. 136, National Library of Scotland, sadly refers to Forbes's large debt; Andrew Millar, "To John Forbes," June 16, 1761, MS Laing Add. 3, Edinburgh University Library, includes discharge of £120 interest owed on £3,000 debt (remainder of total £4,000 borrowed from Millar). Thomson, "To George Ross," November 6, 1736, *Letters and Documents*, ed. McKillop, p. 108. Quotes from *The Castle of Indolence* will be taken from Thomson, *Liberty*, ed. Sambrook.

71. Thomson, "To George Ross," January 12, 1737/8, *Letters and Documents*, ed. McKillop, p. 117; see Thomson, *Castle*, ed. McKillop, p. 196n; Thomson, *Liberty*, ed. Sambrook, p. 389n; Grant, *James Thomson*, pp. 162–163. Murdoch edited Colin McLaurin's *An Account of Sir Isaac Newton's Philosophical Discoveries* (London: A. Millar and J. Nourse, 1748), and wrote the memoir of McLaurin to prefix the volume. His other scientific and mathematical works included *Mercator's Sailing, applied to the true figure of the Earth* (1741); *Neutoni genesis curvarum per umbras* (1746); trans. Anton Friedrich Büsching's *A New System of Geography* (1762); *On the best form of geographical maps* (1751); and [ascribed] *A plain account of the old and new stiles* (1751).

72. Murdoch, "To John Forbes," May 1754, in Thomson, *Letters and Documents*, ed. McKillop, p. 202n; Thomson, *Works*, ed. Murdoch, vol. 1, p. xv; see note 65 above.

73. Thomson, *Letters and Documents*, ed. McKillop, pp. 202–203n; Warrender matriculated in William Scott's humanities class in 1720 and in Charles Mackie's history class in 1721, Matriculation Rolls, Edinburgh University Library, MS Dc.5.24². Boswell, *London Journal*, p. 46, described "Seymours" as a "travelling governor."

74. Thomson, *Letters and Documents*, ed. McKillop, pp. 198–199n; Paterson matriculated in Laurence Dundas's class in 1716, Matriculation Rolls, Edinburgh University Library; see Chapter 5 on the tropical descriptions in "Summer"; [Parke], "Gleanings," *Bee* 6 (1791): 286; Thomson, *Works*, ed. Murdoch, vol. 1, p. xxxi; Tobin, *Plays by Scots*, pp. 152–153; Grant, *James Thomson*, p. 191.

75. Thomson, "To William Paterson," [mid April 1748], *Letters and Documents*, ed. McKillop, p. 197: "You have an Apartment in it [*Castle*] as a Night-pensioner . . ."; see Thomson, *Castle*, ed. McKillop, pp. 192–193n; Thomson, *Liberty*, ed. Sambrook, pp. 172, 387n.

76. See McCosh, *Scottish Philosophy*, pp. 95–106; further references to Turnbull in Chapter 2 (Edinburgh University), Chapter 6 (*Seasons*), Chapter 8 (*Liberty*), and Chapter 9 (*Castle*). Turnbull wrote *The Principles of Moral Philosophy* (London: A.

Millar, 1740); *A Treatise on Ancient Painting* (London: A Millar, 1740); *Christian Philosophy* (1740); preface and appendix to Heineccius's *Methodical System of Universal Law* (1740; publ. 1763); *Observations Upon Liberal Education* (1742); "De Pulcherrima Mundi Materialis tum Rationalis Constitutione" (while at Aberdeen, 1726); *Thesis on the Connection of Natural and Moral Philosophy* (ca. 1726); *A Philosophical Inquiry Concerning the Connection between the Doctrines and Miracles of Jesus Christ* (1726); *A Curious Collection of fifty Ancient Paintings* (1740); and a translation of *Vertot, Three Dissertations* (1740).

77. Grant, *James Thomson*, p. 163; Armstrong also wrote *Benevolence, an Epistle* (1751); *Taste, an Epistle to a young Critic* (1753); *The Forced Marriage* (a tragedy, 1754; publ. 1770); *Sketches or Essays on Various Subjects* (under pseudonym Lancelot Temple, 1758); and *Miscellanies* (2 vols., 1770); Thomson, *Letters and Documents*, ed. McKillop, p. 173n; Thomson, "To William Paterson," [mid April 1748], ibid., p. 198; see Thomson, *Castle*, ed. McKillop, pp. 193–194n; Thomson, *Liberty*, ed. Sambrook, pp. 387–388n; Appendix 2, and Chapter 4.

78. Grant, *James Thomson*, pp. 76–77; Ramsay, *Works*, ed. Kinghorn and Law, vol. 6, pp. 214–215; Dr. William Robertson, interviewed by [Parke], "Gleanings," *Bee* 6 (1791): 285.

79. Johnson, "Mallet," *Lives*, vol. 3, p. 403; William Robertson, interviewed by [Parke], "Gleanings," *Bee* 6 (1791): 284; Mallet's major works included *The Excursion* (1728); *Eurydice* (1731); *Alfred* (with Thomson, 1740); *Mustapha* (1739); *Amyntor and Theodora* (1747); *Elvira* (1763); and *Collected Works* (3 vols., 1759). James Boswell, Andrew Erskine, and George Dempster tried to hiss *Elvira* off the stage, claiming that Mallet had "forsaken" his Scottish nationality in the play; see Tobin, *Plays by Scots*, pp. 147–150; and Chapter 2 (Edinburgh), Chapter 4 (descriptive influence), and Chapter 8 (London years, *Alfred*).

80. Tobin, *Plays by Scots*, pp. 144–146, cites Anon., *Remarks on the Tragedy of Eurydice, in which It is endeavoured to prove the same TRAGEDY is wrote in favour of the 'Pretender' and is a scurrilous Libel against the present Establishment* (1731); also see Loftis, *Politics*, pp. 108, 108n.

81. Grant, *James Thomson*, pp. 65–66; Thomson, *Liberty*, ed. Sambrook, pp. 280, 408n; Joseph Mitchell, "To Mr. Thomson, the Author of *Winter*," in *Poems*, vol. 2, p. 283; Mitchell, "The Charms of Indolence," ibid., vol. 1, pp. 55–66; also see Chapter 2 (Edinburgh clubs).

82. Thomson, *Letters and Documents*, ed. McKillop, p. 149n, citing John Ramsay, *Scotland and Scotsmen*, vol. 1, p. 23n; Charles Knight, ed., *London* [1842], vol. 3, p. 331; and the marginalia of Lady Phillipina Knight, in C. G. Osgood, "Lady Phillipina Knight and her Boswell," *Princeton University Library Chronicle* 4 [1943]: 48–49. Grant, *James Thomson*, pp. 210, 243; Thomson, "To Elizabeth Young," [March 10, 1743], *Letters and Documents*, ed. McKillop, pp. 147–148; William Robertson, interviewed by [Parke], "Gleanings," *Bee* 6 (1791): 282, 285; Thomson, "To Jean Thomson," October 4, 1747, *Letters and Documents*, ed. McKillop, p. 191. Thomson's love-lyrics to

"Amanda" are collected in Thomson, *Liberty*, ed. Sambrook, pp. 305–313, 431–435n.

83. Thomson, "To Mrs. Jean Thomson," October 4, 1747, *Letters and Documents*, ed. McKillop, p. 191; ibid., p. 204n cites Mitchell's note to Murdoch, August 27, 1748, *Culloden Papers*, p. 306.

9 THE CASTLE OF INDOLENCE

1. The edition used here is Thomson, *Liberty*, ed. Sambrook; Thomson, *Works*, ed. Murdoch, vol. 1, p. xiv; Thomson, *Seasons and Castle*, ed. Sambrook, p. xv.

2. Spacks, *Poetry of Vision*, p. 46; Thomson, *Castle*, ed. McKillop, p. 3. On Thomson's subjective and psychological expression in *The Castle*, also see Golden, *Self Observed*, pp. 17–25; Greene, "Accidie to Neurosis," pp. 131–156; Thomson, *Liberty*, ed. Sambrook, pp. 165–172.

3. Morel, *James Thomson*, pp. 489–490.

4. Macaulay, *James Thomson*, p. 216, calls Thomson's introduction of grotesque, more negative supernatural description in *The Castle* "the most serious fault in connection with the imitation of Spenser" in the poem.

5. Thomson, *Castle*, ed. McKillop, pp. 15–16, cites *FQ* VI.iii.29-6 and II.xii; Thomson, *Liberty*, ed. Sambrook, pp. 166, 383n, cites *FQ* I.i.34, 41.

6. Spacks, *Poetry of Vision*, pp. 59, 47.

7. Thomson, *The Seasons and The Castle of Indolence*, ed. Robertson; Thomson, *Castle*, ed. McKillop, p. 33; Wendel, *Calvin*, pp. 233ff.; Boston, *Fourfold State*, pp. 173ff.

8. Thomson, *Castle*, ed. McKillop, pp. 15ff., cites influence of Spenser's "Bower of Blisse," *FQ*; also Thomson, *Liberty*, ed. Sambrook, p. 166.

9. Taylor, "James Thomson," p. 274, notes that there was such a biblical tapestry at Hagley; Hunt, *Figure in the Landscape*, p. 43, notes that one of the earliest landscape paintings to reach England from Italy was Claude Lorrain's "Landscape with Psyche at the Palace of Cupid" ("The Enchanted Castle")—might this work of "intensely elegiac colouring" have influenced Thomson's literary conception of his *Castle?*

10. Thomson, *Castle*, ed. McKillop, p. 51.

11. Turnbull, *Ancient Painting:* see especially Chapter 2, p. 27, Chapter 8, pp. 164–166; Scots subscribers to *Ancient Painting* included the dukes of Argyll, Athol, and Queensberry, John Armstrong, M.D., Mr. William Adam (architect), John Forbes, Esq., Mr. Henry Hume, Andrew Mitchell, Esq., earls of Stair, Aberdeen, Bute, Marchmont, et al., and, of course, James Thomson, Esq. Turnbull refers to Thomson's *Liberty*, p. 183n, as an example of the uplifting, ennobling influence of arts on the "Heart." See Thomson, *Castle*, ed. McKillop, pp. 190–191n.

12. Thomson, *Castle*, ed. McKillop, p. 30.

13. Ibid., pp. 16–17, 28, and appendix "The Harp of Aeolus," pp. 206–209; Thomson, *Liberty*, ed. Sambrook, pp. 437–438n; Thomson was intrigued with the aeolian harp

and wrote an "Ode on Æolus's Harp," published in Dodsley's *Collection of Poems* (1748), vol. 4, p. 129; in Thomson, *Liberty,* ed. Sambrook, pp. 314–315. Smollett, acquaintance of Thomson and Oswald, also wrote of the aeolian harp in *Ferdinand Count Fathom* (1753). For more on Oswald, see Johnson, *Music and Society,* pp. 61–62, 127, 216; and Johnson, "James Oswald," in *New Grove Dictionary of Music,* vol. 14, p. 15. Oswald is also thought to have contributed to the music for the theater production of *Alfred, A Masque.*

14. Thomson, *Castle,* ed. McKillop, pp. 35–36, does not cite significant influence of Martin Martin here but attributes Thomson's description of second sight chiefly to Border folklore; Smith, "Thomson and Burns," p. 185.

15. Thomson, *Castle,* ed. McKillop, pp. 201n, 203n; Taylor, "James Thomson," p. 304n. There are two Rivers Dee in Scotland, one in Kincardineshire and Aberdeenshire, and one in Kircudbrightshire; there is also a River Devon in Kinross. The similar archaic place-name "Devana" or "Devanha," too, is Scottish; Ptolemy's Devana (possibly from the Gaelic for "hilly") was at Normandikes, near Aberdeen: Johnston, *Place-Names of Scotland,* p. 101. Thomson, *Liberty,* ed. Sambrook, p. 392n, notes that in *Lycidas* the Dee is associated with druids and bards.

16. Thomson, *Castle,* ed. McKillop, p. 48, cites *FQ,* "Acrasia's Bower"; Thomson, *Liberty,* ed. Sambrook, p. 389n.

17. Thomson, *Castle,* ed. McKillop, p. 198n; Thomson, *Liberty,* ed. Sambrook, pp. 164, 389n. Armstrong's original versions of these stanzas are included in his *Miscellanies* (1770), i, 164.

18. Thomson, *Castle,* ed. McKillop, pp. 54–55, second stanza echoes Spenser's "Cave of Despair," *FQ* I.ix.33–36; Thomson, *Liberty,* ed. Sambrook, p. 396n.

19. Thomson, *Castle,* ed. McKillop, p. 55; Thomson, *Liberty,* ed. Sambrook, p. 396n, also cites influence of *Paradise Lost.*

20. Speirs, *Scots Literary Tradition,* pp. 169–171; Wittig, *Scottish Tradition,* p. 149; see Chapter 4.

21. Lt. John Forbes was once stationed at Brentford. Thomson, *The Seasons and The Castle of Indolence,* ed. Robertson, p. 401n, says the scene alludes to *Comus;* Thomson, *Castle,* ed. McKillop, pp. 204–205n; Thomson, *Liberty,* ed. Sambrook, p. 397n, comments on Brentford's bad reputation.

22. Taylor, "James Thomson," pp. 218–220, hails Thomson's "new orthodoxy," or return to some form of religious orthodoxy in *The Castle,* as does Hamilton, "Nature's Volume," p. 487; Thomson, *Castle,* ed. McKillop, pp. 52–53.

23. Thomson, *Liberty,* ed. Sambrook, p. 393n.

24. Hamilton, "Nature's Volume," p. 487; Taylor, "James Thomson," p. 298.

25. Thomson, *Castle,* ed. McKillop, p. 55, cites general influence of Spenser's *FQ* I.x, "House of Holiness," on the theme of penitence and relief.

26. Wendel, *Calvin,* p. 277; Boston, *Fourfold State,* pp. 157, 403–404, 354.

27. Boston, *Fourfold State,* p. 406; Smout, *History of the Scottish People,* p. 89; Weber, *Protestant Ethic,* pp. 157–158ff.; Weber's thesis that Calvinism and the Protestant

work ethic fostered the capitalistic economy has been the subject of much controversy of late; however, a recent study, Marshall's *Presbyteries and Profits*, clarifies Weber's position and vindicates him, especially regarding the rise of *Scottish* capitalism.

28. Turnbull, *Moral Philosophy*, vol. 1, pp. 24ff.; Hutcheson, *An Inquiry*, ed. Kivy, p. 21; Fairchild, *Religious Trends*, vol. 1, p. 532.

29. Aden, "Scriptural Parody," pp. 574–575.

30. Thomson, *Liberty*, ed. Sambrook, p. 384n; Thomson, *The Seasons and The Castle of Indolence*, ed. Robertson, p. 432n, quotes *Scots Paraphrase*, X, "How long, ye scorners of the truth, / Scornful will ye remain?" Also compare the juvenile fable "The sick Kite."

31. Hamilton, "Nature's Volume," p. 487; also Thomson, *Castle*, ed. McKillop, pp. 52–53.

32. See Wendel, *Calvin*, pp. 242ff.; Boston, *Fourfold State*, pp. 173ff.; Thomson, *Castle*, ed. McKillop, p. 8.

33. Boston, *Fourfold State*, pp. 147–148, 185–186.

34. Ibid., pp. 320–321, 326, 324.

35. Sher, *Church and University*, pp. 41ff.; Chitnis, *Scottish Enlightenment*, p. 59.

36. Thomson, *Castle*, ed. McKillop, p. 2; Fairchild, *Religious Trends*, vol. 1, p. 531.

37. Boston, *Fourfold State*, pp. 23ff.; also see Chapter 7 on primitivism.

38. MacQueen, *Progress and Poetry*, pp. 64–65.

39. Thomson, *Castle*, ed. McKillop, p. 46; Thomson, *Liberty*, ed. Sambrook, p. 387n.

40. McKillop, *Background of 'Seasons'*, p. 106; Chalker, "*Seasons* and *Georgics*"; also see Chapter 7 on primitivism and progress; Barrell, *History*, pp. 79ff.

41. Prof. John MacQueen suggested to me that Thomson and his Scottish circle, as castle inmates, might represent deliberate Scottish noninvolvement in the Jacobite troubles of the '45; their "indolence" is understandable in the circumstances, yet Thomson ultimately condemns it; see also MacQueen, *Progress and Poetry*; Sher, *Church and University*, p. 44; Chapter 8 on Thomson's attitudes toward Jacobitism.

42. MacQueen, *Allegory*, pp. 62–63; Thomson, *Castle*, ed. McKillop, pp. 23–24.

43. Oliver, "Scottish Augustans," p. 148, mentions particularly William Julius Mickle and James Beattie as well as William Wilkie and John Armstrong.

44. King, "'The Castle of Scepticism,'" pp. 32–33, shows how, for Beattie and his fellow members of the Philosophical Society, the castle in Aberdeen had literal significance even as he portrayed it in the allegorical essay as standing for sceptical philosophy in Scotland. For Thomson, Edinburgh Castle or some other real Scottish castle may have helped to suggest the "castle" symbolic motif, especially as Scotland itself was associated with indolence in the poet's mind.

45. Taylor, "James Thomson," p. 280; Bawcutt, *Gavin Douglas*, p. 51.

46. Bawcutt, *Gavin Douglas*, p. 48; Priscilla Bawcutt, ed., *The Shorter Poems of Gavin Douglas*, Scottish Text Society, 4th series, vol. 3 (Edinburgh and London, 1967), pp. lv–lviii, lxi–lxiii. The MS of *King Hart* has been at Magdalene College, Cambridge (MS. 2553) since 1724, so it is remotely possible that Thomson saw it.

47. Mackenzie, *Scottish Literature*, p. 101.

48. Bawcutt, *Gavin Douglas*, pp. 50, 61–63, 66–67.

49. Mackenzie, "The Renaissance Poets," p. 36.

50. Bawcutt, *Gavin Douglas*, p. 52.

51. Mackenzie, *Scottish Literature*, p. 101.

52. MacQueen, *Allegory*, pp. 68, 72.

53. Jack, *Italian Influence*, pp. 185–189, discusses Thomson's "cultural internationalism"; Thomson, *Liberty*, ed. Sambrook, pp. 167–168.

54. Thomson, *Castle*, ed. McKillop, pp. 40–41; Thomson, *Liberty*, ed. Sambrook, p. 168. The original French works of Rabelais were among Drummond of Hawthornden's books given to Edinburgh University Library. Urquhart translated the first three books of Rabelais's works (1653 and 1693), Motteux the remainder.

55. Thomson, *The Seasons and The Castle of Indolence*, ed. Robertson, p. 428n; in 1719, Duncan Forbes of Culloden, along with Lord Justice Clerk Minto, subsidized the first printing of "Hardyknute": Bushnell, *William Hamilton*, p. 17.

56. See Scott, "Scottish Language."

57. Thomson, *Castle*, ed. McKillop, p. 14.

58. Bawcutt, *Gavin Douglas*, p. 145.

59. Duncan, *Ruddiman*, appendix 2 ("Influence of the 1710 Edition of Douglas's 'Aeneid,'" pp. 166–167); also see [Thomas Ruddiman], "Glossary," in *Virgil's Æneis*, trans. Gavin Douglas (Edinburgh, 1710), n.p.; Ramsay, ed., *The Ever Green*, "Glossary," vol. 2, pp. 265–286.

60. Thomson, "EXPLANATION *of the obsolete Words used in this POEM*," in *Liberty*, ed. Sambrook, p. 174, lists the author's own definitions; "inly": Thomson, *Castle*, ed. McKillop, p. 188n; "weet": *Roxburghshire Word-Book*, p. 325; "Wonne": ibid., p. 332; "felly": Beattie, *Poetry and Music*, p. 220; "spill": Thomson, *The Seasons and The Castle of Indolence*, ed. Robertson, p. 435n; "unkempt": ibid., p. 436n; "Tract": Thomson, *Castle*, ed. McKillop, p. 89; Thomson, *Liberty*, ed. Sambrook, p. 193, gives "Trace," from second edition, September 1748.

61. "Louting": Thomson, *The Seasons and The Castle of Indolence*, ed. Robertson, p. 435n, and *Roxburghshire Word-Book*, p. 204; "Lubbard": Thomson, *Castle*, ed. McKillop, p. 198n; "Rabblement": Thomson, *The Seasons and The Castle of Indolence*, ed. Robertson, p. 435n; "Tradesman": Beattie, *Scoticisms*, p. 89, and Thomson, *Castle*, ed. McKillop, p. 187n.

62. "Glaive": Thomson, *The Seasons and The Castle of Indolence*, ed. Robertson, p. 434n, and [Ruddiman], "Glossary," *Æneis*, trans. Douglas, n.p.; "Coil": Thomson, *The Seasons and The Castle of Indolence*, ed. Robertson, p. 403n.

EPILOGUE

1. Clive, "The Social Background," p. 240.

2. Robert Burns, "To Alexander Cunningham," February 25, 1794, quoted by Snyder, "Notes on Burns and Thomson," p. 307; see Smith, "Thomson and Burns."

Robertson (Thomson, *The Seasons and The Castle of Indolence*) points out many parallels with Burns, as does McKillop (*Castle*), pp. 185ff. One Scots follower of Thomson worth mentioning is David Davidson, who wrote the Scots *Thoughts on the Seasons, Etc. Partly in the Scottish Dialect* (London, 1789).

3. Wittig, *Scottish Tradition*, p. 192; Thomson, "Gaelic Writers," p. 39; Alexander Macdonald (ca. 1700–1770) wrote "Ode to Winter" and "Ode to Spring." Other Gaelic poets influenced by Thomson were Rob Donn Mackay, Ewen MacLachlan, William Ross, and Dugald Buchanan.

4. Johnson, "Thomson," *Lives*, vol. 3, pp. 298–299.

BIBLIOGRAPHY

〰〰〰

I MANUSCRIPT SOURCES

Edinburgh University Library

LAING MSS

Bell, Rev. James. Letters (copy) to eleventh earl of Buchan. June 10, 1791; June 29, 1791; September 14, 1791. MS La.II.330.

Forbes, John of Culloden, and Capt. Hugh Forbes. Bond £1,000 Sterling, to Mr. Andrew Millar, Bookseller. November 15, 1753. MS La.Add.2, fol. 120.

Forbes, Margaret. Letter to eleventh earl of Buchan. June 14, [1791]. MS La.II.330.

Millar, Andrew. Letter to John Forbes of Culloden. June 16, 1761. MS La.Add.3.

MISCELLANEOUS MSS

Bell, Elizabeth. Letter to Mrs. Stewart. January 20, 1829. MS Dc.6.111, fol. 145–147.

"A Catalogue of All the Genuine Houshold Furniture, Plate, China, Prints and Drawings, Etc. of Mr. James Thomson, (Author of the *Seasons*), Deceased . . ." Photostat; original in Mitchell Library, Glasgow. MS Df.3.49. Catalog is printed in Munby,ed., *Sale Catalogues*.

Hamilton, Professor William. Notebook (containing class lists and assignments, Divinity College, 1707–1727; also list of books of theological library). Reid Bequest, Uncataloged.

Mackie, Professor Charles. Class lists (1719–1744), History and Roman Antiquities. MS Dc.5.24^2, fols. 203ff.

Register of Members of Edinburgh University Library, 1635–1753. MS Da.2.1.

National Library of Scotland

CULLODEN PAPERS

Millar, Andrew. Letters to John Forbes. August 13, 1741; October 10, 1744; January 14, 1746–47; March 17, 1747–48 (with P. Murdoch); April 24, 1760; July 16, 1762. MS 2968, fol. 160, 268, 77–78, 104–105, 136, 145–146.

Murdoch, Patrick. Letter to John Forbes. May 16, 1754. MS 2969, fol. 128–129.

Symmer, Robert. Letter to Patrick Murdoch. November 20, 1760. MS 2969, fol. 140.

Thomson, James. Various letters, notes, and clippings relating to the Thomson birthday celebrations given at Ednam. MS 9848.

Newberry Library, Chicago

Thomson, James. "Newberry Manuscript" of Thomson's juvenile poems. Photostat; original MS is now missing.

Scottish Record Office (Register House), Edinburgh

Jedburgh. Town Council Minutes, vol. 1 (1715–1735). MS B.38/7/1.

Trotter, Beatrix [Thomson]. Testament. Executrix Margaret Thomson. June 17, 1725. Register of Testaments, MS CC8/8/90.

II PRIMARY SOURCES AND EDITIONS

"T." [Thomson, James]. Poems "Of a Country Life," "Upon Happiness," "Verses on receiving a Flower from his Mistress." In *The Edinburgh Miscellany.* Edinburgh: 1720, pp. 193–204.

Thomson, James. *The Castle of Indolence,* ed. George Parfitt. London: 1748; repr. Menston, Yorks.: 1973.

———. *The Castle of Indolence and Other Poems,* ed. Alan Dugald McKillop. Lawrence, Kans.: 1961.

———. *James Thomson: Poetical Works,* ed. J. Logie Robertson. Oxford Standard Authors. Oxford: 1908; repr. 1971.

———. *James Thomson (1700–1748): Letters and Documents,* ed. Alan Dugald McKillop. Lawrence, Kans.: 1958.

———. Letters to Mrs. William Robertson of Richmond (sister of Elizabeth Young). In *The Bee, or Literary Weekly Intelligencer* 8 (1792): 149–150, 324–329.

———. *Liberty, The Castle of Indolence and Other Poems,* ed. James Sambrook. Oxford: 1986.

———. *Plays,* ed. Percy G. Adams. From *The Works of James Thomson,* vols. 3 and 4. Edinburgh: A. Donaldson, 1768; repr. New York and London: 1979.

_____. *The Poetical Works of James Thomson*, ed. Sir Harris Nicolas. Aldine Edition of the British Poets. London: 1830, 1847.

[_____]. Preface. In *Areopagitica*, by John Milton. London: A. Millar, 1738, pp. iii–viii.

_____. Previously unpublished poems: "Verses to Miss Young" ("Ah! urge too late"); "On the Death of His Mother"; fragment, "Go, little book"; "To Amanda" ("Accept, lov'd nymph"); "To Myra"; "Psalm civ Paraphrased"; "Hymn to God's Power"; "Upon the Hoop"; "An Elegy Upon James Therburn, in Chatto"; and fragment, "A Pastoral Entertainment." In *The English Gentleman's Library Manual*, by William Goodhugh. London: 1827, pp. 282–294.

_____. *The Seasons*. London: 1730.

_____. *The Seasons*, ed. John Aikin. Leipzig: 1781.

_____. *The Seasons*, ed. Bolton Corney. London: 1852.

_____. *The Seasons*, ed. James Sambrook. Oxford: 1981.

_____. *The Seasons and The Castle of Indolence*, ed. J. Logie Robertson. Oxford: 1891.

_____. *The Seasons and The Castle of Indolence*, ed. James Sambrook. Oxford: 1972.

_____. *Thomson's Poetical Works*, ed. Rev. George Gilfillan. Edinburgh: 1853.

_____. *Thomson's 'Seasons': Critical Edition*, ed. Otto Zippel. Berlin: 1908.

_____. "Three New Letters of James Thomson," ed. Alan S. Bell. *Notes and Queries* (October 1972): 367–369.

_____. *The Tragedy of Sophonisba*. London: 1730.

[_____]. ["The Works and Wonders of Almighty Power."] In *The Plain Dealer*, [ed. Aaron Hill and William Bond]. First publ. August 28, 1724. London: 1730. Vol. 1, pp. 394–396.

_____. *The Works of James Thomson*. 4 vols. in 2. Edinburgh: J. Robertson, 1768.

_____. *The Works of James Thomson*, ed. Patrick Murdoch. 2 vols. London: 1762.

III SECONDARY SOURCES

Adams, Percy G. *Graces of Harmony: Alliteration, Assonance, and Consonance in Eighteenth-Century British Poetry.* Athens, Ga.: 1977.

Addison, Joseph, Richard Steele, et al. *The Spectator*, ed. Donald F. Bond. 5 vols. Oxford: 1965.

Aden, John M. "Scriptural Parody in Canto I of The Castle of Indolence." *Modern Language Notes* 71 (December 1956): 574–577.

[Amhurst, or Amherst, Nicholas]. "Caleb D'Anvers." *The Craftsman*. 4th ed. London: 1728.

Anderson, David R. "Emotive Theodicy in The Seasons." In *Studies in Eighteenth-Century Culture*, vol. 12, ed. Harry C. Payne. Madison, Wis.: 1983, pp. 59–76.

_____. "Milton's Influence on Thomson: The Uses of Landscape." In *Milton Studies* 15, ed. James D. Simmonds. Pittsburgh: 1981, pp. 107–120.

Anderson, William. *The Scottish Nation*, 3 vols. Edinburgh and London: 1860.

Anon. "Authentic Particulars Respecting the Family and Connections of Mr. Thomson,

Author of the Seasons, Etc." *The Bee, or Literary Weekly Intelligencer* 7 (1792): 235–237.

––––––. "A Biographical Memoir of the late Right Hon. Duncan Forbes of Culloden." *Scots Magazine* 64 (1802): 531–540, 653–666.

[Apperley, Charles James]. "Nimrod." *Nimrod's Northern Tour, Descriptive of the Principal Hunts in Scotland and the North of England*. London: 1838.

Armstrong, John. *Miscellanies*, 2 vols. London: 1770.

Armstrong, Norma. "The Edinburgh Stage, 1715–1820." Dissertation, Library Association, 1968, 3 vols. Copy in Edinburgh (Central) Public Library, Edinburgh Room.

Arnot, Hugo. *The History of Edinburgh from the Earliest Accounts to the Year 1780*. Edinburgh: 1816.

Aubin, Robert Arnold. *Topographical Poetry in XVIII-Century England*. New York: 1936.

"B., T." *A Criticism of the New Sophonisba, a Tragedy*. London: 1730.

Barrell, John. *English Literature in History, 1730–80: An Equal, Wide Survey*. London: 1983.

––––––. *The Idea of Landscape and the Sense of Place 1730–1840: An Approach to the Poetry of John Clare*. Cambridge: 1972.

Bate, W. Jackson. *Samuel Johnson*. New York and London: 1977.

Bawcutt, Priscilla. *Gavin Douglas: A Critical Study*. Edinburgh: 1976.

Bayne, Thomas. "Allan Ramsay and Thomson (1)." *Notes and Queries* 9th ser., 10 (1902): 245.

––––––. "Thomson and Allan Ramsay (3)." *Notes and Queries* 12th ser., 2 (1916): 72–73.

Bayne, William. *James Thomson*. Famous Scots Series. Edinburgh and London: [1898].

Beattie, James. *Essays on Poetry and Music, as they Affect the Mind; On Laughter, and Ludicrous Composition; on the Usefulness of Classical Learning*. London and Edinburgh: 1779.

––––––. *The Minstrel: or, The Progress of Genius*. In *The Poetical Works of James Beattie*, ed. Alexander Dyce. Aldine Edition of the British Poets. London: n.d.

––––––. *Scoticisms*. Edinburgh and London: 1787.

The Bee, or Literary Weekly Intelligencer, ed. James Anderson, vols. 5, 6 (1791), 7, 8 (1792), 18 (1793).

Bennet, Sir William, of Grubbet. "Letters from Sir William Bennet of Grubet to the Countess of Roxburghe (1721–25)." *MSS of the Duke of Roxburghe*. Historical MSS Commission, 14th report (1894).

Bisset, Andrew, ed. *Memoirs and Papers of Sir Andrew Mitchell, K.B.*, 2 vols. London: 1850.

Blackmore, Sir Richard. *The Creation*. 3rd ed. London: 1715.

––––––. "Happiness Discover'd." In *Poems on Various Subjects*. London: 1718, pp. 413–418.

Blair, Hugh. *Lectures on Rhetoric and Belles Lettres*. London and Edinburgh: 1824.

Blair, Robert. *The Grave*, ed. James A. Means. The Augustan Reprint Society, no. 161. London: 1743; repr. Los Angeles: 1973.

Boston, Thomas. *The Complete Works of the Late Rev. Thomas Boston, Ettrick,* ed. Rev. Samuel M'Millan, vol. 12. London: 1853.

———. *Human Nature in its Fourfold State.* Glasgow: 1771.

Boswell, James. *Boswell's Life of Johnson,* ed. Mowbray Morris. London and New York: 1894.

———. *Boswell's London Journal 1762–1763,* ed. Frederick A. Pottle. London: 1950.

Bower, Alexander. *The History of the University of Edinburgh,* 3 vols. Edinburgh and London: 1817.

Brooke, Stopford A. *English Literature.* London: 1876.

———. *Naturalism in English Poetry.* London: 1920.

Buchanan, George. *Opera Omnia,* 2 vols. Edinburgh: 1715.

———. *Poemata quae extant.* Amsterdam: 1676.

[———]. *Tyrannical-Government Anatomized: or, A Discourse concerning Evil-Counsellors, Being the Life and Death of John the Baptist. And presented to the Kings most Excellent Majesty by the Author. [Baptistes].* Trans. [John Milton]. London: 1642.

Bulwer-Lytton, Edward. "The New Phaedo." *The Student,* vol. 2. London: 1835.

Burleigh, John. *Ednam and Its Indwellers.* Glasgow and Dalbeattie: 1912.

Burns, Robert. *Burns: Poems and Songs,* ed. James Kinsley. London, Oxford, and New York: 1971.

Burrow, J. A. *A Reading of Sir Gawain and the Green Knight.* New York: 1966.

Bushnell, Nelson S. *William Hamilton of Bangour: Poet and Jacobite.* Aberdeen: 1957.

Butt, John. *The Augustan Age.* London: 1950.

———. *English Literature in the Mid-Eighteenth Century,* ed. and completed Geoffrey Carnall. Oxford History of English Literature Series. Oxford: 1979.

Cameron, D. "Thomson and Allan Ramsay (2)." *Notes and Queries* 12th ser., 2 (1916): 29.

[Campbell, Archibald] ("Alexander Innes"). *ARETE-LOGIA, or, an Enquiry into the Original of Moral Virtue.* Westminster, London: 1728.

Campbell, Hilbert H. "A Bibliography of Twentieth-Century Criticism and Commentary on James Thomson (1700–1748), with Selected Eighteenth and Nineteenth Century Items." *Bulletin of Bibliography* 31 (1974): 9–22.

———. *James Thomson.* Boston: 1979.

———. *James Thomson (1700–1748): An Annotated Bibliography of Selected Editions and the Important Criticism.* New York and London: 1976.

Campbell, Thomas. *Poetical Works,* ed. W. A. Hill. London and New York: 1868.

———. *Specimens of the British Poets,* 7 vols. London: 1819.

Carlyle, Alexander "Jupiter," of Inveresk. *Anecdotes and Characters of the Times,* ed. James Kinsley. London: 1973.

Carnie, Robert Hay, and Ronald Paterson Doig. "Scottish Printers and Booksellers 1688–1775: A Supplement." *Studies in Bibliography,* ed. Fredson Bowers, vol. 12 (1959): 131–159.

A Catalogue of the Graduates in the Faculties of Arts, Divinity, and Law, of the University of Edinburgh, Since Its Foundation. Edinburgh: 1858.

Chalker, John. "Thomson's *Seasons* and Virgil's *Georgics:* The Problem of Primitivism and Progress." *Studia Neophilologica* 35 (1963): 41–56.

Chitnis, Anand C. *The Scottish Enlightenment.* London and Totowa, N.J.: 1976.

Clark, Ian D. L. "From Protest to Reaction: The Moderate Regime in the Church of Scotland, 1752–1805." In *Scotland in the Age of Improvement,* ed. Nicholas T. Phillipson and Rosalind Mitchison. Edinburgh: 1970, pp. 200–224.

Clerk, Sir John, of Penicuik. *Memoirs of the Life of Sir John Clerk of Penicuik, Baronet, Baron of the Exchequer, Extracted by Himself from His Own Journals 1676–1755,* ed. John M. Gray. Scottish History Society, 1st ser., 13. Edinburgh: 1892.

Clive, John. "The Social Background of the Scottish Renaissance." In *Scotland in the Age of Improvement,* ed. Nicholas T. Phillipson and Rosalind Mitchison. Edinburgh: 1970, pp. 225–244.

Cohen, Ralph. *The Art of Discrimination: Thomson's 'The Seasons' and the Language of Criticism.* London: 1964.

———. Letter to M. J. W. Scott. September 28, 1976.

———. *The Unfolding of 'The Seasons'.* London: 1970.

Collins, William. *The Poems of Collins and Gray,* ed. Austin Lane Poole and Christopher Stone. Oxford Standard Authors. London: 1919, 1961.

Corder, Jim W. "A New Nature in Revisions of *The Seasons.*" *Notes and Queries* (December 1966): 461–464.

Couper, W. J. *The Edinburgh Periodical Press,* 2 vols. Stirling: 1908.

Craig, David. *Scottish Literature and the Scottish People 1680–1830.* London: 1961.

Cross, Wilbur. *The History of Henry Fielding.* New Haven, Conn.: 1918.

Culloden Papers, ed. [H. Robert Duff]. London: 1815.

Cunningham, Peter. "James Thomson—Allan Ramsay." *The Gentleman's Magazine* n.s. 39 (April 1853): 368–370.

———. "James Thomson and David Mallet." *Miscellanies of the Philobiblon Society,* vol. 4. London: 1857–58, pp. 1–43.

Daiches, David. "Eighteenth-Century Vernacular Poetry." In *Scottish Poetry: A Critical Survey,* ed. James Kinsley. London: 1955, pp. 150–184.

———. *The Paradox of Scottish Culture: The Eighteenth-Century Experience.* London: 1964.

———. *Scotland and the Union.* London: 1977.

Davie, George Elder. *The Democratic Intellect: Scotland and Her Universities in the Nineteenth Century.* Edinburgh: 1961.

———. "Hume, Reid, and the Passion for Ideas." In *Edinburgh in the Age of Reason.* Edinburgh: 1967, pp. 23–39.

de Haas, C. E. *Nature in English Poetry of the First Half of the Eighteenth Century.* Amsterdam: 1928.

Despauterius, Johannes. *Ninivitae Gramaticae, Syntaxis, Ninivitae Artis Versificatoriae Compendium, et De Figuris* (with George Buchanan's *De Prosodia Libellus*). Edinburgh: 1702.

Doughty, W. Lamplough. "The Place of James Thomson in the Poetry of Nature." *The London Quarterly and Holborn Review* 174 (6th ser., vol. 18) (1949): 154–158, 249–254.

Douglas, Gavin. *The Shorter Poems of Gavin Douglas*, ed. Priscilla J. Bawcutt. Scottish Text Society, 4th ser., no. 3. Edinburgh and London: 1967.

————, trans. *Virgil's Aeneid, Translated into Scottish Verse*, ed. David F. C. Coldwell. Scottish Text Society, 3rd ser. 4 vols. Edinburgh and London: 1957–1964.

————, trans. *Virgil's Æneis*. Edinburgh: Thomas Ruddiman, 1710.

Douglas, Sir George. *A History of the Border Counties (Roxburgh, Selkirk, Peebles)*. Edinburgh and London: 1899.

————. *Scottish Poetry: Drummond of Hawthornden to Fergusson*. Glasgow: 1911.

Drennon, Herbert. "James Thomson's Contact with Newtonianism and His Interest in Natural Philosophy." *PMLA* 39 (1934): 71–80.

————. "The Source of James Thomson's 'The Works and Wonders of Almighty Power.'" *Modern Philology* 32, no. 1 (August 1934): 33–36.

Drummond, Andrew, and James Bulloch. *The Scottish Church 1688–1843*. Edinburgh: 1973.

Drummond of Hawthornden, William. *The Poetical Works of William Drummond of Hawthornden, With 'A Cypresse Grove'*. Ed. L. E. Kastner. Scottish Text Society, n.s. 3–4. 2 vols. Edinburgh and London: 1913.

Duncan, Douglas. *Thomas Ruddiman: A Study in Scottish Scholarship of the Early Eighteenth Century*. Edinburgh and London: 1965.

The Edinburgh Evening Courant. Edinburgh periodical. 1719–20, 1725.

The Edinburgh Miscellany. Edinburgh: J. M'Euen and Company, 1720.

Elliot, George F. S. *The Border Elliots and the Family of Minto*. Edinburgh: 1897.

Erskine, David Steuart, eleventh earl of Buchan. *Essays on the Lives and Writings of Fletcher of Saltoun and the Poet Thomson*. London: 1792.

————. "Eulogy of Thomson the Poet, delivered by the Earl of Buchan on Ednam Hill, when he crowned the first Edition of the Seasons with a Wreath of Bays, on the 22nd of September, 1791." *The Bee, or Literary Weekly Intelligencer* 5 (1791): 200–207.

Eyre-Todd, George, ed. *Scottish Poetry of the Eighteenth Century*, vol. 1. Glasgow: 1896.

Fairchild, Hoxie Neale. *Religious Trends in English Poetry*, vol. 1 (1700–1740). New York: 1939.

Ferguson, William. *Scotland 1689 to the Present*. Edinburgh: 1968, 1977.

Fergusson, Sir James. "The Ballads." In *Scottish Poetry, a Critical Survey*, ed. James Kinsley. London: 1955, pp. 99–118.

Fielding, Henry. *The Jacobite's Journal and Related Writings*, ed. W. B. Coley. Middletown, Conn.: 1975.

[————]. *The True Patriot: and The History of Our Own Times*, ed. Miriam Austin Locke. University, Ala.: 1964.

Forbes, Duncan, of Culloden. *Some Considerations on the Present State of Scotland in a Letter to the Commissioners and Trustees for Improving FISHERIES and MANUFACTURES.* Edinburgh: 1744.

Fowler, Thomas. *Shaftesbury and Hutcheson.* London: 1882.

Freeman, F. W. "The Intellectual Background of the Vernacular Revival before Burns." *Studies in Scottish Literature* 16 (1981): 160–187.

"G., A. B." [Alexander Balloch Grosart?]. "Memorials of the Author of 'The Seasons' and Riccaltoun of Hobkirk." *Gentleman's Magazine* n.s. 40 (October 1853): 364–371.

Gibson, W. J. *Education in Scotland.* London: 1912.

Golden, Morris. *The Self Observed: Swift, Johnson, Wordsworth.* Baltimore: 1972.

Graham, Henry Grey. *Scottish Men of Letters in the Eighteenth Century.* London: 1901.

————. *The Social Life of Scotland in the Eighteenth Century.* London: 1909.

Grant, Sir Alexander. *The Story of the University of Edinburgh during its First 300 Years*, 2 vols. London: 1884.

Grant, Douglas. *James Thomson: Poet of 'The Seasons'.* London: 1951.

Grant, James. *History of the Burgh and Parish Schools of Scotland*, vol. 1. London and Glasgow: 1876.

Greene, Donald. "From Accidie to Neurosis: *The Castle of Indolence* Revisited." In *English Literature in the Age of Disguise*, ed. Maximilian E. Novak. Berkeley, Los Angeles, and London: 1977, pp. 131–156.

Griffin, Dustin. *Regaining Paradise: Milton and the Eighteenth Century.* Cambridge, London, New York: 1986.

Hamilton, Horace E. "James Thomson Recollects Hagley Park." *Modern Language Notes* 62 (1947): 194–197.

————. "Nature's Volume Broad-Displayed." *Times Literary Supplement*, August 28, 1949, p. 487.

Hamilton, William, of Bangour. *Poems on Several Occasions.* Edinburgh: 1760.

Harvey, Sir Paul, ed. *The Oxford Companion to Classical Literature.* Oxford: 1937, 1946.

————, ed. *The Oxford Companion to English Literature.* Oxford: 1964.

Havens, Raymond Dexter. *The Influence of Milton on English Poetry.* Cambridge, Mass.: 1922.

————. "Primitivism and the Idea of Progress in Thomson." *Studies in Philology* 29 (1932): 41–52.

Hazlitt, William. "On Thomson and Cowper" [1818]. In *Lectures on the English Poets*. 3rd ed. London: 1841, pp. 164–200.

Henderson, Thomas. *The Findhorn.* Edinburgh: 1932.

Henryson, Robert. *Robert Henryson: Poems and Fables*, ed. H. Harvey Wood. Edinburgh: 1958, 1972.

[Hill, Aaron, and William Bond], eds. *The Plain Dealer: Being Select Essays on Several Curious Subjects.* 1st publ. 1724. New edition in 2 vols. London: 1730.

Home, Henry (Lord Kames). *Elements of Criticism*, 2 vols. London: 1805.

Hone, William, ed. *The Table-Book*, 2 vols. in 1. London: 1827; repr. Detroit: 1966.

Horn, D. B. *A Short History of the University of Edinburgh 1556–1889.* Edinburgh: 1967.

Hunt, John Dixon. *The Figure in the Landscape: Poetry, Painting, and Gardening during the Eighteenth Century.* Baltimore and London: 1976.

Hutcheson, Francis. *An Inquiry Concerning Beauty, Order, Harmony, Design,* ed. Peter Kivy. International Archives of the History of Ideas. The Hague: 1973.

———. *An inquiry into the original of our ideas of beauty and virtue; in two treatises. In which the principles of the late Earl of Shaftesbury are explain'd and defended, against the author of the Fable of the bees: and the ideas of moral good and evil are establish'd, according to the sentiments of the antient moralists. With an attempt to introduce a mathematical calculation in subjects of morality.* London: 1725.

———. *An Inquiry into the Original of our Ideas of Beauty and Virtue; in Two Treatises.* 3rd ed., corrected. London: 1729.

Hutchinson, John. *An Abstract from the Works of John Hutchinson, Esq.* [Anon. ed.] Edinburgh: 1753.

Inglesfield, Robert. "Thomson and 'Mr. Rickleton's Poem on Winter.'" *Notes and Queries* 26 (February 1979): 27–29.

Jack, R. D. S. *The Italian Influence on Scottish Literature.* Edinburgh: 1972.

———. *Scottish Prose 1550–1700.* London: 1971.

James VI & I, King. *The Essayes of a Prentise, in The Divine Art of Poesie.* Edinburgh: 1584.

Jarvis, Rupert, ed. *Collected Papers of the Jacobite Risings,* vol. 2. Manchester and New York: 1972.

Jefferson, D. W. "The Place of James Thomson." In *Proceedings of the British Academy,* vol. 64 (1978). London: OUP, for the British Academy, 1980, pp. 233–258.

Jeffrey, Alexander. *The History and Antiquities of Roxburghshire,* 4 vols. Edinburgh: 1855–1864.

Johnson, David. "James Oswald," in *The New Grove Dictionary of Music and Musicians,* ed. Stanley Sadie. London: 1980, vol. 14, p. 15.

———. *Music and Society in Lowland Scotland in the Eighteenth Century.* London: 1972.

Johnson, Dr. Samuel. *A Dictionary of the English Language,* 2 vols. London: 1755.

———. *Lives of the English Poets,* ed. George Birkbeck Hill. 3 vols. New York: 1967.

Johnston, James B. *Place-Names of Scotland.* Edinburgh: 1903.

Ketcham, Michael G. "Scientific and Poetic Imagination in James Thomson's 'Poem Sacred to the Memory of Sir Isaac Newton.'" *Philological Quarterly* 61, no. 1 (Winter 1982): 33–50.

King, E. H. "James Beattie's 'The Castle of Scepticism' (1767): A Suppressed Satire on Eighteenth-Century Sceptical Philosophy." *Scottish Literary Journal* 2, no. 2 (December 1975): 18–35.

Kinghorn, A. M. "Literary Aesthetics and the Sympathetic Emotions—A Main Trend in Eighteenth-Century Scottish Criticism." *Studies in Scottish Literature* 1, no. 1 (July 1963): 35–47.

Kinsley, James. "The Mediaeval Makars." In *Scottish Poetry: A Critical Survey,* ed. James Kinsley. London: 1955, pp. 1–32.

Kliger, Samuel. "The 'Goths' in England." *Modern Philology* 43 (1945–1946): 107–117.

––––––. "Whig Aesthetics: A Phase of Eighteenth-Century Taste." *ELH* 16 (1949): 135–150.

Lauder, William, ed. *Poetarum Scotorum Musae Sacrae*, 2 vols. Edinburgh: 1739.

Law, Alexander. *Education in Edinburgh in the Eighteenth Century.* London: 1965.

––––––. Letter to M. J. W. Scott. July 13, 1977.

––––––. Personal interview. February 9, 1976.

Leslie, John, Bishop of Ross. *The History of Scotland*, trans. Fr. James Dalrymple, ed. Rev. Fr. E. G. Cody, O.S.B. Scottish Text Society, 2 vols. Edinburgh and London: 1888.

[Leslie, Rev. W.]. *Manual of Antiquities, Distinguished Buildings, and Natural Curiosities of Moray.* Elgin: 1823.

Linck, Orville F. "Benevolism in the Works of James Thomson." Ph.D. dissertation, Northwestern University, 1941.

Lindsay, Sir David. *Major Poems, Parts I to IV*, ed. J. Small and F. Hall. Early English Text Society nos. 11, 19, 35, 37 (1865–1869); repr. New York: 1969.

––––––. *The Works of Sir David Lindsay of the Mount 1490–1555*, ed. Douglas Hamer. Scottish Text Society, 3rd ser. Edinburgh and London: 1931, vol. 1.

Lindsay, Maurice. *History of Scottish Literature.* London: 1977.

Loftis, John. *The Politics of Drama in Augustan England.* Oxford: 1963.

––––––. "Thomson's *Tancred and Sigismunda,* and the Demise of the Drama of Political Opposition." In *The Stage and the Page: London's 'Whole Show' in the Eighteenth-Century Theatre,* ed. George Winchester Stone, Jr. Berkeley, Los Angeles, and London: 1981, pp. 34–54.

Macaulay, G. C. *James Thomson.* English Men of Letters Series. London: 1908.

McCosh, James. *The Scottish Philosophy from Hutcheson to Hamilton.* New York: 1875.

McDiarmid, Matthew P., ed. *The Poems of Robert Fergusson.* Scottish Text Society, 3rd ser., no. 21, 2 vols. Edinburgh and London: 1954.

McElroy, Davis D. "Literary Clubs and Societies of Eighteenth Century Scotland 1700–1800." Ph.D. dissertation, University of Edinburgh, 1952.

––––––. *Scotland's Age of Improvement.* Pullman, Wash.: 1969.

McEwen, Gilbert D. *The Oracle of the Coffee House: John Dunton's 'Athenian Mercury'.* San Marino, Calif.: 1972.

McGuirk, Carol. "Augustan Influences on Allan Ramsay." *Studies in Scottish Literature* 16 (1981): 97–109.

Mackenzie, Agnes Mure. *An Historical Survey of Scottish Literature to 1714.* London: 1933.

––––––. "The Renaissance Poets (1) Scots and English." In *Scottish Poetry: A Critical Survey,* ed. James Kinsley. London: 1955, pp. 33–67.

Mackenzie, George, of Rosehaugh. *Works*, 2 vols. Edinburgh: 1716–1722.

McKillop, Alan Dugald. *The Background of Thomson's 'Liberty'.* Houston: Rice Institute Pamphlet, English Monograph Series 38, no. 2 (July 1951).

––––––. *The Background of Thomson's 'Seasons'.* Minneapolis: 1942.

––––––. "Local Attachment and Cosmopolitanism—the Eighteenth-Century Pattern."

In *From Sensibility to Romanticism,* ed. Frederick W. Hilles and Harold Bloom. New York: 1965, pp. 191–218.

————. Review of [Eric S. Taylor], "James Thomson's Library" (*TLS,* June 20, 1942). *Philological Quarterly* 22, no. 2 (April 1943): 179–180.

————. "Thomson and the Licensers of the Stage." *Philological Quarterly* 37 (October 1958): 448–453.

————. "Two Eighteenth-Century 'First Works.'" *Newberry Library Bulletin* 4, no. 1 (November 1955): 12–23.

————. "Two More Thomson Letters." *Modern Philology* 60, no. 2 (November 1962): 128–130.

McLynn, Frank. *The Jacobites.* London: 1985.

Macmillan, D. *George Buchanan: A Biography.* Edinburgh: 1906.

MacQueen, John. *Allegory.* Critical Idiom Series. London: 1970.

————. "The Lowland Contribution." Review of Maurice Lindsay's *History of Scottish Literature. Times Literary Supplement,* September 9, 1977, p. 1089.

————. Preface. *Twelve Modern Scottish Poets,* ed. Charles King. London: 1971.

————. *Progress and Poetry: The Enlightenment and Scottish Literature,* vol. 1. Edinburgh: 1982.

————. *Robert Henryson: A Study of the Major Narrative Poems.* Oxford: 1967.

Maidment, James, ed. *Scotish Elegiac Verses 1629–1729.* Edinburgh: 1842.

Mallet, David. *The Excursion: A Poem in Two Books.* London: 1728.

————. "Original Letters of David Mallet, Esq. to Mr. John Ker, Professor of Greek, in King's College Aberdeen." *The Edinburgh Magazine, or Literary Miscellany* 1 (January–June 1793): 3–6, 85–88, 172–174, 413–414.

————. *The Works of David Mallet, Esq,* 3 vols. in 1. London: 1759; repr. Farnborough, Hants.: 1969.

Marshall, Gordon. *Presbyteries and Profits: Calvinism and the Development of Capitalism in Scotland, 1560–1707.* Oxford: 1980.

Martin, J. Burns. "Allan Ramsay," 2 vols. Ph.D. dissertation, Harvard University, 1928.

————. *Allan Ramsay: A Study of His Life and Works.* Cambridge, Mass.: 1931.

Martin, Martin. *A Description of the Western Islands of Scotland Circa 1695.* 1st publ. 1703; revised 1716. Glasgow: 1884.

————. *A Voyage to St. Kilda.* In *Miscellanea Scotica; a Collection of Tracts Relating to the History, Antiquities, Topography, and Literature of Scotland.* Glasgow: 1818, vol. 2, pp. 77ff.

Mason, John. *Kelso Records.* Edinburgh: 1839.

Masson, David. *Drummond of Hawthornden.* London: 1873.

M[asson], D. I. "Sound in Poetry." In *Princeton Encyclopedia of Poetry and Poetics,* ed. Preminger. 1974, pp. 784–790.

Mathieson, William Law. *Scotland and the Union: A History of Scotland from 1695–1747.* Glasgow: 1905.

Matriculation Roll of the University of Edinburgh. Typescript, 4 vols. Edinburgh University Library.

Menary, George. *The Life and Letters of Duncan Forbes of Culloden*. London: 1936.

Miller, Hugh. *First Impressions of England and Its People*. London: 1847.

Mitchell, Joseph, John Callender, et al. *Lugubres Cantus: Poems on Several Grave and Important Subjects, Chiefly Occasion'd by the Death of the late Ingenious Youth John Mitchell*. London: 1719.

——. *Poems on Several Occasions*, 2 vols. London: 1729.

Moore, Cecil A. "A Predecessor of Thomson's *Seasons*." *Modern Language Notes* 34 (1919): 278–281.

More, John. *Strictures, Critical and Sentimental, on Thomson's Seasons; with Hints and Observations on Collateral Subjects*. London: 1777; repr. New York, 1970.

Morel, Léon. *James Thomson: Sa vie et ses oeuvres*. Paris: 1895.

Muir, Edwin. *Scott and Scotland: The Predicament of the Scottish Writer*. London: 1936.

Munby, A. N. L., ed. *Sale Catalogues of Libraries of Eminent Persons*. London: 1971.

Murray, David, of Gorthy. "A Paraphrase of the CIV Psalme." Edinburgh: 1615; repr. in *Poems by Sir David Murray of Gorthy*. Edinburgh: 1823, n.p.

——. *The Tragicall Death of Sophonisba*. London: 1611; repr. in *Poems by Sir David Murray of Gorthy*. Edinburgh: 1823, n.p.

Murray, James A. H. *The Dialect of the Southern Counties of Scotland*. London: 1873.

Murray of Stanhope, Lady [Grisell]. *Memoirs of the Lives and Characters of the Rt. Honourable George Baillie of Jerviswood, and of Lady Grisell Baillie*. Edinburgh: 1824.

Nelson, Bonnie. "The Stage History of James Thomson's *Sophonisba*: The Rise and Fall of a Patriot Queen." *Theatre Survey: The American Journal of Theatre History* 23, no. 1 (May 1982): 103–107.

Nicolson, Marjorie Hope. *Mountain Gloom and Mountain Glory: The Development of the Aesthetics of the Infinite*. Ithaca, N.Y.: 1959.

——. *Newton Demands the Muse*. Princeton: 1946.

Norris, John, of Bemerton. "An Idea of Happiness." In *A Collection of Miscellanies*. 4th ed. London: 1706, pp. 317–354.

Norton, David Fate. *David Hume: Common-Sense Moralist, Sceptical Metaphysician*. Princeton: 1982.

"O., J." "Scotch Professors of Divinity: Messrs. William and Robert Hamilton, Professors of Divinity in the University of Edinburgh." *The Edinburgh Christian Instructor* 113. Vol. 25, no. 8 (August 1826): 523–531.

Oliver, A. M. "The Scottish Augustans." In *Scottish Poetry: A Critical Survey*, ed. James Kinsley. London: 1955, pp. 119–149.

Oliver, John W. "The Eighteenth Century Revival." In *Essays on Scots Literature*. Edinburgh: 1933.

——. "Scotland since the Union: Literature." *Saltire Review* 3, no. 9 (Winter 1956): 12–16.

[Parke, Thomas]. "Gleanings of Biography" (interview with Dr. William Robertson of Richmond). *The Bee, or Literary Weekly Intelligencer* 6 (1791): 281–287.

Phillipson, Nicholas T. Personal interview. May 25, 1976.

———, and Rosalind Mitchison, eds. *Scotland in the Age of Improvement*. Edinburgh: 1970.

———. "Sir John Clerk in His Time." Lecture delivered for symposium "A Treasure of Learning and Good Taste—Sir John Clerk of Penicuik Tercentenary." University of Edinburgh. May 15–16, 1976.

Pinkerton, John. *Letters of Literature*. London: 1785.

Poems on the Royal-Company of Archers. Bound with *Selecta Poemata Archibaldi Pitcairnii, Gulielmi Scot a Thirlstane, Thomae Kincadii, et Aliorum*. Edinburgh: 1727.

Pope, Alexander. *The Poems of Alexander Pope*, ed. John Butt. London: 1970.

Ramsay, Allan, ed. *The Ever Green*, 2 vols. Edinburgh: 1724; repr. Glasgow: 1874.

———. *Poems by Allan Ramsay and Robert Fergusson*, ed. A. M. Kinghorn and Alexander Law. Edinburgh: 1974.

———, ed. *The Tea-Table Miscellany*, first 3 vols. London: 1730.

———, ed. *The Tea-Table Miscellany*. 10th ed. 4 vols. in 1. London: 1740.

———, ed. *The Tea-Table Miscellany*. Repr. from 14th ed. 4 vols. in 2. Glasgow: 1871.

———. *The Works of Allan Ramsay*, ed. Alexander M. Kinghorn and Alexander Law. Scottish Text Society, 4th ser. Edinburgh and London: 1961, 1970, 1972, 1974. Vols. 3–6.

———. *The Works of Allan Ramsay*, Ed. Burns Martin and John W. Oliver. Scottish Text Society, 3rd ser. Edinburgh and London: 1945, 1953. Vols. 1 and 2.

Ramsay, John, of Ochtertyre. *Scotland and Scotsmen in the Eighteenth Century, from the MSS of John Ramsay of Ochtertyre*, ed. Alexander Allardyce, 2 vols. Edinburgh and London: 1888.

Reed, James. *The Border Ballads*. London: 1973.

Reid, John. *The Scots Gard'ner*. Edinburgh: 1683; repr. London and Edinburgh: 1907.

Reisner, Thomas A. "Dryden's 'Metamorphoses' and Thomson's 'Paraphrase of Psalm CIV.'" *Notes and Queries* 25 (February 1978): 31.

[Riccaltoun, Robert]. "A Winter's Day." *The Gentleman's Magazine* 10 (May 1740): 256.

———. *The Works of the Late Rev. Mr. Robert Riccaltoun*, 3 vols. Edinburgh: 1771–72.

[Robertson, J. Logie], "Hugh Haliburton." "James Thomson: A Poet of the Woods." *Good Words* 34 (1893): 467–477.

Rogers, Pat. *The Augustan Vision*. London: 1974.

———. "The Perfect Year." Radio talk. BBC-3. November 6, 1975 (transcript).

Ross, Ian Simpson. *Lord Kames and the Scotland of His Day*. Oxford: 1972.

Røstvig, Maren-Sofie. *The Happy Man*, vol. 2. Oslo and New York: 1971.

Rothstein, Eric. *Restoration and Eighteenth-Century Poetry 1660–1780*. The Routledge History of English Poetry, vol. 3. Boston, London, and Henley: 1981.

Ruddiman, Thomas. *The Rudiments of the Latin Tongue, or a Plain and Easy Introduction to Latin Grammar*. Edinburgh: 1714; repr. Menston, Yorks.: 1970.

Schmidt-Wartenberg, Hans. "Das Newberry Manuskript von James Thomsons jugendgedichten." *Anglia* n.f. bd. 11 (1901): 129–152.

Scobie, Matthew. Map of Roxburghshire (1770). Edinburgh University Library Map
  Room.

Scotland, James. *The History of Scottish Education*, 2 vols. London: 1969.

Scott, Hew. *Fasti Ecclesiae Scoticanae*, 7 vols. Edinburgh and London: 1866; revised 1917.

Scott, John. *Critical Essays on some of the Poems of several English Poets*. London: 1785; repr.
  Farnborough, Hants.: 1969.

Scott, Mary Jane W. "James Thomson and Gavin Douglas: Some Continuities in Scottish Augustan Verse." *Postscript* (Publication of the Philological Association of the
  Carolinas), no. 1 (1983): 106–114.

———. "Scottish Language in the Poetry of James Thomson." *Neuphilologische Mit-
  teilungen* 4/82 (1981): 370–385.

Scott, Mary Jane, and Patrick Scott. "The Manuscript of James Thomson's Scots Elegy."
  Studies in Scottish Literature 17 (1982): 135–144.

Scott, Paul Henderson. *1707: The Union of Scotland and England*. Edinburgh: 1979.

———. "*Severitas:* The Romano-Scottish Ideal." *Blackwood's Magazine* 320, no. 1933
  (November 1976): 412–419.

Scott, Tom. "Observations on Scottish Studies." *Studies in Scottish Literature* 1, no. 1 (July
  1963): 5–13.

[Scott, Sir Walter]. "Drama." In *Supplement to the Encyclopaedia Britannica*. 4th, 5th, and
  6th eds. Edinburgh and London: 1824. Vol. 3, pp. 629–671.

Shairp, J. C. *On Poetic Interpretation of Nature*. Edinburgh: 1877.

Sher, Richard B. *Church and University in the Scottish Enlightenment: The Moderate Literati of
  Edinburgh*. Princeton: 1985.

[Shiels, Robert]. "James Thomson." In *Lives of the Poets of Great-Britain and Ireland*.
  [Theophilus] Cibber and Other Hands. London: 1753. Vol. 5, pp. 190–218.

Simpson, James. "A Judge of Architectory." Lecture delivered for symposium "A Treasure of Learning and Good Taste—Sir John Clerk of Penicuik Tercentenary." University of Edinburgh, May 15–16, 1976.

Simpson, John M. "Who Steered the Gravy Train?" In *Scotland in the Age of Improvement*,
  ed. Nicholas T. Phillipson and Rosalind Mitchison. Edinburgh: 1970, pp. 47–72.

Sinclair, Sir John, ed. *Statistical Account of Scotland*, 21 vols. Edinburgh: 1791–1799.

Sitter, John. *Literary Loneliness in Mid-Eighteenth-Century England*. Ithaca and London:
  1982.

Smith, David Nichol. *Some Observations on Eighteenth Century Poetry*. Toronto: 1960.

———. "Thomson and Burns." In *Eighteenth Century English Literature: Modern Essays in
  Criticism*, ed. James M. Clifford. New York: 1959, pp. 180–193.

Smith, G. Gregory. *Scottish Literature: Character and Influence*. London: 1919.

———. *Specimens of Middle Scots*. Edinburgh: 1902.

Smith, Janet Adam. "Some Eighteenth-Century Ideas of Scotland." In *Scotland in the Age
  of Improvement*, ed. Nicholas T. Phillipson and Rosalind Mitchison. Edinburgh:
  1970, pp. 107–124.

Smout, T. C. *A History of the Scottish People 1560–1830*. Bungay, Suffolk: 1973.

Snyder, Franklyn Bliss. "Notes on Burns and Thomson." *The Journal of English and Germanic Philology* 19, no. 3 (1920): 305–317.

Somerville, Thomas. *My Own Life and Times: 1741–1814,* ed. "W.L." Edinburgh: 1861.

Spacks, Patricia Meyer. *John Gay.* New York: 1965.

_____. *The Poetry of Vision.* Cambridge, Mass.: 1967.

_____. *The Varied God: A Critical Study of Thomson's 'The Seasons'.* Berkeley: 1959.

_____. "Vision and Meaning in James Thomson." *Studies in Romanticism* 4, no. 1 (Autumn 1964): 206–219.

Speck, W. A. *Society and Literature in England 1700–60.* Dublin: 1983.

Speirs, John. *The Scots Literary Tradition.* London: revised, 1962.

Stock, R. D. *The Holy and the Daemonic from Sir Thomas Browne to William Blake.* Princeton: 1982.

Tait, A. A. (Professor of Fine Art, Glasgow University). *The Landscape Garden in Scotland 1735–1835.* Edinburgh: 1980.

_____. Letter to M. J. W. Scott. April 23, 1981.

Tait, James. *Two Centuries of Border Church Life.* Kelso: 1889.

[Taylor, Eric S.]. "James Thomson, from a hitherto unpublished crayon portrait by William Aikman." *Times Literary Supplement,* August 29, 1942, pp. 421, 429.

_____. "James Thomson: Poet of Nature and Reason." Ph.D. dissertation, University of Edinburgh, 1943.

[_____]. "Thomson's Library." *Times Literary Supplement,* June 20, 1942, p. 312.

Thomson, Derick S. "Gaelic Writers in Lowland Scotland." *Scottish Literary Journal* 4, no. 1 (May 1977): 36–46.

Tillotson, Geoffrey. "Eighteenth-Century Poetic Diction." In *Essays in Criticism and Research.* Cambridge: 1942, pp. 53–85.

Tobin, Terence. *Plays by Scots, 1660–1800.* Iowa City, Iowa: 1974.

_____. "School Plays in Scotland, 1656–1693." *Seventeenth-Century News* 27, no. 3 (Autumn 1969): 49.

Turnbull, George. *Observations Upon Liberal Education.* London: 1742.

_____. *The Principles of Moral Philosophy.* London: 1740.

_____. *A Treatise on Ancient Painting.* London: 1740.

Tytler, Alexander Fraser. *Memoirs of the Life and Writings of the Honourable Henry Home of Kames,* 2 vols. Edinburgh and London: 1807.

Veitch, John. *The Feeling for Nature in Scottish Poetry,* 2 vols. Edinburgh: 1887.

_____. *The History and Poetry of the Scottish Border,* 2 vols. Edinburgh and London: 1893.

Warrand, Duncan, ed. *More Culloden Papers,* vol. 3. Inverness: 1927.

Warton, Joseph. *Essay on the Genius and Writings of Pope,* vol. 1. London: 1756.

Watson, George. *The History of the Jedburgh Grammar School.* Jedburgh: 1909.

_____. *The History of Southdean.* Transactions of the Hawick Archaeological Society. Hawick: 1926.

_____. "Rev. Thomas Thomson, M.A., the Father of the Poet of the 'Seasons.'" *Border Magazine* 8, no. 92 (September 1903): 176–178.

————. *The Roxburghshire Word-Book*. Cambridge: 1923.

Watson, James. *Jedburgh Abbey: Historical and Descriptive*. Edinburgh: 1877.

————, ed. *Watson's Choice Collection of Comic and Serious Scots Poems*, 3 parts. Edinburgh: 1706, 1709, 1711.

————, ed. *Watson's Choice Collection of Comic and Serious Scots Poems*, ed. Harriet Harvey Wood. Scottish Text Society, 4th ser., no. 10. Repr. of Glasgow (1869) repr. of original. Edinburgh: 1977.

Watts, Isaac. *Horae Lyricae and Divine Songs*, ed. Robert Southey. Boston: 1854.

————. *The Psalms of David*. Boston: 1787.

Weber, Max. *The Protestant Ethic and the Spirit of Capitalism*, trans. Talcott Parsons, foreword R. H. Tawney. New York and London: 1952.

Wells, John Edwin. "James Thomson and Milton." *Modern Language Notes* 24, no. 2 (1909): 60–61.

Wendel, François. *Calvin*, trans. Philip Mairet. Glasgow: 1976.

Wilson, James Grant, ed. *The Poets and Poetry of Scotland*, 4 half-vols. London, Glasgow, and Edinburgh: n.d. [1876–1877].

[Wilson, John], "Christopher North." "Winter Rhapsody." *Blackwood's (Edinburgh) Magazine*, Fyttes I and II, vol. 28, no. 174 (December 1830): 863–877, 878–894; Fyttes III and IV, vol. 29, no. 177 (February 1831): 285–328.

Wittig, Kurt. *The Scottish Tradition in Literature*. Edinburgh: 1958; repr. 1978.

Wodrow, Robert. *Analecta: or, Materials for a History of Remarkable Providences; mostly relating to Scotch Ministers and Christians*, 4 vols. Edinburgh: 1843.

Youngson, A. J. *The Making of Classical Edinburgh*. Edinburgh: 1966.

INDEX

Aberdeen, 206, 240, 245, 262, 340 (n. 44)
Adam, Robert, 250
Adams, Percy G., 13, 319 (n. 19)
Addison, Joseph, 38, 88, 110, 152; on "The Pleasures of the Imagination," 41; *Cato*, 212
Aeolian harp, 260–61, 338 (n. 13)
Aeschylus, 228
Aesop, 70–71
Agamemnon, 214, 227–29, 230, 236
Agriculture, 20, 173–74
Aikin, John, 4
Aikman, Jocky, 214
Aikman, William, 52, 53, 135, 205, 214, 240, 259
Alexander, Sir William, 73, 84; *Monarchicke Tragedies*, 210–11
Alfred, A Masque, 230, 235
Allegory: in folk literature, 23; in school plays, 25; in "Upon Happiness," 90–92; in Henryson, 99–100; in *Liberty*, 221; in *Castle of Indolence*, 279–83
Alliteration, 103, 126; in "Autumn," 195; in Scottish tradition, 97–98, 100, 120, 321 (n. 1)
Alps, 120, 213, 225
"Amanda." *See* Young, Elizabeth
Ancrum, 28, 29; in "Autumn," 142–43
Angling, 78, 133

Anglo-Scot: defined, 3
Anglo-Scottish poetry, 50–51; influence of Addison on, 41; and Athenian Society, 56–61
Animals, 70, 100, 134, 138, 194
Arbuckle, James, 60
Archers, Royal Company of, 27, 28, 51, 59
Arctic, 122
Areopagitica, Thomson's preface to, 163, 227
Argathelians, 48–49
Argyll, John Campbell (duke), 53, 174, 205, 214, 240
Aristotelianism, at Edinburgh University, 38
Armstrong, Dr. John, 243, 247, 280, 286; "Imitation of Shakespeare (Winter)," 106–8, 246, 301–6 (text); and blank verse, 182; subscribed to 1762 *Works*, 241; caricatured in *Castle*, 246, 262; *Oeconomy of Love*, 246; *Art of Preserving Health*, 246; contributes stanzas to *Castle*, 246, 264; works of, 337 (n. 77)
Arne, Thomas, 231
Arthur's Seat, 140
Athenian Society (Edinburgh), 56–61, 75, 76, 88, 218
Athenian Society (London), 57–58, 88
Augusta. *See* London

Augusta, Princess, 231
Aureation, 50, 65, 188, 287; in "Upon
   Beauty," 69; in Dunbar and
   Drummond, 82; in Douglas, 100–101;
   in "Winter," 121–22; in "Summer," 130
Aurora borealis, 40, 122, 130, 131, 143
"Autumn," 40, 194–96, 208, 224; fogs in,
   32, 255; hunting in, 74, 77, 103, 138–
   39, 262; natural description in, 136–
   44; Scottish sections in, 141–42, 171–
   73; Scotticisms in, 198; and Mallet's
   Amyntor, 248. See also Seasons
Aytoun, Robert, 60

B., T.: A Criticism of the New Sophonisba,
   209
Baillie, George, 205, 214
Baillie, Lady Grisell (nee Home), 19, 25,
   62, 214, 234
Baillie, Rachel, 205
Ballads, 10, 20, 22–23, 139, 186, 256,
   283; Thomson's mother teaches, 19;
   fatalism in, 128; and natural
   description, 102–3, 118; "Daemon
   Lover," 266
Barbados, 127, 227, 245
Barbour, John, 23
Barclay, Alexander, 280, 281
Barrell, John, 329 (n. 30)
"The Battle of Otterburne," 139
Bayne, William, 10, 12
Beattie, James, 4, 41, 195, 198, 292; on
   Seasons, 165; The Minstrel, 167;
   Scoticisms, 200–201, 285–86; "The
   Castle of Scepticism," 340 (n. 44)
The Bee, 6, 8
Bell, Elizabeth. See Thomson, Elizabeth
Bell, Rev. James, 52
Bell, Rev. Robert, 241
Bellenden, John, 284
Bennet, Elizabeth, 71, 72, 73, 129
Bennet, Sir William (the elder), 28
Bennet, Sir William (the younger), 22,
   26–29, 48, 50, 51, 214, 240;
   Thomson's "Poetical Epistle" to, 28, 71,
   72–73, 178; Ramsay's Gentle Shepherd

and, 52; letter to, 62; Latin poems of,
   247, 311 (n. 21)
Benson, William, 85
Bible, 22, 23, 25, 43, 147; Riccaltoun on
   interpreting, 31–32; as poetry, 110;
   Thomson's paraphrases from, 83–85;
   as linguistic influence, 189–90; in
   Castle of Indolence, 272–75. See also
   books of Bible
Binning, Lord, 62, 205, 214, 241
Binning, Thomas (later 7th earl of
   Haddington), 205
Blackmore, Richard: The Creation, 84,
   151; "Happiness Discover'd," 90
Blackwood's Edinburgh Magazine, 9
Blair, Hugh, 4, 41, 275
Blair, Robert, 44–45, 57, 60, 90, 130,
   182, 292; The Grave, 44–45, 87, 123,
   158, 191–92
Blind Hary the Minstrel, 171, 287
Border landscape: in The Seasons, 14,
   113–45 passim; classical associations,
   20–21; in Thomson's juvenilia, 67, 69,
   76; in Castle of Indolence, 258, 276
Borders, Scottish: supernatural beliefs
   in, 18, 24, 90, 130; winter in, 78, 119–
   20; floods in, 138; fever in, 309 (n. 4).
   See also Ballads
Boston, Rev. Thomas, of Ettrick, 89, 152,
   155, 160, 167, 268, 273–75, 276;
   Fourfold State of Man, 89, 157–58; on
   aesthetic pleasure, 161; on the Deluge,
   132–33; on work, 270; on wolves, 324
   (n. 12)
Boswell, James, 236, 241
Boyd, R., 57
Boyd, Thomas, 59
Brentford, 267, 275
Bridgetown, 127, 227, 245
Britannia, A Poem, 219, 224, 261
Brooke, Stopford, 10
Brown, James (schoolmaster), 24, 310 (n.
   14)
Bruce, 23
"Bruce, Fergus": on the Grotesque Club,
   55

Buchan, eleventh earl of, 5, 6, 215

Buchanan, George, 24, 210, 230; *Latin Psalms*, 25, 84; *De Sphaera*, 92–93

Buchanan's Head (bookshop), 246

Bulwer-Lytton, Edward, 9

Bunyan, John: *Pilgrim's Progress*, 22, 91

Burel, John: *Passage of Pilgrimer*, 91

Burnet, Thomas, 133

Burns, Robert, 117, 286, 287; poetic tributes to Thomson, 5–6; treatment of animals, 70; "Tam O'Shanter," 139, 144; "Brigs of Ayr," 123, 196; "The Cottar's Saturday Night," 168; influenced by Thomson, 292

Bute, Lord, 240, 309 (n. 1)

Butt, John, 11, 14

Byron, Lord, 287, 293

C., W.: preface to *Edinburgh Miscellany*, 58–59

Callender, John, 56–57, 75; "Epistle to Mr. Mitchell," 56; "Epistle to Robert Blair," 57; in *Edinburgh Miscellany*, 59, 60, 71; Aesopic fable, 71; "The Elevation," 87

Calvin, John, 151, 160

Calvinism, at Geneva, 213

Calvinism, Scottish, 13, 20, 32–33, 70–71, 87, 89–90, 163, 189, 213, 267; Thomson's father and, 17–19; attitudes to literature, 42–45; in "Upon Happiness," 88; and sudden death, 128; in "Autumn," 137, 138; work-ethic in, 137, 269–71, 339 (n. 27); and panergism, 149; and the supernatural, 154–55; on wealth, 222, 223–24; in *Castle of Indolence*, 258, 267–75

Campbell, Archibald (printer), 114, 202

Campbell, Archibald (philosopher), 159, 328 (n. 15)

Campbell, George, 41

Campbell, Hilbert, 13

Campbell, Admiral John, 250

Campbell, Thomas, 9, 293

Cape Club, 4

Carnall, Geoffrey, 11

Caroline, Queen: *Sophonisba* dedicated to, 207; in *Agamemnon*, 228

Carter Bar, 21

Carter Fell, 140

Carthage, 206–8

The Castle of Indolence, 18–19, 138, 139, 156, 157, 161, 165, 166, 170, 194, 198, 200, 209, 215, 224, 225, 226, 230, 233, 235, 236, 239, 250, 253, 254–89; meter in, 65, 183; caricatures in, 74, 242–46, 262–63; and "Upon Happiness," 91–92; winter fog in, 103, 255; work-ethic in, 169; John Armstrong contributes to, 246, 264; influence of Joseph Mitchell on, 249; language in, 257, 283–87; influence of *Eneados* on, 263, 265, 266, 282, 284; influence of *The Palice of Honour on*, 265–66, 277–78, 281–82, 284; biblical allusions in, 272–75; allegory in, 279–83; continuity with Scottish tradition, 288–89

Castleton, Roxburghshire, 107

Catholicism, 213, 279; in *Liberty*, 222

Cato, 177; Addison's play, 212

"Celadon and Amelia," 103, 128–29

Chalker, John, 169

Chapbooks, 22–23

Charles Edward Stuart, Prince, 228, 238

Chatto, 67–68

Chaucer, Geoffrey, 284

Chesterfield, Lord, 121

Chesters, 23

Cheviot Hills, 20, 117, 128, 140

"Chevy Chase," 139

Cincinnatus, 177

Clerk, Sir John, of Penicuik, 240, 329 (n. 41); *The Country Seat*, 53; observes comet, 131

Clive, John: on Scottish provincialism, 290–92

Cliveden, 231

Cobham, Lord, 143

Cohen, Ralph, 13

Colden, Rev. Alexander, 63

Collins, William: on Highland superstitions, 101; "Ode on the Death of Mr. Thomson," 268

Comets, 130–31, 325 (n. 22), 327 (n. 39)

Cooper, Mrs. Mary (publisher), 233

Coriolanus, 208, 238–40, 250, 252

Corneille, 207

Covenanters, 17, 23, 45

The Craftsman, 315 (n. 29)

Craig, James (architect), 36, 220, 241

Craig, Mary Thomson, 241, 250

Craig, William, 241

Crailing, 36

Cranstoun, Rev. John, 29, 67

Cranstoun, John, 29, 37

Cranstoun, Dr. William, 29, 241; Thomson's letters to, 37, 61, 105, 111, 114, 118, 142, 153, 154, 212

Cranstouns of Ancrum, 29, 63

Crawford, Robert: "Leader Haughs and Yarrow," 72

Culbin Sands, 127

Cunningham, C., 57

"The Daemon-Lover," 103, 266

Dalrymple, Hon. Hugh, 240

"Damon and Musidora," 129

Dante, 263; *Inferno*, 282

Davidson, David: *Thoughts on the Seasons*, 342 (n. 2)

Dee, River, 262, 339 (n. 15)

Defoe, Daniel, 119, 160; *Caledonia*, 174; *Robinson Crusoe*, 229

de Haas, C. E., 14

Deluge, 148, 155; Hutchinson on, 32, 325 (n. 25); Ray, *On the Chaos and Deluge*, 46; Boston on, 132–33. *See also* Floods

Derby, 238

Derham, William, 46; *Physicotheology*, 151

Descartes, 92

"A Description of ten a-clock of night in the town," 73–74

Despauter: Latin grammar, 24; on periphrasis, 187

Devanha, 262

Deva's Vale, 259, 261–62, 271, 278

"A Dialogue in praise of the pastoral life," 82

Didacticism, 18–19, 67, 110, 144, 156; in "Winter," 114, 120; in "Autumn," 139; on social issues, 164; in *Liberty*, 215–16, 221; in *Castle of Indolence*, 264–65. *See also* Pulpit rhetoric

Dido, 207

"Discourse of the Power of the Supreme Being," 86

Dodington, George Bubb, 140, 215, 232, 241

"The Dog and a Piece of Flesh," 70

Donne, John, 26

Dorset, 140

Douglas, Gavin, 10, 184, 188, 254; *The Palice of Honour*, 90, 91; *Eneados*, 100–101, 103, 179

Drama: school plays, 25, 211; as urban phenomenon, 167; Thomson's plays, 206–12, 227–31, 235–40, 251–53, 255, 275; Thomson's views on, 209, 212; limitations in Scottish tradition of, 209–12; Scottish church opposition to, 211, 332 (n. 13); and Opposition Whigs, 229

Drennon, Herbert, 13

Drinking, 139

Drumachose, 246

Drummond, Professor Colin, 38

Drummond, George, 240

Drummond, William, of Hawthornden, 11, 73, 74, 81, 90, 102; "The Praise of a Solitarie Life," 77; "To the Exequies of the Honourable, Sr. Antonye Alexander," 75; "The Angels for the Natiuitie of Our Lord," 82; "For the Natiuitie of Our Lord," 82; "What Haplesse Hap had I now to bee borne," 87; "Why (Worldlings) doe ye trust fraile Honours Dreames," 87

Drury Lane (Whig theater), 209, 212, 231

Dunbar, William, 10, 70, 99, 284; *The Golden Targe*, 69; "Of the Natiuitie of

Christ," 82; "The Dance of the Sevin
    Deidly Synnis," 139, 264, 267
Duncan, Robert, 57
Dundas, Professor Laurence, 38
Dundas, Robert, 240

East Barnet, 205
Ecclesiastes, 87, 157, 189, 272
Eden, River, 16
Edinburgh, 166, 169, 241, 247;
    Thomson's mother moves to, 19; the
    beau monde of, 37; literary clubs in, 52–
    61, 71; poetic criticism of, 74, 77–78;
    New Town of, 220; *Tancred and
    Sigismunda* staged in, 237; Lord
    Provost of, 240; Castle, 280
Edinburgh Divinity Hall, 41–47, 314 (n. 25)
Edinburgh Evening Courant, 200
Edinburgh Miscellany, 42, 58–61, 66, 76,
    87, 88, 187, 233, 244, 249, 316 (n. 48);
    Aesopic fable in, 71; pastoral in, 74, 81
Edinburgh Review, 9
Edinburgh University, 17, 35–42, 192,
    240, 244, 291
Edmonstoune, Andrew, 16
Ednam, 16, 17, 19
Ednam Club, 6
Edward and Eleanora, 214, 229–31, 237,
    244, 277
"An Elegy upon James Therburn in
    Chatto," 11–12, 67–68
"An Elegy upon Parting," 73
Elliot, Sir Gilbert (the elder), 26, 29
Elliot, Sir Gilbert (the younger), 26, 29,
    52, 53, 240
Elliot, John, 62–63
Elliots of Minto (family), 22, 48, 63
Elliots of Stobs (family), 18
English Men of Letters Series, 12
Erskine, David Steuart, earl of Buchan,
    5, 6, 215
Euripides: *Alcestis,* 230
Exorcism, 18

"The Fable of a Hawk and Nightingale,"
    70–71

"The Fable of a sick Kite and it's Dame,"
    70, 71
Fair Intellectual Society, 60
Fairchild, Hoxie Neal, 13
Fairies, 24, 130
Famines, 20
Famous Scots Series, 12
Farquhar, George: *The Constant Couple,* 212
Ferguson, Adam, 275
Fergusson, Robert, 5–6, 74, 117; "The
    Daft Days," 139
Fielding, Henry, 232–33
Floods, 20, 196–97; in "Winter," 117; in
    "Autumn," 138. *See also* Deluge
Fog, 140–41, 255, 264–66
Fogo, 19
Folklore, Scottish, 23, 120, 121, 144, 256,
    266
Folk music, Scots, 260
Foord, Mr., 57
Forbes, Duncan, of Culloden, 32, 48–49,
    52, 53, 89, 205, 214, 232, 233, 239,
    240, 242, 280; *Some Considerations on
    the Present State of Scotland,* 174
Forbes, John ("Jock"), 53, 242–43, 244,
    262, 336 (n. 70)
Fowler, William, 73, 206
"Fragment: Upon a Flower given me by
    ———," 73
France, 213
Frederick, Prince of Wales, 214, 228,
    230, 231, 236

Gaelic poets: and Lowland literature, 10;
    and animals, 70; natural description
    in, 97–99; personification in, 116;
    sound effects in, 193–94; formal
    intricacy in, 280; influence of
    Thomson on, 293, 342 (n. 3)
Gardens, 134, 259; Thomson's gardener
    relatives, 16, 29, 241, 335 (n. 67); at
    Marlefield, 26–27, 72; at Minto, 29; at
    Richmond, 127, 241–42; at Hagley
    Park, 135; at Stowe, 143; in Douglas's
    Palice of Honour, 265; landscape
    gardening, 309 (n. 1)

Garrick, David, 238
Gawain and the Green Knight, Sir, 97
Gay, John, 54, 74, 76–77, 205; *Rural Sports,* 77–78, 178
Genesis, 132, 141, 148, 155, 189, 272
Geneva, 213
Gentleman's Magazine, 9, 105, 299
Geology, in "Spring", 135
George II, King, 228, 231, 236
Golden, Morris, 14
Golden Age, 32, 132, 147, 155, 167
Graham, Henry Grey, 11
Grand Tour, 225, 242–43, 259
Grant, Douglas, 12–13
Gray, John, 206, 241
Greek, 25, 41, 131, 176
Greenhouse, at Marlefield, 72
Gregory, Professor David, 39, 312 (n. 6)
Gregory, Professor James, 41
Gringore, Pierre: *Castell of Laboure,* 280–81
Grotesque, 125; in "Autumn," 103, 139; in *Agamemnon,* 229; in *Castle of Indolence,* 256, 258, 262–67
Grotesque Club, 54–56, 66, 76, 85, 248
Grove, Henry, 88
Grubbet, 26
Gusthart, Rev. William, 36, 241

Hadrian's Wall, 219
Hagley Park, 131, 135, 162, 338 (n. 9)
"Haliburton, Hugh," 11
Hamilton, Baillie Gavin, 241
Hamilton, Professor William, 45–46, 84, 86, 151, 189, 237, 313 (n. 20), 314 (n. 25)
Hamilton, William, of Bangour, 324 (n. 12); "Contemplation, or the Triumph of Love," 320 (n. 36)
Hamilton, William, of Gilbertfield: *Wallace,* 144, 171
Happy Man, the, 77, 164, 179, 229, 261, 277
Harvest: 20, 126, 325 (n. 32)
Hazlitt, William, 9
Hebrew, 32, 45, 322 (n. 20)

Hebrides, 118, 141, 224, 261
Henryson, Robert, 10, 99; *Morall Fabillis of Esope the Phrygian,* 70, 71; "The Preiching of the Swallow," 71, 99–100; *Robene and Makyne,* 74; *Testament of Cresseid,* 99
Hepburn, Mr., 60
Heron, Robert, 4
Hertford, Lady, 214
Hill, Aaron, 86, 107, 241; and the Grotesque Club, 55–56; publishes a Thomson poem, 62; letters to, 159, 173
Hobkirk, 29–30
Hogg, James, 140
Home, Lady Grisell. *See* Baillie, Lady Grisell
Home, Henry, Lord Kames, 4, 41; *Elements of Criticism,* 4, 61; *Edinburgh Miscellany,* 60
Home, John: *Douglas,* 238
Home, Margaret, 19
Homer, 177; *Odyssey,* 228
Horace, 24, 38, 56, 77, 167
Hughes, John, 26, 88, 280, 284–87
Hume, Alexander (grammarian): *Bellum Grammaticale,* 25
Hume, Alexander (poet): "Of the Day Estivall," 43, 102
Hume, David, 30, 247, 311 (n. 27)
Hume, J., 57
Hunting: in "Of a Country Life," 78; in "Autumn," 138–39, 194–96; in Scotland, 326 (nn. 33, 34)
Hutcheson, Francis, 33, 42, 88, 110, 150, 152, 159–60, 161, 162, 180, 221, 271; *An inquiry into the original of our ideas of beauty and virtue,* 159–62; "Inquiry concerning Moral Good and Evil," 177; on social love, 208–9; influence in *Tancred,* 236
Hutchinson, John, 148, 312 (n. 31); influence on Riccaltoun and Forbes, 32; on the Deluge, 133, 325 (n. 25)
"The Hymn on the Seasons," 144, 148, 149, 189–90

"A Hymn to God's Power," 84, 148
The Hyp-Doctor, 229

Improvement, 20, 220, 222, 329 (n. 36);
    Thomson on, 170–73; in *Castle of
    Indolence,* 277–78
Inglesfield, Robert, 322 (n. 12)
Innes, Alexander, 328 (n. 15)
Ireland, 173, 246
Italy, 213–214, 216
Italian literary influence: in *Castle of
    Indolence,* 282

Jacobitism: 27, 175, 177, 206, 231; the
    1715 rising, 36, 38; Thomson's attitude
    to, 38, 219–20; links with neo-latinists,
    50; in *Edinburgh Miscellany,* 59–60; the
    1745 rising, 131, 234, 255; in
    Thomson's dramas, 228, 231–32, 235–
    36, 238–39; in Mallet's *Eurydice,* 247–
    48; in *Castle of Indolence,* 278–79; and
    Opposition Whigs, 315 (n. 29); and
    Thomson's circle, 340 (n. 41)
James I, King: *Kingis Quair,* 201
James V, King, 173
James VI and I, King, 207: psalms, 84;
    sonnets on the four seasons, 102
James VIII and III, King ("the Old
    Pretender"), 228
Jamieson, John: *Dictionary,* 286
Jed, River, 24, 133, 142
Jedburgh, 19, 23, 105, 140; Roman
    remains in, 22; Abbey, 24; library at
    English School, 26; presbytery of, 37
Jedburgh, Lord, 240
Jedburgh Grammar School, 17, 23–26,
    291
Jed valley, 140
Jerviswood, 205
Job, Book of, 32, 87, 92, 111, 126, 144,
    151, 154, 157, 162, 189, 192
Johnson, Dr. Samuel, 194, 197, 294; on
    Thomson's revisions, 7–8; on blank
    verse, 183; *Dictionary,* 201; on *Liberty,*
    215; on *Edward and Eleanora,* 229; on
    Mallet, 247

Juvenal, 180; dramatized by schoolboys,
    25
Juvenile poems, 64–95, 216; reedited by
    James Sambrook, 13; manuscript of,
    66, 317 (n. 3), 318 (n. 4)

Kames, Lord, 4, 41; *Elements of Criticism,*
    4, 61; and *Edinburgh Miscellany,* 60
Kelso, 27; library, 241
Ker, Professor John, 50, 55, 105
Kew Lane, Richmond, 241
King Hart, 281
King's College, Aberdeen, 240

Landscape, Scottish: Thomson contrasts
    with England, 111; in *Seasons,* 113–45.
    See also Borders
Landscape gardening. *See* Gardening
Landscape painting, 259–60
Language: Scots, 49, 173; rejection of
    Scots, 50–51; Scots in Thomson's
    poems, 8, 10, 11, 65, 67–68, 79, 84,
    194–202, 284–86; poetic, 79–80, 184;
    in Scottish makars, 96; in *Liberty,* 216;
    in *Castle of Indolence,* 283–87; archaic,
    280, 284–87. *See also* Scotticisms,
    Latin, etc.
Laplanders, 167, 179
Latin: Scottish vernacular tradition of,
    24–25, 28, 32, 41, 49–50, 187–88,
    292; lectures at Edinburgh in, 38;
    Scottish psalms in, 319 (n. 23); and
    Scottish poetic diction, 101, 294; and
    Thomson's diction, 11, 14, 79–80, 134,
    176, 186–88, 216, 225–26, 257, 283
Lee, Nathaniel, 207
Leeward Islands, 227, 244
Leith, port of, 63
Leslie, Alexander, 219
Leslie, Bishop John, 120–21
Liberty, 6, 18–19, 130, 157, 166, 167, 168,
    170, 177, 178, 200, 201, 208, 209, 213,
    214–27, 231, 239, 244, 251–53, 254,
    255, 261, 275, 288; universal history
    in, 41; rainbow in, 132; chauvinism in,
    175; as "poetical landscape of

Liberty (continued)
  countries," 213; influence on Turnbull,
  259
Lindsay, Sir David, 99, 284; in
  chapbooks, 22; *The Dreme,* 90, 141–42,
  171, 173, 221, 282, 324 (n. 12); *The
  Monarche,* 132, 156, 222, 282; *Ane
  Satyre of the Thrie Estatis,* 282
Lindsay, Maurice, 14
Lindsay, Rt. Hon. Patrick, 240
"Lisy's parting with her cat," 66, 74, 86
Literary societies, 41, 52–61
Livy, 207
Locke, John, 30
Loftis, John, 235
London, 166, 169; Thomson in, 115,
  204–6; in *Seasons,* 129, 131; analogy
  with Rome, 176; Scots in, 231–35,
  240–50, 279
Longinus, 38
Lord Chamberlain, 227, 229, 244
Lorrain, Claude, 225, 259–60; "The
  Enchanted Castle," 338 (n. 9)
Lovat, Simon, Lord, 240
Lucan, 24
Lucretius, 180; *De Rerum Natura,* 178
Lugubres Cantus, 57–58, 75
Lyttelton, George, 135, 137, 162, 232,
  241, 244, 250; on Thomson's religion,
  163; appoints Thomson to sinecure,
  227; and *Castle of Indolence,* 262, 263;
  anglicized Thomson's text, 286

Macaulay, G. C., 12
MacDiarmid, Hugh, 293–94; *A Drunk
  Man Looks at the Thistle,* 139
Macdonald, Alexander, 293
McEuen, James, 316 (n. 48)
McIntyre, Duncan ban, 293
Mackenzie, Agnes Mure, 14
Mackenzie, George, 60; *Caelia's Country
  House and Closet,* 71; "The Praise of a
  Country Life," 77; version of Psalm
  104, 84–85
Mackie, Professor Charles, 41
McKillop, Alan D., 13, 258, 333 (n. 26)

McLaurin, Colin, 131, 244; *Account of Sir
  Isaac Newton's Philosophical Discoveries,*
  243, 247
Macpherson, 292; *Ossian,* 141, 248
MacQueen, John, 14, 130, 321 (n. 1), 340
  (n. 41)
Maecenas: and Sir William Bennet, 72
Malcolm, Alexander, 54
Mallet, David, 48, 50, 54, 55–56, 179,
  182, 205–6, 239, 241, 247–48; and
  Tea-Table Miscellany, 52; contributes to
  Edinburgh Miscellany, 60; has Newberry
  manuscript, 66; "Ode to the Rev. Mr.
  Isaac Watts," 83; Riccaltoun's "Winter's
  Day" attributed to, 105; *Excursion,* 106,
  108–9, 248; and suppression of
  Armstrong's "Winter," 107–8; and
  Thomson's "Winter," 205; prologue to
  Sophonisba, 206–7; *Mustapha,* 229; and
  Alfred, A Masque, 231; claims
  authorship of "Rule, Britannia," 231;
  Scottish hostility to, 247, 337 (n. 79);
  Jacobitism in *Eurydice,* 247–48; *Amyntor
  and Theodora,* 248
Mallock, David. *See* Mallet, David
Mandeville, Bernard, 159
Mantua, 21
Marchmont, earl of, 19
Marischal College, Aberdeen, 206, 245
Marlefield House, 26–29, 51, 52, 71–72
Marlowe, Christopher, 144
Marrow Men, 17
Marshall, Gordon, 340 (n. 27)
Marston, John, 207
Martin, Martin, 167, 224, 261; *Description
  of the Western Islands of Scotland,* 118,
  128, 141, 173–74; *A Late Voyage to St.
  Kilda,* 141
Mavisbank, 329 (n. 41)
Metathesis, 201, 315 (n. 38)
Meteors, 143–44
Metrical forms: in juvenilia, 65; blank
  verse, 74, 182–83; heroic couplets, 75;
  Spenserian, 280
Middle Scots poetry, 10, 96–97, 256; in
  chapbooks, 23; in Edinburgh

University library, 41; flyting in, 68;
Aesopic fables in, 70; personification
in, 116; adjectival contractions in, 186;
hell and grotesque in, 262, 264–66;
Spenser and, 280; aureation in, 287;
winter in, 321 (n. 1)
Millan, John (publisher), 114
Millar, Andrew (publisher), 227, 233,
243, 245, 246–47
Millar, Rev. Robert, 246
Miller, Hugh, 10, 135
Milton, John, 72, 74, 82, 85, 92, 113,
132, 147, 152, 154, 163, 184, 263;
editions owned by Thomson, 26;
Paradise Lost, 32, 115, 143–44, 148,
282; *Lycidas,* 75, 141, 224, 267;
L'Allegro, 76, 124; *Comus,* 90, 267; and
pastoral, 123; *Areopagitica,* 163, 227; as
heir to Homer, 177; and blank verse,
183; influence on Thomson, 187, 189;
translates Buchanan, 209
Minto, 26, 29
Mitchell, Sir Andrew, 174, 232, 240, 241,
243, 244, 250, 335 (n. 65); on
Thomson's dramas, 236
Mitchell, John, 57
Mitchell, Joseph, 56–57, 75, 241, 248–
49; *Jonah,* 83; "The Charms of
Indolence," 249; "To Mr. Thomson,"
249
Moderates, 150–51, 154, 163, 221, 222,
236, 313 (n. 13); Riccaltoun and, 30–
33; attitude toward literature, 31–32;
influence of, 42, 45; in Thomson's
poetry, 81, 156, 255, 267–68, 271, 275;
and Neoplatonism, 89–90; on
justification, 161; in *Edward and
Eleanora,* 230; and Jacobitism, 233–34
Montgomerie, Alexander, 101–2; *The
Cherry and the Slae,* 90, 102, 126, 128,
282
Montrose, marquis of, 60
Montrose, duke of, 205
Moray, 127
More, John, 7, 308 (n. 12)
Morel, Léon, 11, 199

"The Morning in the country," 76, 124
Muir, Edwin, 212, 294
Murdoch, Patrick, 4, 46, 53, 59, 61, 206,
241, 242, 243–44, 250, 280, 336 (n.
71); on Thomson's father, 17; on
Thomson's orthodoxy, 154, 165; edits
Works (1762), 240–41, 243–44, 247;
and *Castle of Indolence,* 243, 254, 262
Murray, David, of Gorthy: version of
Psalm 104, 84; *Sophonisba,* 207
Murray, J. A. H., 287

Natural description: in Alexander
Hume, 43; in Thomson's early poems,
76–80; in Scottish poetry, 96–108;
Ramsay on, 103–4; Newtonianism
and, 104; in *Seasons,* 113–45; and
religion, 147–48; in *Castle of Indolence,*
255–58; in later Scottish poets, 293–
94
Neoplatonism, 83, 87, 88, 90, 124, 131,
147, 148, 163, 189
Newberry Manuscript, 66–67, 317 (n. 3),
318 (n. 4)
Newhall House, 54
New Light Calvinists, 45
Newton, Sir Isaac, 88, 92, 93, 245;
Riccaltoun's interest in, 30; Thomson's
poem to, 39–40, 125, 206; *Optics,* 39,
125, 140, 224; *Principia,* 39, 125, 224;
in Mallet, 108; on the rainbow, 132; in
"Summer," 130; as linguistic influence,
192–93
Newtonian science, 13, 113, 131, 148,
149, 221; at Edinburgh University, 39,
312 (n. 6), 313 (n. 8); and Scottish
nature poetry, 104; in "Summer," 124–
25; at Watts' Academy, 206
Nicolas, Sir Harris, 9
Norris, John, of Bemerton, 92; "An Idea
of Happiness," 88

"Of a Country Life," 60, 66, 76–80, 119,
121, 133, 138, 167, 178, 194, 200
Oliver, A. M., 14
"On his Mother's Death," 317 (n. 53)

"On the death of Mr. William Aikman,"
213
Opposition Whigs, 27, 48, 168, 214,
227–28, 230, 277; and *Liberty*, 220; and
drama, 229; and Jacobitism, 232, 315
(n. 29); in *Tancred and Sigismunda*, 235
Orkney and Shetland, 128, 141
Orkneyinga Saga, 121
Oswald, James, 260–61
Ovid, 24, 180; dramatized by schoolboys,
25

"Palemon and Lavinia," 137–38, 178
Paraphrases, 83–85, 272. *See also* Bible,
Psalms
Pastoral, 73, 74–80, 110, 123, 134–35,
262; in "Spring," 131
"A Pastoral betwixt Damon and Celia
parting," 73
"A Pastoral betwixt David Thirsis and the
Angell Gabriel upon the birth of Our
Saviour," 82–83
"A Pastoral betwixt Thirsis and Corydon
upon the death of Damon," 46, 66, 74–
76, 262
"A Pastoral Entertainment described," 82
Paterson, William, 126–27, 227, 241,
244–45, 246, 262, 280, 336 (n. 74)
Pennicuik, Dr. Alexander, 54; "William
Lithgow, his epitaph," 68; "To my
friend inviting him to the Country," 77
Pennicuik, Alexander, 54
Petrarch: *Trionfi*, 206, 207
Petrarchanism, Scottish, 73, 74
Philips, Ambrose, 57–58, 184
Philips, John: *Cyder*, 140
Physicotheology, 32–33, 151–52; in
Divinity Hall library, 46–47; in early
poems, 84, 86; language of, 189
Pinkerton, John, 4
Pitcairne, Archibald: *Poemata*, 247
The Plain Dealer, 55, 66, 85
Pliny, 180
Plutarch: *Lives*, 177, 238
"A Poem sacred to the Memory of Sir
Isaac Newton," 39–40, 125, 206

"A Poetical Epistle to Sir William
Bennet," 28, 71, 72–73, 178
Pope, Alexander, 74, 177, 205, 242;
Windsor Forest, 71; *The Rape of the Lock*,
74; pastoral on "Winter," 75; and
prologue to *Sophonisba*, 206–7
Poussin, Nicholas, 225, 259–60
Primitivism vs. progress, 122, 123, 166–
75, 220–21; in *Castle of Indolence*, 275–
78
Progress, 178; in *Liberty*, 215; in *Alfred*,
231; religious ideas of, 271; and
corruption, 277. *See also* Improvement
"Progressivism, nostalgic," 169, 277, 329
(n. 30)
Proverbs, Book of, 71
Providence, 20, 62, 149, 150, 154, 165,
222–23, 268; Riccaltoun on, 33
"Psalm 104 Paraphrazed," 84–85, 200,
319 (n. 23)
"Psalm 148," 84
Psalms, 20, 189, 272; divinity exercise on,
46; Psalm 104, 84–85, 319 (n. 23);
Psalm 148, 84, 144, 148–49, 189
Ptolemy, 92, 262
Pulpit rhetoric, 18–19, 92, 148, 189;
Edinburgh classes in, 46; in juvenilia,
67; in "Winter," 123, 157–58; in
Thomas Boston, 158; as linguistic
influence, 190–92; in plays, 209, 230,
in *Liberty*, 223–24; in *Castle of Indolence*,
264, 272–73. *See also* Didacticism

Quasi-adverbs, 185–86, 195, 196, 201,
229, 283
Quin, James, 238, 262
Quintus Curtius, 24

Rabelais, 283, 341 (n. 54)
"Race," linguistic, 11, 194, 257; Johnson
on, 8; in Thomson's revisions, 117,
196, 197–98, 201–3
Ramsay, Allan, 49, 51–53, 76–77, 233,
240, 247; at Marlefield, 28; *The Gentle
Shepherd*, 28, 52–53, 77, 110, 129, 137,
237–38; as editor, 41; *The Ever Green*,

51, 52, 103–4, 283–87; *Tea-Table Miscellany,* 51, 129; *The Morning Interview,* 60, 74; influence in Thomson, 67–70, 91; "Maggie Johnstoun," 68; "Lucky Wood," 68; *Tartana, or the Plaid,* 68–69; "On our Ladies being dressed in SCOTS manufactory at a publick Assembly," 69; "In praise of Scottish Ladies," 69; "The Happy Man," 77; Aesopic fables, 70; "Richy and Sandy," 75; "Keitha, a Pastoral," 75; *Content: A Poem,* 91; on Scottish nature poetry, 103–4; "Scotch Drink," 139; "Pleasures of Improvement in Agriculture," 174; portrait of "Lethargus," 264

Ramsay, John, of Ochtertyre, 249

Ray, John: *Wisdom of God Manifested in the Works of Creation,* 46, 151

Reid, Thomas, 42, 160, 162, 245

Revisions, Thomson's, 8, 113–14, 121, 136–37, 196, 197–98, 201–3

Rhetoric, classical, 24, 38

Rhetoric, Scottish, 4, 41–42, 188–89, 292

Rhyme-words, Scots, 79, 84, 316 (n. 38)

Riccaltoun, Rev. Robert, 22, 26, 29–34, 48, 148, 152, 154; "A Winter's Day," 30, 104–6, 297–99; "Essays on Human Nature," 30–31; "Essays on Several of the Doctrines of Revelation," 31–32; and physicotheology, 47; "Of Happiness and Perfection, in general, absolute and limited," 88; on natural revelation, 149, 151; works of, 311 (n. 26)

Richmond, 127, 169, 241–42, 267

Riddell, William, 46, 66, 74–75

"Rising mind," the, 31, 88–89, 93, 131, 158, 223, 268; in Scottish Calvinist writers, 152–54

Robertson, J. Logie, 8, 11–12, 130, 199–200, 285, 286, 287

Robertson, Principal William, 235

Robertson, Dr. William, 241, 247, 249, 250

Rome, 208, 215, 239; Roman remains in Roxburghshire, 22; antiquities subject of Edinburgh lectures, 41; Empire, 48, 176, 216–18; Republic, 48, 175, 177, 252; Thomson visits, 213–14; Scottish resistance to, 218–19; Thomson's changing attitudes to, 238, 252; influences in England, 329 (n. 41). *See also* Scoto-Roman connections

Rosa, Salvator, 225, 259–60

Ross, George, 174, 240, 241, 243

Roxburghe, duke of, 48, 214, 240

Roxburghshire, 16, 20, 107, 202; Roman remains in, 22; blizzards in, 119

Ruberslaw Hill, 105, 140

Ruddiman, Thomas, 41, 49, 50, 90, 100, 284, 286; *Rudiments,* 24

"Rule, Britannia," 231, 334 (n. 45)

Ruth, Book of, 137

St. Kilda, 14, 134, 167, 248

Sallust, 24

Sambrook, James, 11, 13

Sandstorms, 108, 127, 324 (n. 18)

Sargent, John, 241

Savage, Richard: *Miscellany,* 105

Science, 13; and religion, 31–32, 39, 46; at Edinburgh University, 38–40; in "Upon Happiness," 92; in "Summer," 125. *See also* Newtonian science

Scoto-Roman connections, 22, 28, 48, 72–73, 175–76, 208, 239, 252, 288; and language, 186–88

Scots Magazine, 131

Scots Miscellany, 56

Scott, Alexander, 200

Scott, John, 4

Scott, Tom, 1

Scott, Sir Walter, 287, 293; *Triermain,* 201

Scott, Professor William, 38

Scott, Sir William, of Thirlestane, 27

Scotticisms: discouraged, 41, 54; in early writings, 54, 80; in 1726 preface, 109; in *Seasons,* 198–203; in *Liberty,* 226; in *Castle,* 284–87. *See also* Language, Scottish

"Scottishness," 1–3, 294–95; in critical discussion of Thomson, 3–14
The Seasons, 18, 19, 30, 31, 32, 34, 64, 93, 206, 210, 212, 215, 216, 217, 221, 226, 229, 248, 254, 257, 268, 275, 287–88; critical reputation of, 3–14; revisions in, 8, 11, 113–14, 121, 126, 136–37, 141, 156, 196, 197–98; preface of 1726, 32, 52, 147, 152; religion in, 43, 67, 147–57, 189–92; profits from, 62; meter in, 65; Scottish background to, 96–112; and Scottish landscape, 113–45; first collected edition of, 136, 240–41; interpolated tales in, 128–29, 137–38; "Hymn," 144, 148, 149, 189–90; moral philosophy in, 157–61; political views in, 165–75; as Scottish neoclassical poem, 175–80, 186–88; language of, 182–203; and Scottish rhetoric, 188–89; scientific language in, 192–93; sound-effects in, 193–97; Scotticisms in, 198–203; Scottish subscribers to early editions, 240–41. *See also* "Autumn," "Spring," "Summer," "Winter"
Selkirk, Alexander, 229
Seneca, 228
Shaftesbury, earl of, 33, 88, 150, 152, 156, 157, 159, 160, 162, 183, 221; *Moralists,* 86
Shairp, J. C., 10
Shakespeare, William, 138, 212; *A Midsummer Night's Dream,* 90; *Twelfth Night,* 90; Armstrong's imitation of, 106, 301–6; *Julius Caesar,* 143; *Hamlet,* 212; *Coriolanus,* 238
Shenstone, William, 241
Shiels, Robert, 4
Shorter Catechism, 22, 23, 25
Siberia, 168
Simson, Professor John, 160
Skeat, Walter W., 199
Slavery, 127, 163, 166, 208
Smith, Alexander, 293; *A Summer in Skye,* 286
Smith, David Nichol, 11, 14

Smith, G. Gregory, 10, 11
Smollett, Tobias, 119, 139
Snowstorms, 108, 119–20
Somerville, Rev. Thomas, 105
Somerville, William, 203; "Epistle to Mr. Thomson," 184
"Song of Solomon chap:I ver:7," 84
Sophonisba, 206–9, 212, 216, 218, 227, 228, 252
Sound-patterning, 79–80; Riccaltoun on, 30–31; in *Seasons,* 193–97; in *Castle of Indolence,* 257, 260–61
Southdean, 17, 19, 20–22, 23, 116
Southdean Law: Iron Age fort at, 135, 170
Southerne, Thomas: *Oroonoko,* 212
Spacks, Patricia M., 13, 327 (n. 8), 328 (n. 24)
The Spectator, 38, 41, 88–89; influence on 1726 preface, 109; on the supernatural, 320 (n. 35)
Spenser, Edmund, 26, 69–73, 254, 255, 256, 258, 262, 263, 265, 292; "An Hymne of Heavenly Beauty," 91; *Faerie Queene,* 257, 266–67, 270, 277, 279–80, 281, 292, 284; archaisms from, 284–87
Spiers, John, 1, 14
"Spring," 73, 78, 142, 237; revision of, 249; natural description in, 131–36. See also *Seasons*
Squadrone Whigs, 27, 48
Stage Licensing Act, 227; *Edward and Eleanora* banned under, 229–30; *Tancred and Sigismunda* eludes, 236
Stag hunting, 138–39
Steele, Richard, 88
Stewart, Professor Robert, 38–39
Stirling, James, 206, 331 (n. 31)
Stock, R. D., 327 (nn. 2, 7)
Stowe, 143
Stradishall, 243
Stuart, house of, 177, 231, 238; in *Liberty,* 219–20; in *Tancred,* 236; in *Castle of Indolence,* 277, 278–79
Suffolk, 243

"Summer," 69, 108, 136, 223, 229, 230, 277; and Hume's "Of the Day Estivall," 102; natural description in, 123–31; comet in, 130–31; Scottish passage moved from, 141; pulpit rhetoric in, 190–91. See also *Seasons*

Supernatural, the, 14, 18, 37, 90; in folk literature, 23; and folk beliefs, 24, 108, 120; Riccaltoun on, 33; in Virgil, Gavin Douglas, and Collins, 101; in Mallet, 109; in *The Seasons*, 118, 121, 130; and heavenly phenomena, 131, 143–44; religious attitudes to, 154–55; in *Agamemnon*, 229; in *Castle of Indolence*, 256, 261, 264; in *The Spectator*, 320 (n. 35); in Scottish writing, 321 (n. 7); R. D. Stock on, 327 (nn. 2, 7)

Susanna and the Elders, 129

Sweden, 218

Swift, Jonathan, 74, 173

Switzerland, 213; and Calvinism, 218

Symmer, Robert, 241, 244; in *Edinburgh Miscellany*, 60

Talbot, Charles Richard, 212, 242

Talbot, Charles, Lord, 213, 214; death of, 227

Tancred and Sigismunda, 210, 230, 235–38, 249, 252, 275, 279

Tasso: *Gerusalemme Liberata*, 282

Tate and Brady, 84

The Tatler, 41

Taylor, William, 234–35

Temple, Sir William, 8

Terence, 24, 25

Teviot, river, 29

Teviotdale, 6

Thames, river, 129, 250

Theocritus, 74, 75

Therburn, James, of Chatto, 67–68

Thomson, Andrew (grandfather), 16

Thomson, Beatrix Trotter (mother), 19, 36, 205; death of, 115, 317 (n. 53)

Thomson, Derick, 10

Thomson, Elizabeth (sister), 74, 238, 241

Thomson, Gilbert, 241, 309 (n. 1), 335 (n. 67)

Thomson, James: in critical discussion, 3–14; and Scottish language, 8, 11–12, 22, 67, 182–202; and religious beliefs, 13, 42–47, 80–93, 164–65, 192, 268–69; childhood and youth, 16–34; at Edinburgh University, 35–42; at Divinity Hall, 42–47, 314 (n. 25); and poetic language, 46, 65, 67–68, 185–86; and authorship of *Gentle Shepherd*, 52–53; and Edinburgh literary societies, 52–61; move to England, 61–62, 204–6, 317 (n. 53); juvenile poems, 64–95; on "Native poetry," 110; homesickness for Scotland, 115, 261, 333 (n. 26); continuities of attitude, 164–65, 204, 241, 250–53, 268–69; attitudes to Union and "Britain," 165–78; as dramatist, 206–12, 227–31, 235–40; on the Grand Tour, 212–14; secretary of the briefs, 214; and the Jacobites, 231–35; and Fielding's *True Patriot*, 232–33; Scottish circle in London and at Richmond, 241–50; influence on later Scottish poets, 292–94; lesson of, for literary nationalists, 294–95. *See also titles of works*

Thomson, James ("B.V."): "Lord of the Castle of Indolence," 293

Thomson, Jean (sister), 238, 241, 250

Thomson, John (brother): as amanuensis, 241

Thomson, Mary (sister), 241, 250

Thomson, Robert, 241

Thomson, Thomas, 241, 309 (n. 1), 335 (n. 67)

Thomson, Rev. Thomas (father), 17–19, 22, 27, 48; death of, 18, 128

Thorburn, James. See Therburn, James

Thulè, 128, 141

Tobin, Terence, 14

Tonson, Jacob, 246

Tories, 139, 168

Trissino, 207

Tropics, 126–27, 163
Trotter, Alexander (grandfather), 19
Trotter, Beatrix. *See* Thomson, Beatrix Trotter
The True Patriot, 232–33, 279
Turnbull, George, 39, 42, 61, 89, 135, 152, 160, 161, 162, 180, 185, 245–46, 247, 271; *Principles of Moral Philosophy,* 159, 245–46; *Treatise on Ancient Painting,* 162, 225, 245, 246, 259, 338 (n. 11); in *Castle of Indolence,* 262; works of, 336 (n. 76)
Tweed, river, 54, 77, 117, 142
Tweeddale, marquess of, 240

Union of 1707, 21, 35, 135, 140, 208; Sir William Bennet on, 27–28; and crisis of national identity, 47–49; Thomson's attitude toward, 165–75, 217–18; compared to Roman Empire, 176–78; in *Castle of Indolence,* 276
Universal history, 41
"Upon a Flower given me by ———," 73
"Upon Beauty," 68–69, 130
"Upon Happiness," 60, 87–93, 153, 159, 279; echoed in *Liberty,* 224
"Upon Marle-feild," 28, 71–72
"Upon Mrs. Elizabeth Bennet," 71, 73, 129
"Upon the Hoop," 68–69, 130
"Upon the Sparkler!," 73
Urquhart, Sir Thomas, of Cromarty, 283

Veitch, John, 10, 11
"Verses on receiving a Flower from his Mistress," 60, 73
Victor, Benjamin, 235
Virgil, 20, 21–22, 24, 72, 75, 76, 79, 102, 113, 138, 144, 146, 167, 169, 176, 177, 207, 213, 225, 229, 261, 262, 275, 277–78, 288; Riccaltoun on, 32; and pastoral, 74; *Aeneid,* 100, 216, 282; *Georgics,* 101, 111, 117–18, 134, 144, 168, 178–80, 187; *Eclogues,* 126; on perpetual spring, 131; on Golden Age, 132

Voltaire, 237
Volusenus, Florentius. *See* Wilson, Florence

Wales, 128
Wallace, William, 171
Walpole, Sir Robert, 168, 205, 214, 217, 227, 228, 230, 249; anti-Scottish policies of, 214, 217–18
Wardlaw, Lady: "Hardyknute," 283
Warrender, Hugh, 61, 241, 244, 336 (n. 73)
Warton, Joseph, 4
Watson, George, 202, 285, 286
Watson, James, 41, 49, 283; *Choice Collection,* 60, 68, 71, 91
Watts, Dr. Isaac, 47, 56, 73, 75, 83, 87, 88, 90, 92, 152, 160, 163; "The Nativity of Christ," 82–83; "Two Happy Rivals: Devotion and the Muse," 83; paraphrase of Psalm 148, 84
Watts, Thomas and William, 205–6, 241
Weber, Max, 339 (n. 27)
Westminster Abbey: monument to Thomson, 247, 250
Whigs, 27, 48–49, 209, 215, 231. *See also* Opposition Whigs
Whiston, William, 143
Wideopen (or Widehope), 19, 20, 26, 36, 67
Wilson, Florence, 320 (n. 33); *De Animi Tranquillitate,* 90
Wilson, John ("Christopher North"), 6–7, 9
Winnington, Mr., 232
"Winter," 23, 54, 136, 142, 144, 158–59, 196–97, 223; Joseph Mitchell on, 56, 248, 249; and "Of a Country Life," 77; and Gavin Douglas, 100; and Riccaltoun, 104–6; compared to Armstrong's "Winter," 106–8; and Mallet, 108–9; preface to second edition, 109–11; natural description in, 113–23; publication of, 114; wolves

in, 120–21; success of, 147; pulpit
rhetoric in, 191–92; Scotticisms in, 198
Wittig, Kurt, 10, 14, 20
Wodrow, Robert, 45
Wolflee House, 17
Wolves, Scottish, 120–21, 323 (n. 12)
Woodward: *Essays on Natural History,* 46
Wordsworth, William, 6
"The Works and Wonders of Almighty

Power," 66, 74, 85–87; in Hill's *Plain Dealer,* 55
Works of James Thomson (1762), 247
Worthy Club, 29, 52–54

Young, Edward, 107; and *Lugubres Cantus,* 57–58
Young, Elizabeth ("Amanda"), 133–34, 135–36, 210, 237, 239, 249–50